THE
PARTNERS

---

*Inside America's
Most Powerful Law Firms*

JAMES B. STEWART

SIMON AND SCHUSTER

NEW YORK

Published by Simon and Schuster
A Division of Gulf & Western Corporation
Simon & Schuster Building
Rockefeller Center
1230 Avenue of the Americas
New York, New York 10020
SIMON AND SCHUSTER and colophon
are registered trademarks of Simon & Schuster
Designed by Edith Fowler
Manufactured in the United States of America

10   9   8   7   6   5   4   3

Library of Congress Cataloging in Publication Data

Stewart, James B.
  The partners.

  Includes index.
    1. Law partnership—United States.   2. Law
firms—United States.   3. Practice of law—United
States.
I. Title.
KF300.S73   1982   338.7'6134973   82–16792
ISBN 0–671–42023–2   338.7'613473

Grateful acknowledgment is made to Cravath,
Swaine & Moore for permission to reprint material
previously published in The Cravath Firm and Its
Predecessors, 1819–1948, by Robert T. Swaine.
Privately printed, New York, 1948, Ad Press Ltd.

Acknowledgments

Many of my close friends are lawyers, and years of sharing our professional experiences provided the inspiration for *The Partners*. I deeply appreciate their continuing trust and friendship, and their many contributions to this book.

My editor at Simon and Schuster, Alice Mayhew, provided precisely the right support and guidance at crucial times in my writing and research. Ann Godoff also offered valuable assistance. My agent, Amanda Urban, has been a valued and supportive confidante and an effective advocate.

Steven Brill, editor of *The American Lawyer*, has given me invaluable advice, encouragement and support from the inception of this book. He and the staff members of *The American Lawyer* acted as an important sounding board for my thoughts and discoveries. Margot Cohen tenaciously fact-checked my work.

The following published sources were especially useful in my research: *The American Lawyer Guide to Law Firms*, 1981–1982 edition, Am-Law Publishing Company, New York, for statistical information about law firms and the identity of many of their major clients; *Martindale–Hubble Law Directory*, 1982 edition, Martindale–Hubble, Inc., Summit, N.J., for biographical information about many lawyers mentioned; and Peter Collier and David Horowitz, *The Rockefellers*, 1976, Holt, Rinehart & Winston, New York, for information about members of the Rockefeller family.

I am indebted to my family and friends, especially my parents; my sister, Jane Holden; my brother Michael; and Jane Berentson for their unflagging personal support and encouragement.

TO MY PARENTS

Contents

Author's Note

The Partners is the result of two years of reporting, consisting almost entirely of personal interviews with the people involved in the cases and transactions that are the subject of the book, as well as a review of the many related documents. The book is not based on any other published sources.

Many of my initial interviews for each chapter were conducted on a not-for-attribution basis. Lawyers were concerned that their identification as sources for my book would adversely affect their careers, even if their quoted comments reflected favorably on their firms. The information I gathered from these interviews was used primarily to persuade others to discuss their work with me on an on-the-record basis. My policy was not to use information in the book unless it was confirmed on the record by someone directly involved in the matter.

Many of the sources who did speak to me on the record did so reluctantly. In some cases, lawyers were barred from disclosing client confidences by the Code of Professional Responsibility, and limited their comments accordingly. Although nearly all the principal lawyers involved eventually agreed to be interviewed, no one described in this book sought to be included or sought publicity.

Most quotations which do not come directly from my interviews are taken from court transcripts or from notes made by participants at the time statements were made. Otherwise, the quotes represent the speaker's recollection of the statement or the recollection of someone who heard the statement at the time it was made. Similarly, the thoughts and states of mind of various participants described in the book are as they recall them.

I was an associate lawyer at the New York firm of Cravath, Swaine & Moore from 1976–1979. I did not work on the IBM antitrust cases or any other IBM client matter while I was employed by the firm, and the information about IBM and Cravath that appears in this book is based solely on reporting which took place after I left the firm.

Introduction

On December 12, 1980, lawyers from law firms representing America's richest and most powerful banks gathered secretly in the 32nd-floor conference room at the midtown offices of Shearman & Sterling in New York City's Citicorp skyscraper. For most of the lawyers attending, the circumstances were unique but the cast of characters familiar: the same senior partners from the same law firms they had been working with or against in major financial transactions for years. The meeting's host, John Hoffman, the Shearman & Sterling partner representing Citicorp, greeted his colleagues like old friends: Bruce Nichols, from Davis Polk & Wardwell representing Morgan Guaranty Trust; Frank Logan, from Milbank, Tweed, Hadley & McCloy representing the Chase Manhattan Bank; Richard Simmons from Cravath, Swaine & Moore representing Chemical Bank; and others, together representing the country's twelve largest banks.

Then Hoffman dropped a bombshell on the assembled bank lawyers: acting on behalf of his client, Citibank, he was secretly negotiating with the revolutionary government of Iran for the release of the American hostages. These negotiations were being conducted not by the State Department, not by the President, not by the Pentagon, but by John Hoffman—a partner in a New York law firm that most Americans had never heard of and, throughout the hostage ordeal, never would hear of. In his hands, and the collected hands of the partners from the elite law firms gathered together that day, would ultimately rest the fate of American lives, power, prestige and money.

If Alexis de Tocqueville were describing American lawyers today as an "aristocracy," as he did more than 150 years ago, he would mean the kind of partners from the kind of law firms meeting at Shearman & Sterling that day. There are about 500,000 lawyers practicing in the United States today; among them are personal injury, criminal, divorce and real estate lawyers, practicing in towns and cities, alone and in small groups as partners. Only a tiny fraction of that number—roughly 3,000—practice in the elite blue chip corporate firms which occupy the pinnacle of the profession. From their plush offices high in skyscrapers in the nation's financial centers, these lawyers survey the rest of the profession with at least a touch of arrogance and disdain.

Binding together these lawyers and law firms and distinguishing them from all others is their representation of America's major banks, financial institutions and corporations, the country's greatest concentrations of economic power. Only such clients can afford the elite corporate law firms and the kind of law practice for which the firms pride themselves—one in which no stone is left unturned, no matter how seemingly insignificant, and with virtually no regard for time or money. Indeed, if pressed, this is the explanation most often offered by top corporate lawyers to justify their representation of wealthy clients: it permits them to perfect the craft of lawyering to an extent that poor clients cannot possibly afford. It is what makes them, in their own eyes, the best. The representation of such clients is concentrated in the hands of the partners in the elite corporate firms to an extraordinary degree. At nearly all of the largest, most important and most complicated financial transactions and conflicts which take place, partners from the same small group of elite law firms are present. It is no coincidence that such events are among the country's most significant economic, social and political events as well.

These law firms dominate the legal affairs of their principal clients, even though large banks and corporations always have lawyers within their corporate staffs, known as "in-house" counsel. The firms have developed the capacity to handle a very wide range of the kinds of specialized legal problems which arise in corporate and financial transactions, as well as the manpower to handle very large and complex problems. As a result, the elite corporate firms are themselves large and diversified. None is smaller than 150 lawyers; the largest, Shearman & Sterling, is almost 350 lawyers. Most have at least 200, with a support staff at least as large.

At all such firms, lawyers are divided into partners, the more senior and experienced lawyers who share the profits and risks of the firm and make the management decisions; and associates, younger lawyers who are employed by the firm at an annual salary and may ultimately be tapped for partnership. Most of the legal problems handled by this kind of firm are so large that they require a number of lawyers, which gives rise to what is known as "pyramid" staffing—a single partner or small group of partners who preside over a larger pool of associates. Within the firms, as a whole, there are always more associates than partners. More than any other factor, it is the capacity of the firms to staff matters in such a fashion—and to bill clients for associates' work at rates that far exceed associate salaries—which produces the firms' immense profitability. Their partners earn incomes that rival and often exceed those of the top executives in their client corporations— upwards of $350,000.

There is an aura about the elite corporate law firms that is not quite duplicated anywhere else. It makes itself felt in the tastefully conservative, even faintly shabby, office decor; in the oil portraits of the long-dead founding partners; in the prestige addresses; in the polite but cool formality displayed by the lawyers in the firm, who invariably wear dark suits and dignified ties. The firms project an image of unshakable prosperity and security, of tradition and excellence, of permanence. It is the image of the old-line WASP financial establishment, one that is carefully burnished and maintained.

It is a world for which lawyers are well prepared at the country's most prestigious law schools. At nearly all of the elite corporate firms, many of the partners have been educated at Harvard Law School, itself a bastion of the kind of values reflected in the blue chip firms. Harvard Law graduates have dominated the upper reaches of the legal profession to a far greater degree than any other school or college, and their similar professional training has in turn influenced other lawyers at their firms. As Robert Swaine, a partner in Cravath, Swaine & Moore, wrote unapologetically in 1948, "The firm has taken most of its associates from the law schools of Harvard, Columbia and Yale, although . . . there was a conscious effort to take at least one man a year from other law schools of high repute such as Pennsylvania, Cornell, Virginia, Michigan and Chicago." To that list today would be added Stanford, California (Berkeley) and probably New York University. Despite occasional gestures of hiring an associate from a "lesser" local law school, graduation from one of the top ten law schools is almost a prerequisite for employment at one of the elite firms.

The similar educational background helps explain the homogeneity of the lawyers in the firms despite the absence of any overt discrimination in hiring and promotion. To interview at the prestigious law schools, all firms today sign statements that they do not discriminate on the basis of race, creed, ethnic origin, sex and, in many cases, sexual preference. Historically, there was discrimination, especially against Jews. (Virtually no blacks or women applied.) If there is discrimination today, it is extremely subtle, even unconscious, reflecting a generalized preference for people who will "fit in" and work well with clients. All of these firms now have lawyers who are Jewish, black, female; vestiges of discrimination are, ironically, most apparent in the degree to which some such lawyers have aped their WASP counterparts. There is little, if any, affirmative action at any of the most prestigious firms.

The elite corporate firms are also old; their traditions have been handed down from one generation of lawyers to another, and they have deep roots in the business and financial communities they serve. Most were founded before the turn of the century, with established clients who took advantage of the boom in the American economy which ensued. No firm founded since the Second World War has managed to enter these elite ranks; some old established firms have, however, slipped out of them.

Of these traditions, one of the most deeply rooted is secrecy. As Alexander Forger, a partner at Milbank, Tweed, Hadley & McCloy, explains: "Our clients tell us that one of our great attributes is an ability to cope with problems in a low-profile way. We *never* seek public attention. Discretion is essential. Clients never even have to ask for confidentiality. We assume that our clients don't even want it known that they are consulting counsel."

The elite corporate firms have never needed publicity to attract clients; indeed, their reputation for secrecy is more valuable in that regard. Such a policy has also had the effect of almost entirely shielding such firms from public scrutiny, since knowledge of how and what they do has been largely confined to their partners and, to a much lesser degree, their clients.

The deals, cases and transactions which will unfold in detail in these pages reveal the roles of the partners, associates and their firms in the most significant legal events of recent years. Taken together, they represent the range of specialized work performed by any one of these firms, and they are intended as a composite portrait of the elite corporate firms and their partners—not any one firm in particular. The similarities between an antitrust case or a stock offering overwhelm any differences in approach which might exist from one of the firms to another.

These examples have been viewed within the legal profession as some of the most exciting and significant work that has been performed by major law firms. Obviously, they account for only a small fraction of the work performed by these law firms, most of which is "not of sufficiently romantic nature to be of general interest," as one partner described his work. In that sense, these examples are not typical of the work of the large law firms. But to the extent that it is only at times when the stakes are high that a law firm stretches to the full limits of its power, these examples provide the true measure of the institution.

CHAPTER ONE

IRAN

Shearman & Sterling;
Davis Polk & Wardwell

Deep in the Iranian desert, in the darkness of early morning, chaos swept the American military rescue mission. As a C-130 troop transport plane lumbered down a dark abandoned runway, one of the helicopters struggled in vain to get out of its path. The crash sent flames leaping into the desert night, illuminating the bodies of eight Americans left behind in the wreckage.

It was April 25, 1980. The United States military attempt to rescue the American hostages in Teheran had ended in humiliating failure. The fifty-two hostages were dispersed from the American Embassy into secret locations, and the likelihood of their release seemed more remote than ever. In the wake of the raid, all contacts between the United States government and the revolutionary regime in Iran abruptly ceased.

Most Americans reacted to the failed attempt with feelings of frustration and anguish, but it was particularly worrisome for John Hoffman, a partner at the New York law firm of Shearman & Sterling. Lately, it seemed, nearly everything that happened to the fifty-two American captives in Teheran had a direct bearing on the interests of his own most important client, Citibank, the nation's second-largest bank. Citibank was caught squarely between the United States government and the Iranians. The bank had millions of dollars in outstanding loans to Iranian entities; the Iranians, in turn, had additional millions in Citibank deposits, which had been

19

frozen by President Jimmy Carter shortly after the hostages were seized the previous November.

The main leverage the United States still seemed to have with the Ayatollah and his revolutionary government was the frozen assets in American banks like Citibank. It had become obvious to Hoffman that without a satisfactory settlement of the hostage situation, the Iranian assets would remain frozen, the Citibank loans to Iran would not be repaid, and there was nothing he or the bank could do about it. Now that settlement looked hopeless.

On the Tuesday morning after the raid, Hoffman dutifully called 29-year-old associate Margaret Wiener into his office for their weekly strategy conference on the Iranian situation, though it was hard to know now what strategy could possibly do any good. Citibank had been sued by the Iranians in Paris soon after the freeze. Hoffman was overseeing the litigation. Wiener and he began to discuss the impact of the raid on the already tortuous progress of that case. Shortly after they began, the phone rang. Hoffman paused, waiting for his secretary to answer; when the rings continued, he motioned for Wiener to pick up the extension on the end table next to the sofa where she was sitting in his spacious corner office.

As soon as Wiener heard the excited voice of Peter Mailander, a German lawyer in Stuttgart who often worked with Shearman & Sterling on Citibank matters, she motioned to Hoffman to pick up his phone. Mailander told the Shearman & Sterling lawyers that he had been contacted by lawyers representing revolutionary Iran, and they wanted him to get in touch with Hoffman to "explore an economic solution to the worldwide litigation problems." Hoffman was electrified by the news. For months he had been casting lures in every direction he could think of, desperately hoping that he would make some kind of contact with the Iranians themselves. Was this a long-awaited breakthrough? He peppered Mailander with questions. What was his source for the inquiry? The context?

Mailander explained that he had been contacted by Herbert Wagendorf and Peter Heineman, two German lawyers who were representing the government of Iran and Bank Markazi, Iran's central bank. Wagendorf and Heineman claimed that they had been instructed by Iranian President Abolhassan Bani-Sadr; Nasir-O-Sadat Salami, Iran's Minister of Finance and a board member of Germany's Krupp industry, in which the Iranian government was a principal stockholder; and Behzad Nabavi, the head of Bank Markazi. The Iranians had asked their German lawyers to begin settlement negotiations with Citibank on the following conditions: Iran would not put forward any more money as collateral, and the existence of their negotiations must be kept absolutely secret. They emphasized that any leak would produce emphatic denials from the Iranian officials and the negotiations would be terminated.

Hoffman's voice was calm when he told Mailander that he would consider the proposal, but when he hung up and turned to Wiener, elation sparkled in his face. He reiterated the need for secrecy, then raced to Shearman & Sterling's library, where the two lawyers fed the names of Bani-Sadr, Nabavi and Salami into the firm's computerized information banks. What they discovered reinforced the plausibility of the German approach. Salami and Nabavi were in Hamburg that day for a meeting of the International Monetary Fund, and could easily have been in close contact with their German lawyers. Bani-Sadr was in Paris, where he could have spoken on an untapped telephone. Of course, it wasn't clear that the Ayatollah himself knew anything about the approach or would support it, and it was hard to know the status of any of the various factions struggling for power within Iran. But recent news reports indicated that the Bani-Sadr faction, which included Nabavi and Salami, was in the ascendancy.

Hoffman immediately called Hans Angermueller, Citibank's senior executive vice president and a former partner at Shearman & Sterling, who in turn pulled Walter Wriston, Citibank's chairman, out of a board meeting. The bank executives gave Hoffman their authority to pursue the Iranian approach. Hoffman then notified one other senior partner at his firm, Robert Clare, Jr., the head of the firm's banking department, and notified and obtained approval from officials at the State Department, Treasury Department and the White House, all of whom were then stalemated in their own efforts.

Ten days later, Hoffman stood in Kronberg, West Germany, looking up at the mock-medieval battlements of the Schloss Hotel, a castle built by Kaiser Wilhelm II for his mother. Inside this fantastic and unlikely setting were the German lawyers who were representing Iran. And on Hoffman's shoulders rested the fate of the $8 billion in frozen Iranian assets and, as later events would demonstrate, the fate of the fifty-two Americans held captive in Iran.

There is no better bedrock for a major corporate law firm than a great and powerful bank as a client; it is, in fact, practically a prerequisite for inclusion among the most elite law firms in the country. Obviously, the larger the bank, and the more comprehensive a law firm's grasp on its outside legal work, the better. Two law firms so dominate the outside work of major banks that they would belong in the first rank of law firms for that reason alone: Shearman & Sterling, which represents Citibank, and Davis Polk & Wardwell, which represents Morgan Guaranty Trust.

The importance of a major bank client to a large corporate law firm is based on the sheer volume and regularity of its legal needs. The major American banks today represent some of the greatest concentrations of wealth in the world. Because of the power which stems from such economic resources, they are also among the most heavily regulated institutions in the country, subjected to an unending stream of statutes and regulations from foreign, federal, state and local governing bodies, covering everything from interest rate ceilings to foreign currency exchange regulations. While banks like Citibank and Morgan Guaranty may be officially based in New York, they do business all over the world and have to comply with legal restrictions in every location. A bank can make hardly any decisions that do not have legal implications. Citibank, the country's second-largest after Bank of America, has an in-house legal staff of ten; Shearman & Sterling has almost 350 lawyers, more than half of whom work on Citibank matters at one time or another, their work ranging from reviews of mundane loan agreements to restructuring the Polish national debt.

Representing a major bank like Citibank or Morgan Guaranty also guarantees a major law firm vital exposure in the sophisticated financial markets which generate other legal business as well. In addition to its principal work for Citibank, Shearman & Sterling has added thirty other foreign and domestic banks as clients, including the Bank of Montreal in Canada and the Japanese Fuji Bank. Its extensive international banking work in such areas as Eurodollar financings and transactions has brought it into contact with many foreign governments and foreign corporations; such clients today include the Saudi Arabian Royal Commission; De Beers Consolidated Mines, the South African mining and manufacturing concern; Sonatrach, the North African oil company; the government of Abu Dhabi; and many others. The international scope of the firm's work is reflected in its far-flung network of branch offices located in San Francisco, Paris, London, Abu Dhabi and Hong Kong; overall, about 60 percent of the firm's work is international. Citibank, of course, is also in-volved in many major domestic financial transactions. Expertise derived from this work has enabled Shearman & Sterling to ex-pand into fields like mergers and acquisitions, refinancings and work-outs, and securities and note offerings—the crucial main-stays of a blue chip legal practice.

For these principal reasons, bank work at Shearman & Sterling, at Davis Polk, and at some of the other firms which dominate the outside legal work of the major banks is done at something of a discount. Usually, the banks pay the firms a large annual retainer, and hours are charged against the retainer at a rate discounted slightly from the law firms' usual formula hourly rate. This does not mean that bank work is not highly profitable. In many cases, it is the custom for someone else to pay the bank's legal fees—a buyer from the bank's customer, for example, who is charged at the firm's full rates. Much bank work also lends itself nicely to the pyramid staffing pattern. A single partner, for example, can easily oversee a large number of associates who review loan agreements. And the discount encourages bank executives, as one partner put it, "to just pick up the phone any time they feel like it and talk to us without worrying about our hourly rates." Picking up the phone, of course, triggers the clock for the time which will eventually be deducted from the retainer, but such indirect billing is relatively painless. Furthermore, much of the work performed for a bank does *not* qualify for the discount. Generally, litigation does not qualify, nor does any work requiring the kind of expertise which could not be developed in a client's in-house staff. Though law firm partners do not like to emphasize this aspect, one obvious reason for the discount is to discourage the major banks from keeping most of their legal work in-house. Nonetheless, the exis-tence of the discount for bank work—at a time when the work of the blue chip firm has otherwise evolved exclusively into fields for which a *premium* can be charged—is a strong indication of how important such work is to the overall economic health and vitality of the firm.

Citibank and its predecessors have been Shearman & Sterling's most important client since 1891, about thirty years after the firm was founded by Thomas Shearman and David Field, the author of the "Field Code" of civil procedure for New York State. James Stillman, the son of a prominent cotton merchant, became president of New York's National City Bank, and brought the bank's work to his own lawyer—John Sterling, then a young lawyer at the firm. National City Bank had assets of only about $14 million, but under Stillman's leadership, it evolved into one of the country's largest and most important banks. Shearman & Sterling has always acted as its general outside counsel.

On November 13, 1979, bank telexes carried the news that President Carter had frozen all Iranian deposits in American banks in retaliation for the seizure of the United States Embassy in Teheran and the taking of American citizens as hostages. That step immediately sent outside counsel for the banks scurrying to bank conference rooms across the country. Citibank naturally turned to Shearman & Sterling, which already had some experience with freezes and asset seizures. It had represented Citibank when the Soviet government seized Citibank assets in Russia in 1917, and had represented the bank in previous American freezes: against China in 1950, against Cuba in 1963 and against Vietnam in 1975. None of those freezes had involved such sums of money, however, and none had been ordered in such politically volatile circumstances.

In fact, within the White House there had been a great deal of reluctance to impose the freeze in the first place. In strategy meetings in Washington, presided over in large part by presidential counsel Lloyd Cutler, previously a partner in the Washington firm of Wilmer, Cutler & Pickering, and a former associate at Cravath, Swaine & Moore, there was concern that the freeze would "trigger the Great Depression of 1979," according to Cutler. Not only did the government of Iran and its various entities have billions of dollars on deposit in American banks, but worldwide faith in the integrity of the American banking system might have been jeopardized, leading any foreign depositors who feared political reprisal to withdraw their assets precipitously.

It was just such a threat, however, which finally led Carter to impose the freeze. At 4:00 A.M. on the morning of November 13, eight days after the seizure of the hostages, the Iranians impetuously announced that they were withdrawing all of their assets from United States banks. "That resolved all doubts," Cutler recalls, and by the time the Iranians tried to collect, the presidential order implementing the freeze had been executed and the Iranians were turned away by the banks.

One of the banks to take the lead in refusing to release the Iranian assets was Morgan Guaranty, which acted on the advice of two of its lawyers at Davis Polk & Wardwell, Bruce Nichols and Bartlett McGuire. Morgan Guaranty, though it is only the fifth-largest U.S. bank in assets, wields an influence disproportionate to its size. It was founded by financier John Pierpont Morgan, as the private banking firm of J. P. Morgan & Co.; and the nature of its clientele—it had traditionally serviced only the wealthiest individuals and corporations—and the secrecy which has surrounded its operations have made it one of the world's most influential and powerful banks. In 1933, federal legislation forced it to divide into what became Morgan Guaranty Trust Co., its commercial banking arm, and Morgan Stanley & Co., which is today one of the country's leading investment banking firms.

Both Morgan Guaranty Trust and Morgan Stanley are still represented almost exclusively by J. P. Morgan's old law firm, Davis Polk & Wardwell. Davis Polk in some ways itself resembles the kind of clients attracted to Morgan Guaranty. Historically, it has epitomized the "white shoe" law firm, and it still has many more partners listed in the Social Register than does Sullivan & Cromwell or Cravath, Swaine & Moore, the two firms with which it is most often compared. During the nineteenth century, Grover Cleveland was counsel to the firm; the Davis in the firm name was John Davis, the 1924 Democratic nominee for President. The other name partners were Frank Polk, the Undersecretary of State in Woodrow Wilson's administration, and Allan Wardwell, son-in-law of the Francis Stetson who did legal work on the organization of U.S. Steel.

Though Morgan Guaranty and Morgan Stanley remain mainstays of Davis Polk's practice, the firm has diversified from that base to an even greater extent than has Shearman & Sterling. Among its major corporate clients are International Telephone & Telegraph, International Paper, Johns-Manville, LTV Corporation, McDermott, Inc., and R. J. Reynolds—a corporate roster rivaled only by Sullivan & Cromwell and by Cravath. In addition to Morgan Stanley, it represents Merrill, Lynch, Pierce, Fenner &

Smith, Inc., and Smith Barney, Harris Upham & Co. in investment circles.

When executives at Morgan Guaranty learned of the asset freeze, they first called Bruce Nichols, the Davis Polk corporate partner who acts as a liaison with the bank and oversees most of its work within the firm. Nichols is something of a legend within Davis Polk. Though he eschews company politics and membership on firm committees, his position at the head of the bank work makes him one of the firm's most powerful partners. Like Hoffman, he graduated from Princeton and from Harvard Law School, and his reputation for legal brilliance within the firm is matched only by his reputation for eccentricity. He is a confirmed bachelor who dresses fastidiously but conservatively and, on the rare occasions he is not working at the firm, cultivates an expensive taste in food, wine and opera. To most associates he seems aloof and distant, preoccupied with weighty legal questions. Many associates are afraid to work for him, intimidated by his brilliance and the great deference he is shown by other partners in the firm. Unlike many of the partners at Davis Polk, he is not particularly adept at handling other people. Associates say that he exhibits an almost constant nervous tension, which they often fear is caused by them, and at times he seems almost painfully shy. He abhors publicity of any kind.

To assist him with the Iran matter, Nichols tapped Bartlett McGuire, a younger litigation partner who had extensive experience handling cases for Morgan Guaranty; and the two headed for the bank's fortresslike offices on Wall Street.

Like the lawyers for the other major banks, the Davis Polk partners had two major questions on their minds: What did the freeze mean in practical terms? and How could Morgan Guaranty protect its own interests? Morgan had what McGuire describes as a "substantial exposure," about $80 million in loans outstanding. Like most of the major American banks, Morgan also held deposits of Iranian entities in its branches in London, Paris and Frankfurt. In fact, two Morgan bankers were in Teheran the same day the hostages were taken, and made their way out of the country surreptitiously.

As for the freeze itself, Nichols and McGuire advised the bankers to issue instructions stopping payment to all its domestic and foreign branches. That decision itself took some deliberation,

McGuire recalls, because the regulations implementing the freeze hadn't yet been issued, and the freeze itself raised some serious legal questions. Foremost among them was the status of Iranian deposits in Morgan's foreign branches. There was no question that the President had the constitutional authority to freeze the assets located in the United States, but most of Iran's deposits were in the foreign branches. Did the President have the power to freeze assets located on foreign soil? No one was sure, but pending litigation of that issue in the courts, the bank decided to assume that the President had the authority. As for the bank's own $65 million in claims, it decided to launch a search for Iranian assets located in countries where litigation by Morgan could secure a judgment against them. The Davis Polk lawyers sent instructions to lawyers in England, France and Germany, including a lawyer in Frankfurt, Bodo Schlosshan, an old friend and a former associate at Davis Polk.

On April 17, another presidential directive appeared, as well as regulations implementing the freeze. These orders enabled the banks not only to freeze the Iranian assets in foreign branches but also to set off their own claims against Iran against the Iranian deposits. The order authorizing set-offs gave rise to various legal problems, and the Davis Polk lawyers were initially reluctant to take such an action. But when Citibank set off its claims, Morgan Guaranty and the other American banks with European branches followed suit. Cutler now concedes that he and the President knew their authority in this regard was questionable. "If nothing else, we knew we could snarl the Iranian assets for years in the ensuing litigation," Cutler says. (Litigation is still pending related to the Chinese, Cuban and Vietnamese freezes.)

As Morgan Guaranty, Citibank and the other American banks proceeded with the set-offs, Davis Polk's man in Germany, Schlosshan, located a rich cache for any claimant against the government of Iran—the Krupp industrial complex in Essen. Before the Iranian revolution, the Shah's government had made a major investment in the German steel and heavy equipment manufacturer, and much to the delight of the Davis Polk lawyers, that investment was held in the name of the government of Iran. The revolutionary government had become the successor owner, and Salami, the Finance Minister, was a member of Krupp's board of directors.

On Monday morning, April 28, after a weekend of long-distance calls to Davis Polk, Schlosshan was on the courthouse steps armed with the papers necessary to attach Iran's interest in Krupp on behalf of Morgan Guaranty. An attachment, in a sense, is a temporary seizure of property by the court. The court does not actually award the property to the party obtaining the attachment, but it puts the property within the control of the court so that, in the event the party eventually wins a judgment against the owner of the attached property, that property can be used to satisfy the judgment. Thus, in this case, the German court would hold Iran's interest in Krupp. If Morgan Guaranty eventually won a judgment against Iran, the court would turn all or part of the Krupp assets over to Morgan Guaranty.

In the secret proceeding which ensued, Schlosshan and his colleagues at Davis Polk demonstrated that they had successfully anticipated every objection raised by a judge who was understandably apprehensive that the Iranian-American conflict had reached German soil. The attachment was granted. Ten days later, pursuant to West German law, the government of Iran was notified that one of its prized foreign assets had been tied up by an American bank, acting independently of the United States government. Citibank quickly followed Morgan Guaranty's lead and also obtained a German attachment decree relating to the same property.

After learning of the Morgan Guaranty Krupp attachment, Iran had its German lawyers, Wagendorf and Heineman, file a motion in the German court to set aside the attachment. It was clear, however, that the motion was not likely to be granted and that an ultimate resolution of Morgan Guaranty's rights to all or part of the Krupp assets could take years to determine. And Iranian lawyers were already getting a sour taste for Western litigation. Hundreds of claims had been filed against Iran by American companies, with many of the claims running into millions of dollars. Those suits had been stayed—but not disposed of—at the time the Iranian assets were frozen. Iran still remained liable to any of those companies anywhere in the world where it had assets and where a court might issue an order against them.

Furthermore, after the American banks set off their claims against the Iranian deposits in foreign branches, Iran had instituted litigation in Paris to declare such set-offs illegal and to reclaim the foreign deposits, raising many of the questions about presidential authority which the Davis Polk lawyers had feared.

There had been no quick resolution—in fact, it had become obvious to the American bank lawyers, John Hoffman among them, that the French were going to be content to juggle that judicial hot potato as long as necessary to avoid any politically embarrassing outcome.

It was this complicated web of litigation, which had effectively tied Iran's hands in world financial markets, to which the German lawyers evidently referred when they told Hoffman they wanted to negotiate a solution to the "worldwide litigation problems."

At about the same time that they called Citibank's lawyers, Wagendorf and Heineman, the German lawyers for Iran, also approached Davis Polk. They asked to postpone a hearing that had been scheduled regarding Iran's motion to set aside the Krupp attachment, and they also made some vague reference to settling Iran's other litigation problems.

Nichols, McGuire and Donaldson Pillsbury, another Davis Polk partner who often handled problems for Morgan Guaranty, met to consider the Iranian approach through the German lawyers. They had no problem with granting a delay in the hearing on the Krupp attachment—Morgan Guaranty had nothing to lose there, since it retained its attachment, and the Davis Polk lawyers had been advised that the German court would just as soon put off the matter itself, again for international political reasons. But they found the reference to litigation curious. For some reason, Morgan Guaranty had never been made a party to Iran's litigation in Paris. Nor had it been sued in London, and its only other attachments were in New York, out of reach of the Iranians. Partly because they failed to see how Morgan Guaranty would be involved in broader talks, partly because they felt Morgan Guaranty was now adequately protected by its German attachments and the set-offs, and partly because they were suspicious of *any* approach which claimed to come from the Iranian government, the Davis Polk lawyers declined an invitation to travel to Germany to meet with Wagendorf and Heineman.

"Undertaking these negotiations was enormously expensive," Pillsbury says. "We didn't think it was worthwhile for Morgan Guaranty. And frankly, we didn't take this approach terribly seriously." Three weeks later, Pillsbury noticed that the hearing scheduled for Citibank's Krupp attachment was also being postponed, so "I realized Hoffman must have been talking to the

Iranians through the German lawyers, too," Pillsbury recalls. But he didn't talk to Hoffman, nor did he notify anyone in Washington about his own contacts. After the initial flurry of excitement about the asset freeze, life returned to routine at Davis Polk.

Not so at Shearman & Sterling, where Hoffman felt instinctively that something would break—and that he wanted to be there when it did.

Hoffman does little to alter the image of the banking lawyer as the drab, colorless counterpart to his cautious and meticulous banking clients. Shearman & Sterling's midtown offices (the firm also has expansive quarters at 53 Wall Street) are bright and modern, but Hoffman's own corner office is conservatively furnished in somber colors and antique furniture reproductions, decorated with family photos. Hoffman looks younger than his 48 years, despite his gray hair, and dresses in regulation pinstripes. He is all that a bank lawyer is expected to be—thorough, meticulous and cautious—but as one associate puts it, "he has a vision." He loves to tackle the broad complexities of a new project, to "kick ideas around."

As the head of Shearman & Sterling's twenty-seven-lawyer midtown litigation group, he has plenty of opportunity for such intellectual activity. He and his group work almost exclusively on litigation matters for Citibank, but most of it is threatened or prospective litigation, and Hoffman's goal is to head it off before it actually gets to court. Hoffman is the kind of litigator, in fact, who almost never appears in a courtroom. As a result, his principal litigation skill is negotiation, and it is as a hard-nosed negotiator that he has earned his reputation within the firm. Even before the approach from the Iranians came, he was spending his free time daydreaming about possible solutions for what became, after the asset freeze, perhaps the most tangled financial mess in history.

More than any other bank lawyer, Hoffman was also in a position to circulate the results of his thinking. Besides his close friendship with Angermuller, the former Shearman & Sterling partner at Citibank, he had close personal and professional ties to lawyers serving in the Carter administration. Robert Carswell, Deputy Secretary of the Treasury with primary responsibility for the asset freeze, was also a former partner at Shearman & Sterling and had worked closely with Hoffman. Robert Mundheim, general counsel for the Treasury, had been an associate at Shearman &

Sterling before becoming a law professor at the University of Pennsylvania. Lloyd Cutler, whose firm in Washington, Wilmer, Cutler & Pickering, often handles matters in the capital for Citibank, is a friend of Hoffman's.

"I was in contact with the government people on a daily basis," Hoffman recalls. "They wanted to know about the pending litigation [Citibank was sued by Iran in both Paris and London], a matter of great concern to the government because the legality of the freeze in foreign branches was the issue. If we'd lost, the U.S. financial leverage was gone." Hoffman met in Washington periodically with Carswell and Mundheim, keeping them abreast of developments. Hoffman also began sending out his own signals to the Iranians.

In March, for example, Hoffman accepted an invitation to speak at Harvard Law School with Thomas Shack, a Washington lawyer who was representing the government of Iran in its various cases in the United States. "I figured he was at least a link to the Iranians," Hoffman says. "I wanted to float the idea of some kind of settlement." Later in March, Hoffman sat through "a long, dull hearing in French" in Paris, hoping that he would get some kind of signal from Iran's French lawyers, who were radicals known to be sympathetic to the Iranian cause and possibly in touch with the revolutionary leaders. But nothing came until the phone call from the Germans on May 2.

When Hoffman reached Carswell in Washington over the weekend to tell him about the call, Carswell was interested but hardly as excited as Hoffman sounded over the phone. "We had agreed we'd see the bank lawyers whenever they wanted," Carswell recalls, "and they'd march down. We had endless contacts with every conceivable bank lawyer. What really happened for six months was a lot of probing that came to nothing." Carswell understandably felt no great sense of urgency, and when he met with Hoffman the following week was no more persuaded that anything would ever come from a contact that to him looked like a slender and indirect thread. "The U.S. government wasn't talking to Iran then," Carswell says. "The raid had killed every approach we had under way. Sure, I told Hoffman to go ahead and talk. But I didn't have any great expectations."

Although Carswell won't talk about it, Hoffman was not the only bank lawyer who contacted him that week claiming to have had feelers from revolutionary Iran, but Carswell was not so willing to bestow the support to others that he had given Hoffman. Bank of America had also been contacted by Iran's German lawyers and given much the same message as Hoffman. They were told—indeed, ordered—to have no further contacts with lawyers purporting to represent Iran.

Bank of America is the country's largest bank, and it was also exposed to the greatest risks in the Iranian situation— $2.5 billion in deposits. Unlike the other major banks involved, however, it did not turn most of the legal work over to its outside counsel. Although it retained Washington, D.C.'s Steptoe & Johnson and San Francisco's Pillsbury, Madison & Sutro, the lawyer in charge was Thorne Corse, the bank's senior in-house counsel for international matters.

Bank of America and First National Bank of Chicago are the only major banks in the country which do not rely principally on a single law firm as outside counsel. In the case of Bank of America, according to Corse, "A. P. Giannini, the bank's founder, was not enamored of lawyers. He hired Samuel Stewart away from Cravath, Swaine & Moore to become the bank's inside general counsel, a position Stewart was only willing to accept if he became the bank's principal lawyer. This was fine with Giannini." Today, Bank of America has 140 lawyers on its staff, and spreads its outside work among a number of law firms.

So it was Corse himself who told Carswell about the approach from the Iranians; and according to Corse, Carswell told him that "no negotiations will be permitted as long as the hostages are still being held." In retrospect, Corse isn't sure why Hoffman got the go-ahead and he didn't, especially since Bank of America had more at stake. "It may have been that Citibank was approached slightly before we were," Corse says. "On the other hand, there was speculation that Hoffman was tapped because he and Carswell and Hans Angermueller [the Citibank executive vice president] were all former partners at Shearman & Sterling. I didn't know Carswell nearly as well as Hoffman did, obviously. But this may be unfair—it may just have been a matter of timing." Corse soon forgot about the Iranian approach.

Hoffman, on the other hand, went to work immediately, flying to Washington for a briefing and meeting with Carswell. At their meeting, Carswell reminded Hoffman that, given the government freeze, any settlement would be subject to the approval of the United States government, and asked him to keep the government informed. He also made clear what had become an implicit condition of Hoffman's daydreams: There would be no United States government approval of any financial settlement that did not include the release of the United States hostages. When Hoffman returned to New York, he cabled the German lawyers to state the conditions for negotiations. He accepted the Iranian demand for secrecy, and added another condition to those stated by Carswell: Citibank would not enter into an agreement which did not contain an across-the-board settlement for all the United States banks that were holding frozen Iranian assets. One day later, the Iranians accepted his conditions.

Hoffman's diplomatic efforts were shrouded in the most careful security precautions ever taken at Shearman & Sterling. Hoffman always traveled alone and rarely used the telephone to discuss his progress. He used fictitious names to make hotel reservations. Within the government, only Carswell, Mundheim, Owens, Christopher, Cutler, Treasury Secretary William Miller, Secretary of State Cyrus Vance and President Carter were informed; at Shearman & Sterling, Hoffman told only senior banking partner Robert Clare, Jr., Wiener, and his secretary. Unknown to these participants, he also began discussions with one other lawyer: Frank Logan, a partner at New York's Milbank, Tweed, Hadley & Mc-Cloy, which represents Chase Manhattan Bank, the financial citadel of the Shah.

Although the Chase Manhattan Bank had acted as the agent bank in more syndicated loans to Iran than any other bank in the world, it had no independent contacts with representatives of Iran after the revolution. The mere mention of the Chase Manhattan Bank or its chairman, David Rockefeller, was enough to make a revolutionary Iranian see red. Rockefeller, after Carter, was probably the American most hanged in effigy by Iranian militants. It was risky for Hoffman to talk to Logan. If the Iranians found out, negotiations might be quickly terminated.

That risk was minimized in the person of Francis Logan. Modest, almost self-effacing, he is the kind of lawyer for whom secrecy is instinctive. He considers even the name of his client to be confidential information, and for 25 years has never spoken to a reporter. Associates at Milbank are intimidated by his rectitude, his taciturnity and above all by his encyclopedic knowledge of banking law and procedure. He is a pillar of professional responsibility, and typically his first concern when Hoffman called him about the Iranian approach was his professional obligation.

"I couldn't get involved in any conflicts of interest," Logan recalls thinking. "I didn't want to get involved in anything which might embarrass my client. It was also clear to me that this was a matter of great importance, and we would have to bear in mind the public interest. I hope history's verdict will be that we served the public interest without sacrificing our duty to our clients, and our duties as officers of the court." Those reservations aside, Logan began to help Hoffman work through the issues and formulate strategy. When Hoffman reached Germany for the first meeting with the lawyers representing Iran, he was armed with what was called Plan C—a complex arrangement for a simultaneous financial settlement and release of the hostages, the joint product of their efforts. (Plans A and B had been discarded early on; Plan A had been jotted down on a paper napkin.)

Hoffman's goals for that first meeting in the quiet and secluded Schloss Hotel in Kronberg were modest. Only five lawyers were present: the two German lawyers representing Iran; Citibank's two German lawyers, Mailander and Klaus Gerstenmaier; and Hoffman, with Gerstenmaier's wife acting as translator. The group focused on a few of the mechanical problems, but Hoffman was more interested in establishing a rapport with the lawyers for Iran. The meeting made little substantive progress—Hoffman never brought out Plan C—but Hoffman recalls the atmosphere as being enthusiastic and cordial. "I was ready to lay some plans on the table," Hoffman says, "but I wanted some clear signals from their Iranian principals to continue. I wanted evidence of real authority." Hoffman considered asking for some kind of written grant of authority but decided against it. "Even asking for that might have upset the balance of the negotiations," Hoffman says. "We decided that if we had to, we would just go ahead in the dark." In the meantime, the participants took a breather and scheduled their next meeting for the following September.

The summer of 1980 was a period of confusion within Iran. The hostages had been dispersed from the American Embassy in Teheran, the United States had renounced further attempts to retrieve them by force, and there were no negotiations between the American and Iranian governments. In Iran, the struggle for power between the clerics, led by Prime Minister Mohammed Ali Rajai, and the so-called moderates, led by President Bani-Sadr, continued, with few signals to the outside world indicating who was in the ascendancy.

During that summer, Hoffman, the German lawyers and Roger Brown, an English solicitor who represented Bank Markazi and had been called into the negotiations by the lawyers for Iran, continued to hammer out details of Plan C in a series of meetings in Paris, London, Bermuda and even Hoffman's own home in suburban Chappaqua, New York.

Though it eventually required voluminous paperwork and dealt with an extraordinarily complex financial situation, the basic principles of Plan C were relatively simple. Iran basically faced two kinds of financial claims by the major American banks: "liquidated claims," whose amount and existence were really not in dispute, and "unliquidated claims," which included claims by a large number of American corporations, as well as letters of credit and performance bonds executed by the banks. Such unliquidated claims were not only difficult to verify and assess, but would require elements of proof too complicated for a negotiated settlement that would coincide with release of the hostages.

As a result, Plan C envisioned that Iran would pay off all of its syndicated loans with its assets that had been frozen in the foreign branches of the American banks. Iran's frozen domestic assets—those already located in the United States—would be held pending resolution of the unliquidated claims against Iran. Since Iran had more in foreign branch deposits than the liquidated claims against it, the excess—about $1.8 billion—would be unfrozen and deposited in the Iranian central bank, Bank Markazi. Plan C had obvious appeal for Citibank, and Hoffman assumed that it would be equally appealing to the other American banks, which, except for Chase Manhattan, didn't even know the negotiations were proceeding. The American banks' syndicated loans, which represented the vast amount of debt owed by Iran to American banks, would be paid off in full.

The Iranian lawyers never made a counterproposal. Over and over, Hoffman and the German lawyers repeated the details of Plan C, explained its implications, and sought to reassure the

Iranians. In September, Ayatollah Khomeini announced formal conditions for the release of the hostages, which Hoffman viewed as a positive step toward settlement. The Iranian lawyers continued to shuttle back and forth between Teheran and the meetings with the bank lawyers, but there were communications problems after the outbreak of the Iraq-Iran war in November. Two of Iran's English solicitors arrived in Teheran two hours before the Iraqi attack and were trapped there for ten days. But by late November 1980, a final Plan C was ready. Iran's German lawyers took it to Teheran, and Hoffman flew to Düsseldorf in anticipation of a favorable response.

He was bitterly disappointed. Shortly after his overnight flight from New York, Iran's German lawyers called with the message that Plan C—Hoffman's cherished product of six months' effort—was unconditionally rejected. They offered no comment or explanation.

Hoffman's first thought was that he wanted to go to bed. Instead, Gerstenmaier and Mailander took him out for a heavy German dinner, and the lawyers tried to make some sense out of the unexpected rejection. As they talked, a theory began to emerge which contained the germ of an alternative plan that might be acceptable. The three lawyers felt that the plan's failure must have stemmed from opposition by the clerics as a result of the Iraqi war. The war had placed enormous strain on Iran's crippled financial reserves; and, they reasoned, Plan C called for paying off the loans too quickly, further depleting Iran's financial strength. But no solution to that problem seemed evident, and their spirits sagged. "Let's not sit around and mope," Hoffman finally said, and the lawyers left the restaurant. "I felt we were back at Ground Zero," Hoffman says. "It was grim."

At seven the next morning, the lawyers reconvened, and Hoffman felt new determination. Overnight he had had a new idea—what was to become Plan D—and he decided that he had gone too far to stop trying now. "There didn't seem any alternative," he says. "It was obvious that there would be no hostage release without a financial settlement." The essence of Plan D was an attempt to accommodate what the lawyers assumed was Iran's reluctance to pay back all of its syndicated loans to the American banks at once out of its frozen assets. Plan D called for Iran to pay only the current overdue interest on its syndicated loans. The banks would then continue the loans with repayment guarantees from the government of Iran and the central bank of Iran, and Iran's assets would be unfrozen.

If Iran was prepared to accept the existence of further financial ties to American banks, Plan D was obviously a much more favorable proposition. But for that very reason, Hoffman no longer felt that he could act alone for banks other than his own client, Citibank. The German lawyers agreed that Plan D posed such financial risks that the acquiescence of the other American banks couldn't be taken for granted; and they agreed that, to as limited an extent as possible, the time had come to lift the veil of secrecy from their activities.

On December 12, lawyers for the country's twelve most powerful banks gathered in Shearman & Sterling's 32nd-floor conference room. Later dubbed "the gang of twelve," or simply "the twelve," the lawyers represented an extraordinary concentration of banking expertise. Nichols and Pillsbury were there from Davis Polk on behalf of Morgan Guaranty, as was Milbank's Logan for Chase Manhattan. Richard Simmons, a partner at Cravath, Swaine & Moore, attended for Chemical Bank; Thomas Cashel, from New York's Simpson Thacher & Bartlett, represented Manufacturers Hanover Trust. Hamilton Potter, Jr., from New York's Sullivan & Cromwell, appeared on behalf of both European American Bank and Marine Midland. Bank of America was represented by Thorne Corse. Rounding out the twelve were Bankers Trust (represented by White & Case in New York), Irving Trust (represented by Winthrop, Stimson, Putnam & Roberts in New York), First National Bank of Chicago (represented by Debevoise & Plimpton in New York) and Continental Illinois (represented by Mayer, Brown & Platt in Chicago).

The meeting followed two days of furious phone calls by Hoffman: first to Carswell and Mundheim in Treasury, to Warren Christopher in the State Department, and then to the chairmen and principal lawyers for each of the syndicate banks. To each, he outlined briefly the nature of his undertaking and stressed the need for secrecy. Even so, the lawyers weren't prepared for the scope of Hoffman's efforts when he explained them in detail at the meeting. Pillsbury, in particular, says he was "amazed" that the contact he had earlier discounted "proved to be a more direct pipeline than anything the United States government had."

Corse was a little piqued, annoyed with Carswell for letting

Hoffman proceed even though Bank of America had the largest stake in the outcome. But he had to admit he was impressed with Hoffman's efforts, and he too was amazed by the tight secrecy which had been maintained.

After explaining the exhaustive preparation of Plan C and its sudden, unexpected demise, Hoffman began to outline his concept for Plan D and passed out copies of a draft. With surprising speed, but with bank lawyers' typical appetite for mechanical detail, the group of lawyers absorbed the concept and turned to a discussion of some of the practical details of working out a Plan D financial settlement which would coincide with a release of the hostages.

Those practical problems proved to be simple in concept but enormously complicated in the execution. Where were Iran's frozen assets? How much was there? What kind of transfer would be necessary, and how could it be executed? What kind of authority and what kind of documents could initiate the payments? It was obvious, for example, that simply identifying Iran's assets would be an enormously difficult task. Although the twelve banks had acted as agents for the syndicated loans, more than 300 banks had actually participated in those transactions, some domestic and some foreign. The Treasury Department had been trying for months to locate the Iranian assets located in literally hundreds of American financial institutions and their foreign branches and subsidiaries. Revisions of their figures were being made on nearly a daily basis, and no one had any confidence that the proper total had yet been reached.

"There was an immediate appreciation of the hard technical problems," Logan recalls. "But the meeting was businesslike, low key. Everyone immediately pitched in." There were no strangers in the group; many of the lawyers had known one another for twenty-five years or more and had attended the same law schools (most had gone to Harvard and Columbia). Lawyers involved repeatedly echo Logan, who says, "One of the most important factors was the fact that we knew each other well. We trusted one another. We had confidence in everyone's legal skills and judgment." That first meeting in December did indeed end in a spirit of camaraderie, of a shared challenge.

At the end of the meeting on December 12, the lawyers divided into working specialty groups. Hoffman assumed a general oversight role. Logan became the head of a "drafting" group, with responsibility for preparation of all the documents which would eventually be necessary to transfer the assets. Cashel, the Simpson, Thacher partner, agreed to head the "figures" committee, in charge of assembling data on the location and extent of the Iranian assets. To help him, the banks retained the accounting firm of Peat, Marwick, Mitchell & Co., whose offices were around the corner from Citibank's, at 345 Park Avenue.

Shortly after the December 12 meeting, the Citibank negotiations with the German lawyers representing Iran, known in Washington as the "bank channel," and the United States government's own negotiations, which had resumed through Algerian intermediaries, began to coalesce. Carswell at Treasury was still reluctant to rely too heavily on the bank channel—he didn't know who was on the Iranian end of it, and he was pressing Warren Christopher in Algiers to have the Algerians take up financial negotiations with the Iranians—but he recognized that whatever the source of a financial settlement, the banks would have to be involved, and the same back-up work would eventually be necessary. The government didn't have the manpower, so he directed the Federal Reserve Board of New York to work with the lawyers representing the twelve. By mid-December, the mechanisms were in place so that a settlement could be implemented. Among the bank lawyers painstakingly assembling the components of Plan D, a cautious optimism was taking hold.

Then, on December 21st, "the whole thing blew up," Carswell recalls. That day, the Iranians publicly announced the terms of the financial settlement they had in mind—payments by the United States which totaled an astounding $24 billion. The Algerians themselves were stunned, since they had not negotiated any terms of a financial settlement. Though the Iranians had assured them that they represented the only negotiating channel, they had avoided the topic of the frozen assets. Then suddenly the Ayatollah dropped this bombshell of a proposal, which even the Algerians recognized was grossly overreaching.

Hoffman and the bank lawyers were equally surprised. The outrageous financial demands appeared to have the support of Behzad Nabavi, the Bank Markazi head and Bani-Sadr ally who they assumed was among those Iranians on the other end of their negotiating channel. While they knew that the German lawyers also had contacts within the clergy, they had always presumed that

the Bank Markazi faction would predominate in a financial settlement. Yet they had had no portents of the kind of demands
which suddenly appeared. Even more surprisingly, negotiations
through the bank channel continued as though the demands hadn't
been made.

The importance of the bank channel finally became clear to
Carswell and the Carter administration shortly before New Year's
Day. The Algerians had returned to Teheran on December 26,
and during discussions in the next three days the Iranians told the
Algerians that negotiations intended to reach a financial settlement were already taking place with the American banks. Since
the Algerians had made no headway in that area, they suggested
merging the United States and bank negotiations into the bank
channel. On January 3, 1981, Carswell flew to New York to brief
Hoffman; and on January 8, Shearman & Sterling became the
official site of the financial negotiations. Hoffman cancelled his
twenty-fifth wedding anniversary trip to the Seychelles Islands
scheduled for that week.

Beginning January 8, lawyers for the twelve began intensive
round-the-clock negotiating and drafting. Computer runs were
being performed at least twice a day to update the financial data.
Daily meetings were held with the team of lawyers representing
Iran: Roger Brown and Nigel McEwen from Coward Chance in
London; the two German lawyers; and Leonard Boudin, the well-
known American antiwar lawyer who was retained by Bank Markazi. Hoffman and several lawyers moved into the Waldorf-
Astoria Hotel, but few were actually finding any time to sleep
there. Clean clothes were at a premium, and Shearman & Sterling
secretaries kept running out to buy shirts at a nearby Bancroft
clothing store.

By Saturday night, January 10, most of the details had been
hammered out. That night, in a series of twenty-minute sessions
with Iran's lawyers in a Shearman & Sterling conference room
dubbed the "dentist's chair," a lawyer for each of the banks sep-
arately negotiated the rate of interest each bank would pay Iran
on the frozen assets it had held. Late that night, the deal was
complete.

Sunday morning, the lawyers waited. An eerie calm prevailed in
the Shearman & Sterling offices; the typewriters, the telexes, the
computers were quiet. Hoffman put in a few calls to Boudin and

to the Iranian lawyers; they were unavailable. Around 2:30 that afternoon, the lawyers for Iran arrived with an Iranian national— Iran's delegate to the International Monetary Fund and the only "real" Iranian the lawyers would ever meet—and asked to speak with Hoffman. Taking only Logan, Cashel and Corse into his office with him, Hoffman, the Iranian and the lawyers for Iran sat down.

Hoffman suddenly had haunting memories of the baffling rejection of Plan C months before. The Iranian banker did not look like someone about to conclude the $8 billion deal which had been painstakingly finished the night before. The Iranian's first statement confirmed Hoffman's premonition. He rejected outright any notion that Bank Markazi or the Islamic Republic of Iran would guarantee repayment of the loans which were being deferred.

The American lawyers were stunned. Guarantees of repayment —a Koranic guarantee from the Islamic Republic and a full guarantee from Bank Markazi—had been a cornerstone of Plan D, and it had never been questioned by any of the negotiators for Iran. It had been made clear at the outset that the American banks wouldn't *consider* deferring Iran's repayment of the outstanding loans without a guarantee of eventual repayment.

Unfazed, the Iranian proceeded to demand the American lawyers' "last written offer." Hoffman, slightly confused, said that Plan D *was* their last written offer. This seemed to make no impression; the Iranian simply kept parroting his demand for their "last written offer," almost like a record stuck in a single groove, as the German and English lawyers for Iran looked uncomfortable. Finally, Hoffman cut him short. "I can tell you that nothing further will develop," he said. "This meeting is closed and we probably will not be speaking to you again." As the Iranian and his counsel filed out, Hoffman felt overwhelmed by frustration and disappointment.

"It was the low point," Hoffman recalls, "and I wanted them to know it. They had overplayed their hand." Hoffman had emphasized all along that if no agreement was reached by Inauguration Day, the slate would be wiped clean, and negotiations, if any, would begin from scratch. Now there were only nine days left, and "I had no optimism that we could put a new deal together in nine days," Hoffman says.

But thirty minutes later, the English solicitor Brown and the

German lawyers for Iran were back at Shearman & Sterling, minus their Iranian client. "Let's talk," Brown told Hoffman. The lawyers for Iran told the Americans that the Iranian banker was in tears by the time he got off the elevator after the meeting, unable to understand what had gone wrong. He had simply adopted an Iranian merchant's style of negotiating. By the time the lawyers for Iran left this time, Plan D was alive again.

Hoffman called Carswell after the meeting to brief him on their progress; and for the first time, Carswell sounded a little desperate. He exhorted the bank lawyers to "cut a deal they could live with" and then "sell it to the Iranians." The people in Washington, too, had now realized that time was running out.

In the meantime, intensive work proceeded on the mechanics of the fund transfer. Carswell called Mundheim (who had retired from the Carter administration to resume teaching at the University of Pennsylvania but agreed to return for a few weeks to help with the hostage crisis) on January 7 and asked him to travel to Europe to arrange for a depository bank that would act as an intermediary in the transfer of funds from the United States to Iran. Pursuant to the plan then under consideration, worked out by the bank lawyers and the Treasury Department, American banks would transfer by telex all the Iranian funds held in foreign branches to the Federal Reserve Bank of New York, which would in turn transfer those assets, in gold if necessary, to an intermediate depository bank. When the Iranian authorities received word that the assets were in the hands of the intermediary bank, according to the plan, the hostages would be released, and the intermediary bank would forward the assets to any bank Iran designated, presumably Bank Markazi.

Mundheim interviewed officials of both the Bundesbank in Frankfurt, and the Bank of England in London, two international banks with the stature to handle such a transaction, and finally settled on the Bank of England. English law makes the attachment process more difficult, and Mundheim felt that, given the Iranians' unhappy attachment experience earlier in Germany, they would be less apprehensive about attachment of the assets while on deposit in the intermediary bank if that bank were in England. London now looked as though it would be the center of any movement of assets which might occur; so Logan, in charge of drafting the transfer documents, left the group in New York and flew to London on January 13, along with Davis Polk's Pillsbury and Thorne Corse from Bank of America. To cover Bank of America's interests in New York, the bank called in Timothy Atkeson, a partner from Steptoe & Johnson in Washington. By Thursday morning, the mechanisms were in place in London and New York to execute the modified Plan D.

That day, Hoffman had just returned to his office after lunch when Cutler and Carswell got on the phone from Washington to report a major breakthrough in Algeria. The Algerian negotiators had just presented Christopher with a new financial proposal, a proposal which, much to their amazement, looked something like Hoffman's old Plan C. Hoffman grabbed his briefcase and a couple of files, ran out the door, calling to his secretary not to tell anyone where he was going, and caught the Eastern Airlines shuttle.

By the time he arrived at Cutler's White House office for further briefing, more details of the plan had been received. Iran proposed paying off all the syndicated loans out of its deposits in the foreign branches of United States banks. These it valued at $3.7 billion. As for the unliquidated claims, which it valued at $5.1 billion, it proposed creation of an escrow fund out of which payments would be made once the merits of the claims were determined. The balance of the frozen assets would be returned to Iran, and the hostages would be released.

In principle, it was Hoffman's Plan C. Only the numbers were significantly different and, as it turned out, erroneous. Though Hoffman didn't know it at the time, the earlier Plan C had not been rejected by the clerics, as Hoffman had assumed, but by the Bani-Sadr faction, which was then in decline and apparently believed it needed a spectacular financial coup to re-establish its power and legitimacy. The settlement that Bani-Sadr had originally embarked upon looked too favorable for the American banks. This time, the clerics embraced Plan C as a solution which solved the hostage crisis and left it with no lingering financial obligations to the American banks.

Besides the erroneous figures, there seemed only one area of difference: the interest owed on the frozen assets. The Iranian proposal asked $800 million; the banks' plan, worked out in the "dentist's chair" negotiations over Plan D, called for payments of only $670 million. After the frustrations Hoffman had already endured, those differences seemed minor. It looked as though action might be at hand. He, Cutler and Carswell scheduled a meeting at the State Department for 11:00 A.M. the next day. It was time for the lawyers for the twelve to act.

Secretary of State Edmund Muskie opened the meeting, which convened that morning in the State Department's elaborate briefing room. Cutler did most of the initial presentation, stressing that the deal promised to be almost incredibly favorable for the United States banks—full, accelerated repayment of the outstanding syndicated loans. He stressed the fate of the hostages, emphasizing tacitly that public opinion might easily blame the banks for their fate. Nonetheless, the proposal posed some problems for the bank lawyers who, until hours before, had been immersed in Plan D. The first of these was the priority to be given the syndicated loans. Such an arrangement favored the banks with large syndicated loans—like Chase Manhattan and Morgan Guaranty—at the expense of those banks whose unliquidated claims against Iran were more substantial, such as Bank of America and Bankers Trust. The practicalities of the situation, however, tended to minimize that problem. While the syndicated loans had been accurately determined by the figures committee at $3.7 billion, no one had been able to figure out the amount of the unliquidated financial obligations. If some allocation had to be made, the deal simply couldn't go through.

Interest rates posed a greater problem. Iran had asked for $800 million in interest on the frozen assets held by the banks, and while no one knew for sure where that figure had come from, it looked like it might be the highest interest rate negotiated by the lawyers for Iran in the individual sessions in New York applied to all the banks. This was approximately a 17 percent annual rate spread over a 14-month period, and some of the American banks —especially Bank of America and Bankers Trust—didn't want to pay such a high rate, because they had larger interest-bearing deposits. Tension mounted as Atkeson, the lawyer from Steptoe & Johnson representing Bank of America, refused to concede the interest rate question.

After lunch, Nichols took Cutler aside. "Why don't you, Muskie, Carswell and the government people stay out of the meeting?" Nichols asked Cutler. "Give us an hour to have a little dogfight."

Cutler followed his advice, and when they returned, an agreement had been reached. The $130 million difference would be paid by the banks into an escrow account on a pro rata basis based on the size of interest-bearing Iranian deposits, and the interest question would later be submitted to international arbitration.

Government representatives began drafting a formal reply which was, in its essential elements, an acceptance. But amidst the euphoria of the agreement was a nagging anxiety on the part of some of the lawyers present. The debate over the interest rates was the first crack in the united front that had been maintained by the bank lawyers—a reminder that the public interest was not necessarily foremost, and that the client's was. Even the fate of the fifty-two hostages had not obscured that fact at the meeting.

Back in London, Mundheim was on his way to dinner at the American ambassador's residence when he was told of the break-through in the financial negotiations and Iran's offer to accelerate repayment of the syndicated loans. When Mundheim arrived at the ambassador's, he learned that the deputy governor of the Bank of England was on the guest list, and asked Ambassador Kingman Brewster, Jr. to arrange a secret meeting between them during the course of the evening. When the somewhat bewildered English banker was brought into the ambassador's study, Mundheim explained the turn in the negotiations and the implications for the Bank of England: instead of merely being a conduit for the funds, the bank would be required to act as a stakeholder—to keep much of the frozen assets on deposit in an escrow account—until the non-syndicated loan claims were ultimately settled, a process which could take years. Would the Bank of England—and Britain itself—be willing to become involved in the crisis for such a long period of time?

Mundheim left the dinner at about 1:00 A.M. feeling that he had nearly persuaded the deputy governor. At his hotel, Carswell called him from Washington with the news that the Algerians had insisted that the Bank of Algeria act as the final conduit and that the closing take place in Algiers. Could he, the deputy governor, and some of the bank lawyers in London be in Algiers the next morning?

Mundheim spent the night on the telephone and, with the active help of ambassador Brewster, secured the consent of the Bank of England. At 10:00 A.M. the next day, Warren Christopher's State Department plane landed at a private airstrip outside London. Waiting to board were Mundheim, the Bank of England's deputy governor and head cashier, Logan and Corse. Abbreviated though it was, they had all had their last good night's sleep before the resolution of the crisis.

On the plane, Logan and Mundheim began working out the mechanics of the new deal on scraps of paper, stuffing important notes into their pockets. At about 1:00 P.M., the plane touched down in Algiers and taxied to a remote corner of the airport where the lawyers were hustled into armored police cars. Then, at what Logan calls "excessive speeds," the caravan careened through the center of Algiers with horns blowing, scattering a flock of chickens when it reached the United States Embassy.

The next five days Logan remembers only as a blur. As soon as they arrived, Warren Christopher, the Deputy Secretary of State, briefed the lawyers on the plan which had been proposed by the Iranians the day before. Logan and Corse, too, quickly recognized it as Hoffman's Plan C.

Shortly after, the lawyers and Mundheim were introduced to the Algerian negotiators, who politely shook their hands and then told Mundheim that they wanted the bank lawyers out. For some reason, they didn't trust anyone who was not a U.S. government official, so Corse and Logan were excluded from the ensuing negotiating sessions.

It made their drafting efforts considerably more difficult. Corse and Logan were responsible for the actual preparation of most of the documents and for collecting the financial data from their colleagues in New York. But they were implementing political agreements which were constantly changing in meetings from which they were barred. "We'd get it on paper," Corse recalls with some irritation, "and then we'd get word that 'it didn't mesh' with the political agreement. We'd ask why—and get no answer. They saw all of our work, but we couldn't see theirs, even though their negotiations were going on right upstairs in the embassy."

According to Logan, "We were in the trenches—we couldn't see what was going on around us. We just kept going. You had to. Desperation and elation alternated as we struggled through, hour by hour. It was a continuous mental and physical effort, with little to eat and even less sleep. A kaleidoscope of work was produced and jettisoned. Phones, connections kept breaking down." Then, in midafternoon of January 20, the final drafts were finished. The frenzied pace ground to a halt. The waiting began.

Following the breakthrough on January 16, an excited Hoffman flew back to New York to supervise the last hurried attempts to complete the inventory of Iranian assets and to arrange the financial transfer out of the Federal Reserve Bank of New York. Lawyers for the twelve resumed round-the-clock drafting at the offices of Shearman & Sterling. But the heightened time pressure, the lack of sleep, and the prospect of a final resolution to the agonizing crisis all contributed to a tinderbox atmosphere. It nearly exploded on January 17.

That Saturday, lawyers for the twelve regrouped for a final review of the transfer mechanism and asset data. Some of the lawyers—Hoffman, Nichols—would be meeting with the government people the next morning to work through the last details with them and to be on hand in case of any last-minute snags. But during the discussion of the transfer procedures, a problem resurfaced which had pervaded all of the negotiations, that of attachment.

The plan which had been worked out for the mechanical transfer of the assets was designed to alleviate the mistrust between the Iranians and the U.S. government. According to the plan, a single payment order for the $5.3 billion in Iranian assets on deposit in the foreign branches of U.S. banks would be sent by Bank Markazi to the London office of Coward Chance, Citibank's English solicitors. Copies would immediately be sent to the twelve banks, which would in turn instruct the Federal Reserve Bank in New York to debit their accounts for the respective amounts. Once the Federal Reserve Bank of New York had done so, it would credit the Bank of England.

The Bank of England in turn would credit the Central Bank of Algiers, a step which, together with the transfer of some gold and securities, it certified to the Algerian government. When copies of the Bank of England's certification reached the U.S., Iranian and Algerian governments, the Iranians were required to release the hostages. As soon as they cleared Iranian air space, the Algerian government would instruct the Bank of England to release $3.7 billion back to the New York Federal Reserve Bank, which would in turn pay off Iran's loans from the U.S. banks. The Bank of

England would hold an escrow account for the disputed unliquidated claims, and the residue would be transferred to Bank Markazi.

Though all of these transfers would take place electronically in a matter of hours, the assets would, in a physical sense, be moving from Europe, to the United States, to England, to Algeria, and finally to Iran. During the fleeting period when those assets touched down in the United States, they could be subject to an attachment order issued by any U.S. federal court—just as Citibank and Morgan Guaranty had attached Iranian assets that were physically present in West Germany—and there were hundreds of American companies with big claims against Iran, greedy for the chance to tie up Iranian funds which might eventually be awarded to them by a court decree.

The lawyers for the twelve had recognized this problem from the beginning, but the likelihood of an attachment—and the resulting halt in the flow of assets which would undoubtedly destroy the entire hostage release arrangement—was considered remote. No one knew that billions of dollars in Iranian assets would be briefly exposed to attachment as they touched down in the United States, and they wouldn't know where or when. That is, except for the obvious—the lawyers for the twelve knew the plan, and knew exactly when and where the assets could be seized.

One lawyer at that meeting on Saturday evening recalls that Bank of America's lawyer Timothy Atkeson from Steptoe & Johnson seemed particularly subdued, even uneasy. Suddenly Atkeson plunged into the discussion, talking vaguely about the fact that he and his law firm also represented some major industrial clients with outstanding contract claims against Iran. Such clients were precisely the kind who would, under ordinary circumstances, be interested in the possibility of attachment. As this realization dawned, silence fell over the assembled lawyers, then Hoffman, his voice grave, ordered Atkeson out of the room. Had he dallied, another lawyer says, he would have been forced out the door.

"We had to get him out," Hoffman recalls, even though he and Atkeson were close friends and Steptoe & Johnson often handled Washington, D.C., matters for Shearman & Sterling. "We had no margin for error. These stakes were very, very high."

Atkeson had to be stopped, and urgently. He was a live wire that could ignite the entire hostage deal with a simple piece of paper in any federal court. The bank lawyers knew they had a legal handle for action against Steptoe & Johnson in the event it tried an attachment: if the law firm tried to stop the assets on behalf of one or more of its other clients, it would be jeopardizing the chance for its bank client, Bank of America, to recover its outstanding syndicated loans. That was a case of conflict of interest on a global scale, a violation of the lawyers' Code of Professional Responsibility.

They, in turn, notified Cutler, Civiletti and Muskie. The attachment problem was one that had been anticipated—and feared —at the highest levels of government. Some months previously, Steptoe & Johnson had actually obtained an attachment order on behalf of one of its clients with claims against Iran, Electronic Data Systems, but it had been set aside when it and similar cases were stayed. In a reference to the problem aimed directly at Atkeson, Muskie had sternly warned at the previous day's meeting that "the full resources of the U.S. government would be deployed against anyone who attempted to block the transfer."

Now that threat was made more specific. Word was passed to Atkeson and the other lawyers that both Air Force I and Air Force II were standing by, ready to fly a squad of Justice Department lawyers anywhere in the country if Steptoe or any other firm tried to interfere. Justice Department lawyers were already on location, armed with the necessary papers, in Washington, New York and Boston, the most likely sites for an attachment attempt. If Steptoe acted on behalf of one of its industrial claimants, it would be charged with conflict of interest.

In the unlikely event that an attempt by Steptoe actually succeeded, the government was prepared to obtain review by the U.S. Supreme Court in less than four hours. The Supreme Court had immediately been alerted to the potential problem and justices were standing by. Muskie and Cutler didn't need to say that it seemed inconceivable that the Supreme Court would permit such a disruption of the solution to the long and painful crisis.

Despite the warning, Steptoe & Johnson made one last attempt to keep tabs on plans for the asset transfer. On Sunday afternoon, bank lawyers in Washington noticed that another Steptoe partner was hanging around the Treasury Department room where coffee and sandwiches had been made available adjacent to the room where the bank lawyers were working. When Nichols from Davis

Polk arrived, he ordered the Steptoe partner out of the building. According to another lawyer present, Nichols said, "We threw your partner out, and we'll throw you out, too."

By Sunday evening, all was ready for the asset transfer. The computers in New York, which take four hours to warm up, were turned on. Twelve phone lines from the banks were open to Hoffman in Washington and to the Shearman & Sterling conference room, as well as lines connecting Washington, New York, London and Algiers. Because the Iranians didn't want a plane leaving the Teheran airport at night during the Iraqi war, the target time was set for dawn on Monday, Teheran time. The lawyers waited for the single telex order to London from the Iranians, the signal to set the asset transfer in motion. By now, all the basic agreements had been signed by the bankers and government representatives, including President Carter's own order unfreezing the Iranian assets. Carter went on national television to announce the imminent release of the hostages.

The morning dawned in Teheran, but nothing happened. Where was the telex? Hoffman called Algiers; there had been no information. He called the lawyers in Germany representing the Iranians; they had heard nothing. Then the snag appeared. Through the Algerians, Hoffman learned of an eleven-page appendix to the escrow agreement which had been drafted by Logan and Corse in Algiers and attached to the final papers. Basically, the attachment contained technical instructions related to the escrow account which would be maintained by the Bank of England, and the language had already been approved by the government negotiators in Iran. Someone, however, had needlessly inserted Bank Markazi as a signatory to the escrow agreement—and Nabavi seized this as a last opportunity to upset the deal. He claimed that the language in the appendix implied some kind of general release by Iran to the American banks. Once they learned the problem, Logan, Corse and Hoffman solved it in thirty seconds by simply dropping the language and deleting the Iranian bank as a signatory. But in all the confusion, and because of bad connections, an entire day was lost. It was now 10:30 P.M. on Inauguration eve. The waiting recommenced.

For Hoffman, the waiting had become an agony. Nightfall was approaching in Teheran, after which there would be no hostage release. Hoffman would have felt better if, as he had advocated all along, there had been a standard formal closing in London, with all the lawyers and representatives involved. Then he could simply have sat down with the Iranians, and if there were any last-minute problems they could have been dealt with on the spot. But the principals acting on behalf of Iran—whoever they were—had refused to budge from Teheran. As a result, Hoffman and the lawyers had had to work out the cumbersome telex arrangement. The language of the triggering telex had been sent from London to Teheran, where the Iranians had to retype it, beginning with a secret numerical test code to prove its authenticity.

At midnight, Hoffman set up an open line to the Coward Chance conference room in London. Someone stayed on the phone at all times, in touch with a lawyer who watched the telex machine for the red warning light indicating that a transmission was in progress; but nothing happened. Then, at 2:40 A.M., Hoffman shouted to his colleagues in Washington, "The light's on!" and everyone jumped to his feet and gathered around the phone. Hoffman told London that he wanted the transmission read instantly as it came over the wire, but there was nothing. In London, the light blinked out. Frantic inquiries soon revealed that the machine had been triggered by a wrong number a sleepy and unsuspecting caller had haphazardly dialed.

But shortly after, the light blinked on again, and this time a transmission began. "Read the test number," Hoffman shouted, and the lawyers waited breathlessly as they listened for the series of numbers. As they were read over the phone, Hoffman couldn't believe what he was hearing. The code number was wrong. As he later described it, "It was like being handed a forged check."

What was happening at the Iranian end of the transmission remains a mystery. But as the telex transmission continued, it soon became apparent that practically nothing had been accurately recorded and transmitted by the Iranians. The typed reference to First National Bank of Chicago, for example, emerged as "First -589,-)?,(." The amount it was to pay "0,000,-000." The amount to be paid by Morgan Guaranty was overstated by $300,000.

As soon as the wrong test code appeared, Hoffman got on the phone to the lawyers in London, who were able to reach the Iranian transmitters by telephone. The Iranians claimed the erroneous code had resulted from simple typing errors, and they agreed to transmit a corrected test code, which finally appeared on the London telex at about 3:00 A.M. But as for the garbled names and figures, the Iranians refused to make any corrections. Instead, the lawyers received a final threatening message over the telex: "Responsibility for the fate of the 52 American hostages rests entirely with you."

Ordinarily, no bank lawyer would authorize the transfer of $8 billion on the strength of such documents. Even simple typographical errors have derailed closings and caused associates to be disciplined. But these were not ordinary circumstances, and as patriotic duty and the fate of the hostages swept aside reservations about client obligations and prudent behavior, the usually calm and cautious lawyers became militant. As secretary Miller stood at his side, Davis Polk's Nichols yelled into the telephone that London was to ignore all errors of less than $1 million. "Who gives a damn about $300,000?" he finally shouted. When a mechanical hitch prevented Chemical Bank from making the transfer, Treasury Secretary Miller threatened to deduct its share of the frozen assets out of its Federal Reserve deposits. The problem was hurriedly straightened out. Finally, at 6:44 A.M., January 20, the money completed its global circulation and flowed into the Bank of England. There had been no sign of Steptoe & Johnson that night, and no attachment attempts had been made as the assets flowed through the New York Federal Reserve Bank.

Six hours later, the plane carrying the American hostages took off from the Teheran airport. The $3.7 billion in assets were electronically credited to the accounts of the twelve American banks whose lawyers, in a sense, had just bought the hostages' release.

CHAPTER TWO

IBM

Cravath, Swaine & Moore

Thomas Barr, then a 42-year-old partner at New York's Cravath, Swaine & Moore, waited anxiously by the telephone at the International Business Machines Corporation headquarters in Armonk, New York. Across a large desk sat IBM's general counsel, Nicholas Katzenbach, in the leather chair he had occupied as Attorney General under President Lyndon Johnson. It was September 17, 1973, three months after the end of the trial of *Telex* v. *IBM*, an antitrust case brought against the giant computer manufacturer by Telex Corporation, a fledgling competitor in Oklahoma City. Barr had personally conducted the 29-day trial, and he and Katzenbach had just been notified that the New York Stock Exchange had suspended trading in IBM stock. They knew that the judge's verdict in the Telex case must be imminent.

Barr told Katzenbach he was beginning to feel more optimistic about the outcome, even though on the day the trial ended Barr had gotten a phone call from Bruce Bromley, Cravath's eminent senior litigation partner and Barr's mentor, who scoured the transcripts of each day of trial and was always Barr's harshest critic. "You stupid bastard," Bromley had shouted at Barr in his usual blunt fashion. "You haven't proved any damages."

Barr had to admit that Bromley was right. During the trial, Barr had counterattacked against Telex with a claim that the company had stolen valuable trade secrets from IBM, but he hadn't made clear to what extent IBM had been hurt by the theft. But as he thought about the problem, Barr decided that Telex's lawyers had done an even worse job with the problem of damages. The judge had been given no coherent theory for calculating them even if he believed IBM had violated the antitrust laws. If Barr had to bet, he told Katzenbach, the damages problem would be the undoing of Telex.

Moments later the light blinked on the telephone, and Katzenbach grabbed for it. As he listened, he turned pale. The judge had found IBM guilty of violating the Sherman Act, he tersely told Barr. Then Katzenbach switched on the speaker phone and called in Frank Cary, IBM's chairman, so all could hear the news. The judgment awarded Telex was $350 million in damages—the first time in history a plaintiff had been awarded more than one-third of a billion dollars. It was a loss of staggering proportions. And with an intensity that is nearly consuming, Tom Barr hates to lose.

Within days, the repercussions of the Telex loss were felt, and they were even more threatening than the prospect of paying out a billion dollars. Buoyed by the success of Telex, other companies in the computer business filed complaints modeled very closely on Telex's in courts around the country. The West German government and the European Economic Community began investigations of IBM. More ominously, the United States government, which had filed an antitrust suit to break up IBM in 1969 but had done little to prosecute it, suddenly started calling for accelerated discovery and an early trial date. The future of the most successful company in American history suddenly looked bleak—if IBM survived to have a future. In a short period of time, the price of IBM stock fell more than $60 per share on the New York Stock Exchange—which some Cravath lawyers dubbed the "Barr market."

No one felt responsibility for the Telex loss more keenly than Katzenbach, and there were those within IBM who wanted Cravath dropped from the case. But he elected to stand behind Barr and his colleagues at Cravath. Cravath would reward that decision with what may be the most brilliant and sustained legal representation in history, at a cost that is staggering both in financial and human terms. IBM became a case that so taxed the institution of the corporate law firm that neither Cravath nor any other firm like it will ever be the same again.

•

If a recognition poll were to be conducted, Cravath, Swaine & Moore would surely emerge as the best-known corporate law firm in the country. Paul Cravath, the partner who most shaped the identity of the modern firm, had explicitly and coherently articulated the principles which he believed should regulate the large corporate firm. Because those principles were recorded in a three-volume history of the firm published shortly after World War II—a rare firsthand account of the development of such a firm—Cravath has come to epitomize the large Wall Street firms and their progeny in other parts of the country. Though it has had its share of celebrated partners—Roswell Gilpatric, the Deputy Secretary of Defense under John F. Kennedy, and Carlyle Maw, Kissinger's legal adviser in the State Department, are two—Cravath was the first of the large firms to become known first and foremost as an institution.

Though Cravath partners have been as secretive as their counterparts in similar firms, myths have accumulated about the firm that have contributed to its pre-eminence. During the mid-1960s, Cravath was the first major firm to pay associates something considerably more than a living wage. It dramatically raised starting salaries in a single year, and ever since has had the reputation for paying lawyers more than any other firm in the country. It has, occasionally, actually been topped by Sullivan & Cromwell, by Davis Polk & Wardwell and by others; but it has never lost its reputation for being at the top. By extrapolation, it is perceived as offering young lawyers a lavish calendar of social activities and an array of fringe benefits, although the fact is the firm's attitude toward social activities is virtually Spartan; and, particularly for summer associates, other firms offer far more lavish perquisites.

It is also known for hiring only the best and the brightest law school graduates, usually members of law reviews from the most prestigious schools. That, too, is not always the case. But a mystique has grown up around Cravath to which no one firm could possibly measure up. When lawyers today speak loosely of "Cravath," they often mean it as shorthand for all the large and illustrious corporate firms.

Cravath traces its roots to 1819, making it one of the oldest law firms in the country. An early partner was William Seward, Lincoln's Secretary of State, whose writing desk and papers are today located in Cravath's "treasure room" located just off the firm's dark-paneled reception area furnished with antiques at 1 Chase Manhattan Plaza, the downtown skyscraper it shares with Davis Polk and with Milbank, Tweed, Hadley & McCloy. Paul Cravath was the dominant influence from the turn of the century until his death in 1940, and his portrait dominates the reception area. The name of the firm was fixed in 1944; all of the name partners are now deceased.

Though the firm has a long and eminent history, its continued vitality is due primarily to the incomparable stable of clients the firm maintains, many of which have become closely identified with Cravath only since the end of World War II. Despite its old-line reputation, the firm has had remarkable success at seeking out leading companies in high-growth fields. In the oil and energy sector, it represents Royal Dutch Shell and Ashland Oil; in banking, Chemical Bank; in media, CBS, the *Washington Post*, and Time Inc.; in investment banking, First Boston, Paine Webber, Inc., and Salomon Brothers; in chemicals, Allied Chemical; in steel, Bethlehem Steel; and in computers, of course, International Business Machines Corporation.

No one can quite recall the genesis of the relationship between Cravath and IBM, but it is one which has been extremely close since the early 1950s. IBM had its first brush with government antitrust regulators in 1952, when the company had annual revenues of only $150 million; and Cravath's Bromley—recognizing the potential of the computer industry—successfully handled the resolution of the case through a consent decree. IBM was so delighted that Bromley was named to IBM's board, where he remained until his retirement. During those years, IBM's legal needs burgeoned, and other Cravath partners, especially corporate partner George Turner, devoted much of their practice to IBM matters. But by the late 1960s, this first generation of IBM partners at Cravath was nearing retirement, just when IBM faced the gravest legal threats in its history.

On January 17, 1969, the last business day of the Johnson administration, Attorney General Ramsey Clark, in his last official act, signed a complaint charging IBM with monopolization, a violation of Section 2 of the Sherman Act. Within the practice of the large corporate firm, there are three kinds of antitrust cases: the price-fixing case, a violation of Section 1 of the Sherman Act; the private monopolization case, a violation of Section 2 of the

Sherman Act; and the government monopolization case. Of these, the government case poses by far the most ominous threat. The government antitrust case is as close as litigation ever comes to economic and social planning.

When the government brings a Section 2 case, it is probably not content to seek an injunction or fines—it wants divestiture, a breakup of the offending company into an economic structure that, the government believes, will enhance competition. To the threatened company, it is a step only slightly less horrifying than outright nationalization, and it must be fought with every resource at its disposal. It is a battle for survival in which the aggressor is not some small plaintiff's litigation firm hoping for a contingency fee, but the U.S. government and its vast resources. It is a battle whose stakes make money no object, and it is, naturally, a favored preserve of the large corporate law firm.

Because the Sherman Act is so broad itself and because government lawyers have tried to embrace almost every conceivable legal theory that could be derived from it, it is difficult to summarize with any precision the government's legal allegations against IBM. Essentially, IBM was charged with monopolizing and attempting to monopolize the electronic data processing industry, an industry which embraces computer equipment (commonly called "boxes") but not computer programs, or "software." Electronic data processing consists of five basic functions: input, storage, processing, output and control—functions which may be performed all in one box or in an assemblage of boxes. IBM was alleged to have driven competitors out of this broad market through its pricing and leasing practices, by frequent technological and design changes in its products, and by making its products technically incompatible with function boxes manufactured by competitors for attachment to IBM equipment. The only way to restore competition in this field, the government argued, was to break IBM up into at least four separate companies.

Because vast resources are necessary to prosecute such cases, there have been relatively few government Section 2 cases filed, and fewer have resulted in divestiture. The case against IBM was singular in the novelty of its legal theory. There was no allegation of collusion or price fixing—the traditional antitrust wrongs found at the root of Section 2 cases like that against American Tobacco —and the government aggressively sought—indeed, insisted upon

—divestiture. It was thought by many to be a radical and wrong-headed application of antitrust law and theory—later extended in government antitrust attacks on AT&T and companies in the cereal industry—and it called, therefore, for a radical legal defense.

On Christmas Day 1968, Tom Barr stretched his short, stocky frame in the blazing Virgin Islands sun. It was his first real vacation since he had become a Cravath partner three years earlier; and, characteristically, he was restless, anxious to get back to New York and a new assignment at Cravath. For the past six months, he had been spending most of his time in Washington with Lloyd Cutler as deputy director of the National Commission on the Causes and Prevention of Violence, an investigation triggered by the assassination of Robert F. Kennedy that June. Barr was deeply disturbed by what he saw as a continuing breakdown of the fabric of American society. As a former Marine Corps lieutenant, it offended his sense of order and discipline; at the same time, as a Yale Law School graduate, he recognized the injustices that seemed to be at the root of the problems. After Kennedy was shot, Cutler called Barr and asked his help in probing the sources of violence in America. And Barr welcomed a break from the Wall Street firm.

But now he was ready to go back. His overriding impression of government service had been inefficiency and political infighting that he had been powerless to control. After six months of Capitol Hill, he wanted back in the courtroom, an arena where combatants played by the same rules and where he could be in command. Barr got his wish even sooner than expected. The day he returned from vacation, Bromley came into his office and asked him to leave immediately for St. Paul, Minnesota. The next day, Barr was in a snowbound Minnesota courtroom as counsel for IBM.

During the winter of 1968–69, the prospect of a government suit against IBM was not the only IBM problem that worried Bromley and his Cravath partners. By the end of 1968, it was clear that the government investigation of IBM—which had been going on for more than three years—would probably result in a lawsuit against the computer maker, and Cravath lawyers weren't the only ones aware of that likelihood. Whenever there is a major govern-

ment investigation, word leaks out, and numerous plaintiffs' lawyers are invariably lurking on the fringes ready to bring a private
antitrust suit if they sense that the government is onto something.
Then, the plaintiffs' lawyers can wait for the government to sue
and ride its coattails to a verdict and a large contingency fee in
their own parallel suits.

Sometimes, however, the private plaintiffs jump the gun, as did
Control Data Corporation when it sued IBM on its own in December 1968. When Bromley learned of the suit, and knowing of
the impending government suit, he realized that he himself
couldn't keep his finger in the dike much longer. He was 75 years
old, and given Cravath's skill with litigation techniques, which he
himself had pioneered, he knew the developing IBM litigation
would take years, if not decades. With his assignment of Barr,
Bromley leaped over several more senior litigation partners for
someone to assume his mantle, a partner who would see the cases
through and who would ensure the transfer of one of the firm's
most important clients from one generation of partners to another.
In that one gesture, he had passed the crown of firm litigation
leadership to Barr. Those waiting for Barr to fumble with his
sudden stature and authority were to be quickly disappointed.

Shortly after the filing of the Control Data suit in December
came the government complaint in mid-January 1969. Predictably, the filing of the government case unleashed a flurry of suits
by competitors of IBM. Greyhound Computer Corporation filed a
private antitrust suit in Illinois; Telex filed its suit in Oklahoma.
With Bromley standing firmly behind him, Barr took command
of discovery in all the cases, though he soon discovered that not
much was happening in the government case. With the exit of
Ramsey Clark, interest in the suit seemed to lag in the new Nixon
administration, and the private plaintiffs found that, far from
riding on the government's coattails, they had no alternative but
to take the lead with discovery themselves.

In Minnesota, Control Data's suit was assigned to Federal District Court judge Phillip Neville, who happened to be a close
friend of John Robertson, a senior partner in the leading St. Paul
law firm of Oppenheimer, Hodgson, Brown, Wolff & Leach, which
represented Control Data. Neville seemed to view Barr as an arrogant, brash outsider almost from the start, and his dislike
hardened after Barr dared to appeal an interim order by Neville to

the Eighth Circuit Court of Appeals, where Neville was reversed. That incident had led to Neville screaming at Barr in court and then walking off the bench.

But even if the Oppenheimer firm had caught the judge's sympathy, there was little Neville could do to forestall the sorry demise of Control Data's case. During discovery, Barr and his Cravath colleagues produced a mass of IBM documents for the Control Data lawyers and demanded a mass in return. It is a common misperception that large firms always try to withhold producing evidence; the truth is that it is often far more effective to overwhelm the opposition by overproducing documents. Floundering in IBM documents, Robertson, Control Data's lead lawyer, gathered together twenty-five boxes of Control Data documents to hand over to the IBM lawyers. But in doing so, he committed a fatal error. No matter how many documents IBM produced, not one was turned over that hadn't been read by a Cravath lawyer—often by Barr himself—to make sure that privileges would not be applicable and to determine if anything potentially detrimental to IBM's case was revealed. Robertson did not take this simple but time-consuming precaution. Instead, as Robertson later admitted to Barr, the firm hired scores of paralegals to read and index documents. Whether he was too busy (or too bored), he didn't read them all himself.

Barr and the other Cravath lawyers pounced on the documents, and they found devastating evidence of plans by Control Data to join a "multinational club" to fix prices and allocate markets to undermine IBM. Shortly after the discovery, IBM was able to file a counterclaim in Control Data's suit which, if successful, would probably have driven Control Data into bankruptcy. Judge Neville was furious, and indicated that he would let Control Data claim those documents were privileged even though the company's lead counsel had already turned them over to Cravath. But even Control Data knew such a ruling would not withstand review by the Eighth Circuit Court of Appeals. The day that Barr filed his counterclaim, Robertson took Barr out to lunch and said, "Let's settle."

Meanwhile, interest in the government antitrust case within the Nixon Justice Department began to rise, and a new antitrust division lawyer, Raymond Carlson, was assigned as lead counsel. Noting the progress of the private suits, Carlson had the novel idea that the government could ride the coattails of the private plaintiffs in this case, turning the tables on the plaintiffs' lawyers. In particular, he had his eye on the computerized data base that Control Data had put together, which catalogued and analyzed thousands of the documents that IBM had produced in its litigation, and he recommended that the government purchase Control Data's data base for use in its own suit.

On a Sunday evening in mid-January 1973, Carlson got a phone call from Richard Lareau, a lawyer for Control Data, notifying him that Control Data and IBM had reached a settlement of the litigation which would be publicly announced the next morning. Among the provisions of the settlement were Control Data's dropping of its antitrust suit in return for IBM dropping its counterclaim and a payment of $15 million by IBM to pay for Control Data's attorney's fees and litigation expenses. Negotiating the settlement for IBM were Cravath corporate partners George Turner and John Hunt. Carlson immediately asked about the government's acquisition of Control Data's data base, and was furious to learn that one of the secret provisions of the settlement was an agreement by Control Data to destroy its data base. Lareau and his colleagues from Control Data, overseen by several Cravath lawyers, had just spent the weekend shredding the accumulated documents, tapes and computer printouts that Carlson was so desperate to have. Though Carlson rushed into Federal Court in Manhattan to protest, and continued for years to argue that Cravath had violated a court order and should be sanctioned for its role in the data base destruction, there was nothing that could be done to retrieve the destroyed work product. Carlson had simply been outmaneuvered by Cravath.

Barr's stunning performance in the Control Data case—it was the unanimous opinion that the settlement ended the case on extremely favorable terms for IBM and it was largely attributed to Barr's aggressive use of the counterclaim—was soon followed by an even greater triumph in the Greyhound suit. After it had been filed initially in Illinois, Barr moved successfully to have the case transferred to Phoenix, Greyhound's headquarters. Access to Greyhound documents and witnesses would be easier, and Greyhound's lawyers, the large Chicago firm of Winston & Strawn, would not be on their home turf, as the Oppenheimer firm had been in St. Paul.

Considering the scope and complexity of the litigation IBM faced, Cravath still had a relatively small team of lawyers working under Barr. Frederick A. O. "Fritz" Schwarz, Jr., who started working as an associate with Barr on the Control Data and government cases, became a partner a year later. The other senior associate on the case was David Boies, and he became a partner a year after Schwarz. They worked with a handful of young associates. Among them were Joseph Sahid, a lawyer who had impressed Barr while working on the violence commission with him and whom Barr had brought into the firm, and who had also worked with him as a summer associate; Ronald Rolfe, a recent Columbia Law School graduate; and Robert Mullen, a year ahead of Rolfe at Columbia. At Cravath, new associates were all assigned to a single partner for a period of 18 months, and then rotated to another partner. Except for Sahid, none of the young associates had worked for Barr before and had come to him from other partners in the firm. At firms like Cravath, the clout of a partner is often measured by the number of associates he commands. Although Barr could have used some additional manpower, he was not then in a position to acquire any more associates.

The shortage was such that as the Greyhound case headed rapidly toward an actual live courtroom trial, Barr had to gamble and shift all his personnel to Phoenix, leaving no one behind to man the government suit in New York. And it was in Phoenix that the intensity of work on the case began to fuse an identifiable IBM "team" within the firm. Although Barr and local counsel from the Phoenix firm of Brown & Bain (Jack Brown, one of the firm's founders, is a former Cravath associate) handled all the actual in-court cross-examination of witnesses, other Cravath lawyers were intimately involved in trial preparation, often sitting at Barr's elbow in court and working 20-hour days preparing exhibits, witnesses and outlines for examination and cross-examination, oblivious of everything outside the confines of the hotel and the federal courthouse. Barr's performance in cross-examining the Greyhound witnesses was, by all accounts, brilliant, and after an intense two months of the Greyhound case, Judge Walter Craig took the dramatic step of granting Barr's motion for a directed verdict in IBM's favor without even hearing IBM's own evidence. It was beginning to look as though the IBM war would be over after only a few skirmishes. By the time that Telex came

to trial only three months later, the IBM Cravath team was beginning to feel invincible.

And then Barr and his colleagues ran into Floyd Walker.
Walker is no pale imitation of the Wall Street lawyer, but an old-
fashioned plaintiff's litigator who, if he had been living in Oklahoma City at the turn of the century rather than now, would have
worn a holster and pistol. His style was the antithesis of the
laborious, methodical team approach embraced and perfected by
Cravath. He made relatively few discovery demands, choosing to
ignore the thousands of documents that IBM would have been
happy to drop on him and, much to the amazement of the Cravath
lawyers, seemed to pull his trial strategy out of thin air. Almost
single-handedly, and working for a contingency fee, Walker put
together a more effective case than had the scores of lawyers from
the larger St. Paul and Chicago firms in the cases that had gone
before.

Like Control Data, however, Telex and its flamboyant chairman, Roger Wheeler (later murdered in an alleged underworld
killing), had some embarrassing secrets in their closets, and the
Cravath lawyers exploited them. After the Control Data settlement and the end of the Greyhound trial in Phoenix, the same
IBM trial team, headed by Barr, moved to Oklahoma, using the
same system that had worked in Phoenix.

Sahid was overseeing document production by Telex, which
took place in a hotel on the outskirts of Tulsa because Telex
didn't want any of the Cravath lawyers to get inside its plant; and
after several days, he became convinced that everything had not
been produced for inspection. There were files on some of Telex's
personnel, for example, which had practically nothing in them.

Late in the week, Sahid confronted Telex's general counsel, J. B.
Bailey, claiming that all the documents hadn't been produced.
Bailey insisted that they had. "Then let me look at your plant,"
Sahid demanded. "Let me look around." Bailey refused, but the
next morning Sahid hammered at him further with his requests.
Finally Bailey gave in, and allowed Sahid and one IBM business-
man into the plant.

That Saturday morning the Telex plant was deserted, and
Bailey tried to lead Sahid into a central filing area. Instead, Sahid
veered directly into the office of a former IBM employee who was
now working for Telex and whose file had looked suspiciously

scant. In the engineer's top desk drawer Sahid found three inches of documents stamped "IBM confidential"—documents the engineer had obviously stolen when he left IBM's employ. Sahid was elated. He grabbed a nearby trash cart and began to stuff documents into it.

The Telex general counsel was alarmed, but there was no stopping Sahid now. During the day, the Cravath associate raced through thousands of documents, forcing custodians to open locked offices and desks, and dropped whole file drawers into the trash cart. Bailey was reduced to the lame argument that he was going to be late for a dinner party, and practically begged Sahid to leave. Finally Sahid did, but only after arranging delivery of his bulging trash cart.

Barr realized immediately that Sahid's discovery was extraordinary and meant that Telex—a company that had long had an unsavory reputation within the computer business—had actually stolen IBM trade secrets. Sahid's discovery soon formed the core of an IBM counterclaim against Telex for theft of trade secrets. His exploit also became one of the most talked-about subjects among associates at Cravath. No one could remember when an associate—someone who had only been with the firm for eight months—had pulled off such a coup. There were some questions raised about the ethics of Sahid's action. His methods had been, to say the least, unorthodox, indicating bad and impulsive judgment to some. But such grumbling was interpreted, for the most part, as sour grapes by envious associates. For Sahid had demonstrated dramatically that he was prepared to take daring risks to win, an attitude that found great favor with Barr. It was obvious to all after the Telex discovery that Sahid became one of Barr's favored associates.

The discovery of the trade secret documents was to assume an even greater importance in the months to come. The trial of the Telex case began in April, and Floyd Walker conducted a brisk, straightforward trial before Federal Judge A. Sherman Christensen that lasted less than a month. At the close of his case, Barr made a motion similar to the one that had so effectively ended the Greyhound case. But this time, the judge indicated that Walker had done an effective job of raising questions in the judge's mind. Christensen denied Barr's motion and said he wanted to hear IBM's case.

It was the first time that Barr had actually had to present IBM's evidence in court, and despite Cravath's reputation for delay, he demonstrated that he could conduct an efficient and effective trial. He also had the opportunity to make the most of the evidence of Telex's tactics against IBM, demonstrating a pattern of theft, bribery and hiring of IBM personnel in order to keep pace with IBM's technical breakthroughs. Barr worked hard. During the last 48 hours of the trial, he spent all of one night locked in a window-less room with his partners and associates, cite-checking Cravath's post-trial briefs, a tedious task usually delegated to the most in-experienced lawyers. At the end of the trial, Christensen praised both Barr and Walker for their handling of the case. It was only that next September that they all recognized what Bromley had spotted immediately and had bawled out Barr for. With re-spect to damages, the judge had been given practically no evidence or guidance on how to calculate them.

On the day of Christensen's fateful decision against IBM, a group of Cravath associates got a firsthand look at the impact of the adverse $350 million verdict. Some IBM office space in White Plains, New York, not far from the company's headquarters, had been set aside for work on the government antitrust case, and that day a group of IBM businessmen assigned to work on the matter and a handful of Cravath associates were in the offices when news of the verdict came in. The Cravath lawyers, especially those who had been in Oklahoma for the trial, were shocked, their image of Cravath's invincibility shattered. But they were even more shocked by the reaction of the IBM businessmen, who were apoplectic. Some looked suicidal; one burst into tears. Some IBM employees are partly compensated in stock options, and many had put their life savings into IBM stock. For the young lawyers especially, in whom institutional loyalty to Cravath was only just taking hold, it was disturbing to watch the impact of a threat to the company on company men.

Many now mark the loss of the Telex trial as the end of an era at Cravath. The IBM litigation could no longer be viewed as just another big government antitrust case with a handful of private suits on the fringes. With the surge of new cases on the West Coast, appeals of the Greyhound and Telex cases, European in-vestigations, and the end of the sitzkrieg in the government case, the IBM litigation became global in scope, the largest antitrust case in history, with the future existence of the company seriously at stake. Furthermore, the loss of Telex seemed to galvanize IBM, Katzenbach, Cravath and Barr in a way that nothing else had. From now on, no stone was to be left unturned, no matter what the cost. Barr went to his partners at Cravath and told them that IBM wanted—and expected—all of its needs to be met by the firm. In return, it would pay a premium above the rates normally charged the firm's clients. Support for IBM also meant support for Barr. With the acquiescence of his partners, the power conditionally bestowed by Bromley upon Barr was now secure.

Perhaps the most telling symbol of a new era in the IBM litigation was the rise of the White Plains office. In January 1974, a contingent of associates was assigned to the case—Barr's requests for additional lawyers were no longer questioned or challenged—and they moved to the IBM White Plains office building, a nondescript modern edifice on Hamilton Avenue, to be close to IBM documents during a period of discovery depositions that the associates assumed would last for the summer. They never returned to New York City, at least as long as they continued to work on the IBM case.

White Plains, far removed from the influences of the rest of the Cravath firm at 1 Chase Manhattan Plaza, became a world of its own, a firm within a firm that was the unchallenged domain of Barr. Napoleonic in stature, Barr here presided over a clearly defined militaristic hierarchy that consisted of a layer of more junior partners: Boies, Schwartz, and a new addition, Paul Dodyk, a former Columbia law professor who became a partner at the same time as Boies; a layer of associates who had already been through the Telex and Greyhound cases: Sahid, Rolfe, Mullen and several others; and a new, larger layer of the most junior associates, about twenty in all. For the young associates in particular, their experience was considerably different from that of the associates who had preceded them on the case. While Sahid, Rolfe and the others of their generation had worked closely and directly with Barr, most of the new associates had their work filtered through those senior associates who still surrounded Barr, and through the partners working on the case. For many, their only contact with Barr came at weekly Saturday lunches where everyone reported on his work during the week, or at sporting events like the frequent touch football games or tennis matches arranged by Barr.

Barr's emphasis on military discipline and team spirit, as well as the isolation of the office, gave rise to a life-style that was peculiarly identified with the White Plains office and the IBM litigation, one that differed dramatically from the norms that prevailed in the Cravath office downtown. One of the first Cravath principles to vanish—though it was always officially maintained—was the notion that associates were rotated to other partners after an approximately 18-month period. To Rolfe, Sahid and Mullen, for whom the IBM cases had been the most significant experiences of their professional lives, a move seemed unthinkable. They wanted to stay on the cases and Barr wanted to keep them. At lower levels, commitment to the case became accepted evidence of commitment to the firm, as associates sought to emulate the behavior of the senior associates who had found favor with Barr. When other partners at the firm raised the issue, they were quickly rebuffed by Barr, who argued that IBM's needs for experienced lawyers on the case came first. In any event, it became obvious that those assigned to White Plains rarely came back.

Other changes were more obvious. The White Plains office did not look anything like a law firm; Cravath's quarters there were not even identified in the building directory. Most lawyers had only cubicles to work in, and Coke machines lined the hallways. The only "clients" on the premises were IBM businessmen, so the need to wear the formal dark suits and ties that prevailed downtown became less and less important. Gradually any notion of a dress code faded, and the IBM litigation team increasingly donned blue jeans and sports clothes. To ease their transportation problems, IBM rented a fleet of cars and gave them to the Cravath lawyers, a rare luxury for young professionals in Manhattan. Some found it easier to live in Westchester County, especially in the summer. Eventually IBM paid for associates to have summer houses in the White Plains vicinity, which for some translated into rambling mansions on the Connecticut coast complete with tennis courts and pools. Following Telex, Cravath also broke its cardinal rule that all associates be paid the same: it distributed annual IBM "bonuses" of up to $10,000 to all associates on the IBM case.

But if there were perquisites which became associated with the IBM case, there was a price to be paid as well, which was translated most directly into hours worked. At the White Plains office, there was no sense of weekends or free evenings. Eighteen-hour days became normal. In the wake of the Telex decision, the Cravath lawyers faced an enormous burden of work.

Shortly after the Telex case, Raymond Carlson and his team of government lawyers in the Justice Department sensed a potential victory. After years of relative inactivity, they pressed for expedited discovery and for setting a trial date.

Since the case was filed in 1969, Cravath had shrewdly used the tactics which have given rise to the firm's reputation for delay. After discovering that the Control Data documents had been destroyed by the Control Data lawyers, Carlson tried to obtain copies of those documents directly from IBM. Not surprisingly, the Cravath lawyers refused, claiming that they were protected from disclosure by the work-product or attorney-client privileges, standard protective claims for litigation-related documents. Eventually, Cravath lawyers raised claims of privilege for approximately 100,000 documents sought by the government. The government lawyers protested that they couldn't even read all of those documents within the lifetime of the lawsuit.

This was one of many claims of being burdened by Cravath tactics that seemed to impress the federal judge presiding in the government case, David Edelstein. The chief judge of the Southern District of New York in Manhattan, Edelstein has a reputation for erratic, sometimes even bizarre comments and behavior. Almost from the beginning, however, he had shown great sympathy for the government lawyers and an almost unmitigated hostility toward Barr and his Cravath colleagues. Carlson attributes the judge's attitude to Edelstein's outrage over destruction of the Control Data documents. More probably, however, it stemmed from his pique over the realization that the IBM case alone might occupy the remainder of his career on the bench, and for that he seemed to blame Cravath.

Dealing with the claims of privilege, Edelstein ordered the appointment of three prominent lawyers as special masters to review each of the documents, thereby relieving the government lawyers of that exhausting job and of making a preliminary determination on the merits of the privilege claims. The results of that enormous task provided the fuel for more arguments over findings and procedures, accompanied by what seemed an endless exchange of briefs and motions.

By the time of the Telex decision, the work of the special masters had barely gotten under way when Carlson and the government lawyers started clamoring for a deposition campaign and fixing a date for the start of trial. Although Barr argued strenuously that the case was not nearly ready for trial—that the government case was so disorganized that his opponents needed more time—the judge granted Carlson's requests and fixed a trial date for April 1974, only four months away.

That order launched the most hectic period of the IBM cases, even though the April trial date was soon jettisoned with the consent of the government. And if charges of delay could be laid at Cravath's feet for its conduct over the document production, blame for the scope and length of the deposition campaign belongs equally to the government. One of the crucial aspects of any antitrust case is the determination of the relevant market and the number of competing companies within it and their respective market shares, all indices of monopoly power. To aid the court's determination of those issues in the Control Data suit, lawyers for both sides sent a questionnaire to 2,700 companies requesting information about the scope of their activities in the computer industry. The lawyers had received 1,800 useable responses, and the data produced by the survey had been used in both the Greyhound and Telex cases, obviating the need to call hundreds of witnesses to the stand to supply simple data on a company's activities in the industry. At the time the survey was taken, government lawyers had been invited to participate and they had declined.

Now, in the government case, Barr wanted to use the survey data in the same way that they had been used in Greyhound and Telex. Much to his astonishment, Carlson refused to agree to use the data, claiming that the government would be deprived of its right to cross-examine the sources of the data. Instead, he insisted that Cravath take depositions to establish the same data that had been provided in the questionnaire survey. During the next four months, Cravath lawyers took 800 depositions of witnesses related solely to the questions in the survey. At many of those depositions, no government lawyer even bothered to attend; at others, someone from the nearest Justice Department field office attended, usually with virtually no knowledge of what the case was about. Cravath lawyers also had to take the depositions of the 200 people listed by the government as their witnesses; a list which was frequently changed by additions and deletions, all permitted the government by the judge.

It was a period of intense activity for the Cravath lawyers in White Plains and in cities scattered across the country. Barr recalls it as a period when he was always on an airplane. A typical week took a single lawyer from New York to Tulsa to San Francisco to Los Angeles to Syracuse and back to New York on Saturday or Sunday, if at all. First-year associates were thrown into taking depositions, a level of responsibility at Cravath usually reserved for senior associates. The demands were so great that corporate, tax, and trusts and estate partners and associates were dragged into the effort and sent out to take depositions, maintaining constant phone links for guidance to lawyers in White Plains. Crash courses in computers were conducted at midtown Manhattan hotels and at Armonk on weekends for all Cravath lawyers. In Washington, Ron Rolfe—still an associate—was in the position of instructing John Pickering, the senior partner of Wilmer, Cutler & Pickering, about taking the depositions of officials in government agencies. Pickering took to greeting the young Rolfe as "boss."

As if the intense pressure generated by the discovery schedule weren't enough, internal competition generated by the senior associates on the case made matters worse. Associates at Cravath are considered for partnerships in groups based on their year of graduation from law school, though there may be some spillover from one year to the next. During the period of frenzied discovery in 1974, the group of senior IBM team associates were entering the last crucial year or two before the fateful decision, and competition among them reached a fever pitch. There was Mullen, from the law school class of '68, who appeared to be on his way to an all-time firm record for billable hours logged; and there were four associates from the class of '69: Rolfe, Sahid, Saunders and John Cooper. Competition was especially fierce between Rolfe and Sahid. The feeling was that probably only one or two out of the eligible group would actually be made a partner, and Sahid seemed to have had an edge ever since his Telex counterclaim triumph. When Sahid scored another triumph by billing 24 hours in a single day, Rolfe—in a move that became the subject of legend in the firm—flew to California, worked on the plane and, by virtue of the change in time zones, managed to bill 27 hours in one day.

That competition was not always so benevolent. Rolfe and Sahid eventually were separated from working on the same projects. Rolfe worked closely with Boies on deposing and preparing expert economists; Sahid was assigned to another aspect of the case. Still, they both appeared to their colleagues to engage in a petty campaign to discredit each other and take credit for each other's work. Eventually, perhaps even Sahid and Rolfe realized that their destructive competition might be their mutual ruin. A year before the partnership decision, they seemed to stop undercutting each other and became allies in a major common interest: the pursuit of partnership.

In June 1974, as he had insisted he would do, Judge Edelstein halted IBM's discovery campaign, saying that if he didn't stop it the case would go on forever. However, he allowed the government to continue its own document review and deposition campaign, ordering the start of trial for May 1975. For the next year, the Cravath IBM team prepared feverishly, defending against depositions by government lawyers, mounting appeals of the special master rulings on the privileged document claims, coordinating discovery beginning in the various West Coast private cases, and preparing its own case for trial.

Meanwhile, the Cravath lawyers waited for a decision in the appeals of both the Greyhound case, which had been argued before the Ninth Circuit Court of Appeals in San Francisco in the spring, and the Telex case, which Barr had argued in the Tenth Circuit a month later. Either opinion could prove to be extremely important. Though circuits are not bound by the decisions of other courts of appeal, they are often deferential to the interpretations of sister courts. And whichever opinion appeared first was likely to be the first of the IBM cases to produce a ruling in the Supreme Court that would bind all the other courts hearing IBM suits. At the beginning of January 1975, Carlson amended the government's complaint—more than five years after it was filed—to add all of the claims that had been made successfully by Telex.

Two weeks later, the Tenth Circuit announced its decision in Telex. It was a sweeping reversal of Christensen's opinion, and it turned stunning defeat into total victory for IBM. The Court of Appeals repudiated the lower court's definition of market and went on to say that the " 'acts' of IBM . . . when evaluated under the Sherman Act and when set in the context of the prevailing court opinions do not constitute a violation of law." The court even awarded IBM more than it had ever dared hope for. It upheld the District Court's finding that Telex had stolen trade secrets from IBM and awarded IBM $18.5 million against Telex. Telex promptly announced that it would appeal the decision to the Supreme Court, but it was a devastating loss. If the counterclaim was ultimately upheld, it would force Telex into bankruptcy.

The Telex win, though celebrated in the White Plains litigation headquarters, did not seem to daunt the government lawyers or the plaintiffs in the private cases that had sprung up after the first Telex decision. In fact, the long-awaited opening of the government trial in May 1975 proved to be a false start, because the government wanted to reopen its discovery with respect to the new Telex claims added to the complaint in January, even though they had now been repudiated by the Court of Appeals.

There was, of course, still the hope on the part of government lawyers and private plaintiffs that they would be rescued from the Tenth Circuit's opinion by the Supreme Court; but that too would be dashed by the end of the summer. In October, on the day before the Supreme Court announced the list of cases it would hear during the fall term, IBM and Telex announced that they had settled the case and that Telex was withdrawing its petition for certiorari to the Supreme Court. In return, IBM agreed to drop its counterclaim and give up the $18.5 million in damages awarded by the Court of Appeals. When the Supreme Court's list of rejected cases was issued the next day, it was apparent from a gap that one case had been dropped at the last minute, suggesting that the Supreme Court would not have heard the Telex appeal.

There were rumors at the time that somehow Barr had been leaked the information that the Supreme Court would grant certiorari and, armed with that knowledge, forced settlement with an attractive offer to Telex to drop the counterclaim. Had Barr known that the Supreme Court had granted certiorari, it would have given him an unfair advantage in bargaining with Telex. For all Telex knew, the Supreme Court was going to deny certiorari, locking it into the disastrous outcome imposed by the Court of Appeals. But Barr denies that there was any exchange of confidential information. And the settlement itself was sufficiently favorable to IBM that it casts doubt on the suggestion that, knowing it faced the risk of Supreme Court review, the Cravath lawyers were willing to do almost anything to settle the case. All IBM gave up was its counterclaim. And given the allegations of the government, the last thing IBM wanted was to drive a marginal competitor out of business as a result of its litigation strategy.

In any event, Katzenbach and IBM saw the Telex outcome as a triumph. At a subsequent talk to some of the Cravath lawyers working on the case, Katzenbach said, "The next thing the government will be accusing us of is monopolizing the best lawyers and law firm in the country." In the eyes of IBM, it seemed, Barr and Cravath could do no wrong.

The trial of the government case began in earnest in November 1976, with a series of witnesses from the Memorex Corporation, one of the West Coast private plaintiffs, all of whom Barr expected to supply important witnesses. For the trial, Barr honed the organizational format developed in the Greyhound and Telex cases into a structure which prevailed throughout the government case. Barr remained in overall command of the entire case and, initially, did all of the cross-examination in court except for a few witnesses who were assigned to Dodyk. Part of his commitment to IBM had been that no one but a Cravath partner would actually speak on behalf of IBM in the courtroom; associates had to content themselves with sitting at the counsel table.

Beneath the top partners, lawyers were divided into teams corresponding to broad issues in the case. There were the "market structure" team, the "acts and practices" team, etc. These were headed by senior associates, like Rolfe and Sahid. More junior associates were assigned to narrower issues within the teams, and at the very bottom was the "beachmaster." The beachmaster—named after the first wave of Marines who would land in an amphibious attack and who suffered the highest mortality rate—was responsible for having all the documents and exhibits in place in court, and had to read each day's transcript and correct typographical, spelling and other errors. It was considered the worst assignment on the case. The beachmaster was invariably the first lawyer in the office in the morning, usually around 7:00 A.M., and the last to leave, usually after midnight; and stints as beachmaster sometimes lasted six months or more.

For the conduct of the trial, Barr set up another set of litigation offices at 100 Church Street in downtown Manhattan, not far from the courthouse or from the regular Cravath offices at 1 Chase.

Ostensibly, there wasn't enough room at the 1 Chase offices. Work on the IBM case, however, was also deemed too intense to be subjected to any of the potential distractions which existed in the regular Cravath offices, including the disconcerting presence of other Cravath associates who were not being made to work nearly so hard; and the separate litigation quarters reinforced the sense of a separate "team" identity. Depending on the witness in court on a particular day, the corresponding IBM "team" from White Plains would travel to the 100 Church facility in limousines, followed by trucks carrying any documents needed. On Friday night, the delivery men would come around the 100 Church offices gathering up everything that might be needed over the weekend; the materials would be back on the lawyers' White Plains desks by early Saturday morning.

Saturdays were characterized by their own routine. All associates were expected to be present in White Plains for lunch on Saturday, even on the rare occasions when they had no pressing work, and to sit through the weekly reports of progress on the case. After lunch, lawyers were expected to play football, baseball or volleyball, depending on the season. Barr saw these "games" as an important part of building team spirit, and they were often rough. When one Cravath IBM associate broke his collarbone in a Saturday football game, he demanded workman's compensation for injuries suffered as a condition of his employment.

Managing the documents in the case was a task that kept scores of IBM employees busy full-time. IBM executives—most perceived as having risen above their capacities within the company —were assigned to "litigation analysis," a unit with offices adjacent to the Cravath lawyers in White Plains. There, the businessmen—contemptuously labeled "grundoons" by the Cravath lawyers—served essentially as Cravath paralegals, at the disposal of the lawyers when they needed documents. For the case, IBM had more than 3,000,000 documents recorded in full text in one of the world's largest computer systems. An additional 17,000,-000 documents were in an author-addressee code for ready identification and location. Every day's transcript was also computerized in full text. The programs were shrouded in secrecy, with access available only to those given elaborate security codes. Most of the Cravath lawyers were not given security codes, but when they needed documents, they simply called one of the IBM businessmen. They, in turn, were organized by classes of documents. For example, if a lawyer needed documents related to IBM's efforts to drive out competitors, he called the IBM businessman in charge of "fighting machines," and a binder of the appropriate documents would appear on his desk, all neatly coded and tabulated.

The government's first witness was Sidney Fernbach, a computer industry expert. As he did throughout the trial, Barr arrived at 100 Church Street only about an hour before going over to the courtroom, quickly reviewed the large ring binders of documents related to the witness and the elaborate outlines for cross-examination that had been prepared by his associates, then jotted down a few notes on a piece of paper. Barr amazed associates by his ability seemingly to absorb masses of material and conduct what sounded like an impromptu cross-examination, an entirely different approach from that of Dodyk, who demanded detailed scripts for cross-examination, which he studied and revised painstakingly and virtually memorized.

"Barr never lost sight of the few important points he had to establish with each witness," recalls one of the lawyers who worked closely with him during the trial. "He'd respond to the witnesses' answers, sometimes going off on what seemed like long diversions, but he always came back to those points. He was relentless, and he didn't stop until the witness had told him what he wanted to hear."

In Fernbach's case, however, it took no brilliant cross-examination to establish the point that Barr wanted to make. A basic rule of examining one's own witness is never to ask a question when the answer is unknown, and that rule was seemingly violated by Carlson, the lead government lawyer. A major point to be established by Fernbach was the number of producers of general purpose computers, which the government, in its trial brief, claimed was five. So during his direct examination, Carlson asked Fernbach for the definition of a general purpose computer and then asked how many manufacturers there were, a subject he had presumably discussed at length with Fernbach before the trial. Fernbach answered that more than a hundred companies manufactured them, rather than the hoped-for five. Carlson looked stunned and asked for a break. "I would have walked out of the courtroom never to return," Barr later told his Cravath colleagues as he lectured them about never making Carlson's mistake themselves. In a sense, Carlson never did return. Ultimately he examined only three witnesses; and he turned most courtroom work over to his young Justice Department staff. Barr frequently used examples from the government lawyers' work on the case to teach his associates how *not* to try a case.

Barr's success in undermining government witnesses on cross-examination, and the government lawyers' own ineptness, however, only seemed to heighten the antagonism displayed by Judge Edelstein toward the Cravath lawyers. One of the government's key Memorex witnesses was Lawrence Spitters, the company's former chairman, who testified for six full days of direct examination about how IBM had nearly driven Memorex out of business. During preparation for his cross-examination, Barr recalled that seven years before, Spitters had been sued by the Securities and Exchange Commission for fraud as a result of distributing false accounting data to potential investors. Barr was outraged that the Justice Department would even put such a witness on the stand, but the information gave Barr devastating material for cross-examination, since it would undoubtedly undermine Spitters' credibility.

When the time came for Barr to cross-examine Spitters, he immediately raised a question about the SEC charges. Burney Boote, the government lawyer, who was only five years out of law school, objected to the question as irrelevant, a preposterous claim that the judge overruled. Then Barr attempted to introduce as evidence of the SEC suit a copy of an article from the *Wall Street Journal* which had exposed Spitters' activities. Again, the government lawyer objected, saying that Barr had to produce the original article—not a copy. Incredibly, Edelstein agreed and ordered Barr to produce an original. Since the article had appeared only in the Pacific edition of the *Wall Street Journal*, there were no originals in New York—not even at the *Wall Street Journal* itself. Even on the West Coast, most libraries had only microfilm copies. Finally a copy was located at the Stanford library, where a librarian sent it on an overnight flight back to New York. The next morning—much to the amazement of both Edelstein and the government lawyer—Barr began his examination by using the original of the 1970 *Wall Street Journal* article, and Spitters' testimony was soon thoroughly discredited.

On another occasion Boote wanted to introduce a document into evidence in conjunction with testimony by a witness who was a Bank of America executive who had come from San Francisco to testify in the trial. Boote conceded that she couldn't establish any foundation for admitting the document—foundation requires demonstrating some connection between the witness and a document, typically that the document came out of the witness's files—but that she wanted the judge to admit the document anyway. Naturally enough, Barr rose and objected. "Received," Edelstein stated, glaring at Barr. When Barr tried to argue, Edelstein ordered Boote to conduct a deposition of the witness to establish a foundation, saying that he would admit it conditionally until she did so. At the subsequent deposition, the witness testified that he had never seen the document, had no recollection of it and knew nothing about it. Several months later, Boote again tried to admit the same document, and Barr objected, noting that at the deposition the witness knew nothing about it. Edelstein was furious and admitted the document anyway. "I said any problems in the deposition were to be brought to me before the witness left town," the judge practically screamed at Barr.

Then there was what became known as the "red pen" incident. During Barr's cross-examination one morning, Judge Edelstein interrupted Barr, who was holding a red pen, with a command to "stop that." Barr asked the judge what he meant, and Edelstein boiled over. "Now look, don't you point any finger or pen at me. What you need is a lesson in good manners." When Barr apologized but said he didn't understand what the problem was, Edelstein finally sputtered: "I think you have had too many indulgences, and you have been a very spoiled brat. Now stop it. Don't you ever point a finger at me again. I consider that threatening and bullying, and stop it."

After the first series of witnesses called by the government, not even the judge's diversions could disguise the fact that the government's case was not going smoothly at all. In evident recognition that Cravath's cross-examinations of live witnesses had done considerable harm to the position they were trying to establish, the government turned, with the judge's permission, to the use of deposition transcripts rather than live testimony. A government lawyer would come to court and simply read directly from deposition transcripts, which would then be retranscribed by the court reporter. That procedure continued for more than a year, and after a few weeks the judge quit attending the trial. Edelstein would open court at 10:00 A.M. each day, and then one of the government attorneys would begin to drone the deposition transcript into the court record. The judge would leave the bench, returning only at 4:30 P.M. to adjourn the day's court session. The proceedings took on only the barest resemblance of a trial.

Though the government's trial tactics eased the pressure in the government case on Barr and his colleagues somewhat during 1976, developments on the West Coast kept the Cravath IBM team working in a constant crisis atmosphere. Following the Telex decision, IBM had been sued by three West Coast computer manufacturers: California Computer Products, Inc., called "Cal-Comp," Memorex Corporation and Transamerica. To help coordinate work on those cases, Barr and IBM retained the Los Angeles law firm of O'Melveny & Myers and one of its top litigating partners, Patrick Lynch.

O'Melveny & Myers is one of the two largest firms in Los Angeles, and although the city has never had the financial or industrial base to support a blue chip corporate firm like Cravath, O'Melveny is the closest firm to that model in Southern California. It is one of the oldest firms in Los Angeles; it represents a major bank, Security Pacific Corporation; it shares CBS with Cravath and does much of its work on the West Coast and most of its entertainment work; it does West Coast work for such major corporations as General Motors and Occidental Petroleum; and it is California's leading municipal bond firm. Warren Christopher, the former Assistant Secretary of State, is its best-known partner; Louis Myers, one of the name partners who is now deceased, was a chief justice of the California Supreme Court.

Pitted against O'Melveny and Cravath were Gibson, Dunn & Crutcher, Los Angeles' largest law firm, on behalf of Memorex; and Maxwell Blecher, the famous plaintiff's litigator, on behalf of CalComp. The Transamerica case was filed in the District Court in San Francisco, and Cravath again tapped O'Melveny & Myers to assist in the defense of IBM. Representing Transamerica was the large conglomerate's regular outside counsel at Orrick, Herrington & Sutcliffe, a large San Francisco firm.

Barr had two principal worries about the California cases. Which of them would come to trial first, and when? With Telex and Greyhound out of the way (Greyhound's appeal still had not been decided by the Ninth Circuit), the first of the California cases was likely to be the next candidate for a test case in the Supreme Court. And as the government's case dragged on, Barr was increasingly worried that one or more of the California cases would go to trial while the government case was still in session in New York. Barr had always been lead counsel in the IBM trials; he couldn't be on both the West and East coasts simultaneously, even with the aid of IBM computers and unlimited money.

Those worries turned to near panic when, in February 1976, Judge Ray McNichols, the presiding judge in both the Los Angeles cases, assigned an October 1976 trial date for the CalComp case. His reasoning was that CalComp's complaint raised the broadest issues against IBM, and that if IBM went to trial and lost it would be more inclined to settle the other pending cases without having to go through a trial. For the same reasons, Barr was particularly alarmed that CalComp had been selected as the test case. And he would be facing Max Blecher on the other side, a well-known plaintiff's lawyer with all of Floyd Walker's toughness and canny instincts and with what Barr expected to be a considerably better understanding of the issues in the case and the workings of the computer industry.

News of the CalComp trial date triggered a hurried high-level conference between Barr and Katzenbach in Armonk. The principal issue was whether Barr dared leave New York and the government case for as long as a year, the time it would probably be necessary to prepare and try the CalComp case. And if he did not, who could do it? The problem had been made worse because, just before the judge set the trial date, O'Melveny & Myers had informed Cravath that it had done some legal work for CalComp itself in the past and hence couldn't act as Los Angeles counsel for IBM because of a conflict of interest. Barr had immediately hired another Los Angeles firm, Kadison, Pfaelzer, Woodard, Quinn & Rossi, but it was relatively small, with about fifty lawyers, and Barr doubted that they could be counted upon to take a major role if the case started in October.

On one point Barr and Katzenbach had never wavered: the company's principal commitment had to be to the government case, which posed a far graver threat than any of the private suits, no matter how much money was at stake. They decided they couldn't let the temptation to send Barr to California for the CalComp case shake that commitment. Dodyk was also too deeply immersed in the government case. Barr urged that David Boies be entrusted with the case, even though he had only been a partner for three years and had never before tried a major case. And if Boies seemed to get into real trouble, Barr promised he would personally go out to California and back him up. Katzenbach was worried, but he agreed with Barr's suggestions.

At first glance, Boies seemed an unlikely choice for what was the most important role on the case after that of Barr himself. He hardly fit the Cravath mold. Boyishly handsome, with slightly unkempt blond curls and blue eyes that made him look far younger than his 34 years, he was the heart-throb of many of the IBM secretaries. He is warm and personable, described by the government lawyer Carlson as "angelic" in his courtroom demeanor. He was actively interested in politics, and had taken several years off while an associate at Cravath to work on civil rights cases in the South. Moreover, he had never acted like a slavish imitator of Barr, preferring an office at White Plains on a different floor from his boss, where he cultivated his own circle of loyal associates. Beneath the surface, however, he could be as demanding as anyone at the firm. When an associate once declined to attend a meeting with Boies in order to take his fiancée to the doctor, Boies was so annoyed that he had the associate transferred to another partner and made clear that he thought the associate had "attitude" problems.

Boies had actually been one of the few to extricate himself from active duty on the IBM team when the CalComp crisis arose. He was in Bombay, India, working on a case for another client against the Indian government, when Barr called and told him that he was placing him in charge of the CalComp case. Boies flew to Tokyo, left Tokyo at 11:00 A.M., and arrived in New York at 11:00 A.M. on Sunday. Sunday evening, a messenger delivered a stack of CalComp papers and documents, which Boies read that night. He was ready for his meeting with Barr on Monday morning.

Continuing with the trial of the government case while preparing for the imminent trial of another major case taxed even the resources of a firm like Cravath. To handle CalComp, Boies actually moved to California in June, taking his family with him and enrolling his children in California schools for the next year. Boies installed his secretary in one of the bungalows at the Beverly Hills Hotel. Drafted for the case were a corporate partner, Thomas Brome, and a tax partner, Richard Hiegel, whose chief functions were to run the special litigation office that Cravath set up in a downtown Los Angeles office building. Two associates in Cravath's London office who had had experience on the IBM matters, Douglas Broadwater and Stuart Gold, were told to leave London indefinitely for California. The assignment was particularly galling for Gold, who had only just arrived in London a few weeks before. In fact, Gold had been thinking about leaving Cravath for another job; he was persuaded to stay with the promise that he would be assigned to the London office. Barr and Boies had a short tug-of-war over Rolfe, but Boies won. Given Rolfe's herculean capacity for work, "He was the one guy I was absolutely intent on getting. I wanted him with me," Boies recalls.

Altogether, about fifteen Cravath lawyers shifted to Los Angeles for all or part of the trial. Some rented houses or apartments; most lived in the downtown Hyatt Hotel, connected to the IBM/Cravath offices by an enclosed shopping mall. They were joined by teams of IBM businessmen from the litigation task force, who ran the computers and performed the document searches; a group of lawyers from Brown & Bain, including Jack Brown and some others who had helped on the Greyhound case in Phoenix; a few lawyers from the upstaged Los Angeles firm, who swallowed their pride and agreed to take commands from Boies; and a crew of secretaries and paralegals.

From mid-April until the case was over in February 1977, the CalComp team worked every day and night. Meals were catered into the office building; fried chicken was a favorite of Boies, so fried chicken was on the menu almost every night. One associate recalls not stepping outside of the hotel/office complex for a solid week. A typical day began at 8:00 A.M. and continued without a break until midnight or 2:00 A.M., with the only relief a visit to the hotel's indoor tennis club. Some associates played regularly on mornings from 7 to 8 A.M.; when Barr was around he liked to arrange matches late in the afternoon.

By the time the trial itself began in October, Boies and the Cravath team were ready, probably better prepared than Blecher realized. Boies was excited and confident, even though he also felt the enormous pressure of a $350 million lawsuit. To needle him, some of the Gibson, Dunn lawyers working for Memorex came up to him in the courtroom just before the start of the trial and asked, "How does it feel to be trying your first jury trial for $350 million against Max Blecher?"

The taunts of opposing counsel only enlivened Boies's interest in the case and whetted his appetite for battle. Boies is not the typically cautious Wall Street lawyer. He loves to take chances and confided to a group of IBM businessmen that if he hadn't become a lawyer, he would like to have become a professional gambler. Indeed, during some of the nights before trial, when associates were toiling long and hard on trial documents, Boies holed up with IBM businessmen and played poker.

An outsider observing Boies in court would not have guessed that he had never tried a jury case before. He quickly displayed the kind of intuitive brilliance which had already marked his work, though in less visible ways. CalComp's principal contention was that its computer manufacturing business had been badly damaged by IBM's business practices, including destructive price cuts on existing products and the introduction of new and changed products. In recent years, CalComp had begun to diversify, and had launched a consumer products division that had nothing to do with computers or computer software. Included among CalComp's consumer products were a Mickey Mouse night light and a rubber Donald Duck lamp which hung from the ceiling. For his opening statement, Boies set CalComp's Mickey Mouse and Donald Duck paraphernalia on one end of the counsel's table. At the other end, he placed one of IBM's complex disc-drive mechanisms. To the jury, he remarked, "CalComp claimed it couldn't compete because of IBM price reductions. But the real reason CalComp couldn't compete was that it went for the quick buck—it went for novelties over technology. IBM has always been dedicated to computers." CalComp's chief executive, Lester Kilpatrick, was furious and was grumbling audibly by the end of Boies's opening remarks. But the Mickey Mouse figures made their mark on the jury.

Kilpatrick became even angrier with Boies later in the trial when he himself took the witness stand. After he testified at length that excessive competition from IBM was damaging CalComp's business, that particularly disc-drive competition in the Los Angeles area had been "fierce," Boies asked Kilpatrick about a speech he had given to some securities analysts in 1971, and read directly from the text of the speech:

"Let's look at the competition in the disc-drive business," Boies read. "I really don't characterize IBM as competition per se, because if they weren't there and hadn't created the market and hadn't made installations we wouldn't have any market at all. So it is hard to call the guy who created your opportunity a competitor —although certainly IBM doesn't give up easily on any particular order. But our real competition isn't IBM." Then Boies asked, "Was it the case, sir, in February 1971 that CalComp's more serious competition on a day-to-day basis was companies like Memorex, Telex and Potter?"

That is the kind of skilled cross-examination question that scores the point no matter what the witness answers. Eventually, Kilpatrick explained what he meant by competition by saying, "If I climb in the ring with Cassius Clay it is not competition, it is exhibition," which only reinforced Boies's point that IBM is a champion in a vigorously competitive industry. Eventually, Kilpatrick seemed obsessed with Boies, constantly referring to his own counsel, Blecher, as "Mr. Boies." Finally Blecher said, "I'm Blecher and he's Boies," pointing at Boies. Kilpatrick smiled and said, "Just wishful thinking."

Just as important as Boies's courtroom performance was the work by the other Cravath associates camped in the Hyatt and the adjoining offices. As soon as each day's transcript was prepared by the court reporters, usually around 9:00 or 10:00 P.M., a team consisting of Rolfe, Mullen, Gold and Marty Edel, another associate, immediately started dissecting it and converting it into proposed findings of fact. The trial team had already completed a master skeleton of the various topics and issues in the case. The Cravath associates converted each statement in court into a single declarative fact, and then plugged it into the category where it supported one of the positions that IBM wanted to prove in the case, preserving a page reference to the actual transcript record. As the proposed findings took shape, Rolfe would go to Boies in court and indicate gaps in the master skeleton where more proof was needed.

During the final days of the trial, the associates worked for three days and three nights without a break, catching up on the transcripts where they had earlier fallen behind, and managing to incorporate even the testimony given on the last day of the trial. On February 11 at 10:00 A.M., Blecher announced that he was resting his case. After a brief recess during which Rolfe rushed from the office building to the courthouse, Boies stood up and made an oral motion to dismiss the case. To support his motion, he handed Judge McNichol the proposed findings that the Cravath lawyers had gleaned from the evidence submitted during Cal-Comp's part of the case. It was voluminous, with thousands of individual citations to the transcript record.

Blecher and the three lawyers in his firm working with him were stunned by the enormousness of the effort expended on a simple motion to dismiss. "I had never encountered anything like that in my life," Blecher recalls. "The sheer manpower that took, the cost, I just felt overwhelmed. I've often wondered how they could operate if the client imposed any cost control at all. Everything showed this attitude. They buried us with paper. They produced reams of paper in futile endeavors. They made requests for admissions of fact that were ridiculous. We stacked up the paper—it was five or six feet tall." There was no way that Blecher could prepare an immediate response. His own staff didn't expect to do such an analysis of the record until the judge asked for proposed findings of fact at the end of the entire case. Blecher's pleas for some additional time to review the Cravath motion and prepare a rebuttal were denied by the judge, who adjourned the trial for lunch at 12:30.

Two hours later, he reconvened the lawyers and announced that he would grant Cravath's motion for a directed verdict on behalf of IBM, taking the case away from the jury. Such a decision is extremely rare, done only in those situations where the judge has determined that even if the jury accepts the plaintiff's evidence, there is no way that the defendant can be found guilty. The Cravath team broke out the champagne at the Hyatt, and IBM later paid for everyone who had worked on the case, even secretaries who had worked behind the scene in New York, to fly to Los Angeles for a cocktail party, dinner and holiday. A few of the associates visited Disneyland—their first trip out of downtown Los Angeles in more than six months.

The CalComp triumph was soon followed by another major victory in the Memorex case, though one that was much closer to the wire. The Memorex case was also different in that, technically, O'Melveny & Myers was lead counsel and handled the entire trial. In truth, Barr was just as much in charge as he had been in Telex and CalComp. The first major clash between the Cravath and

O'Melveny lawyers occurred shortly after O'Melveny completed its draft of IBM's pretrial brief for Memorex. Barr was immediately upset when he read it, worried that O'Melveny might be developing positions that were inconsistent with positions he was taking in the government case and that might later haunt him. Barr, Mullen and three other Cravath lawyers went out to Los Angeles, installed themselves in the same offices that had been used in CalComp, and worked round the clock for four days completely revising the O'Melveny brief. To avoid demoralizing the O'Melveny lawyers, they were prevented from even seeing the Cravath counsel, working just down the street from their own offices. But O'Melveny's Lynch was angry and asked Katzenbach to review both the O'Melveny and Cravath versions of the pretrial brief. It was the Cravath version that prevailed.

From then on, O'Melveny lost whatever independence it might once have had in the case. Cravath lawyers actually prepared scripts to use with the Memorex witnesses; Lynch would typically meet with an IBM witness for only twenty minutes before trial and review the Cravath script that was handed to him by a Cravath lawyer. A Cravath lawyer was always present in the courtroom ready to report on the day's events to Barr—a task that became known to Cravath associates as "babysitting for O'Melveny."

The Memorex case was the first IBM trial to actually reach a jury's consideration. Lynch's motion to dismiss in that case was denied, a development interpreted at Cravath as evidence that their fears about O'Melveny were well founded, and the jury deliberated over its verdict for more than a week before it finally said it was impossibly hung. At that point the judge took the case away from them and directed the entry of a verdict in favor of IBM. A later poll of the jurors showed that IBM had come very close to losing the case. At one point the foreman's poll had indicated an 11 to 1 vote in favor of Memorex; and it turned out that the one holdout also thought that IBM was guilty but felt that IBM should be subjected to even more severe penalties than the other jurors were prepared to award. By the time she explained her position, however, two other jurors changed their minds, and the final jury poll indicated a 10 to 2 vote in favor of Memorex. Perhaps most revealing, however, were the jurors' answers to a series of questions the judge asked them after they had announced they couldn't reach a decision. The answers indicated that the jurors hadn't the vaguest idea what the case was all about. It was then that the judge decided to direct a verdict himself.

Though the work had been incredibly arduous, for many of the Cravath lawyers the victories in CalComp and Memorex were emotional high points in the cases and in their careers that would not be repeated. After the end of the active trials in California, the IBM cases entered their last and, for many of those working on them, their most disturbing phase.

During and shortly after the CalComp and Memorex trials, the personnel configurations within the Cravath team began to undergo some significant changes. During the autumn of 1975, associates from the law school classes of 1968 and 1969 came up for partnership, and the decision that year was viewed as particularly revealing by other associates at the firm. Of the senior litigation associates from those classes working on the IBM case, there seemed three likely candidates: Mullen, Sidney Davis and George Vradenburg. Mullen was known to associates principally for two qualities: an incredible number of hours billed and unswerving loyalty and devotion to Barr. Otherwise, he seemed an unlikely choice as partner. In the presence of strangers he seemed shy and awkward; his appearance was eccentric, with a hair style that sometimes looked as though it had been cut at home. In short, he wholly lacked that indefinable constellation of characteristics that at Cravath meant someone was "partnership material." Davis, on the other hand, was one of the most popular and personable associates in the firm, one who seemed the model for attracting and keeping clients. Vradenburg, while not as outgoing as Davis, exuded skill and competence. All three were bright, imaginative and unquestionably competent as lawyers. But in October, only Mullen was elevated to partnership; the others were never tapped.

Partnership decisions in 1977 reinforced the impression that Mullen's choice had made on other lawyers at the firm. Four IBM litigation associates became eligible for partner that year, and they had been locked in the most intense competition that anyone had ever witnessed at the firm. They were Rolfe, who clearly had the strong support of Boies; Sahid, Rolfe's "ally" who had discovered the basis for the Telex counterclaim; Paul Saunders, an associate who often seemed invisible but who had also billed an astronomical number of hours and did a lot of administrative work for Barr; and John Cooper, an associate who had left the IBM case to work on some CBS matters at the 1 Chase office. All had made major sacrifices in the course of their work for IBM: Rolfe had gotten divorced partly as a result of pressures from the case; Saunders once joked that his children had forgotten his name.

Choosing partners among the four, however, posed a dilemma for the firm. Partners at Cravath have always been chosen democratically, by a full vote of the partnership. Prior to the IBM case, that system had informally shifted to one where partners in each of the firm's departments reached a consensus about who should be elevated, and then the other partners in the firm voted along the lines of their recommendations. Under the system where associates rotated to new assignments every 18 months, there were always at least four or five partners who had worked closely with an associate for an extended period of time. But during their careers at the firm, Sahid had worked *only* for Barr. Rolfe and Saunders had worked for Barr for all but their first years. Only Cooper had had any significant exposure to other partners in the firm.

The results that year surprised even those associates who had begun to perceive the extent of Barr's power within the firm. Rolfe, Sahid and Saunders were all made partners; Cooper was not. For the second year in a row, every new litigation partner was a Barr protégé from the IBM case. The message to other litigation associates: The road to partnership is long hours and loyalty to Barr above all else.

Meanwhile, the government case in New York had been dragging forward. While entire trials in Telex, in Memorex and in Greyhound were conducted in a matter of months, the government's presentation of evidence was now entering its third year. At the request of the government lawyers, so as to give themselves more time to prepare, Edelstein only heard testimony three days a week, and readily granted requests for long recesses in between witnesses. By 1977, the government ended its long and tedious procedure of reading deposition testimony into the record, and testimony by live witnesses resumed. These were to be the government's final witnesses, the economic experts who would tie all of the facts together and demonstrate the unlawful economic impact of IBM's activities.

With practically the full Cravath team back in New York, the economic experts provided a field day for cross-examination. The Cravath system in which no stone was left unturned, which had worked so effectively in the private cases, was solidly in place, working like a well-oiled machine, much to Barr's satisfaction. Barr and Dodyk and now Boies, after his stunning success in California, handled all of the in-court cross-examination, and even though they were now partners, the work of Mullen, Sahid, Saunders and Rolfe continued in much the same way it had when they were senior associates. One of the government experts, however, gave Rolfe the opportunity for his first in-court cross-examination in the case, and he acquitted himself well, painstakingly refuting nearly every point the expert had made in a cross-examination that lasted nearly twice as long as the witness's direct testimony. The curious system developed at Cravath, in which only partners were allowed to appear in court, and which meant that new partners had virtually no courtroom experience, seemed to work for both Boies and Rolfe.

But if Barr and Dodyk had made what seemed to be bad impressions on Judge Edelstein, Rolfe's was even worse. Within the firm, Rolfe is well liked by most lawyers who work with him. Though to his colleagues he seems obsessed with the firm and his work, he is a hearty, friendly type who seems to care what others think of him. But if his inexperience showed in court, it was that he was sometimes too painstaking in his approach, raising technical objections that seemed to annoy the judge, and failing to demonstrate the proper deference to the judge's concerns, no matter how inappropriate he felt them to be. By the end of his cross-examination of the industry expert Frederic Withington, Rolfe was arguing with the judge more than with the hostile witness.

One of the points Rolfe had spent a great deal of time effectively establishing was that the number of competitors in the manufacture and sale of general purpose computer systems was much larger than Withington had testified. Withington had testified that National Cash Register did not compete with IBM in that area. Rolfe wanted to show him during cross-examination a document that was in fact an NCR press release indicating that it did compete with IBM. He wanted to see if he could get Withington to change his opinion. Rolfe was interrupted by Edelstein quickly.

"What is the purpose of showing this witness this document?"

"The purpose, Your Honor, is to—"

"Don't read it yet, Mr. Withington, please," the judge interrupted.

"The purpose, Your Honor," Rolfe began again, "is to contradict the witness's testimony."

"I don't see how you can possibly contradict this witness's testimony by this document. . . . I will not receive it," the judge said, now glaring at Rolfe.

"I haven't offered it, Your Honor."

"Then you can't use it."

Rolfe then asked if the witness could read the document to himself. "He will not read the document until we know why you are asking him to read the document."

"I am asking the witness to read the document, and I will then inquire of the witness—" Rolfe began, his voice beginning to rise.

"I have instructed him not to. That settles that."

The next day, Rolfe again tried to approach the subject of NCR in his cross-examination, and the judge again interrupted him. "You went over that on cross-examination once," he said.

"Your Honor, I asked the witness the question and . . . I want to continue that line with reference to the annual report of NCR."

"Why didn't you do that on cross-examination?" the judge demanded.

"I am still in cross-examination, Your Honor," Rolfe pointed out, but his answer may have been too smart, and it seemed to enrage the judge. Later, when Rolfe tried to have two of the documents simply marked by the court reporter for identification, so that it would be clear what documents the questions and answers referred to, Carlson, the government lawyer handling Withington, objected on the ground that Rolfe had already covered that area of cross-examination.

"Objection sustained," the judge quickly agreed.

"May I respond, Your Honor?" Rolfe asked.

"Mr. Rolfe, I have indicated the ground rules," the judge said angrily. "I have indicated again and again and again if I need any response, I will invite it. Now, you seem to ignore [that] and now I conclude that you are doing that deliberately. Thus, if the record develops that you are deliberately ignoring my instruction, I will apply sanctions. There is no need for any response."

"Very well, Your Honor," Rolfe replied, but the judge seemed to be warming to his subject. "You are also ignoring my instruction about using connectors and then you are falling back on withdrawal. I am getting weary of that, too."

"Those are inadvertent, Your Honor," Rolfe apologized.

"Cure yourself of those inadvertencies."

"I am trying to. Those are constraints I have never had to operate under before," Rolfe protested.

"That is unfortunate," the judge concluded. "You have been taught some very bad habits, and you are not going to use those habits in this court. They are inappropriate. They are undesirable. They are misleading."

The last of the government witnesses was Alan McAdams, the government's chief economist, who was scheduled to give an overview of the entire case. He spent a total of seven months on the witness stand, which, because of the judge's frequent rest periods, actually represented only 38 trial days of direct testimony and 38 trial days of cross-examination. Barr designated Boies to handle the cross-examination; and to the lawyers working with him on the case, it was an even greater triumph than the CalComp victory. A group of associates had been working for months on the McAdams cross-examination, analyzing documents, preparing outlines, and culling through McAdams' direct testimony each day when they received his transcripts. All of this material—about 1,000 pages—had been assembled into notebooks for use by Boies. The day the cross-examination was scheduled to begin, Boies arrived at 100 Church Street only an hour before the start of the trial. He hadn't seen the notebooks and didn't have time to read them. He simply flipped through some of the material and made four handwritten notes on a single page of a yellow legal pad. For the next five days, he cross-examined McAdams without reference to another note, eventually destroying almost every point the economist had made during his direct examination.

Boies's performance was hailed as brilliant, but for some lawyers at the firm who were working on the case, there were some disturbing thoughts. Had Cravath's attention to detail, to exhaustive preparation, become an obsession? Had it become an end in itself that was causing the lawyers to lose sight of the broader issues in the case? Those concerns were intensified at one of the firm's biweekly litigation lunches at the Wall Street Club on top of the Chase skyscraper. IBM lawyers from White Plains only rarely came to the lunches. Bromley, now nearing 80, almost always attended, and he continued to read each day's transcript in the IBM case. Shortly after McAdams left the stand, he lashed out at Barr and the other IBM lawyers for what he termed overcross-examining the witnesses. The government lawyers, in their redirect examination, he said, had used Boies's work to correct the errors McAdams had made and Boies had exposed. A more effective approach would have been simply to attack McAdams' credibility, and use his errors in post-trial briefs, when it was too late for McAdams to correct them. Bromley's criticisms were dismissed by some younger partners as the ramblings of an old man, but to others—including some lawyers on the IBM case—his remarks made a lot of sense.

At the close of the government's direct case in 1977, the major battles for the past few years had all been Cravath victories—the Telex reversal and settlement, Greyhound, CalComp, and even, in a sense, the government's case. But now the tide seemed to turn decidedly against Cravath.

At the end of the government case, Raymond Carlson, the Justice Department's lead counsel, quit. Exhausted and evidently demoralized, he left the Justice Department to pursue a career as a teaching tennis pro. The new lead counsel, Robert Staal, asked the court to reopen discovery for the government, despite the fact that IBM had already produced millions of documents and many of the witnesses the government wanted to depose had already had their depositions taken, some more than once. The judge granted the government's motion, which meant that Cravath needed a crew of lawyers to defend those depositions just as it was beginning to introduce its own case. Barr was further frustrated by Edelstein's refusal to grant IBM any more discovery, stating that to do so would have propelled the trial into "intolerable, never-ending discovery."

On the personnel front, Barr also had to face the defection of his two most important partners on the case, Boies and Dodyk. Boies took a leave of absence from the firm to become antitrust counsel to Senator Edward Kennedy and the Senate Judiciary Committee which Kennedy chaired. He insisted that his departure had nothing to do with disenchantment over the IBM case. His move was nonetheless interpreted by many others at the firm as partly a result of his desire to extricate himself from Barr's orbit.

Boies's rebelliousness had, in fact, aroused the wrath of some of his partners. While he was in California heading up the CalComp effort, he and Brome, the corporate partner working with him, had had stationery printed with the heading *Boies & Brome* and the address and phone number of Cravath's L.A. office, as though it were a separate law firm. When the partnership learned about it, "they hit the ceiling," a Cravath lawyer recalls. "Boies was severely reprimanded." Dodyk, too, was reportedly anxious to handle some cases on his own. Barr was left with only the four new partners, whom, for reasons that would later become apparent, he wasn't willing to rely on in lieu of Dodyk and Boies.

Barr was determined never again to face a manpower crisis such as that which had struck at the time just before the CalComp trial. With IBM fees rolling into the firm at a clip in excess of $15 million per year, his partners at 1 Chase were not in a position to deny his requests. Early in 1978, a large number of existing Cravath partners began taking the IBM training sessions that new associates were given, but there was considerable foot-dragging. Most were not eager to succumb to Barr's authority, and many managed to come up with other work that made them "indispensable" at 1 Chase. In the end, Barr got only three partners: Alan Hruska, a litigation partner, and two corporate partners. Within the firm, all three assignments were viewed as punishments for partners who were not carrying their own weight. Although all partners at Cravath earn an amount based on a formula determined by seniority, there are other ways than money to discipline those who are not holding their own. Unproductive partners may be openly chastised in partnership meetings; assignments to positions of subservience to other partners often follow.

Hruska, in particular, was a problem for Barr. The two had been close friends at Yale Law School, and when Barr was made a partner at Cravath and Hruska was not, Barr lobbied vigorously for Hruska, who was elevated to the partnership a year later. Since then, however, Hruska had come to be viewed by some of his partners as a "mistake." His handling of a large antitrust case for Westinghouse—which Westinghouse settled before it went to trial, but not before Hruska had managed to rack up enormous legal fees that Westinghouse protested—was regarded generally to be the reason that Westinghouse, one of the firm's oldest clients, was shifting most of its work both in-house and to other law firms. Hruska had also recently lost a major trial for CBS, and CBS had not pressed to have him assigned to another CBS case that was pending at the firm. Hruska's assignment to IBM soon followed.

But Hruska was at least a seasoned litigator. He was given responsibility for the direct examination of IBM's opening witness in its direct case, an IBM engineer named Richard Case, and he was credited by the Cravath lawyers assisting him with doing an exceptionally fine job. He kept the testimony moving along at a reasonable pace, helped make technical testimony comprehensible, and was considered to have established the best relationship among the Cravath lawyers with Judge Edelstein because of his gracious and deferential courtroom demeanor.

In a lecture to the associates, however, Barr deprecated Hruska's achievement as he told them they should not look to Hruska as a model. Case, Barr explained, was such a natural witness and had been so well prepared by the Cravath back-up lawyers that all Hruska had to say was "Talk," and Case would deliver near-perfect testimony. It was true that some of Hruska's questions had taken the form of, "Now, what else do you want to say about that?" And at one point, Hruska had said, "I'll just sit down for a while," while the witness was testifying. But Barr's lecture was taken as a sign that Hruska had not redeemed himself.

If there were some problems with Hruska, however, they seemed small compared to difficulties with some of those who had been elevated to partnership just a year or two before. The increased pressure on Mullen, now a partner on the case, seemed to be driving him close to breakdown. Some of his behavior became odd. His driving deteriorated, and after two associates reported that they were nearly killed when Mullen drove them from the Detroit airport, there were always chauffeured limousines to meet him. Nevertheless, Mullen would still occasionally insist on driving himself. Once at the San Francisco airport, he refused to get into the limousine, and associates and the chauffeur had to physically force Mullen into the car in an attention-getting scene accompanied by shouting and abusive language. Some days he was calm and pleasant; on others he would call associates at home and scream at them. He developed a reputation among associates as one of the worst partners to work for.

Deborah Batts, an associate assigned to him on the case, remembers that Mullen would rush in and give her an "urgent" assignment, one that would be based on some hypothetical decision by the judge, and then he would ask for the options open to Cravath. The first time that happened, Batts recalls, "I worked like a fool— nights, weekends. About a week later I took my memo in to him, and he said, 'What's this?' He'd completely forgotten the assignment!" From then on, Batts and other associates working for Mullen often simply ignored his research assignments. "If he ever asked, which was extremely rare, I'd say, 'It's coming.' " Gradually, Mullen spent more and more of his time working on one of Cravath's major *pro bono* cases.

While Mullen was from time to time unpleasant and difficult, Sahid occasionally displayed such bad judgment that he seemed at times positively dangerous. He was evidently so dazzled with his acquisition of the Telex counterclaim documents, that he came precariously close to the line between ethical and unethical conduct. Dealing with documents from IBM files, he once instructed associates to white-out any handwritten comments so that they wouldn't show on Xeroxed copies to be produced in discovery. When Barr was notified, he was furious and countermanded the order. Once in court, Sahid offered Janet Luymes, a young government lawyer, a "clean" copy of a document that had been poorly duplicated and was difficult to read. Sahid was actually substituting a different version of the document, a feat which he bragged about to associates under him, saying, "Wasn't she stupid?" Sahid also introduced associates to what became known as the "tickle" method of taking depositions. He would sometimes make an arrangement with the court reporter at undefended depositions so that when he tapped the reporter's knee under the table the reporter would stop transcribing and Sahid could have an "off-the-record" conference with the witness.

Some of Sahid's transcripts indicated remarkably few pages of testimony in a deposition that might have occupied an entire morning or afternoon. And his deposition techniques, which had always been aggressive, became obstreperous. In San Francisco for the deposition of a computer engineer scheduled to be an IBM witness, Sahid kept interrupting Bernard Meyers, the government lawyer doing the questioning, with comments like "Stop screaming at the witness," when, according even to the Cravath lawyers there, Meyers was speaking in a normal tone of voice. Once he shouted, "You're driving this woman to tears," referring to the court reporter—except the court reporter was a man.

Eventually Sahid simply stomped out, bringing the deposition to a halt. Meyers was so angry that he asked Edelstein to impose sanctions against Sahid for his abusive behavior, and when Barr found out, he was furious. "I'm going to have to save your ass again," associates heard Barr shout at Sahid when he returned from the deposition. Sahid's responsibility for witnesses was reduced, and he spent more of his time on documents in the case. Young associates assigned to Sahid began to demand transfers to other partners; most of those who didn't get them left the firm.

Such problems with members of the "team" were becoming apparent just as developments in the private cases took an ominous turn, once again raising the possibility that Cravath would be forced to try other IBM cases simultaneously with its case in the government suit. In San Francisco, the judge ordered trial of the Transamerica case to go forward. Then, in a major setback, the Ninth Circuit, after deliberating for more than two years, decided the appeal of the Greyhound case in favor of Greyhound. It reversed the directed verdict for IBM and ordered a new trial of the case. CalComp was then on appeal to the same circuit court, and Blecher rushed into court with a supplementary brief arguing that the court's decision in Greyhound now mandated the reversal of CalComp, too. If that were to be reversed, IBM could face retrials in Greyhound and CalComp, the trial of Transamerica and the government case all at the same time.

One of Barr's first steps was to call Boies back from Washington, and Boies took a leave of absence from Kennedy's staff to head up a team to draft new papers in the CalComp appeal. Together, Barr and Boies developed a bold strategy for the appellate position in CalComp. In his papers, Boies conceded a finding that IBM was a monopolist, but argued that even so, its acts— essentially the development of new products and price cutting— were so much the essence of competition that they should be lawful even if performed by a monopolist. The position was risky, since courts had repeatedly held that the scrutiny given any conduct by a monopolist would be intense, and that acts that would be lawful if performed by an ordinary company might be unlawful if done by a company with monopoly power. Even so, Boies saw that strategy as the only hope for harmonizing the court's reversal of Greyhound with the favorable directed verdict in CalComp.

Meanwhile, Barr drafted a large contingent of new associates and other associates working at 1 Chase—practically every litigation associate who wasn't indispensable to another pending case. Those associates found assignment to White Plains to be a far different experience from that which had existed when some of the veterans on the case first arrived there. Beginning around 1978, assignment to White Plains came to be viewed as assignment to Siberia, the ultimate test of an associate's stamina and loyalty to the firm.

One new associate recalls his arrival at Cravath for his first day of work: "New associates were told to wait in the conference room, where Mrs. Fordyce, this older lady who greeted you, would tell you about your assignments. For those of us who were assigned to IBM, it was obvious that she didn't want to tell us. She said, 'It hasn't been decided yet what you'll work on. Mr. Hruska will speak to you.' Speaking to Mr. Hruska, the associate later learned, was code for being assigned to IBM. Later in the day, at the new associates' welcoming lunch, he explained that he had been told to talk to Hruska. "That's terrible," his host, another associate at the firm, told him. That evening, Hruska told him that he'd "be working on the most exciting case in the office," and that he should report to White Plains the next day. After six days of training by IBM businessmen in the issues of the case and the operations of IBM, the new associate spent six months digesting transcripts. "I never knew why I was doing this," he complains.

Another new associate was assigned to work for Sahid. "My first assignment was to draft questions and answers for a prospective witness, the man who had practically invented disc technology. But this project had already been done. I was given copies of four other drafts of Q's and A's for this guy, so mine was going to be the fifth revision. I had no guidance, no insight, and had no idea what this witness was supposed to say. What was I supposed to do? What was my purpose in life? I was in a state of shock," the associate recalls.

"The highest level of achievement for an associate," notes another, "was to take a deposition, and you were lucky to do that. I had prepared three volumes of Q's and A's for a deposition witness. I spent weekends, long hours, about six weeks on this set. My drafts were passed on by two partners, who made a few changes. Then this corporate partner got his hands on it. He re-organized everything. A few of his changes were valid, a lot were just stylistic, quite a few were mistakes. He didn't know the facts in the case well enough. Then I was told that a more senior associate was stepping in to take the deposition using my script. I was furious. And then *he* came in and wanted to know why some of this stuff was in here, and I told him, 'I don't know, I was told to do it.' It was unreal."

While associates had always worked hard on the case in pre-vious years, they had always understood why they were doing it, and had close supervision and contact with Barr and the other partners. Now Barr was insulated by a group of competitive junior partners who jealously guarded their turf, often keeping associates in the dark. Trying to emulate the hardworking partners, young associates often failed to know when they had done enough work on their assignments. One new associate was told to do a short memo on Cravath's ability to get into evidence some testimony about the efficiency of IBM's accounting systems. The associate went off and worked night and day for four weeks, ultimately producing a 220-page typed document that spent 60 pages sum-marizing the witness's testimony—something that hadn't been asked for—and covered all areas of potential testimony from experts such as medical doctors, with only a few pages on ac-countants. Despite the associate's effort, the memo didn't answer the one question the associate had been asked, and a senior asso-ciate who supervised his work told him to redo it and produce a memo that was no more than 25 pages long. The associate came back with 50 pages.

At the weekly Saturday lunches, one or more associates would be called upon to discuss their work during the past week, an exercise designed to keep all the lawyers apprised of developments and to provide an opportunity for public speaking. As associates tried to outdo one another, however, the speeches became longer and more tedious to sit through. One associate droned for 45 minutes on the technical aspects of a computer connection until a partner finally cut him off. "Why would they be stopped," asks one partner, "when no matter how much time and energy they wasted, IBM would pay the bill? The longer they worked, the more IBM paid."

The atmosphere of unreality was reinforced by some of the

young partners' reactions to young associates' own self-doubts
about the value of the work they were doing, or the extent of their
own expertise. When one new associate complained that she
wasn't sure she was experienced enough to oversee the work of
O'Melveny & Myers partners, Sahid told her, "Remember that
you, as a Cravath associate, are the equal, if not the superior, of
partners in any other firm."

Saunders, considered by many to be the easiest of the young
partners to work for, told another associate who had only been at
the firm three months that his former colleague John Cooper, who
had left Cravath to become a partner in another firm but was still
getting IBM business referred to him, would be "helping you. But
you have to tell him what to do. Keep on top of him. Let me give
you a tip," Saunders continued. "You tell people that their work
isn't good, even if it's perfect. Find something and make them redo
it, or they'll give you anything."

Equally stupefying to new recruits to the White Plains office
was the attitude toward expenses. Even the youngest associates
were entitled to fly first class and stay in the best hotels. In San
Francisco, for example, Cravath lawyers stayed at the Stanford
Court, one of the city's most expensive, while IBM businessmen
working with them had to stay at a cheaper hotel in Berkeley. The
lawyers were given cars (though Sahid had his free Oldsmobile
Cutlass replaced with a blue Cadillac at his expense) and summer
houses and annual bonuses. Most of their meals were paid for.
Saturday lunches were always catered into the White Plains offices,
and whenever lawyers worked late in the evening, they were entitled to go to a restaurant and bill IBM for the meal. There was
messenger service, delivery service, laundry service—everything
imaginable to keep the lawyers from being distracted from the
work at hand. In the area of expenses some associates didn't know
where to draw the line. At least two associates were actually fired
for expense account abuse, one for buying a costly leather and
chrome desk chair and charging it to IBM. "It got to the point
where it seemed you could rationalize almost anything as a client
expense," one lawyer on the case recalls.

Barr's morale-boosting tactics—the football games, the tennis
matches, the Saturday lunches—had all worked well when the
Cravath team felt they were working hard for some identifiable
goal. But by 1978, despite Barr's fears that crises in the case

could still arise imminently, there really wasn't enough day-to-day work to do for so many people; and much of what was done was tedious or make-work. The trial of IBM's direct case offered little of the excitement or the unpredictability of cross-examination. The testimony of IBM's expert economists, in fact, was reduced to sworn, stipulated statements negotiated with the government lawyers. The witness simply appeared for a few minutes in court, testified that the stipulated record was what his testimony would be if he were to give it on the stand, and it was admitted into evidence. Even the live witnesses testified from scripts prepared so carefully that the testimony itself was anticlimactic. The aimlessness of it all seemed to be particularly evident in an incident which came to be known as the "Rhode Island affair."

Stacey Moritz was among a group of new associates who had been assigned to the IBM case upon arriving at the firm in 1978, and had been one of the few who seemed to establish a satisfactory working relationship with Sahid. Late one Friday night, Sahid called her at home and, without explanation, told her to be at the 1 Chase office the following Saturday morning. Assuming there had been some problem with one of her recent assignments, Moritz spent most of the night worrying about what might have gone wrong. But the next morning, when she and four other IBM associates arrived at the firm, Sahid explained that their work that weekend had nothing to do with the IBM case. Rather, it turned out that Hruska, a litigation partner, owned land in Rhode Island, and the state was going to build a public path across it to provide access to an adjacent river. Hruska had vowed to stop the project and Sahid blustered to the associates, "They can't get away with this against Cravath."

Moritz and the other associates spent all weekend in the Cravath library researching the issues and looking for a legal mechanism to stop the State of Rhode Island. Their principal problem, however, was with the facts. It turned out that Hruska had known about the state's right-of-way on the land when he purchased the property, and that the purchase price had evidently been deeply discounted in anticipation of the construction which Hruska was now trying to stop.

On Monday night, back in White Plains, Sahid came to Moritz and told her, "You'll pick me up tomorrow morning at seven, then drive Barr and me to Rhode Island." It was the last straw for Moritz, tired from a full weekend of legal research.

"No, I won't," she told Sahid.

"Yes, you will," he insisted, furious that an associate had defied him.

"I can't," she said. "I hate to drive. It's not safe. You don't pay me for this," she pleaded.

"This is a great opportunity for you," Sahid said in a cajoling tone, implying that the time spent with him and Barr would be a chance to make a favorable impression. When she still resisted, he invoked the ultimate authority. "I'm taking you in to Barr."

Moritz felt as if she were facing a firing squad, but Barr only looked at Sahid with what looked like great weariness. "You drive us, Sahid," Barr said.

That was not the end of the matter of Hruska's land, however. When the factual problems became evident, Sahid went in to Barr and, in the presence of several other people, asked if any of the Rhode Island Environmental Commission members were lawyers. "What do you mean?" Barr asked. Sahid answered something to the effect that "I bet some of them could use some Cravath referral business."

One lawyer present recalls, "Everyone nearly died. I mean, this was an open bribe suggestion. All we could do was treat it like a joke and kind of laugh nervously." (Sahid himself says the comment must have been a joke.)

Another associate says that "Joe Sahid was very troublesome. He suggested the most insane things ever thought of as legal tactics. He didn't worry if they were legal or not. Most of the time, you just couldn't believe he was serious. And every once in a while, he came up with a good idea."

Eventually, six Cravath lawyers from the IBM team together with local counsel in Rhode Island worked on the case, researching motions, threatening civil rights actions, and taking appeals before the State Environmental Commission. The road was ultimately stopped. The state had failed to comply with all the provisions of the wetlands protection act. During the following year, Moritz was among the more than forty associates who left Cravath for other jobs. When Moritz told Sahid she was leaving, he told her, "You're a horse's ass."

•

On the government trial front, relations between the Cravath lawyers and Judge Edelstein were nearing the boiling point. In a series of affidavits, various witnesses in IBM's case later described their relations with the judge:

Abraham Briloff, a professor at Baruch College: "Instead of affording me the opportunity of presenting my considered views on the subject . . . the court persisted in a process of rapid-fire questions on an unrelated subject, which can best (if not only) be described as harassment."

Richard Case, an IBM engineer: "I have never in my career been subjected to the explicit and implicit charges of evasion, uncooperativeness, secretiveness and even untruthfulness that I was subjected to by Judge Edelstein."

Red Dunwell, a retired IBM fellow: "I became increasingly conscious that Judge Edelstein was turning toward me for long periods of time, possibly fifteen or twenty minutes at a stretch, to stare and scowl in a manner which I could only interpret as an effort at intimidation. . . . I was terrified that I might through some slip of the tongue say something which he would seize upon to try to discredit me."

Arjay Miller, retired dean of the Stanford Business School: "At no time in my life have I felt so abused and demeaned as I did at the hands of Judge Edelstein."

Thomas Spain, IBM director of industry relations: "I have never seen before or since a human being wield and abuse his granted power and authority in such a demeaning, inconsiderate, abusive and despotic manner. . . . [His] demeanor toward me was characterized from the outset by scowling; by sour looks and cold stares; by shouting at me; by rapidly firing questions at me, often several questions at once, showing impatience when I could not answer them at once or as rapidly as he would like; by violent scribbling and scratching on a pad."

The judge's hostility toward IBM witnesses reflected the continuing deterioration of his relations with Cravath lawyers. On one occasion, Edelstein accused a Cravath partner of having "cued" and "coached" a witness. When that day's transcript appeared, however, "confused" had been substituted for "cued" and "coached." Barr asked the court reporters to retranscribe their notes. When another transcript of that day's testimony was released, "cued" and "coached" mysteriously reappeared.

On another occasion, Edelstein told Hruska that the Cravath lawyers were engaged in a "pattern" of conduct intended to "wreck" his health. That charge, too, mysteriously disappeared from the transcript until Barr insisted that it be restored.

The last straw, however, was Judge Edelstein's handling of discovery with respect to one of IBM's most important witnesses, Frank Cary, the chairman of the board of IBM. By May of 1979, the judge had already ordered IBM to turn over to the government, in what he termed the government's "narrow" discovery program, more than 760 million IBM documents. But that summer, government lawyers renewed a discovery demand with respect to Cary's testimony that asked for every document that had been under Cary's control during his 14 years as the chief executive of IBM. Barr opposed the discovery request, noting that the government had already deposed Cary in 1974 and pointing out that the government was asking for 5 billion additional documents, many of which they had already received, and that it would cost IBM more than $1 billion to retrieve, review and produce them.

Judge Edelstein granted the government's request in its entirety. He noted that "while the inconvenience to be imposed by the Cary subpoena may be substantial on an absolute scale, when compared with IBM's size and resources it is neither unduly burdensome nor oppressive" nor has IBM "demonstrated that compliance would disrupt the day-to-day operation of IBM." Rather than comply with the subpoena, Barr and Katzenbach reluctantly concluded that they had no choice but to drop Cary as a witness in the case.

They also realized that it was time to mount a direct attack on the judge, a tactic that in the bygone days of more genteel litigation would have been unthinkable. With an ample supply of manpower on deck, Barr assigned a dozen lawyers to scour the record and history of the proceeding for evidence of the judge's bias and misconduct. Eventually, practically everyone on the case got involved. The lawyers worked full-time, seven days a week, from mid-March to midsummer. Ultimately they produced a motion to disqualify Judge Edelstein from the case, supported by an affidavit signed by an unprecedented roster of counsel: Katzenbach, Bromley, Barr and eight other Cravath partners, supported by an appendix of excerpts from the trial record of more than 1,000 pages.

"Chief Judge Edelstein's personal, extrajudicial bias and prejudice against IBM and in favor of plaintiff has led him to abandon his role as an impartial trier of fact and adjudicator of law and has brought him to plaintiff's counsel table," the lawyers wrote. Their detailed scrutiny of the record revealed that the judge had virtually taken over the case from the government lawyers:

• Judge Edelstein had asked almost 5,000 questions of IBM witnesses, about 36 percent of the total.

• The judge had interrupted IBM witnesses more than 1,200 times.

• The judge sustained objections by government lawyers 60 percent of the time. He sustained objections by Cravath lawyers less than 3 percent of the time.

Simply counting the rulings had occupied a handful of lawyers most of the summer.

Judge Edelstein was, predictably, enraged by the motion to disqualify him from the case, and promptly denied it. Cravath appealed his decision to the Court of Appeals, where the motion was also denied. Neither result was surprising to Barr or his colleagues. Such motions are typically granted because of financial conflicts, and then usually at the beginning of a case. Granting IBM's motion would have required appointment of a new judge; and Barr had earlier angered Edelstein by refusing to stipulate that if Edelstein became ill or died, he would proceed with a new judge and not insist on starting over. Cravath's motives for the elaborate and costly and probably doomed motion were largely political. The motion was reported in most major newspapers, and the acknowledged mess that the IBM litigation was in was beginning to make a few ripples in the Carter administration Justice Department. And working on the motion seemed to boost the sagging morale of the Cravath IBM team. Hostility that had begun to develop among themselves was effectively focused on the judge. Though the motion was denied, its overall success was deemed to be such that Max Schulman, the senior associate who coordinated the project, was made a partner the following year.

The motion to disqualify proved to be another turning point in the twisted course of the IBM cases. During the next few months, O'Melveny & Myers lawyers tried the Transamerica case for IBM in San Francisco, with only minimal supervision necessary by Cravath lawyers. That proceeding, like CalComp, hopelessly confused the jury; when they reported they couldn't reach a verdict, the judge took the case out of their hands and directed a verdict in IBM's favor. After another full year of preparation, Barr was also ready for the retrial of the Greyhound case, and again moved a trial team to Phoenix. There the case had been assigned to a visiting senior judge, Wesley Brown, who wanted to spend the winter in Arizona, and Barr soon realized that he might be a problem.

In discussing the case in court before trial, the judge had kept referring to the "casual antitrust injury." Barr had argued that the case was too complicated for a jury to understand, and the judge said it seemed very simple to him. "There are just three elements of the case: power, acts, and casual antitrust injury," he read from the complaint. "Well, I guess I'm not sure about this casual antitrust business," he went on, and Barr realized he was in trouble. The word was not "casual," as the judge kept repeating, but "causal," and the mistake suggested the judge knew very little about antitrust law.

The night before the trial was scheduled to begin, Barr met with Edward Foote, the Winston & Strawn partner who had tried the case before, and they settled the suit on what were deemed very favorable terms for IBM. Softening the loss for Foote and his firm, IBM agreed to pay all of their legal fees in the case, which amounted to a hefty portion of the $17 million settlement. But the most encouraging development came in the Ninth Circuit Court of Appeals. Boies's CalComp appeal brief proved to have struck precisely the right note in the Court of Appeals. Despite its reversal of Greyhound, the court upheld the CalComp directed verdict in an opinion that quoted from the Cravath brief—the highest form of flattery in appellate litigation. By the end of 1980, the private cases were over, without a single loss for IBM. And on June 1, 1981, Cravath concluded the testimony of its last witness in the government trial and rested its case.

Even before the formal end of the case, there was a sense in the firm that IBM was winding down. After 1979, fewer new associates were assigned to the case; several experienced associates were able to shift to other assignments with no apparent adverse consequences. When Cravath acquired two additional floors at 1 Chase in 1979, the IBM lawyers were given office space—Barr was accorded a spacious corner office, a visible symbol of his position in the firm—and they began to spend more time there instead of in White Plains.

The offices at 100 Church Street were dismantled, and IBM associates were no longer given the use of summer houses. Perhaps most significantly, supreme loyalty to Barr no longer seemed to be the chief criterion for making partner. One senior associate pushed for partnership by Barr was actually passed over, rejected by the other litigation partners. One of them says, "It was finally perceived that Tom Barr may be a superb lawyer, but he is not always the best judge of character." Those who were now making partner—associates like Max Schulman, Stuart Gold, Richard Hoffman, John Beerbower—were uniformly perceived as excellent lawyers who lived up to the high standards that had seemed to prevail in the past, and some of them even seemed to be independent thinkers.

With the end of the trial itself, hours worked on the case—and the corresponding bills—began to decline. This didn't mean that there was nothing left to be done. Chief among the remaining tasks was the translation of the 114,000-page record, the trial transcript, into proposed findings of fact, the same exercise that had been done by the Cravath lawyers in the CalComp case. For the twenty Cravath lawyers laboring in White Plains, however, the task was much more laborious and tedious than it had been for the lawyers in California, where the CalComp case had been completed in a tiny fraction of the time spent on the government case. It was also difficult for Barr and his partners to keep morale high among the associates in White Plains who were doing the drafting, since there were suspicions among them that their work would prove to be superfluous. Given the attitudes displayed by the judge, some of them doubted that he would even read Cravath's proposed findings, let alone adopt any of them in his conclusions. And although they didn't expect it to happen at such a late date, there was still the possibility that a settlement would be reached in the case, bringing it to an end before the findings had to be submitted.

Speculation about a possible settlement of the case had picked up after the last day of the trial, when Barr had stated in open court that he was willing to enter into settlement negotiations with William Baxter, the conservative Stanford antitrust professor who had just been appointed to head the Justice Department's antitrust division by President Reagan. But among most associates and partners on the case, there was little hope that this offer or any resulting negotiations would be more successful than previous attempts, all of which had failed. In fact, settlement hopes had really reached their peak toward the end of the Carter administration, when IBM had an ally in Lloyd Cutler in the White House, and negotiations with Sanford Litvack, the Donovan, Leisure partner who was Baxter's predecessor, seemed close to what Barr believed would be a successful resolution of the case. But when Carter lost the election, progress stopped. Litvack evidently preferred to leave IBM as a thorn in the side of the Reagan administration.

Neither Barr nor Clark Clifford, the former Secretary of Defense and Washington lawyer who was retained to advise IBM in the capital, had approached Baxter or others in the Reagan administration about settlement prior to the closing day of the trial, but they felt that Barr's public statement in court would assure some kind of high-level response. By mid-July they had heard nothing, but then Barr got a call from Baxter.

Baxter and Barr began by discussing the schedule for submitting the proposed findings and final briefs in the case. Barr reminded Baxter that they faced an October 1 deadline, and suggested that if they were going to be negotiating during that period, it would be hard to meet that deadline. At that point, the Assistant Attorney General told Barr that his problem in responding to Barr's trial offer was due not only to the schedule but also to the fact that he wasn't sufficiently familiar with the facts and theories in the case. Otherwise, he was open-minded about the possibility of disposing of all or part of the case before it had to be submitted to the judge. Barr leaped at the opportunity he sensed Baxter was offering, proposing to Baxter that he and his colleagues at Cravath assume the burden of educating the Assistant Attorney General about the case in a series of weekly meetings in Washington. Baxter was impressed by the offer and tentatively agreed.

The Justice Department lawyers working on the case were not impressed, and in fact were outraged. They argued to Baxter that they should do the "educating," that he was being railroaded by Cravath, that the Cravath lawyers would only try to divert his attention from the merits of the case with horror stories about Judge Edelstein. But Baxter wanted to hear both sides. The only concessions he made to his trial staff were that they would be allowed to attend all of the meetings, that they could submit any memoranda, documents or other material that they wanted him to see, and that they would be allowed to schedule the topics to be addressed at the series of meetings. Barr would have preferred to meet with Baxter on his terms, but he agreed to those concessions.

Barr also told Baxter that if Barr or another Cravath lawyer went before the judge to ask for the extra time to carry out the sessions, Edelstein would almost surely deny the request, so Baxter went personally to the judge and asked for an extension. Edelstein quibbled with the timing, but essentially granted his request, obviously pleased at the homage represented by the new Assistant Attorney General's trip to his courtroom in New York.

The first of what would be eight Friday meetings with Baxter took place in Washington in early October. The topic for that week had been selected by the government, and it had been designated as "fighting machines," the aspect of the case which the government lawyers believed was their strongest. These issues were some of the oldest—part of the original 1969 complaint—and included the allegations that IBM had introduced new products at low prices for the purpose of keeping other manufacturers out of the market. "Fighting machines" was followed by topics in what the government lawyers believed was a descending order of strength: "unbundling," "leasing practices and educational discounts," "peripheral products," "market measurement," "market share," and finally, "power and profits." Each week Cravath lawyers prepared a relatively short memorandum for Baxter which summarized the evidence and appropriate cases for interpreting it.

To the extent that Baxter's "educational" sessions were a contest between Cravath and the government lawyers, it was another woeful mismatch. Although Robert Staal, the lead government counsel, attended every meeting, the sessions seemed almost as much an educational session for him as they were for Baxter. Staal had to rely heavily on McAdams, the government's chief economic expert, and members of his staff. At the meeting on "peripherals," for example, a member of McAdams' staff talked non-stop from 10:00 A.M. to 4:30 P.M. At around two, Barr interrupted and noted that the economist was not reciting the facts properly, adding, "But then, he's not a lawyer." Baxter seemed shocked. "What are you, then?" he asked the flustered witness as Staal said nothing and looked uncomfortable.

To the extent that the government lawyers did participate in the sessions, they seemed to blunder from one meeting to the next. One of the issues in the first session was whether IBM's preannouncements of its new products were misleading. Baxter immediately said that if that were true, he wanted evidence that customers had been deceived by the announcements and had been hurt by them. Staal seemed to squirm a little, but said that the government lawyers would produce the evidence, although, "We don't have it with us today." The next week, Baxter asked for it, and Staal replied, "We're still getting it." Eight weeks later, they still hadn't managed to get it. Probably because it didn't exist.

Another issue which arose was whether IBM's System 370 leasing and purchase terms undercut its own prices on the System 360 which it replaced. IBM had claimed that the prices, when properly analyzed, were the same. Baxter said that the issue should be a simple one to resolve. Simply make a graph showing the leasing and purchase price lines over time of both the System 360 and the System 370. McAdams objected briefly with the peculiar argument that the graphs wouldn't work because Baxter "knew too many facts," but Staal said that he would make the graph. Again, eight weeks later no graph had appeared.

The contrast with Cravath was striking. At the meeting on peripheral products, Barr made the point that every other court which had considered whether IBM's introduction of peripheral products was anticompetitive had ruled in IBM's favor, finding that, on the contrary, IBM's behavior had been the essence of competition. For the first time that day, the government lawyers changed their theory about the peripheral issue, arguing not that the peripheral manufacturers' *sales* had been hurt by IBM's activities, but that it had prevented the peripheral manufacturers from *expanding* into computer systems manufacturing, which was anticompetitive. Baxter asked them who specifically was prevented from expanding, and they said Telex and Memorex. After the government elaborated the theory all day, Barr spoke for thirty minutes. He presented a document written by Telex's chairman saying that the company was not and had never been interested in expanding into computer systems manufacture. And he had an admission from Memorex that because of the company's accounting irregularities, it couldn't obtain financing for expansion even if it had wanted to. He promptly handed both documents over to Baxter, demolishing the government's contention.

To hear the Cravath lawyers describe them, the meetings with Baxter were developing into a major triumph. Each week, those lawyers who had attended the meeting—always Barr and Evan Chesler, his current favorite associate, usually Boies, as well as other partners who attended from time to time—presented reports to other lawyers working on the case. Each week, the reports became more glowingly optimistic. If the previous week's meeting had been described as a "devastating victory," then the next week's had to be an even more devastating victory. As one participant described it, "It was the most outrageous boasting I'd ever heard during the case."

The accounts became so hyperbolic that many of the lawyers working on the findings quit paying attention. They were working round the clock on their task, and some of them resented the way the lawyers dealing with Baxter were giving them short shrift. By mid-December, they had actually completed a draft of the proposed findings—several thousand pages of text.

On December 4, Baxter, Barr and the government lawyers met for their last session. Barr expected a lull at this point, and went ahead and scheduled some knee surgery. He had just checked into Greenwich Hospital in Connecticut on Wednesday morning, January 6, when the telephone rang. His call was from Abbott Lipsky, one of Baxter's top assistants in the Justice Department, who told Barr that the government was ready to make a settlement offer of unprecedented scope: it was willing to drop the IBM case.

Barr swung into action. He told Lipsky to fly to New York immediately to meet with him at the Cravath offices at 1 Chase. He canceled his surgery. Of all his fellow partners on the case and at the firm, he called only Mullen—who had overcome many of his personal problems—and told him to go immediately to Armonk to notify Cary, IBM's chairman; Opel, its president; and Katzenbach. Barr himself sped to the IBM headquarters at Armonk, where he met Mullen. Then the two partners flew to 1 Chase in the IBM helicopter in time to meet Lipsky.

Despite the almost total capitulation of the government, the Cravath lawyers negotiated for another day and a half, trying to squeeze even more out of the Justice Department. The main sticking point was that the government wanted the case dismissed "without prejudice," meaning that it would be free to bring suit again against IBM, alleging the same violations, if anyone in the government would ever be so foolish as to do so. Mullen wanted the case dismissed "with prejudice," meaning that the government would be barred from suing IBM again for all or part of any of the same offenses.

Mullen, however, was asking more than Lipsky was in a position to give. Because of Justice Department administrative regulations, consent to a dismissal with prejudice requires the consent of the Attorney General—Baxter alone is not empowered to consent to such a disposal of a case. Since Attorney General William French Smith was disqualified from any rulings in the IBM case (he is a former partner at Gibson, Dunn in Los Angeles, the firm that had represented Memorex), it meant that President Ronald Reagan himself would have to approve the dismissal. The last thing Barr wanted was to have Reagan grappling with the intricacies of the case.

On Thursday afternoon, when that point had been sufficiently impressed upon Mullen, the Cravath lawyers abandoned their demand. Instead, Lipsky agreed that the Justice Department would concede that the suit had been "without merit," a cosmetic gesture, but a humiliating one for the government nonetheless. Lipsky flew back to Washington with the completed settlement, met Baxter at the airport, and Baxter signed it. Late Thursday night, the word was spread by telephone among Cravath partners that the IBM case was over.

When the Cravath associates arrived in White Plains the next morning, they were told only that "something had happened" and they should report to Cravath's 58th-floor conference room at 1 Chase for a noon meeting. That morning, Barr called Judge Edelstein, read him the text of the stipulation and asked for a special court session at 4:00 P.M. that day. Edelstein said nothing, other than to agree to the court appearance. Shortly after, a lawyer came into the office where Barr and Lipsky were sitting and announced that the Dow Jones wire had just carried an item saying that the AT&T case had been settled. Lipsky confirmed the report, and the Cravath lawyers realized that the Justice Department's eagerness to bury the loss of the IBM case in the successful resolution of AT&T had probably given them even more bargaining leverage than they had realized.

Barr called Judge Edelstein back to tell him about the AT&T

settlement, but the judge didn't want to hear about it and, in fact, had become nearly apoplectic since the earlier phone call. He told Barr that a "horde" of Cravath lawyers was descending on him at the courthouse, which he said was "outrageous." Then he shouted at Barr to "call off your lawyers." Actually, one Cravath associate had simply walked over to the courthouse to file a copy of the settlement with the clerk, and hadn't even seen Judge Edelstein.

By the noon meeting, it seemed everyone in the firm, including secretaries and messengers, had heard the news. Partners and associates crowded and stood around the conference table, spilling out into the corridor. Barr entered to applause. "It was his moment of triumph, of complete victory," one lawyer there recalls. Barr didn't say much, but then he didn't need to. He simply read the text of the settlement order. At 4:00 P.M., the Cravath lawyers trooped to the courthouse for their session with Judge Edelstein. Though the judge sputtered and fumed over Baxter's failure to appear personally before him, it was obvious that the court session was an anticlimax, a mere tidying up after the real end of the case at the Cravath offices. Friday night, IBM executives and Cravath lawyers who worked on the case—even former Cravath associates who had since left the firm—partied into Saturday morning at Regine's, the expensive Manhattan discotheque and restaurant. Two weeks later, Cravath's White Plains office was closed.

In the wake of such an unqualified victory, it was easy to forget that the IBM litigation had taken a toll on the firm and its lawyers that no victory could entirely erase, a toll most evident in the high divorce rate among the IBM lawyers. Barr, who concedes he has spent minimal time with his own family during the past decade, recalls that Carroll Bumpers, the Greyhound chairman, told him, "It really bothers me that my lawyer is going home to be with his family while Tom Barr is figuring out how to kick the shit out of me."

And Barr is the first to concede that his approach to litigation isn't for everyone, and that there has been unhappiness for some of his Cravath lawyers. "I don't know any good lawyer who doesn't work his ass off," he says in typically blunt fashion. "Until you've done everything you can do to win, you're not free to stop. There isn't any other way to do it. If you don't want this, you shouldn't be a litigator."

There was never any doubt in Barr's mind, or Katzenbach's, or really anyone else's, for that matter, that IBM would win the case in one way or another. Raymond Carlson, the principal government lawyer through the years, acknowledges Barr as "one of the dozen most able lawyers I have ever come up against. David Boies and Paul Dodyk are two of the other twelve. They did things marvelously well, a first-class job on everything. Of course, everything was done in a way that cost a fortune. If they wanted ten people working on one motion, they assigned ten lawyers. They always had company jets or flew first class; they had the best of everything."

Of course, it is difficult to separate Cravath's effectiveness from the vagaries of Judge Edelstein and the incompetence of the government lawyers or, indeed, what the government now admits was a weak case from the beginning. In a memorandum Lipsky wrote and circulated within the Justice Department just before the settlement, he urged dropping the case because, since IBM did not achieve its dominance of the computer field illegally, "the likelihood of success on appeal is small" and, because of changes within the computer industry, no "appropriate" relief could be obtained. These were reasons which have nothing to do with Cravath or the effectiveness of the defense it mounted for IBM. The case also took its toll on the resources of the government; expenditures exceeded $50 million. In terms of manpower, there wasn't a single Justice Department lawyer working on the case at its conclusion who was there when the case began.

Nonetheless, the Cravath approach in IBM has become the model for complex litigation at nearly every other major firm. And Barr says that, for the past ten years, "There is no job I would rather have had, nothing I would rather have done. I'm sure my partners feel the same way. This has been the biggest and most important case in the country."

The week after the settlement, the Cravath litigation partners met to plan the firm's transition to the post-IBM era. Barr began by saying that he'd always planned on taking time off after the end of the case, that he wanted "to relax and take it easy." He said that he had spoken to Samuel Butler, Cravath's presiding partner, who agreed that the IBM partners should all take some time off. Jack Hupper, the firm's other leading litigation partner, said he agreed, and others chimed in saying it was time for the non-IBM partners to "carry the weight" for a while. During these pronouncements, Rolfe began to turn red. Finally he burst out, "I don't care about the rest of you. I'm not taking any time off. I'm eager to get to work. I want to work just as hard." And one by one, the young IBM partners picked up the Rolfe line. Not one took a vacation.

CHAPTER THREE

GENENTECH
Pillsbury, Madison
& Sutro

Michael Ostrach, a 29-year-old corporate associate at Pillsbury, Madison & Sutro in San Francisco, took a breath, picked up the telephone and called Blyth Eastman Paine Webber, Inc., the New York brokerage and investment banking firm. The message he received: all systems were go. It was 6:58 A.M. in California, October 14, 1980; the sun was beginning to peek into the narrow streets of San Francisco's financial district.

In New York, it was going on 10:00 A.M., and the anticipation and excitement had already reached a pitch on Wall Street. Two minutes after Ostrach's call, a million shares of common stock of Genentech, Inc., the genetic engineering concern, were offered to the public for the first time. At 10:01 A.M., all the million shares were sold, the fastest public offering in history. In that minute, Genentech had acquired $35 million in working capital.

Investor excitement—in some cases, mania—hadn't stopped with the initial public sale. The public price of Genentech climbed in a whirlwind of trading. As Ostrach stayed glued to the telephone throughout the day, he listened in amazement as the price rose beyond his expectations, from $35 a share to $50, to $60, to $89. Investors were doubling their money in a single day's trading. Late in the afternoon, Henry Kaufman, Salomon Brothers' influential financial analyst, made a public statement complaining about the speculative fever that had swallowed up the Genentech offering.

Almost instantly, the share price dropped $20 but it closed at a phenomenally high $71¼.

The day after next, Ostrach came into his office late, after the first full night's sleep he'd had in more than a week. He was about to leave for the monthly lunch meeting of Pillsbury, Madison's corporate securities lawyers when he got a call from Bud Coyle, the investment banker at Blyth Eastman who had handled Genentech. Coyle's voice was strained as he asked Ostrach whether he had read that morning's *Wall Street Journal*. Ostrach had not. And when he heard Coyle's précis, he felt chest pains. That morning, the *Wall Street Journal* disclosed that there had been substantial changes made in Genentech's final prospectus—information that could easily form the basis for allegations of securities fraud against Genentech and Pillsbury, Madison for failing to recirculate the final prospectus prior to the public offering. The price of the stock had started to plummet. There could be millions of dollars in liability. Ostrach sat at his desk stunned, his mind racing. He started going back over the Genentech deal step by step. Had he erred? Had his judgment been wrong?

Ostrach first thought he might skip the securities lunch, but then decided that his absence would be more conspicuous than if he got there late. At 1:10 P.M., as the securities partners were starting on their dessert, Ostrach arrived at the meeting. They had all read the article. There were no smiles, no words of reassurance. In fact, the collected partners looked green. There was only one question on everyone's mind: Would Pillsbury, Madison & Sutro be sued?

Pillsbury, Madison & Sutro is the only law firm west of the Mississippi which rises truly into the rank of the country's most eminent and powerful law firms. Although its location in San Francisco—traditionally the financial center of the West—has isolated it from its more numerous rival firms in the east, the eastern firms have never had the hegemony Pillsbury, Madison has had over California and the western United States.

San Francisco is an old city, and Pillsbury, Madison is as old as most of the blue chip firms in the East. Evans Pillsbury, its founding partner, started practicing in California in 1865; and the firm acquired its present name in 1905. Pillsbury, Madison's offices were destroyed in the San Francisco earthquake in 1906.

Like many of the New York firms it resembles, Pillsbury, Madi-

son rose to prominence through close relationships with corporations which grew into powerful national and international institutions. Its most enduring and most important client relationship has
been with Standard Oil of California, a company which it incorporated in 1906, and the firm today maintains a separate department devoted almost exclusively to the legal problems of the giant
oil company. Traditionally, the general counsel of Socal has come
from the ranks of the Pillsbury, Madison partners, and the current
vice-president–legal, William Mussman, is a former Pillsbury, Madison partner. Socal still prefers to send most of its legal work to
Pillsbury, Madison rather than handle it with in-house lawyers.
Pillsbury, Madison today occupies seven floors in the Italian Renaissance palazzo which serves as Socal's headquarters in downtown San Francisco.

Pillsbury, Madison once had a similar client relationship with
Pacific Telephone & Telegraph, and for many years, partner John
Sutro had his own office within PT&T's headquarters building in
San Francisco in addition to his office at the firm. Though PT&T
remains one of the firm's major clients, unlike Socal it has been
using inside counsel for a high percentage of its legal work; and
Pillsbury, Madison billings have declined correspondingly. The
firm has also had long-standing relationships with such California-
based companies as Del Monte, Pacific Lumber Company and
Safeway Stores. Though banking has never played as important a
role at Pillsbury, Madison as it has at some of the major New
York firms, Pillsbury represents the Bank of California and has
done extensive work for Bank of America, the nation's largest,
including work on the Iranian crisis.

Pillsbury, Madison's prominence and geographical location
have made it the firm of choice for the large eastern law firms
which need to refer matters to a California law firm. Pillsbury
does extensive work for IBM and Time Inc., both clients of Cravath, Swaine & Moore; for Morgan Guaranty Trust and Morgan
Stanley, clients of Davis Polk & Wardwell; and for Equitable Life,
a Debevoise & Plimpton client. It also represents in the West such
national corporations as FMC, Ford, General Motors, Joseph E.
Seagram & Sons and DuPont.

The principal difference between Pillsbury, Madison and the
blue chip firms in New York is the partner-associate structure.
There are slightly more associates than partners at the 245-lawyer

firm, which eliminates some of the fierce competition among associates to become a partner, and also makes impossible the kind of pyramid staffing which occurs frequently on matters in the New York firms.

Pillsbury, Madison is also more dependent on local clients and, therefore, local contacts than are the New York firms, with their proximity to the national financial capital. Lawyers at Pillsbury tend to be more prominent and socially active in San Francisco; the firm itself has counseled, on a *pro bono* basis, the Junior League of San Francisco, the San Francisco Ballet, the San Francisco Opera Association; and the firm's partners sit on the boards of an array of charitable and civic organizations. In some cases, client ties are cemented by marriage: John Bates, the chairman of the firm's management committee, is married to Nancy Witter, who is related to Dean Witter, the San Francisco financier whose brokerage firm became one of the firm's important financial clients.

One of the mainstays of Pillsbury, Madison's practice, as it is in the case of almost all of the country's leading corporate firms, is its corporate securities practice. Though it is geographically far from Wall Street, Pillsbury, Madison is the rival of any blue chip New York firm in the field; in recent years, it has done more first public offerings of securities than has any other firm. In addition to Dean Witter, Pillsbury, Madison has represented Lehman Brothers Kuhn Loeb, Inc.; L. F. Rothschild, Unterberg, Towbin; E. F. Hutton; Kidder, Peabody; and Salomon Brothers among the major investment banking houses, even though all are New York–based.

Securities work has long been the preserve of the corporate blue chip firms. Investment banking has remained remarkably centralized in the hands of a few houses, almost all based in New York; they have become even more concentrated as a result of mergers during the past few years. The brokerage firms and investment banking firms turned naturally to law firms that were the most financially sophisticated, and these, in turn, tended to be the law firms that represented major banks or major corporations which were active in the financial markets; in short, the blue chip corporate firms.

The key to a securities practice is the Securities Acts of 1933 and 1934, intended to prevent the kinds of wholesale frauds which had plagued the public and contributed to millions of dollars of losses during the Depression. It remains the principal governing statute in the securities field, and virtually guarantees that every offering of securities will be accompanied by a battery of lawyers. The need for underwriters' counsel, in particular, stems directly from the statute; it makes underwriters as fully liable as the issuing company for any registration statement containing "an untrue statement of a material fact" or which "omitted to state a material fact . . . necessary to make the statements therein not misleading." Courts have been even more explicit about the legal burden placed upon underwriters. The Second Circuit Court of Appeals (which includes New York) wrote in 1973 that:

> No greater reliance in our self-regulatory system is placed on any single participant in the issuance of securities than upon the underwriter. He is most heavily relied upon to verify published materials because of his expertise in appraising the securities issued and issuer, and because of his incentive to do so. He is familiar with investigating the business condition of a company and possesses extensive resources for doing so. Since he often has a financial stake in the issue, he has a special motive thoroughly to investigate the issuer's strengths and weaknesses. Prospective investors look to the underwriter —a fact well-known to all concerned and especially to the underwriter—to pass on the soundness of the security and the correctness of the registration statement and prospectus.

Especially when the price of a security falls, the purchaser is inclined to claim that he or she was misled or defrauded rather than admit an error of judgment. Underwriters have been sued frequently. Though they have been found liable only rarely, even a few instances of being made to assume the full price of a stock offering are enough to ensure that every underwriter will consult lawyers on every offering of securities, who, in turn, share the underwriter's liability.

Like the other fields of legal practice in which such firms have concentrated, securities work is lucrative. In such transactions, huge sums of money change hands. This enables a law firm's fees, however large, to remain a relatively insignificant percentage of the overall transaction, and it tends to mean that the fees charged will not be subjected to much scrutiny. When a law firm represents the underwriter in an offering of securities, the law firm's fees are generally subtracted from the percentage the underwriter charges the offering company; in some cases, the fees are among the costs simply passed on by the underwriter to the company. In either event, the underwriter has no major financial incentive to hold down the fees, since they are covered by the percentage charged or paid directly by the offering company. Although all the major firms charge an "hourly rate" for their services, they are not limited by it in securities work. The underwriter is customarily charged a flat fee, derived by the law firm partners in charge from considerations of the hourly rate, the amount of time spent, the complexity of the deal, the risks assumed, and the success of the offering. Customarily, no breakdown of the bill by hours spent is provided, and in practice, the "hourly rate" tends to set only a floor for the amount of the entire bill.

For the offering company, a few hundred thousand dollars will usually seem a small price for an infusion of millions of dollars in capital. Initial public offerings are only one aspect of a corporate securities practice in the blue chip firms. Their large regular corporate clients may issue additional stocks, bonds, notes and other financial instruments which provide a steady flow of work for the firm's outside lawyers. Though that work may be more routine than an initial public offering, the legal problems and billing procedures are much the same.

In the case of an initial public offering, the elite corporate law firms generally represent one of their large underwriting clients, and not the company offering the stock. The principal reason is financial. Most new companies cannot afford a law firm like Pillsbury, Madison or its leading securities partner, Bruce Mann. As Mann explains: "It is hard for us to approach an emerging company the way a small law firm can. A small firm will often take a reduced fee, even no fee, in return for stock participation. A lot of lawyers have become very wealthy that way. But we have a high overhead and a large number of partners who have different investment goals. You can't split up 1,000 shares of a company among a group of partners. We work only on a cash basis, and most new companies want to preserve their capital. Even if the company says it will pay our normal fees," Mann continues, "we have to be careful. The client's ability to do so may depend on its future success. Obviously, we can't take those kinds of risks."

Of course, some emerging companies will become the IBMs of

the future—and large law firms will tend to make exceptions for them. And large corporate law firms all have extensive securities practices for corporate clients which have already become established. Thus, the securities bar tends to be concentrated among a handful of prominent law firms and lawyers who are either representing the underwriter or the offering company, and who work with one another on deal after deal.

Pillsbury, Madison owes much of its current prominence in the securities field to two factors: the rapid growth of new high-technology companies in what has become known as "Silicon Valley," which runs from Palo Alto to San Jose near San Francisco, and to Bruce Mann. Mann made a name for himself in the securities field while still an associate at Pillsbury, Madison.

During the summer of 1968, Pillsbury, Madison partners were approached by a group of investors who wanted to incorporate Intel, one of the first successful manufacturers of semiconductors. Intel was the kind of emerging company for which Pillsbury, Madison was readily willing to lift its usual reluctance to represent new companies. Among the Intel investors were Arthur Rock, one of the country's most prominent and uncannily successful venture capitalists, who also happens to be married to a partner at Pillsbury, Madison; and a representative of the Rockefeller family who was referred to Pillsbury, Madison by the Rockefellers' lawyers, the New York firm of Milbank, Tweed, Hadley & McCloy. Intel's underwriters were L. F. Rothschild Unterberg Towbin, an investment banking firm specializing in high-technology corporations, which was represented in the deal by Cravath.

Although Mann didn't have the vaguest idea what semiconductors were, he recognized a "hot" issue when he saw one from the personnel surrounding it. Intel became one of the most successful new stock offerings ever, and went on to become a successful company and a stalwart client of Pillsbury, Madison. In the meantime, Mann made a favorable impression on the New York lawyers and investment bankers he worked with, and the Intel offering attracted widespread attention in New York financial and legal circles. Rothschild Unterberg began to steer some of its work in California in Mann's direction, and in 1967 he was made a partner.

Mann is the kind of lawyer, as Pillsbury, Madison is the kind of law firm, that East Coast lawyers and investment bankers feel comfortable with. He exudes none of the kind of casual offhand style often associated with California. Though personable, he is thoroughly professional, even cool and detached. In dealing with Easterners, who often suspect Californians of being relaxed to the point of laziness, Mann gives off the reassuring air of always having more to do than he has time for. There is nothing flashy about his appearance; he dresses in conservative suits, parts his clipped light brown hair neatly, and shows only a hint of suntan.

Mann is not particularly popular with associates who work at the firm. He ignores new, inexperienced associates, and there is no stampede among senior associates to work for him. Many of those who have been tapped for his assignments do not measure up to what some complain are his unreasonably high standards. "Associates are generally afraid of him," one Pillsbury, Madison associate explains. "He's not communicative at all. He never praises you directly; you're lucky to hear a favorable comment second- or thirdhand." Another associate who worked extensively for Mann says, "It's an in-joke that Bruce is always busy. I would go into his office after carefully organizing my questions so as to take a minimal amount of time. Usually, Bruce would be on the phone, and I'd just stand there. Never in the time I worked for him did he ever ask me to sit down. It was as if I did, I might not leave. I always had to be ready to leave his office at a moment's notice."

Mann rarely volunteers any instructions to associates, and most of them are reluctant to ask what they fear might be stupid questions. "You just had to learn by watching him, and then doing it yourself," one former associate recalls. On the other hand, Mann bestowed some nice touches. He didn't like to talk with associates on the telephone and instead would often walk down to their offices to discuss a problem or ask questions. Any interaction on a purely personal level, however, was almost nonexistent. "Fundamentally, I think Bruce is very shy" is one associate's assessment.

Part of Mann's success has been his active participation in the professional equivalent of the lecture circuit, speaking to groups of lawyers about legal issues in securities practice for organizations such as the Practicing Law Institute, where Mann is a regular lecturer. Such sessions are far more than purely educational sessions; they tend to establish reputations in the field and provide a meeting ground for the leading practitioners in a field such as securities. If Mann is sometimes shy on a personal level, the professional seminars and lectures provide a format in which he is entirely comfortable and in which he can give free rein to some of his own more scholarly impulses.

He is a popular and sought-after participant at such conferences. Following one of his presentations at a conference in San Diego in 1978, Harold Williams, the chairman of the Securities and Exchange Commission in Washington, D.C., approached him and suggested he consider coming to work at the SEC. "Why don't you see what you can do if you think you've got the answers," Williams told Mann. Mann was not eager to leave his hard-won Pillsbury, Madison partnership for an extended stint as a bureaucrat, but he recognized how valuable exposure to the inner workings of the SEC might be for his practice. The SEC is, of course, never far from the thoughts of a securities lawyer; it is the agency charged with enforcing the securities laws and the myriad regulations it has promulgated pursuant to them. So Mann took Williams up on his offer, agreeing to become an unpaid consultant to the agency, which, under applicable laws, didn't necessitate his withdrawal from the firm while he worked in Washington.

At the beginning of 1979, Mann returned to San Francisco and, armed with new expertise and contacts and with a steady flow of business from his underwriter clients, thought he might be given a seat on Pillsbury, Madison's management committee. Pillsbury, Madison's management structure is closer to the Sullivan & Cromwell than to the Cravath model, with almost all important decisions made by the management committee, including the distribution of the firm's income and partnership shares. The firm itself is divided into "practice groups" rather than the broader departments found in most firms, and a representative of each of the practice groups sits on the management committee. In theory this gives the committee a somewhat democratic cast, with the members soliciting opinions of the partners in their practice groups and taking them into account in their committee voting.

In practice, however, the members of the committee tend to be selected less for their political skills than for their age. Following the pattern set by Evans Pillsbury and more recently by Jack Sutro, the firm has always shown great respect for seniority, in its decision making and in its distribution of profits. Members of the committee are, almost without exception, simply the most senior members of the practice group; the members of the committee are themselves selected by the chairman of the management committee and by the firm's ten most senior partners, most of them semi-retired. When Mann asked to be given a position on the committee, there were two corporate securities partners in the firm more senior than he. He was politely told by the management committee that his ascension was out of the question.

By the spring of 1980, few recent scientific developments had so gripped the popular imagination as had gene splicing. Although much popular attention was being given to such science-fiction notions as cloning and runaway bacteria, molecular biologists had successfully developed techniques for inserting segments of DNA into micro-organisms which reproduce following the genetic code which has been planted in them.

A pioneer in the commercial application of these techniques has been Genentech, a small company founded in April 1976 by a University of California professor active in the field and by a venture capitalist. Genentech was the first company to demonstrate that gene-splicing technology was commercially feasible. In 1977, it mass-produced Somatostatin, a hormone ordinarily found only in the human brain, which may play a role in the treatment of diabetes and human growth disorders. Since then, the company has produced human insulin and interferon, a virus-fighting substance which many scientists believe will play a significant role in the treatment of cancer.

During its early years, Genentech limped along on some infusions of venture capital (its founders had made only nominal capital investments) and some joint research and development contracts with major drug companies. But to exploit its research breakthroughs, it needed a major addition of capital for investment in new plant and facilities, for expensive clinical testing programs on human subjects, and eventually, to finance inventory and receivables for sale of its products. A logical move for a company in such a position is to offer stock to the public.

It seemed that only one major obstacle stood in Genentech's way: a lawsuit in which the United States government claimed that patents could not be awarded to inventions that happened to be living things. Since all of Genentech's products are living bacteria, and failure to patent its inventions could mean that other, larger companies would quickly copy and exploit them, Genentech's future earnings potential might be seriously restricted. Then in June 1980, the United States Supreme Court ruled that living things could be patented. It was the breakthrough that Genentech's executives had been waiting for.

Members of the investment and financial community had already been keeping a close eye on Genentech, waiting for signs that a public offering might be in the offing and offering advice and expertise in marketing the securities. When Robert Swanson, Genentech's president, learned of the Supreme Court decision and decided that it was time to think seriously about a public offering, he called Hambrecht & Quist, an investment banking firm based in San Francisco. Hambrecht & Quist had been pursuing Genentech almost since the company was founded. The investment banking firm was just a short distance from Genentech's offices in south San Francisco, and Hambrecht & Quist had made a national name for itself specializing in underwriting for high-technology companies, including many of the computer and semiconductor companies in Silicon Valley. Hambrecht & Quist was, nonetheless, still a regional firm, and lacked the nationwide distribution network which would be needed for an offering of the size contemplated by Genentech. For breadth in national and international distribution, and for its research back-up in dealing with a complex and untested field such as genetic engineering, Hambrecht & Quist referred the company to Blyth Eastman Paine Webber, the New York–based investment banking firm, to act as lead underwriter.

Customarily, the lead underwriter selects the law firm that will act as counsel for all the underwriters and brokers involved in an offering of securities, and Blyth Eastman Paine Webber ordinarily chooses Cravath, Swaine & Moore, particularly one of its leading corporate partners, Samuel Butler. But in the Genentech deal, Thomas Volpe who was working on the offering at Blyth Eastman, and would later move to Hambrecht & Quist, insisted that Pillsbury, Madison, and not Cravath, act as underwriters' counsel.

"This was a once-in-a-lifetime deal, and we wanted the best," Volpe recalls. "I think Bruce Mann is the best. He's done more of these deals, and he has good relations with the SEC. Frankly," Volpe continues, "Pillsbury runs rings around Cravath, Davis Polk, and Sullivan & Cromwell. I've worked with all of them.

New York firms think they're the fountain of all legal wisdom. But they send in their top partner, who presses the flesh and then never shows up again." Volpe could also have mentioned that Mann and William Hambrecht, the co-founder of the investment banking firm, are close personal friends.

In August 1980, Hambrecht asked Mann if he was interested in working on what Hambrecht believed would be one of the hottest deals of the decade: the initial public offering for Genentech, the pioneering company in the burgeoning genetic engineering field. Mann had his mind on other things that summer, specifically, his forthcoming marriage to Naomi Rattner, a professor of Victorian literature at the City College of San Francisco. But when Hambrecht suggested that genetic engineering would be the semiconductor industry of the 1980s—and Genentech a bigger deal than Intel had been—Mann took notice. Hambrecht impressed one other point on Mann: the need for secrecy. Genentech's greatest reluctance to enter the public markets stemmed from its fear that it might have to expose some sensitive commercial secrets; the company was not yet certain it would be willing to offer securities publicly, and any premature publicity could cause it to pull back from the deal altogether. Such was Mann's concern that he did not even circulate the customary "new matter memo" informing his partners that he was working on a new project in the office. Even though another one of Pillsbury, Madison's and Mann's clients was actively pursuing Genentech's underwriting business, Mann gave no sign that another investment banking firm had already been tapped for the assignment.

The prospective Genentech deal could not be kept entirely secret, of course, even though it would be what Mann liked to refer to as a "high profile" deal. For whatever the impressions of the investment bankers at Hambrecht & Quist, Mann—like his counterparts at the New York firms—relies heavily on associates who actually do most of the legal work involved in a securities offering. At a meeting concerning one of Mann's "low profile" offerings, the chief executive of the issuing company commented acidly that if Mann bothered to attend their meetings he would find it unnecessary to ask questions and raise issues about matters that had already been discussed and resolved. On high profile deals Mann was more careful, making sure that important telephone messages passed through him and that letters bore his signature, even if the underlying work had been performed by an associate. And apart from the skill with which he discharged such subterfuges, there was nothing unusual about Mann's reliance on more junior lawyers. Much securities work is boring, technical and routine, as effectively handled by beginning lawyers as by an experienced partner. And the more associates who can be involved, and the greater the time they spend on the matter, the more profitable is that work for the firm, particularly at a firm like Pillsbury, Madison, where the partner/associate ratio is high.

When he finished his phone conversation with Hambrecht, Mann walked downstairs to Michael Ostrach's office. Ostrach was the associate he wanted most to work on the Genentech deal. Indeed, he was the associate he had come to rely upon most heavily in the firm. Ostrach was the kind of associate Mann liked: he worked hard, putting in long hours; he didn't bother Mann with questions or conversation; he could be counted on to handle all but the most complicated problems. In short, Ostrach made Mann's life much easier and added to his efficiency.

Ostrach also had the right attitude and demeanor. Though he had attended Stanford Law School, he was born in Rhode Island and had begun his legal career as a corporate associate at Debevoise & Plimpton in New York. Despite his move to California, he still looked like an Easterner, with his scholarly wire-rim glasses, dark hair and dark wool suits, and was bright and energetic. Although he had only been an associate at Pillsbury since moving to San Francisco in 1978, he had already worked on more than twenty securities offerings with Mann, and several investment bankers had commented favorably to Mann on Ostrach's work.

When Mann stopped by Ostrach's office to broach the assignment to him, the associate jumped at the chance to work on the deal. Mann hardly had to explain that Genentech would provide unusual challenges for the securities lawyers working on it. It was the first company in the genetic engineering field to go public, which meant that the lawyers had no comparable registration and offering statements to use as models. The success or failure of its offering would have a major impact on the fate of the entire genetic engineering industry. And there were bound to be problems with the Securities and Exchange Commission. The public interest which had focused on the company and the genetic engineering field meant that the potential for investor disappointment was great, and meant that the deal would receive unusual scrutiny from the SEC.

Mann cautioned Ostrach to say nothing about the proposed offering, and said that there was still a possibility that the deal would not go forward. Mann was on his way to a meeting of the company's board of directors to discuss some "roadblocks" which had arisen, and Mann expected that he'd have a pretty good idea whether the deal would go after he returned from the meeting that afternoon.

When Mann arrived at Genentech's offices, a 15-minute drive south from Pillsbury's offices, he would hardly have known he had arrived at the headquarters and operating plant for the world's leading genetic engineering company. The company's small, unimpressive facilities in a seedy warehouse district were a far cry from the plush Socal executive suite upstairs from Mann's own office. Mann was given a tour of the facilities, which left him largely bewildered. "It just looked like a laboratory," Mann recalls. "They held up this test tube of white powder and told me it was pure interferon. For all I knew, it was salt."

At the board meeting, Mann was introduced to Genentech's president and chief executive officer, Robert Swanson; its in-house general counsel, Thomas Kiley, a patent lawyer; and several of the outside directors. Also present was the company's outside general counsel, Lee Benton, from the San Francisco firm of Cooley, Godward, Castro, Huddleson & Tatum. Cooley, Godward is the kind of relatively small and new firm that is happy to take on a promising new client, even if the initial work is at a reduced rate or in exchange for stock participation. Benton and Mann had worked on several deals together before and knew each other well; Pillsbury had been responsible for steering several new offerings to Cooley, Godward in instances where it represented the underwriters. One of Cooley, Godward's young partners is John Bates, Jr., the son of Pillsbury's chairman. (It is common for the children of partners in firms which have antinepotism policies to be partners in other major firms.)

It didn't take long for Mann to recognize that Genentech's greatest asset was its extraordinary *promise*. For the fact was that the company had not yet sold a single product to an end user. Here was a company hoping to market securities in the public market that had no revenue from sales of its products. Further-more, Genentech had already accumulated a deficit of nearly $700,000.

A timid securities lawyer might have left the meeting at that point, but one of the qualities that has made Mann so appealing to underwriters is that such problems do not seem to deter him. He is as much a businessman as a lawyer, and he looks for ways to go forward rather than for factors which might derail an offering. And on the positive side, Genentech did have some income; it had several long-range research and development contracts with major companies.

These contracts, however, provided the major "roadblock" that Mann had mentioned to Ostrach. Swanson and the Genentech executives did not want these development contracts to be made public, principally for what they saw as serious competitive risks. They were afraid that if the identities of Genentech's contracting partners and the terms of the deals became known, Genentech's competitors—especially Cetus, another genetic engineering con-cern in the San Francisco area—would attack the arrangements and underbid them. The company also feared that if the terms of the deals became known, future contracting partners would be in a position to drive a much harder bargain, knowing what Genentech had settled for in other deals. Swanson felt so strongly about preserving the secrecy of the contracts, in fact, that he said flatly that if they had to be disclosed, Genentech would not go forward with the public offering.

His insistence posed a serious problem for Mann. After all, the principal purpose of filing a registration statement with the SEC is to make sure that the investing public has access to all the material information it needs about a company in order to make an informed decision about whether to invest in its securities and in the company's future. And there was no question in his mind that Genentech's research and developments contracts were ma-terial information; they accounted for nearly all of the company's present earnings. On the other hand, Mann recognized that the information was genuinely sensitive for the fledgling company, and he told Swanson and Middleton that he thought he could bring the SEC around to the company's point of view.

His strategy for accomplishing that involved what is known as a prefiling conference, a rarely invoked procedure which permits securities counsel to meet with SEC staff members to discuss potential problems before they arise in conjunction with the filing of a preliminary registration statement. Such conferences are generally avoided by sophisticated securities lawyers. They already know the usual mechanics and strategies for steering a registration statement through the commission, and a prefiling conference often only tips off the commission staff to problems that they might otherwise overlook. In the Genentech case, however, Mann knew that without the information about the development contracts in the preliminary statement, there would be an uproar from the commission. Shortly after his meeting with the Genentech directors and officers, he called to arrange a meeting with the SEC. It was here that his contacts in Washington would come in handy. Mann and William Wood, the SEC's associate director for corporation finance, had worked together when Mann was in Washington.

Late in July, Mann, Benton and Kiley flew to Washington armed with a memorandum co-authored by Benton and Mann which argued that Genentech should be entitled to keep confidential the details of its existing contractual arrangements. In their telephone conversations, Wood had already insisted that the SEC be allowed to see some of the contracts, and Mann had forwarded edited copies of Genentech contracts with Hoffmann–La Roche, Eli Lilly, and Kabi AB, all large drug manufacturers, on the condition that the SEC staff make no copies of them, return them following their conference, and not consider them "filed" with the commission for any reason.

Mann was at his most diplomatic and persuasive at the meeting, his arguments cleverly appealing to the concerns of the SEC and downplaying the hard competitive reasons why Genentech wanted to protect its contractual relationships. Mann expressed concern for a potentially gullible investing public. He argued that "premature disclosure" of the company's development deals might "unduly raise" investor expectations about the outcome of the research before any real achievement had been realized and might contribute to "speculative interest" in the company's securities. He also argued that the information was not "material" since the arrangements could be canceled on short notice and would only be a source of significant future income if the projects were successful. In essence, he argued that more information would mislead rather than educate the public; that the SEC would in fact be performing a public service by permitting Genentech to conceal these contractual relationships.

Wood and his staff members swallowed the arguments with surprising ease, or so the Genentech lawyers thought, especially since the arguments, though well phrased to appeal to the commission, weren't terribly persuasive. Couldn't the danger of the public being misled be obviated by the kind of warnings that Mann had articulated to the commission? And isn't the investing public sufficiently sophisticated to make its own evaluations of how "material" information about long-term research and development contracts are? But such nagging questions were quickly brushed aside in the wake of Mann's success at the meeting. He had the assurances he sought, and the deal could now go forward.

On August 1, 1980, a stream of investment bankers, lawyers and accountants began to assemble in Genentech's offices in south San Francisco for the "all hands" meeting for Genentech, the corporate securities equivalent of the kick-off in football. Representatives of both Blyth Eastman and Hambrecht & Quist attended, as did lawyers from Cooley, Godward and Mann and Ostrach from Pillsbury, Madison. A series of executives from the company lectured them on Genentech's technical processes, recombinant DNA and the company's financial picture. Then, tasks were assigned to groups of participants along with a timetable intended to result in a preliminary registration being filed with the SEC by mid-August. Mann ticked off some of the usual problems that arise in an offering of new securities: problems with valuing assets, how to treat loans to officers of the company, offering of cheap stock, all of which tend to be scrutinized closely by the SEC. But the meeting's discussion tended to focus on two areas: the risks that should be disclosed in the prospectus, and the need to avoid publicity.

Problems with the media have been a particular thorn in the side of securities lawyers in recent years, and were bound to be an even greater problem with a high-interest company like Genentech. From a legal perspective, the problem is that securities may only be sold pursuant to a prospectus which has been studied and approved by the Securities and Exchange Commission and circulated to the public. Yet various courts have ruled that press releases, press conferences, publicity campaigns and the like prior to approval of the registration statement constitute an "offer to sell" in violation of the Securities Act, and for which the underwriters can be held liable. The SEC itself has issued guidelines that strictly limit the permissible publicity surrounding a company which contemplates issuing securities. Practically the only exceptions permitted are the dry announcements known as "tombstones" which announce the offering of securities and litter the financial pages of major daily newspapers, especially the *Wall Street Journal*. Mann strongly urged all concerned to avoid contact with the press.

The next two weeks were a period of intense activity directed toward the filing of a preliminary prospectus, or "red herring," with the SEC. Lee Benton and his associates had responsibility for the first draft of the document, but the process quickly became committee drafting in six lengthy, tedious meetings of all the lawyers involved, which resulted in rewriting almost the entire document. Some of the discussions were important substantively, such as whether to include a section of high-risk factors and, if so, what should be included. At one of the meetings, for example, an underwriter expressed his anxieties about fluctuations in the price of the stock after it was issued, and Mann agreed that this could be a problem. Finally, they agreed on a section they would entitle "Certain Factors to Be Considered." Among the seven factors was "the possible Volatility of Share Price. Because of the foregoing factors, the market price of the Company's Common Stock may be highly volatile," the prospectus read. At the same time, the drafters had to bear in mind that the prospectus is a selling document, which, at its most effective, persuades investors to purchase the stock.

As a result, some of the warnings were couched in language that was as optimistic as possible: "Technological developments are expected to continue at a rapid pace in the Company's industry. Although the Company has announced the development of more products using recombinant DNA technology than any other company, the successful development of the Company's products will be dependent upon its ability to continue on the leading edge of this technology and its ability to attract and retain scientific and technical personnel," the lawyers wrote. And there were the ongoing discussions and arguments about how to treat the confidential research and development contracts, with the resolution a brief statement saying, "It is Genentech's policy not to disclose the nature of specific projects prior to the demonstration of a product with commercial potential."

The novelty of the company also made the process more complex, but also more interesting, than usual. Prospectuses always contain a general description of the offering company which is usually boilerplate language to the effect that the company "designs, develops, manufactures, sells and distributes" a certain product. But all Genentech had done was develop and produce—it had yet to sell or distribute. The sessions also had their share of tedium: the discussions of punctuation, shifting of sentences, and a lengthy debate over whether to include a glossary, and if so, what terms should be explained. (The glossary was then abandoned, but an index and cross-reference were included.)

Most of the drafting at Pillsbury fell to Ostrach, although Mann was attending the meetings because of the importance and visibility of the deal. Ostrach hurried into Mann's office one afternoon with a revision of his draft of the "company" section, and he was surprised to find Genentech's general counsel, Tom Kiley, huddled with Mann over the conference table in the office, talking in whispers. Mann looked distressed, and stopped talking when he saw Ostrach, but Kiley motioned the associate over and said, "You should hear about this."

"This" threatened to be a major wrench in Genentech's efforts to pass muster with the SEC and sell its securities on the open market. In Kiley's hand was a copy of a complaint filed in a lawsuit by Dr. David Golde, a professor of medicine at the University of California in Los Angeles, against Hoffmann–La Roche, the drug manufacturer. During the summer of 1978, Dr. Golde had derived a cell line from a patient who subsequently died, and had sent some of the cells to a colleague, Dr. Robert Gallo, at the National Cancer Institute in Bethesda, Maryland, along with a letter saying that the cell line was for his use exclusively. Gallo was then engaged in a joint research project with Hoffmann–La Roche, which was in turn engaged in a major research and development project with Genentech—the subject of one of the very contracts that the company had been so anxious to keep confidential. Dr. Gallo, the lawsuit claimed, had taken the cell line furnished him by the University of California, turned it over to Hoffmann–La Roche for commercial exploitation, and had used it to produce interferon.

Of greatest concern to Kiley and Mann was the additional fact that dead cells from Dr. Golde's cell line had been supplied to Genentech by Hoffmann–La Roche pursuant to their joint development agreement, and that Genentech had used DNA extracted from that cell line in its own production of interferon. The complaint had not yet been filed, but the lawyers were worried about the implications of the lawsuit for Genentech, and specifically, the cloud it might put over the company's rights to any proceeds from its manufacture of interferon, potentially one of its most lucrative products.

In the best of circumstances, a company about to enter the securities market is not anxious to air its dirty laundry, and some lawyers might have swept an unfiled lawsuit under the rug. But Mann and Kiley gave no serious thought to concealing the Hoffmann–La Roche matter, if for no other reason because the suit was bound to be given a great deal of attention in the press and because Genentech's involvement could not be kept under wraps for long. They decided to confront the problem head-on and present the SEC with as favorable a prognosis for the outcome of the case as they could muster.

Genentech was in a relatively good position in that regard, since it maintained close relationships with both Dr. Golde, the scientist who produced the cell line and whom it employed from time to time in its own research efforts, and Hoffmann–La Roche, the company that had given it the allegedly stolen cell line. After brief negotiations, Genentech obtained a letter from Dr. Golde stating that "I have no information indicating any wrongdoing by Genentech," as well as a commitment from Hoffmann–La Roche that they would indemnify Genentech in the event it were found liable for appropriation of the cell line. Genentech's negotiations with the University of California were not so successful. Despite its claims that it had no way of knowing the source of the cells furnished it by Hoffmann–La Roche, the university replied that it intended to name Genentech as a defendant in its suit.

Finally, Genentech obtained a legal opinion that "There is no reasonable likelihood that the company will be subjected to injunctive relief [such as a ban on further production of interferon] in the event of such litigation." That opinion was provided not by Mann or Pillsbury, Madison, but by the patent law firm of Lyon & Lyon in Los Angeles, the firm where Kiley had been a partner before joining Genentech as general counsel. Patent law is one of the specialty areas avoided by the large corporate law firms. The field is highly specialized, and nearly all its practitioners are trained scientists or engineers as well as lawyers. Though aspects of the practice of the large corporate firm have become nearly as specialized, lawyers in such firms still preserve the notion that they are "generalists," and almost all of them have liberal arts undergraduate degrees. The patent bar has historically been monopolized by a group of small regional, highly specialized firms. Furthermore, the practice is not particularly lucrative, and much of it is technical, tedious and routine. Large companies handle most of their patent matters with their own legal staffs.

Mann gathered the letters and opinions regarding the Hoffmann–La Roche suit and sent them directly to the SEC as exhibits. As for the prospectus, he and his associates artfully drafted: "The Company has been made aware of a claim stated by the University of California against Roche alleging unauthorized use of certain materials in connection with its interferon project with the Company. Counsel for the University has stated that its claim against Roche will be extended to the Company, in which case Roche has agreed to indemnify the Company against any money judgment the Company might incur. Lyon & Lyon, patent counsel to the Company, has expressed the opinion that there is no reasonable likelihood that the Company will be subject to injunctive relief in the event of litigation against it. The Company cannot predict whether its future income from interferon sales would be adversely affected if a claim were established against Roche."

Mann's disclosure of the potential claim by the University of California is part of what is generally called a "due diligence" investigation by the underwriters, much of which, in practice, is conducted by the underwriters' counsel. Indeed, in the eyes of many practitioners in the field, making sure that the underwriters have discharged their "due diligence" responsibilities is the single most important obligation of the underwriters' lawyer.

"Due diligence" has, nonetheless, never been defined with any precision. According to the Securities Act, an underwriter will not be liable for any misstatements or misrepresentations contained in a prospectus if he has "after reasonable investigation, reasonable ground to believe and did believe . . . that the statements therein were true." Underwriters have not been permitted by the courts to simply accept a company's or its officers' or its counsel's assertions that statements about it are true, but are required to make some kind of independent investigation. Thus, in between the drafting sessions, Mann made his own review of the company's various contracts, checked to see if it was involved in any other pending litigation that it had not disclosed to him, checked accounting records to see if any suspicious payments had been made, and generally learned about the company to make sure that its claims rang true.

"Genentech was a particular problem because we had no other models to look at in the field," Mann explains. "Ordinarily, part of the due diligence investigation is to look at the claims that similar companies have made. Is the current example generally in line, given industry standards? In genetic engineering, there was a Regulation A offering from a small company called Enzo Biochem, Inc., that was totally inadequate—not nearly enough about the industry, or the risks. However, a lot had been written generally in the field: articles in *Fortune, Forbes, Scientific American,* hundreds of articles. I and my associates read all this material."

Generally Mann, other Pillsbury, Madison securities lawyers and, indeed, the profession in general have shrouded the due diligence and prospectus-drafting process in secrecy as a precaution against future lawsuits alleging that they have not discharged their due diligence obligations. "We used to prove our due diligence by keeping detailed notes of everything we did," Mann explains. "We kept every scrap of paper. But during the past ten years we have moved in the opposite direction, because of the threat of litigation. Some of this stuff could be devastating taken out of context in discovery, in the hands of some plaintiff's lawyer." The lawyers' discussion of the Hoffmann–La Roche suit, for example, might be used as evidence that the final prospectus did not go far enough in warning of the potential liability to Genentech.

Meanwhile, as Mann's and his associates' work resulted in fewer and fewer changes to the draft prospectus at the group discussions and drafting sessions, more and more of the work was transferred to associates working on the deal, Ostrach in particular. And Ostrach began to shift more and more of his work from his office at Pillsbury to the offices and plant of Bowne, a financial printer that Pillsbury, Madison uses in San Francisco.

The printer practically becomes any corporate associate's second home, especially so for those frequently involved in offerings of securities. Because the prospectus is circulated to dealers who use it as a selling document, it must be formally printed; in the case of Genentech, it also contained a glossy four-color insert. Life at the printer is a curious combination of boredom and excess. For the most part, the work is painstaking and routine—it is essentially proofreading. Mann himself almost never goes to the printer. "By the time you're there, the work is routine. The language has essentially been resolved. You must proofread, and it doesn't take a senior partner to do that," Mann explains. "On the other hand, Pillsbury, Madison never participates in a filing or registration without having a lawyer at the printer until the filing package is mailed off. I know another law firm where, just in the past two months, a lawyer left the printer early and the printer shipped the registration statement without the signature pages." The prospect looks as though it gives Mann considerable distress. "It took an entire day to straighten that out. Given the precise timing of these deals, you can't afford to have that happen." Work at the printer usually occurs at night, especially in New York. Since the SEC opens at 9:00 A.M., associates at large New York firms typically work all night until about 7:00 A.M. at the printer and still have time to send the registration or filing materials to Washington, D.C., with a messenger or on the air shuttle. At least in San Francisco, the last flight to Washington leaves the night before, meaning that corporate associates have to be finished at the printer by around 8:30 P.M.

Then again, an associate's life at the printer isn't all work. "Pillsbury, Madison usually uses Bowne," according to Ostrach. "It's the most expensive printer in San Francisco. They take you out to dinner anywhere you want to go, to all the expensive restaurants. They get you lunch, drinks, snacks, cigarettes, just about anything. They have a color TV set—not all the printers in San Francisco do—and some printers also have a few video games." The bills for these diversions are simply included in the printers' bills, which are paid by the issuing company—in this case, Genentech—and not the law firms. Genentech's bill from Bowne for its new offering was close to $200,000. Of course, it also paid the lawyers' hourly rate for the time they spent at the printer.

And some trips to the printer do not involve any work at all. A former associate at Cravath, Swaine & Moore in New York recalls that "I was always dragged along to these sessions at the printer because I didn't drink. Everyone else would get drunk, and then I'd be the only one there sober enough to proofread." Ostrach was once treated to dinner with a pro football player and given tickets to celebrity tennis events.

There was little time for drinking on the Genentech deal, however. As the lawyers rushed to complete the preliminary prospectus for the SEC, Ostrach stayed in touch by telephone with Mann and other lawyers working on the deal so that he could immediately relay last-minute changes and adjustments to the printer. Finally, after several all-night printing sessions, the document was finished and on a plane for Washington. On August 19, it was filed with the SEC. The lawyers' work was far from over, however.

By the very next day, they realized that the Genentech deal was going to be fraught with greater peril than they had anticipated. As required by SEC regulations, Genentech and the underwriters issued a short press release the day they filed the preliminary prospectus announcing that Genentech intended to make a public offering and that the preliminary prospectus had been filed that day with the SEC. Expecting some inquiries from the press, Mann again cautioned all concerned that they should not speak with representatives of the media, and should refer all requests for information to Fred Middleton, the company's vice president of finance, who would be permitted to "clarify" statements contained in the prospectus. But Mann hadn't anticipated the deluge of phone calls which poured into Genentech's offices, keeping Middleton constantly on the telephone. Among them were calls from the *Wall Street Journal*, the *San Francisco Chronicle* and the *Examiner*, the *Oakland Tribune*, the *Economist* of London, *Newsweek*, *Science*, the *New York Daily News* and a score of others.

The next day, August 20, Mann's worst fears about the media were borne out in a front-page article in the *San Francisco Examiner* trumpeting Genentech as the glamour company of the decade. Worse than the publicity itself was a quote attributed to Swanson, the company's chairman, containing wildly optimistic projections for the company's sales and earnings in future years— for example, $100 million in sales by 1985—exactly the kind of speculation likely to whet investor appetites and arouse the wrath of the SEC. Mann immediately launched an inquiry to find out how a statement from Swanson had crept into a news article, since Swanson himself insisted that he had not made any comments to the press.

That inquiry had not yet solved the mystery when Lee Benton, the Cooley, Godward partner, received a call on September 5 from John Roycroft, the SEC branch chief who had been assigned the Genentech–Hoffmann–La Roche–University of California dispute informed Benton that he had received copies of the *Examiner* article, as well as two *Wall Street Journal* articles and a *Newsweek* article. Roycroft said that he was especially disturbed by Swanson's remarks in the *Examiner*, and he wanted more information about the extent of company contacts with the media, about the sources of the information, and what steps the company was going to take to ensure compliance with the SEC's regulations governing publicity and to limit the impact of the publicity. It was obvious from the thrust of Roycroft's remarks that he was contemplating the dread possibility of what is called a "cooling off period," an indefinite delay during which the SEC holds up an offering in the hope that the effects of publicity will dissipate. In practice, a "cooling off" period is often fatal to a public offering.

Benton, eager to deflect the SEC's suspicions, emphasized that Swanson had not been interviewed by the *Examiner* and volunteered that the source of the quote attributed to him came from remarks Swanson had made in a speech in Los Angeles early that summer, prior to the current offering, and which had been reported in the *Los Angeles Times*. Roycroft was not mollified. Three days later, Benton received more calls from three of Roycroft's assistants, asking for copies of the *Los Angeles Times* articles and announcing that they had turned the matter over to the SEC's enforcement division, meaning that there would be an investigation to see if any regulations or laws had been violated and, if so, a lawsuit. What all had hoped would be a model offering was threatening to come apart at the seams.

As if matters weren't bad enough, on September 6, just one day after the preliminary registration statement was filed, the Genentech–Hoffmann–La Roche–University of California dispute over the interferon cell line burst into public view. The *San Francisco Chronicle* reported that "A threat of legal action by the University of California, charging two drug firms with 'unauthorized use' of a UC scientific discovery, has thrown the companies and the government's cancer-fighting agency into turmoil, the Chronicle learned yesterday. . . . The legal threat was raised by UC against Hoffmann–La Roche . . . and against Genentech, Inc., the four-year-old south San Francisco company that is producing human growth hormone, insulin, and the protein called interferon." And for a company in the registration process, Genentech's general counsel, Kiley, responded in a rather flip manner: Kiley noted that Swanson, the company's chief executive, would not interrupt his honeymoon in Paris. "That should indicate how seriously we are taking the issue," the Chronicle quoted Kiley.

A meeting among the lawyers was hurriedly convened to plot strategy for salvaging the deal, and the first development was another setback. When copies of the Los Angeles Times articles—which, according to Benton, had been plagiarized by the Examiner to get its quote from Swanson—didn't contain the projections the Examiner had attributed to Swanson, Mann was annoyed. Now the lawyers would have to go back to the SEC and retract their prior explanation, a maneuver which would do nothing to bolster their credibility at such a sensitive juncture. But in the meantime, the lawyers had apparently uncovered the source of the Examiner's information. Prior to the registration process, Genentech had prepared a publicity brochure, called "The Genentech Story," for distribution to the media. Despite Mann's lectures on publicity, no one reviewed the brochure and no one told Genentech's public relations people to stop distributing it. The day the registration was announced, Genentech had routinely sent a copy of the brochure to the Examiner, where an editor, eager to come up with a quote from the company's chairman, simply attributed statements in the brochure to him.

But Mann felt that the lawyers' credibility had already been so damaged that a massive and unprecedented effort to explain the publicity which had arisen around the deal had to be undertaken. He proposed that every article which had appeared be copied and sent to the SEC with explanations of how the articles had been initiated and whether any company interviews had been granted. While Ostrach began a crash effort to assemble and explain the voluminous materials, Mann drafted an explanatory memorandum setting forth in detail the steps he had taken to try to avoid publicity. More importantly, he argued to the SEC that "To cause a delay in the proposed public offering because of this publicity would not only penalize the issuer and the underwriters for events beyond their control, but would serve no purpose under the federal securities laws. Each business development involving genetic engineering can be expected to result in media attention. Because additional product developments by companies and research centers involved in genetic engineering can be expected to continue to occur and in all probability increase in their frequency, there is no basis to assume that the level of such attention would be reduced by any delay in the proposed offering. Indeed, a delay itself would be viewed as a newsworthy event and would generate additional publicity."

Benton prepared a similarly detailed memo explaining Genentech's media contacts and his own mistake with respect to the *Examiner* article, adding that distribution of the company's background brochure had been stopped. Attached as exhibits were twenty articles concerning Genentech which had been collected by Ostrach and other associates working on the deal.

Meanwhile, the lawyers seemed to be suffering a setback on an even more sensitive front. Despite the agreement Mann believed he had obtained at the July prefiling conference at which Genentech's commercially sensitive contracts were discussed, the SEC now said that it wanted to examine uncensored copies of all of Genentech's research and development contracts and expressed concern about their omission from the registration materials. This was precisely what Genentech executives and Mann had been trying to avoid in their prefiling conference. Mann was now furious.

Part of the problem was that Wood, the associate director for corporation finance at the SEC who had agreed to the earlier arrangement, was now no longer in charge of the Genentech application, and his successor in that capacity, Gerald MacFarlane, took a much more critical attitude and was prepared to drive a harder bargain. MacFarlane and the Genentech lawyers—principally Benton, this time—began an exchange of letters and phone calls which the company considered so sensitive that even those letters and notes were eventually sealed from public view. Genentech eventually had to produce for SEC inspection the full texts of the agreements with Hoffmann–La Roche and the large drug companies with which it had previously announced it had contractual relationships, as well as three previously secret development agreements with the City of Hope National Medical Center and the regents of the University of California.

Unfortunately for Genentech, those previously secret agreements revealed that the company had not been quite so open as it had publicly proclaimed, and that its reasons for protecting its contracts might have had something to do with concerns other than the competitive impact of disclosure. Part of the company's agreement with the University of California was a settlement of a dispute over whether Genentech had unlawfully used information belonging to the university. The university claimed that two postdoctoral fellows hired by Genentech had funneled information to Genentech while still employed by the university. Such allegations were not only uncomfortably similar to the claims made in the Hoffmann–La Roche suit, but they involved two of Genentech's employees. To potential investors, the allegations might raise legitimate questions about the character and integrity of some of Genentech's research scientists, and thus affect their investment decisions.

Nonetheless, Benton argued to the SEC that "The allegations of impropriety affecting these individuals were without substantial basis. Particularly in view of the settlement of the issue, disclosure of the dispute is not material to investors." The lawyers were treading a very fine line.

As the days following the filing of the registration statement became weeks, the lawyers waited anxiously for the SEC's official comments, which would indicate whether the deal was in serious trouble. The SEC staff members were giving no hints; several phone calls proved fruitless.

In the meantime, Ostrach turned his attention to what is known in the securities practice as "blue sky" work. A public offering of securities requires not only a successful registration and approval from the SEC, but also the approval of the securities commissions which exist in each state, often under the aegis of its secretary of state. Securities can only be marketed in those states from which approval has been obtained by the time the offering becomes effective at the SEC, and each state subjects the offering to varying degrees of scrutiny and imposes different requirements.

The legal work involved in blue sky work (so-called because of the states' attempts to prevent sales of thin air to the public) is mechanical and routine, consisting principally of knowing the various timing and filing requirements and making sure that they are complied with. In most of the large corporate law firms, blue sky work is performed by a small cadre of lawyers who are known somewhat euphemistically as "permanent associates." Permanent associates are known to everyone in the firm as lawyers who will never be made partners. In some cases, they are hired by the firm at the outset with the understanding that they will never be considered for partnership. They form a subclass of lawyers who lack the prestigious credentials of the firm's regular associates, and they are paid less. In rarer cases, a lawyer who begins at a firm as a regular associate, but who does not exhibit partnership potential yet stays at the firm year after year, drifts into permanent associate status. In the eyes of most regular associates, permanent associates lead their lives and careers in a state of humiliation.

The whole notion of permanent associates is inconsistent with the firms' up-or-out philosophy, and though most of the firms employ a handful of them, it has never seemed a comfortable arrangement. Over the past decade or so, Pillsbury, Madison has been phasing out its permanent associates, failing to replace them when they retire or leave the firm. As a result, the blue sky work has largely been handed over to young associates at the firm and to paralegals.

In the twenty deals he had worked on with Mann, Ostrach had easily mastered the technical requirements of the blue sky registrations, and found that the work didn't intrude too heavily on the more interesting aspects of the deals on which he worked. But just as Genentech was not a typical SEC registration, its blue sky problems were more complicated and time-consuming than Ostrach had anticipated. Because he recognized certain problems at the outset, Ostrach decided not even to attempt to get blue sky clearance from ten states which are notorious for their strict standards in securities offerings, such as Iowa and Missouri. That left forty jurisdictions where Ostrach had to prepare and submit filing packages.

From past experience, Ostrach also knew that the state securities officials were apt to move slowly on his applications, so he tried to anticipate their problems in his original submission. In his view, the chief of these was the offering price of the Genentech stock. Company executives and the underwriters had tentatively determined that the asking price for the shares would be $25 to $30, which Ostrach disclosed to the states. Price is a factor that often makes state officials nervous, especially in a case like Genentech.

Subjected to the ordinary tests by which stock prices are judged, Genentech's price seemed outrageously high. At $30 a share, Genentech stock's price/earnings ratio was about 3,000; most New York Stock Exchange stocks trade at a price/earnings ratio of from 5 to 12. Genentech also posed what looked like some "cheap stock" problems, since insiders had already purchased shares at a far lower price. The $500 Swanson had invested in 1976, for example, would be worth $30 million following the public offering at $30 a share. These factors were likely to make some state officials view Genentech stock more as a patent medicine than a safe investment.

In this instance, however, the wildly optimistic publicity Genentech had been receiving was likely to be helpful. Ostrach culled a selection focusing on the company's great earnings potential, and used it to show how the proposed earnings would easily bring Genentech's price/earnings ratio into line. The states were much less concerned than the SEC about publicity, where it came from, and whether it constituted an "offering" in the SEC's terms. Ostrach's only risk was that, had the SEC known, it might have frowned on such an affirmative use of the publicity that Genentech was supposedly trying to avoid.

By the time the blue sky filings had been sent out, Genentech was beginning to look like an unusually troublesome deal. Though all of the initial steps in the typical offering were now complete, and Mann's principal responsibilities over, problems loomed on nearly every front. Moreover, they were likely to come at the most sensitive time in a securities offering, when delay—or even rumors of delay—can cause investor interest and confidence to evaporate. But these factors didn't seem to make any great impression on Mann. Somewhat to Ostrach's dismay, Mann proceeded with plans for his honeymoon, which would take him to Europe beginning in mid-September.

Mann had, in fact, seemed a little distracted at times throughout the Genentech deal, for reasons that were obvious: on August 31, he and Naomi Rattner were to be married, each for the second time. Mann was determined to take the honeymoon to France that he and his new wife had been planning for months. Ostrach didn't dare say anything, but he wished that Mann wouldn't go, particularly since he showed no signs of bringing another Pillsbury partner into the deal. Ostrach would be left as the lawyer principally in charge. Whatever the personal considerations, he knew that at Debevoise or any of the major New York law firms it would have been unthinkable for the lead partner—no matter how supervisory his actual involvement in the deal—to leave town at such a time for *any* personal reason. But Mann seemed confident that, despite some of the blustering from the SEC people, the offering would proceed smoothly without him. He and his wife left for Europe as scheduled.

Then, on October 1, not long after Mann's departure, the SEC issued its official comments on the initial registration filing. It was even worse than Ostrach had feared: more than fifty comments calling for revisions in the registration statement. Furthermore, the SEC was still insisting on disclosure of the sensitive contracts. "The names of the two non-profit institutions, and their affiliation if any, should be set forth. Moreover it would appear that such agreements should be filed as an exhibit in the amendment," Roycroft at the SEC wrote. He also asked for much fuller disclosure of the Lilly, Hoffmann–La Roche, and KabiGen contracts, and gave the lawyers no comfort about the publicity concerns that had been raised earlier. "The staff has reviewed your letter of response and supplemental information dated September 12, 1980," Roycroft wrote.

Our areas of concern still lie with the following:
1) when the company first decided to go public and the circumstances surrounding the company's decision;
2) the date the "Genentech Story" was first completed and the dates of material revisions should be supplied, and;
3) whether prior to August 19, 1980, the *Los Angeles Times* published an article regarding the company. If so, please provide a copy of the article.

Obviously, there would have to be a thorough revision and resubmission of the registration statement, and even then it looked like the same problems could derail the offering. The comments were sufficiently serious and extensive that another "all hands" meeting was scheduled to plan the company's response. This time, there was an even greater sense of urgency, since the lawyers had only a week to file an amended registration statement. Ostrach nearly moved into the printer's around the clock, supervising the changes at the same time he was taking phone calls from state securities officials who started deluging him with questions about the offering. Benton continued to haggle with SEC officials in Washington about the sensitive contracts, right down to the inclusion of particular three-word phrases, but increasingly he was capitulating on the very issue that the Genentech executives had once vowed would preclude the offering. There was really no question now that Genentech would pull out of the deal over the disclosure issue—not with $30 million in the offing.

In fact, the underwriters were whetting Genentech's appetite for even more money with reports that they could market the shares at a price even higher than the $30 they had previously envisioned. After the announcement of the registration in mid-August, the investment bankers had gone on what is called the "road show," a multicity tour in which they pitch the new securities to local dealers. Although they aren't allowed to disclose any information not contained in the prospectus filed with the SEC, they are permitted to embellish the facts somewhat with a prepared statement that had been reviewed and approved by Mann.

In their presentations in New York, Boston, Chicago, San Francisco and Los Angeles in the United States, and in London, Edinburgh, Geneva, Paris and Zurich abroad, the investment bankers had encountered unusual investor excitement. In fact, Blyth Eastman's Volpe couldn't recall an offering that was so easy to sell, in which the road show participants actually had to make sure that investor optimism didn't get out of hand. Ostrach had been telling the state securities authorities that the stock would be offered in the $25 to $30 range. Now the underwriters called and asked him about the possibility of $35, which meant he would have to call every state where a blue sky filing was pending. His first effort was not very successful: the securities commissioner in Pennsylvania laughed at the suggestion. By the time the amended registration statement had to be filed, no final decision had been reached, so the new draft was sent to the SEC with the pricing information left blank.

Ostrach had the amended registration statement ready to send to the SEC by the following Monday morning, after a full weekend of work. That draft gave the SEC almost everything it asked for, including most of the sensitive contract provisions, and Ostrach also provided a memorandum on behalf of Pillsbury, Madison assuring the SEC that the underwriters and their counsel had discharged their due diligence responsibilities, though somewhat testily he had written that "We do not believe such an explanation should be required in view of the numerous initial public offerings which the Representatives have managed."

Ostrach's principal worry now was whether the changes made in the amended registration filing were so extensive that the entire prospectus would have to be recirculated to securities dealers and prospective purchasers, a move which could delay the offering by weeks and might cause a crisis in investor confidence. There are no hard rules for what constitutes a "material" revision which requires the underwriters to recirculate the prospectus. Ostrach was extremely worried about making that decision himself on behalf of Pillsbury, Madison, since that firm might be liable for a wrong decision, and Mann couldn't be reached. So he took the problem to Albert Brown, a senior securities partner at Pillsbury, Madison. Brown didn't know that much about the Genentech deal and its history, but he supported Ostrach in his tentative decision that, pending additional comments from the SEC, he could take the position that the prospectus didn't need to be recirculated. It was that decision which would later be called into question by the *Wall Street Journal*.

Genentech was not the only deal that Mann had left in Ostrach's hands during the partner's honeymoon. Pillsbury, Madison and Mann were also representing the underwriters for People Express Airlines, which was also in registration then for an initial offering of securities. At 10:00 P.M. on Sunday, just a short time after finishing the Genentech amendment, Ostrach boarded a plane for New York, arriving at 6:30 the next morning. He took a cab straight to Pandick Press, a financial printer near Wall Street, where he worked on the People Express registration with a former Cravath associate all day and all night—until 5:00 A.M. Tuesday morning. When he arrived at the Waldorf-Astoria, not having had any sleep for two days, he was told that his room had been given to someone else. Ostrach took the next available flight back to San Francisco, where, exhausted, he faced a barrage of calls from the media on developments in the Genentech filing.

This time the media were not interested in Genentech's great success but its potential failure with the SEC. Financial reporters had noticed how long it had been since the initial registration was announced, and it made them suspicious. On October 7, the day the amended registration statement was filed, the *Los Angeles Times* headlined that "SEC Concern Delays Offering of Hot High-Technology Issue," writing that "One of the most eagerly awaited new stock issues in more than a decade, Genentech, Inc., which was to be offered this week, has been postponed because of Securities and Exchange Commission concern about publicity surrounding the offering, informed sources said Monday." Other reporters were quick to pick up the hint that the Genentech offering was in trouble, and Ostrach was powerless to say anything to the contrary, other than to insist that if reporters went with that story, they would be making a mistake. Though not identified, Ostrach was quoted in a *Newsweek* story which predicted that Genentech would not be able to go forward with its stock offering. In the article, Ostrach complained that the problems with the offering had been the media's creation, not Genentech's, a comment which earned him several compliments in the corridors of Pillsbury.

The underwriters reported that, despite the bad publicity, investor enthusiasm was continuing to mount, and in fact, by the time the *Newsweek* article appeared, the deal was poised to go forward. A member of the SEC staff called Genentech with only minor comments on the amended registration statement and a request that the missing price information be filled in; and on October 8, the commission granted Genentech's pending request for confidential treatment with respect to their negotiations and certain still undisclosed aspects of the company's contractual relations. Ostrach braced himself for another weekend at the printer's, the last push to get out the final registration statement.

The public offering itself was finally scheduled for 10:00 A.M. on October 14, the moment when the SEC registration would become effective, and the underwriters alerted their network of dealers. But on the afternoon of October 13, as the final proofs were about to be printed for shipment to Washington, a group from Blyth Eastman and from Hambrecht & Quist burst in on Ostrach at the printer's. The investment bankers had heard reports from the field that the offering was going to be way oversubscribed, even at the $35 price that Ostrach had finally managed to clear with all but four of the forty states targeted for sales. "We've got to price to meet demand," the underwriters insisted to Ostrach. "We can get $50 a share."

Ostrach could see their excitement getting out of hand, and although he was only an associate, he decided that he had to stop them. It was already 4:00 P.M. in many of the states where the offering had been approved, and Ostrach told the underwriters that it would be impossible for him to reach all the state securities authorities before they left for the day. Even if he succeeded, he emphasized, he wasn't sure he could secure their approval. He'd had enough trouble getting approval for the increase to $35 a share. The underwriters seemed to be wavering when Ostrach made a judgment that further derailed their hopes. The section of the registration statement dealing with price, he noted, did not talk about "pricing to meet demand," but rather, pricing in accord with long-term expectations for Genentech's performance. If pricing to meet demand was the position that the underwriters now wanted to take, that section of the registration statement would have to be redrafted, and possibly recirculated, jeopardizing the SEC approval that had been finally obtained, and delaying the offering.

The underwriters gave in. Ostrach's insistence had just cost Genentech $15 million in additional proceeds, and had cost the underwriters their additional percentage. But as he put the finishing touches on the filing package that evening, Ostrach didn't much care. He realized that during the past year, he had billed clients about 2,500 hours for his $41,000 salary, usually doing three deals at a time, rarely having a free weekend or evening, spending countless hours on overnight flights to the East Coast. With the Genentech filing package now in his hands, he was turning Swanson, Kiley and a group of what seemed like ordinary investors into multimillionaires. He felt he had a right to assert himself.

The final closing for the Genentech deal was held in San Francisco at 7:00 A.M. on October 21, a week after the initial sale. That night the underwriters held a celebratory dinner at L'Etoile, an elegant and expensive French restaurant on Nob Hill. Ostrach didn't attend either event; in fact, he wasn't invited. He feels that senior partners didn't want to call attention to the fact that much of the legal work on this "high profile" deal had been handled by a relatively young associate at the firm. And, in any event, the focus of the toasts for Pillsbury, Madison that evening was Bruce Mann.

Soon after Mann returned to San Francisco from his honey-moon, the glamour faded from Genentech, and the price of its stock began its slide. Mann had read the threatening *Wall Street Journal* article which discussed the changes in Genentech's pro-spectus. Although he told Ostrach that he supported his associate's judgments, Mann's prognosis was not very reassuring: Mann told Ostrach that he believed there was a two out of three chance that Pillsbury, Madison would be sued. But in the meantime, there were plenty of new deals in the wings, and there was no time to dwell on hypothetical lawsuits. Ostrach turned almost immediately to the initial public offering for Cetus, another San Francisco–area genetic engineering company, and one of Genentech's prin-cipal competitors.

At Pillsbury, Madison that autumn, there were rumblings in the partnership that helped to deflect attention from the Genentech deal and its possible consequences. Among some of the younger partners, there was growing dissatisfaction with the firm's policy of putting the lion's share of its profits and power in the hands of a few of the most senior partners. Two partners had actually de-fected from the firm, moving to rivals like Morrison & Foerster—and defections are almost unthinkable in firms like Pillsbury, Mad-ison. While senior partners like Wallace Kaapcke, the firm's chairman, were reputedly making $350,000 a year, junior partners were said to be making only about $70,000—barely more than the firm's senior associates. And the firm's ossified decision-making structure did not seem to be responding to challenges from newer, smaller firms in San Francisco; to aggressive competition from the large and growing Los Angeles firms; and, of particular concern to Mann, the growing presence of those rival firms in Silicon Valley, the source of much of his business.

Late in 1978, Kaapcke stepped down from his post as firm chairman, ostensibly as a result of an understanding reached among the firm's most senior partners, including Jack Sutro, who at 76 still made a daily appearance at the firm. There is little doubt that he was forced out to make way for John Bates, the head of the firm's litigation department, who, though less senior, is more dynamic and flexible than Kaapcke. Bates named Mann to the firm's management committee, even though he had to create a second position on the committee for a corporate securities lawyer to do so. More significantly, he allowed Mann to negotiate a merger with a small San Jose firm in order to establish a direct Pillsbury, Madison presence in Silicon Valley, staffed with locally known lawyers. Although Bates personally opposed the merger—the lateral admission of partners, let alone an entire firm, is a long-standing taboo at such firms, and Bates is skeptical of the need for regional offices—it was a measure of the firm's new-found flexibility that the merger was allowed to go through.

Such developments, however, did little to quell associate unrest. One morning during the spring of 1981, Ostrach and Mann were on a plane for Los Angeles to attend a securities meeting and, as usual, Mann wasn't saying much. Ostrach decided that it was time to bring up a topic that he'd been thinking about for some time, but had put off discussing as long as he could. Ostrach nudged Mann. "There's something I'd like to talk to you about," the associate began. "I guess you've heard those rumors at the firm about associates leaving?" Pillsbury had been plagued by rumors of a mass defection of associates ever since a junior partner had openly complained about his salary and taken the issue to a partners' meeting a month previously. Word of the dispute—and of the disparity between senior and junior partners' salaries—had trickled down to the associates, and it had triggered extensive grumbling. "Well," Ostrach continued, "I'm one of those associates." He told Mann that he had already asked for and been given the position of general counsel to Cetus.

Characteristically, Mann betrayed no surprise or emotion, saying only that he wanted to think about what Ostrach had told him. But on the return flight that afternoon, he began to try to talk Ostrach out of his decision, ticking off his points almost as though he were preparing a legal brief. He tried to assure Ostrach that the firm's financial future was secure, adding that changes might be made in the firm's allocation of income, even going so far as to discuss his own partnership draw. And he warned Ostrach that he was taking a risk by going with a new, unproved company, warning him that it was like having only a single client. "What if they don't like you?" he asked.

Ostrach agreed to think again about his decision, but he didn't change his mind. "I earned basically the same as every other associate at my age level," Ostrach explains. "I was doing better work, I had much more responsibility, and much more pressure. I was overworked and I was exploited. Then I looked at the young partners. They weren't earning a hell of a lot more than I was; you had to wait 25 years to get a real share of the money. And I thought, Why not take some risks? Why fall into the easiest thing? I'd gone to college, to law school, into a big firm. Where was my pot at the end of the rainbow? Was this how I wanted to spend my next 25 years?" On May 13, 1981, Michael Ostrach left Pillsbury, Madison for the last time.

Recently, shares of Genentech traded at about $34, approximately the same as the price at which they were offered. Although the company has recorded several more research breakthroughs since going public, it still has not marketed a single product commercially. The stock's fall from the peaks recorded shortly after it was offered caused considerable unhappiness among many investors, but neither Pillsbury, Madison nor the underwriters have been sued. "Why? I really don't know," Mann says. "I like to think it's because our documents thoroughly warned every potential investor of the risks. No one would have bought without realizing the serious risks involved." But Mann acknowledges that the lawyers' efforts usually do not determine whether lawsuits will be brought. "I wrote every prospectus for Occidental Petroleum from 1960 until 1969, when I had to resign as counsel due to a conflict of interest," Mann recalls. "Not one suit was ever brought. After I resigned, suits were brought on every prospectus the company offered. Why? Not because I was a better lawyer. In 1969, Libya nationalized Occidental's oil wells and its stock plunged."

Though no longer at its peak price, Genentech stock has not slipped appreciably below the $35 price at which it was initially offered. Mann, for one, has his fingers crossed that the price of Genentech stock will soon go up.

CHAPTER FOUR

WESTINGHOUSE
Kirkland & Ellis

Kirkland & Ellis partner William Jentes gazed out over Lake Michigan from his 58th-floor office in Chicago's Standard Oil skyscraper. It was a balmy day in May 1975, a few sailboats had ventured out onto the lake, and Jentes thought it might soon be time for a vacation, perhaps a trip with his family to France, where he had been a Fulbright scholar nearly twenty years before. Nothing was further from his thoughts than uranium and nuclear energy.

Jentes pulled himself away from the view to answer his ringing phone, and his reverie was quickly shattered. The call was from Samuel Pitts, a lawyer inside Westinghouse Electric Corporation, one of the firm's most important clients, and he sounded upset. Pitts only would say that a "delicate and confidential" matter had come up, one so sensitive that it couldn't be discussed over the telephone. He wanted Jentes to fly to Pittsburgh immediately. The next day, the Kirkland & Ellis partner learned that Westinghouse faced one of the gravest threats in its history. Like a nuclear reactor running amok, financial disaster within Westinghouse's nuclear fuel division was threatening to destroy the company.

Four months later, on September 8, 1975, Westinghouse teams of in-house lawyers and utility executives made simultaneous calls on fourteen of the largest United States utilities and representatives of the Kingdom of Sweden, with which Westinghouse had uranium supply contracts and to whom it had promised to deliver 80 million pounds of processed uranium ore. The Westinghouse teams carried a simple but devastating one-page announcement: Westinghouse couldn't deliver. The company was defaulting on its contracts with some of the country's largest utilities and some of its most important customers. Accompanying the announcement was a short opinion letter drafted by Jentes and signed by the law firm of Kirkland & Ellis. Invoking a rarely used section of the Uniform Commercial Code, Kirkland & Ellis stated that Westinghouse's performance of the uranium supply contracts had become "commercially impracticable" and that, as a result, Westinghouse was excused from fulfilling its contractual obligations.

It was a default of unheard-of proportions, an assault on the citadel of contract, the code by which businessmen have conducted their affairs for centuries. Normally cautious utilities executives were successively stunned and outraged. In less than a month, they rejected outright Westinghouse's attempts to renegotiate the uranium deals and began scrambling into courts all over the country. Facing the potential of nearly $2 billion in damages from the lawsuits—an amount which many business commentators predicted would plunge Westinghouse into bankruptcy —Westinghouse placed its fate in the hands of Kirkland & Ellis.

Kirkland & Ellis is one of only a few law firms outside of New York which, lacking proximity to the Wall Street financial community, has nonetheless established itself in the ranks of the elite blue chip firms. It has had impeccable ties to the Chicago establishment since its founding in 1908 by Colonel Robert McCormick, grandson of financier Joseph Medill, owner of the *Chicago Tribune*. As Chicago grew into one of the country's major industrial centers, Kirkland & Ellis cultivated a base of Chicago- and Midwest-based corporate clients to rival the leading New York firms: International Harvester, Firestone, Santa Fe Industries, Motorola, Inland Steel, Marshall Field and, most importantly, Standard Oil of Indiana, whose Chicago skyscraper Kirkland & Ellis today symbolically inhabits. But many of those clients continued to use New York law firms for important financial and corporate transactions (International Harvester, for example, often uses Cravath, Swaine & Moore for such work), and it has been through exploitation of the post–World War II litigation boom that Kirkland & Ellis has secured its position in the first rank of law firms. Under the leadership of senior partner Hammond Chaffetz, who came to the firm after eight years in the Justice Department, the firm's premier specialty became litigation; and Chaffetz and his litigation protégés came to dominate the firm's decision making. Today, more than half of the firm's nearly 290 lawyers are litigators.

Although the firm's prestige and the range of its practice equal those of the other eminent law firms which are the subject of this book—Kirkland & Ellis is, for example, practically the only non–New York law firm which has made significant inroads into the hostile takeover practice—the relative importance of litigation within the firm is one of several distinctions which set it apart from the New York firms like Cravath and Shearman & Sterling. The most important of these are the firm's partner/associate ratio and the way it allocates income.

At Kirkland & Ellis, there are only slightly more associates than partners, making the pyramid staffing pattern common to many New York firms unfeasible. Some manifestations of that structure are subtle. There is a less formal distinction between partners and associates (partner-only restrooms are unheard of here), associates feel more a part of the firm and less like employees, and they are given responsibility more rapidly. Though the structure also lessens competition among associates—most of those associates who are still at the firm after six or seven years will make partner, and the notion of the "passed over" associate is not strictly applicable in Chicago—many associates have already been weeded out earlier in their careers.

More significantly, the firm does not even pay lip service to the notion that all partners are equal. The firm has a formal two-tier partnership in which junior partners receive a salary and a bonus and do not directly share in the firm's profits, which go into a pool reserved for "share" partners, whose income and influence depend on the shares they control. Even share partners may have their participation rearranged by the "proposing" partners, the three or four dominant members of the firm who allocate shares and, hence, income. The struggle for power and influence among partners which exists at all the major firms is much closer to the surface at Kirkland & Ellis, and in the context of the Westinghouse litigation, it eventually spilled out into the open.

One function of the firm's staffing structure and the partner status hierarchy is that associates perceive that chances of being made a partner are closely related to the influence of the partner with whom they establish a mentor relationship. In the absence of any formal assignment mechanism, associates openly politic for assignments with a handful of partners perceived as having the power to ensure their own elevation to the partnership. Bill Jentes has, for a number of years now, been perceived as one of the best partners to work for.

Indeed, Jentes seems to come as close as anyone to being the model Kirkland & Ellis partner. His intellectual reputation is impeccable both within the firm and among other lawyers in Chicago; he is also urbane and sophisticated. Yet he tempers those qualities with a Midwestern charm and lack of pretentiousness. He is the partner most likely to be spotted leading a group of the firm's summer associates to classical music concerts at suburban Chicago's Ravinia Festival, and he is popular among the firm's regular associates. Their only complaint seems to be that he can be intimidating, and sometimes shows an uncharacteristic impatience with muddy thinking. If he lacks any quality customarily associated with Kirkland & Ellis litigators, it is aggressiveness. But there are plenty of others who go for the jugular, and it falls to Jentes to lend an air of respectability to the sometimes bloody remains.

Jentes is also a diplomat, perceived by many as the heir to the mantle of firm leadership handed down by Chaffetz, who was himself Jentes' mentor. Indeed, Jentes now tends some of the clients that were once carefully nurtured by Chaffetz: Standard Oil and Westinghouse. One of Jentes' first assignments at the firm was working with Chaffetz and former U.S. Solicitor General Robert Bork, then a Kirkland & Ellis partner, on the electrical equipment price-fixing cases during the 1950s in which Westinghouse was represented jointly by Cravath and Kirkland. Over the years, Jentes had successfully handled a number of cases for the electric company in Chicago and the Midwest.

Nothing Jentes had done for Westinghouse in the past, however, had quite prepared him for the magnitude of the problem that Pitts and the company's general counsel, William Letson, laid out for him at their first May meeting, nor for the technical complexity. Since the early 1960s, Westinghouse had been among the pioneering companies in the production of nuclear power equipment. Its commercial activities consisted principally of the construction of nuclear power plants incorporating steam turbine generators manufactured by Westinghouse, and the manufacture and sale of nuclear fuel.

Nuclear fuel is the end product of a long process of mining and processing which begins with open-pit and underground mining and extraction of uranium ore. The ore is converted into gas, the percentage of unstable uranium-235 is increased through enrichment, and the enriched uranium is fabricated into nuclear fuel assemblies, usually referred to as "rods." All American enrichment facilities are operated by the United States government because of enriched uranium's potential for use in nuclear weapons. Westinghouse purchased uranium ore on the open market, subcontracted its gasification and enrichment, and then manufactured the nuclear fuel assemblies itself. Westinghouse's customers for both nuclear power plants and the nuclear fuel with which to supply them are principally large utilities interested in using nuclear power to generate electricity.

Nuclear power was a glamour industry during the 1960s, long before the "China Syndrome" and Three Mile Island tarnished its image. Westinghouse was eager to establish itself as the dominant manufacturer of nuclear generating equipment, and its willingness to get into the uranium supply business was in part a reflection of that desire. Westinghouse offered utilities not only the power plant itself, but the fuel to keep it running. The contract it entered into with Virginia Power and Electric Company (VEPCO) was typical. VEPCO had bought four Westinghouse nuclear power plants, with fuel to be supplied by Westinghouse.

In 1972, VEPCO opened up its fuel requirements to competitive bidding and entered into a new agreement with Westinghouse. Their contract called for delivery of processed uranium during the period 1975 through 1980 at prices ranging from $21.09 per kilogram to $22.27 per kilogram, or the equivalent of $7.00 per pound to $7.45 per pound of uranium ore. Prevailing market prices for uranium ore were then slightly less than $7.00 per pound. There was an escalator clause for the years 1978–1980, based in part on the wholesale price index and labor cost increases, designed to protect Westinghouse against inflation. The contract specified that over the contract period, VEPCO would purchase no less than 7.7 million pounds of uranium ore and no more than 11.5 million pounds from Westinghouse.

Though the terms of each individual contract varied, Westinghouse had entered into analogous agreements with thirteen other utilities, including New York's huge Consolidated Edison, South Texas Power, and Florida Power & Light, for a total of 80 billion pounds of uranium at an average contract price ranging from $6.00 per pound to $8.00 per pound. Pitts explained to Jentes that day that Westinghouse had on hand 15 million pounds of uranium ore, which meant that it still had to buy 65 million pounds on the open market to meet its contractual obligations. If the market price of uranium had remained at about $7.00 per pound, Westinghouse would more or less break even on the transactions; if the price dropped somewhat, the company would make money; conversely, if the price rose, Westinghouse would lose. Westinghouse's own market studies suggested that the price wouldn't move much either way. Pitts paused, then announced that the market price of uranium that day had just reached $18.00 per pound and that it was still rising fast. Every dollar it rose meant an additional $65 million loss for Westinghouse.

The Westinghouse lawyers didn't deny that the corporation had entered into extensive contractual relationships with the utilities, though there were some legal questions about their scope and finality. For a solution, Jentes had to depend on the law of contracts.

The law of contracts is one of the great glories of the common law, a subject which absorbs beginning law students during a good part of their first year in law school. But the real era of contract law was the nineteenth century, when one scholar could gush that "All social life presumes it, and rests upon it; for out of contracts, express or implied, declared or understood, grow all rights, all duties, all obligations, and all law." Since that era of unbridled capitalist expansion, contract law has been in eclipse. The promulgation of the Uniform Commercial Code, a codification of the myriad common law principles and decisions dating to medieval England, in 1962 did much to rob the field of its mystery, unpredictability and potential for litigation.

For the large corporate law firm, contract drafting now makes up only a tiny and insignificant aspect of its practice. Most contracts relied upon by major corporations are so routine and established that in-house legal staffs can use standard forms and adapt them to particular transactions. Only the complex and unprecedented agreements are now referred to outside law firms. Even Westinghouse's uranium supply contracts were prepared by the company's own legal staff. Similarly, contract litigation has been in a steep decline. Most contracts now contain arbitration clauses in the event of default, designed to resolve conflicts before they reach a court. But those disputes which do persist into litigation tend to be those with the highest stakes. Though they rarely pose the threat of an antitrust suit or a hostile takeover, some, like Westinghouse's problems with the utilities, pose the threat of economic ruin, and these cases are still embraced by the large corporate firm.

Jentes told the Westinghouse lawyers that he would immediately turn his attention to the matter, and he returned to Chicago. He briefed Hammond Chaffetz, who approved taking on the case and assured him there wouldn't be any conflict of interest problems, since Kirkland & Ellis didn't represent any of the utilities. Utility counsel may be perfectly respectable lawyers and law firms, but they tend not to be in the ranks of the most wealthy and powerful. Because all utilities are subject to the scrutiny of state regulatory commissions—and so are the fees they pay to outside counsel—they cannot be depended upon for lucrative fees and are generally perceived to create more trouble than they are worth in income to the firm. His partners' approval in hand, Jentes organized two teams of lawyers, one to examine the facts surrounding the surprising price increase of uranium, the other to examine the Uniform Commercial Code and related contracts cases for some kind of legal escape.

For assistance in analyzing the uranium industry—something about which he knew very little—Jentes turned to Professor James Lorie, a professor of finance at the University of Chicago's school of business who contributed to the "random walk" theory, which analyzes economic performance as a function of chance. Kirkland & Ellis has strong ties to the University of Chicago—it and Harvard have educated the largest number of its lawyers—and the university's conservative economics faculty has influenced both the law school and many government and business leaders. If not an apologist for corporate bigness, the University of Chicago has nonetheless supplied many economic doctrines that have been invoked in its defense, making it a fertile source for expert economic witnesses needed by the major law firms.

At the end of June, Lorie and a Washington consulting firm gave Jentes a report saying that at the time Westinghouse entered into its uranium supply contracts, there was nothing about the industry or its past price performance to suggest the dramatic increase in uranium prices which started in the fall of 1973. The report contained charts showing that the price of fuel oil and coal also increased dramatically at the same time. Based on published sources, it appeared to Lorie that U.S. government actions curtailing enrichment and protective legislation passed by Australia and Canada had had some effect on uranium prices, but that the principal cause of the increase was the Arab oil embargo.

There wasn't anything in Lorie's report which startled Jentes— the effect of the Arab oil embargo on the price of alternative energy sources was well publicized—but it gave him a factual germ for the legal theory he wanted to develop. One of the Uniform Commercial Code's most controversial provisions is one which provides an escape for sellers who would otherwise be locked into their contracts under common law principles, and Jentes had mentioned it as a possibility at the first meeting with the Westinghouse lawyers. It provided that non-delivery is not a breach if "performance as agreed has been made impracticable by the occurrence of a contingency the non-occurrence of which was a basic assumption on which the contract was made." Jentes' was certainly a creative interpretation of impracticability. There was no support in the official comments explaining the section, which stated that "Increased cost alone does not excuse performance. . . . Neither is a rise or a collapse in the market in itself a justification, for that is exactly the type of business risk which business contracts made at fixed prices are intended to cover." Traditionally, such "impracticable" situations have been war or natural disaster, such as an earthquake or hurricane. Furthermore, the provision had almost never been invoked or upheld in a court decision excusing non-performance. Undaunted, Jentes assigned some associates to scour the case law for some support should Westinghouse invoke the commercial impracticability clause.

Legal research, and the related preparation of a memorandum of law, are among the relatively few tasks mastered during the course of law school, and part of that assignment at Kirkland &

Ellis fell to James Goold, a law student at the University of Chicago who was working as a summer associate for the firm. It was an unusually important and challenging assignment for a summer associate, though one of the ironies of the frenzied competition among the top firms for new lawyers is that summer associates are sometimes wooed with better work than that assigned to older and more experienced first- and second-year full-time associates. The task was, nonetheless, laborious.

Goold went first to an annotated copy of the Uniform Commercial Code, one which collects small excerpts of court decisions which have mentioned or interpreted particular sections and which provides citations to the case report. Case reports are usually contained in the rows of buff-colored volumes which line lawyers' offices, the West reporters, collected and published by West Publishing Company. Each opinion is broken into "key words" with corresponding numbers. Once Goold identified the key phrases and numbers for the few cases provided by the annotated code, he turned to the voluminous West digests, which provide citations to *all* cases which have ever mentioned particular key words or phrases. Those cases are then looked up and read, which may give rise to even more key words and phrases that need to be digested. Eventually Goold found his way to several old English cases which arguably said that a price increase of more than 200 percent would serve as the type of unforeseen disaster justifying excuse from a contractual obligation.

Next, Goold turned from the case reports to another legal service, Shepard's citations. Shepard's works in reverse from the West digest. It provides the citation of every case that ever mentions an earlier case, along with a code identifying how that case was treated in the subsequent opinion. Among those codes, an "o" is the most alarming—it means that a case has been overruled or repudiated entirely by another court. Some of Goold's U.S. cases had been cited in other opinions hundreds of times, and he had to read each case to make sure that they had not been rendered useless through subsequent interpretation. Eventually his task of researching the question of impracticability would take a full year —he barely attended class at the University of Chicago in order to complete the research—and resulted in a 200-page memorandum. But by June, he and the lawyers had a reasonably good sense of the requirements for impracticability: There had to have occurred an unforeseen contingency; it had to have worked a substantial hardship on the seller; and the seller could not have assumed the risk that the contingency would occur.

There was considerable debate inside Kirkland & Ellis about whether the facts surrounding the Westinghouse uranium contracts satisfied those conditions. The price of raw uranium ore had more than tripled, but despite that, Westinghouse may have been making money on some of its older uranium contracts. And Westinghouse wanted a formal opinion from Kirkland & Ellis justifying its failure to perform the contracts, one on which the firm would stake its prestige and reputation and for which it would assume liability.

To give Westinghouse the unqualified opinion it wanted, Jentes thought, was going too far, even for a client as large and important as Westinghouse. Instead he offered a compromise. Kirkland & Ellis would issue a formal opinion that Westinghouse had sound legal grounds for repudiating the contracts, but would say that the firm had not evaluated each contract, so that it couldn't say whether, in individual cases, Westinghouse had assumed the risk of the extraordinary price increase. The letter did not expose Kirkland & Ellis itself to much of a risk. It said that Westinghouse was excused from the contracts—but that maybe it wasn't. As for the assumption of risk question, the utilities might reasonably ask why the firm hadn't examined each of the contracts. Indeed, the firm had examined them, rendering the opinion rather disingenuous. It failed to reach any conclusion but provided a convenient way for the firm to hedge its bets.

The opinion was the best that Westinghouse could get, and Jentes sent it off to the company in early July. As uranium prices continued to soar during the summer, pressures on Westinghouse became severe. The uranium situation was actually threatening to plunge the company into bankruptcy. The Kirkland & Ellis opinion, qualified though it may have been, began to look more and more attractive to Westinghouse as a way out of the mounting disaster. At the least, stopping performance of the contracts based on the Kirkland & Ellis opinion might buy time for renegotiations. In September, the opinion was delivered to the utilities.

If the worsening uranium market made the Kirkland & Ellis opinion more attractive to Westinghouse, it seemed to have the opposite effect on the utility clients. As one general counsel for a major utility recalls, he found the Westinghouse default "almost unbelievable," given its scope; the legal opinion he dismissed as "flimsy—obviously grasping at legal straws." The legal opinion may even have been a tactical error. Expected by Westinghouse to be interpreted by the utilities as an indication of how serious Westinghouse's plight had become, it was instead greeted as an audacious attempt by Westinghouse to wriggle out of the contracts rather than admit its own errors and ask the utilities to help restructure the deal. Jentes, however, doubts that the utilities would ever have expressed a conciliatory attitude. "They were not the least bit statesmanlike. They acted like we were repudiating the Bible." One by one, the utilities marched into courts across the country, all filing lawsuits against Westinghouse.

Less than a month after the repudiation meetings and delivery of the Kirkland & Ellis opinion, Jentes received another frantic phone call from Westinghouse. This time it was Raymond Scannell, Westinghouse's inside counsel who supervises litigation, a cautious, solid and normally unflappable lawyer. On this occasion, Scannell was plainly upset. Every day the utilities suits were rolling in from courts around the country. Worse, each of the utilities was asking for a fast preliminary injunction that would prevent Westinghouse from allocating or disposing of the 15 million pounds of uranium ore that it did have. Each utility wanted all of it. How could Kirkland & Ellis help?

The utility lawsuits may not have been expected by the lawyers inside Westinghouse, but they hardly came as a surprise to a seasoned litigator like Jentes. He had considered the possibility that Westinghouse would be faced with simultaneous lawsuits in different jurisdictions, and he had some suggestions for Scannell. Administratively, he urged that Kirkland & Ellis act as lead counsel for all the suits, assigning day-to-day responsibility for them to local law firms located in the cities where the suits had been filed. The major corporate law firms often rely on "local" counsel when handling far-flung cases and deals, and each of the major firms has a network of smaller law firms around the country appreciative of—and in some cases dependent on—the local work sent their way by the big firms. Jentes would coordinate and direct the litigation from Chicago, flying in to various cities when major developments made his presence necessary.

Jentes had also hatched a novel application of an old legal theory with which to bring the various preliminary injunction suits to a halt before some court ordered Westinghouse to turn over all of its uranium to a single utility, thereby losing its last bargaining chip. That theory was interpleader, a device ordinarily used by a defendant in a lawsuit to bring in a third party who, the defendant claims, is really the one who has the dispute with the plaintiff. For example, a plaintiff may sue a bank for money held on account for someone else. The bank might interplead the person in whose name the account is held, saying, in effect, "Yes, the bank has this money, but the two of you must fight it out to decide who gets it." Jentes reasoned that Westinghouse's situation was somewhat analogous to that of the bank. It had the uranium—let the utilities fight among themselves to see who should be allowed to have it. He was also admittedly stretching the theory, for what was there for the utilities to fight with each other about? Their disputes were with Westinghouse, not each other. Westinghouse was not simply the safekeeper of a cache of uranium, like money in a bank.

The next Friday, Jentes rushed to Pittsburgh looking for the Federal Court's chief judge with whom to file his action for an interpleader. (He had to file the suit in Pittsburgh, the location of Westinghouse's headquarters and, in a technical legal sense, the location of the uranium, even though the uranium was actually in the course of being processed elsewhere.) Jentes reached the courthouse around noon, only to learn that Judge Herbert Sorg, the senior judge, was out fishing, planning to stay the night at a motel in the Appalachian foothills south of Pittsburgh. Jentes sent an associate to the telephone to call the motel and warn the judge that he was coming, then drove a rented car over twisting and hilly roads to reach the judge, who, still dressed in his boots and fishing gear, met the lawyers in the motel reception area.

Though discussions between a judge and lawyers for only one side of a case are frowned upon, they are often necessary in the context of a preliminary injunction, and Jentes hastily explained Westinghouse's predicament and the proliferation of suits around the country. Sorg said he understood the gist of their interpleader action and the need to halt the other suits, and told Jentes to draw up the necessary papers for him to sign and to appear before him in court on Monday morning. While the judge returned to his fishing lures, Jentes and two associates raced back to Pittsburgh, where they spent the remainder of the weekend drafting the inter-pleader complaint and the injunctions to halt the other suits. On Monday morning, Sorg signed the papers.

Westinghouse got a much-needed reprieve, but the injunctions brought howls of protest from lawyers for the utilities. Later that week, Sorg scheduled several days of hearings on the injunctions to give the utilities a chance to reply and comment, and they were vehement in their denunciation of the interpleader gambit. Jentes was trying to rebut some of their arguments in the crowded court-room when Roger Wilson, the Kirkland & Ellis associate at his side, tugged at his elbow. Irritated, Jentes whispered to the asso-ciate not to interrupt him, but Wilson shoved a telegram into his hand. Jentes read it hastily, and was surprised to learn that acting on a request by the Tennessee Valley Authority, one of the most aggressive of Westinghouse's utility customers, a federal judge in the Western District of Tennessee had issued a temporary restrain-ing order to halt the interpleader proceeding then taking place in Pittsburgh. It is a measure of Jentes' scrupulous adherence to procedural requirements that he immediately halted his presenta-tion in mid-sentence. He read the telegram out loud to the as-sembled lawyers and the judge, then sat down.

Judge Sorg went back into his chambers, taking some of the lawyers along with him, and called Judge Robert Taylor in the Western District of Tennessee. "Judge," he said, "I've got all of these lawyers here on my hands. Now what am I supposed to do with them?" Sorg and Taylor finally agreed that the Pittsburgh proceeding could continue as long as no action was taken that might affect the rights of the Tennessee Valley Authority. But as the hearing went on, Sorg himself seemed more and more con-fused about the appropriateness of Jentes' interpleader suit. Jentes and his associates would finish a draft of a proposed order, and then Sorg would change his mind about signing it after hearing more protests by the utilities. Finally he said that he thought the matter should be taken up by the multidistrict judicial panel. Since he realized that Westinghouse was concerned about the prelimi-nary injunction suits brought by the utilities, he made the utility lawyers promise on the record that they would take no further steps to pursue those claims until the multidistrict panel had been given a chance to determine how best the cases should proceed and whether they should be consolidated into a single proceeding.

But he refused to sign the injunction orders stopping the suits that Westinghouse had wanted.

Jentes wasn't at all confident that the promises of the utilities' lawyers would hold up. It usually took a long time for the multi-district panel to get around to consolidating cases, and greed for uranium might easily overtake a reluctant promise demanded by a faraway Pittsburgh federal judge. So Jentes and other Kirkland & Ellis lawyers flew to Tennessee, to South Carolina, to Virginia, to Houston, to Kansas City, appearing before each of the judges presiding in the utilities' suits and persuading them to hold off until the multidistrict panel had a chance to consider the issue. Still, Jentes was not certain he had succeeded in heading off all the suits. Some of the federal judges reigned like monarchs in their isolated federal judicial districts, and they might be fickle in the face of demands from powerful local utility interests. Jentes believed his only sure way of stopping them was to get the judicial panel to meet on the uranium cases almost immediately and take the cases away from them.

While he was in Columbia, South Carolina, appearing before Judge Robert Chapman, the presiding federal judge in the South Carolina Electric and Gas suit, it occurred to Jentes to call Judge Edwin Robson, a Chicago Federal District Court judge and a member of the judicial panel who happened to be in Asheville, North Carolina, for a judges' seminar. Robson was an old friend of Jentes' from Chicago who might be able to help expedite the panel's consideration of the consolidation request.

When Jentes reached Robson by telephone, the judge told him to come up to Asheville to talk over the situation. Jentes and a lawyer from Westinghouse jumped into another rented car, this time driving for two and a half hours over the rugged mountains of western North Carolina. When they asked Robson to help arrange an immediate meeting of the multidistrict panel, he assured them he wouldn't have any trouble helping them. He got on the telephone. "John, I'd like you to arrange a little special meeting," he drawled into the phone to Judge John Minor Wisdom, who responded with an invitation to come "right on down to New Orleans," the site of the Fifth Circuit Court of Appeals, where Wisdom is the senior judge. Within two days, the same cast of lawyers that had gathered only a week before in Pittsburgh found themselves in Wisdom's court in New Orleans, the utilities' lawyers visibly baffled by the speed with which the multidistrict panel was taking up their cause.

Multidistrict litigation, which came about because national corporations who do business throughout the country can find themselves sued simultaneously in a variety of jurisdictions, is a phenomenon of the last few decades. It is used most commonly in defective products cases, like the tetracycline litigation, involving most of the large drug manufacturers, or in antitrust cases with a large class of plaintiffs. Though there are often multiple plaintiffs and defendants in such cases, the goal of the multidistrict panel is the same: to determine whether the various suits are so similar that they can be tried in a single proceeding and, if so, to assign the collected cases to a single judge. Though Westinghouse was the sole defendant in the uranium suits, the fact that there were competing lawsuits for the cache of uranium—and the likely chaos that might result from different courts rushing to be the first to enter judgment and award all of it to one utility—made Westinghouse a likely candidate for multidistrict treatment. Though the utilities' lawyers made some halfhearted arguments that the suits among them were sufficiently different—based on different contracts with substantially different terms that would have to be construed by the courts—Judge Wisdom granted Westinghouse's request for consolidation and assigned all the pending cases in federal district courts to Judge Robert Merhige, Jr., in Richmond, the site of VEPCO's suit.

Wisdom's decision left Jentes with only one major and immediate problem on his hands. Because the utilities resided in states other than Pennsylvania, almost all of the cases had been filed in federal district courts, rather than state courts, and Westinghouse was a Pennsylvania corporation. That meant that there was diversity of jurisdiction between Westinghouse and the utilities that allowed the cases to be tried in a federal court. Even if the utilities had first sued Westinghouse in a state court, Westinghouse would have had the right to remove the case to a federal court, wasting the utilities' time in the process. The existence of diversity of jurisdiction—based on the underlying notion that the courts of one state might be hostile toward the claims of litigants from foreign states—is another anachronistic vestige of federalism which pervades the court system. But in one case—Duquesne Light Co., the large Pittsburgh-based utility—there was no diversity of jurisdiction. Duquesne had gone first to the Pennsylvania Court of Common Pleas in Pittsburgh; and Westinghouse, with its headquarters just down the street from the courthouse, was powerless to move the case elsewhere. And since it was a state court plaintiff, Federal Judge Wisdom's order consolidating all of the other federal cases in Richmond had no effect on Duquesne.

Duquesne's lawyer, Harold Schmidt of the smaller Pittsburgh firm, Rose, Schmidt, Dixon & Hasley, knew that the Kirkland & Ellis and Westinghouse lawyers had their hands full trying to stave off the attacks from all the other utilities, so he pushed his own suit for an injunction in the Pennsylvania court as hard as possible. Each time Schmidt got before the presiding judge, I. Martin Wekselman, with Jentes or another Kirkland & Ellis lawyer present, he would loudly insist, "We're ready to go to trial," even when it was obvious that he couldn't possibly be adequately prepared.

By Christmas Eve 1975, Jentes and Schmidt had reached the end of the hearings Wekselman had scheduled to hear arguments and evidence that related to Schmidt's request for an injunction turning the uranium over to Duquesne. Much to Jentes' relief, Wekselman seemed as if he were leaning toward *not* granting Schmidt's request—not so much because of the legal arguments put before him, but because Jentes had, if nothing else, convinced the judge that the whole situation was a mess and that if he granted an injunction it might only make matters worse. Wekselman told Jentes and Schmidt that he didn't want to be forced into making a decision himself; he wanted the two companies to reach some kind of settlement and to find a way of apportioning the uranium among the squabbling utilities. Schmidt was annoyed that his first strike for the uranium was being delayed, but he had little choice but to sit down to bargain with Jentes.

By the time the lawyers for Westinghouse and the utilities gathered for their first meeting before Judge Merhige in Richmond, the negotiations with Duquesne had made little progress. The basic problem was still that Westinghouse had only 15 million pounds of uranium and the utilities wanted 80 million pounds, and Duquesne was not willing to take only the fractional share that would have been the result of an equal division among the utilities.

In contrast to Judge David Edelstein in New York, the judge

who presided over IBM, Merhige is one of the most respected federal judges in the country, an activist who moves cases in and out of his court like a drillmaster and who, if he is criticized at all, is faulted for too readily exercising the considerable power of his judgeship. His is best known for his handling of the Richmond desegregation cases in the early 1970s. Appearing before Merhige, Jentes shrewdly focused on the negotiations that were proceeding with Duquesne, emphasizing not Westinghouse's default on the contracts but the necessity of finding a way to carve up the stockpile of uranium. That issue, even though it wouldn't dispose of the entire case, would at least force all of the parties to the bargaining table; and Merhige rapidly made clear that that was where he thought the lawyers and their clients ought to be. He ordered all of the lawyers to come up with an agreement for allocating Westinghouse's uranium, and he emphasized that while they were at it, they should be settling their other disagreements as well. Merhige was not anxious to plunge Westinghouse into bankruptcy; he did not think that the size and nature of the disputes between the parties was the kind of thing that could best be resolved by the all-or-nothing approach of litigation.

To handle the negotiations, Jentes and Westinghouse hired John Battle, Jr., a courtly Richmond lawyer and senior partner in one of Richmond's two leading law firms, McGuire, Woods & Battle. (The other major Richmond firm, old-line Hunton & Williams, was representing Virginia Electric & Power Co.) McGuire, Woods is typical of the leading regional firms relied upon by the national blue chip firms. Many of their lawyers have attended the same prestigious law schools and know partners in the national firms; they often represent national corporations when they have legal needs in the regions in which they are located; and, most importantly, their partners often know intimately the local judges and their idiosyncrasies. Battle and Merhige are old friends.

Jentes describes Battle as a "smooth southern gentleman"; and though Jentes is fairly smooth himself, he felt that it would be easier for the utilities to face McGuire, Woods at the negotiating table, since neither was the firm directly associated with the offending default letter, nor was it so closely linked to Westinghouse. Not even Battle, however, could make a dent in the ranks of the utilities. Evidently afraid that one utility might get a better deal than another, mindful of the potential wrath of watch-dog public utilities commissions, each utility took the hardest possible line. According to Jentes, they took the position that "We're going to crucify Westinghouse."

After hearing reports that the negotiations were deadlocked, Merhige reluctantly ordered discovery in the massive cases to get under way. Westinghouse's impracticability defense had thrown the entire nuclear industry open for investigation, since the evidence at trial would have to answer the fundamental question of why there had been such a sudden and drastic increase in the price of uranium. The utilities began to prepare long lists of Westinghouse executives to be deposed, and Jentes and the Kirkland & Ellis lawyers had an even longer list of utilities executives and uranium producers that they wanted to question. Even working with large teams of lawyers full-time, the discovery depositions— not to mention the massive production and review of documents that would go along with them—would take months. Kirkland & Ellis assigned four partners and six associates to the case full-time; in addition to McGuire, Woods & Battle, it hired local law firms in Miami (Floyd Pearson Stewart Richman Greer & Weil); in New York City (Donovan Leisure Newton & Irvine); in Houston (Vinson & Elkins); in Hartford, St. Louis, Kansas City and Birmingham. In late May, nearly one hundred lawyers gathered at the Kirkland & Ellis offices in Chicago for the first of a series of seminars on uranium and the nuclear industry. They heard physicists, economists, Westinghouse executives and Kirkland & Ellis lawyers deliver a crash course on the complexities of the nuclear power industry.

Meanwhile, another contingent of Kirkland & Ellis lawyers was assigned to shore up the legal positions. When he had been a student at the University of Chicago, Goold, who had now come to work full-time, had taken a class in contracts with Professor Soia Mentschikoff. Mentschikoff was the widow of Karl Llewellyn, the man who had actually drafted the Uniform Commercial Code which formed the basis for Westinghouse's defense, and Mentschikoff had worked closely with him on the project. Goold hired her as a consultant on the case, and together they began to sift through Llewellyn's files for more clues about the meaning of the impracticability provision.

Eventually they found a bundle of handwritten notes, some of them nearly tattered beyond legibility, and after piecing them together, they derived some small encouragement for the position that a price increase, if it was the result of some unforeseeable event directly related to performance of the contract, might excuse performance. Though Mentschikoff left Chicago shortly afterward to become dean of the University of Miami School of Law, Goold commuted regularly to Florida, keeping Mentschikoff informed of developments in the case and developing with her an outline of testimony she might eventually present in court as an expert witness on the meaning of the Uniform Commercial Code.

If the impracticability section of the code had remained something of an academic mystery, it was nonetheless minor compared to the curious circumstances surrounding the rise of the world price for uranium. That summer, while discovery efforts proceeded, Jentes and his partners were able, for the first time, to return their attention to the merits of the case. The more they studied the analyses of their own economists, as well as additional studies and press reports on conditions in the uranium industry, the more baffling the price rise seemed. And the price continued to march upward, approaching $40 per pound by the fall of 1976. Even taking into consideration the Arab oil embargo and its impact on the price of alternative fuels, the uranium increase was extraordinary.

Late that October, Jentes was walking into the Westinghouse nuclear center in Monroeville, Pennsylvania, with a Westinghouse in-house lawyer when they bumped into L. M. "Mike" Meierkord, a Westinghouse engineer who had been given the assignment of trying to meet Westinghouse's uranium needs through new technology and exploration. Meierkord was familiar with the case, having talked frequently to Jentes about some of the technical aspects of uranium mining and production of nuclear fuel. He mentioned in passing that he had just returned from a trip to Canada, where he was investigating some potential sites for test mining. A Canadian consultant employed by Westinghouse had been talking about some uranium meetings around the world, Meierkord said, where the uranium producers had discussed price, supply and related topics, and he thought that perhaps Westinghouse should get in on the meetings, or at least find out what was being said. Jentes nearly dropped his briefcase. What was this about price and supply? And these meetings in exotic locations

like Johannesburg, Paris, Rio? It all sounded like a script for a
secret price-fixing conspiracy. Did Meierkord think that the consultant might talk some more—to a Kirkland & Ellis lawyer?
Meierkord said he'd see what he could arrange.

The possibility that the uranium price rise might have been
caused by some kind of cartel arrangement had already occurred
to both Jentes and Westinghouse executives, especially given the
attention that had been given to OPEC's price-setting activities. In
fact, Westinghouse executives had undertaken a study to determine if any kind of a price conspiracy was at work in the uranium
industry. They were aware from press reports that occasional
meetings of the world's major uranium producers were taking
place from time to time, but their own investigation of uranium
price bids submitted to utilities showed a pattern of differing price
levels and no sign of fixed prices or price leadership. In 1972, a
spokesman for the French Atomic Energy Commission had dismissed a suggestion that the producers might be attempting to
control prices as "completely false and absurd"; a Uranex executive commented in *Nucleonics Week* that the uranium "industry is
too liberal-minded" to ever engage in price fixing. Westinghouse
had dismissed the notion of price fixing as unfounded rumor. In
any event, though price fixing is a criminal offense in the United
States and forms the backbone of its antitrust laws, it is not illegal
in most countries.

Several days later Meierkord called Jentes and said that William Gilchrist, the Canadian uranium consultant and former head
of Eldorado Nuclear, seemed willing to talk, although he had not
been told anything about the utilities' suits or Kirkland & Ellis'
role in them. Jentes immediately called another of his partners,
George Newton, Jr., and asked him to fly to Toronto immediately
before Gilchrist had a chance to change his mind. When Newton
met him at his hotel room the next day, Gilchrist was initially ret-
icent. But as he talked about his career as a uranium miner in
western Canada and his rise to the top of Eldorado Nuclear, a
Canadian Crown company, it became evident that his reticence
was simply a result of a Westerner's ingrained suspicion of outsiders, and not of any awareness that he was revealing potentially
explosive information. Newton acted blasé, occasionally jotting
down notes in an almost offhand fashion, as Gilchrist gradually
gave details of a long series of meetings beginning in 1972 that, he

said, had stabilized the uranium market and prevented the price from falling. He urged Newton to look into the matter more, since he hadn't actually attended these meetings himself. If anything, he was proud of the way the uranium companies had saved the industry from being ruined by excessive competition.

An astounded Newton hurried back to Chicago, where he reported to Jentes. They again examined Westinghouse's files and other published information on meetings of uranium producers, and found that they fit neatly into the pattern of price escalation in the uranium industry. Their suspicions were heightened by reports that the U.S. Department of Justice was investigating a variety of commodities producers, which they now strongly suspected included uranium. Jentes flew to Washington to meet with Joel Davidow, the Justice Department lawyer handling the investigation, but Davidow refused to provide any information about the government investigation. But Jentes' suspicions were reinforced, and he got the impression that the State Department was hampering Justice's efforts. Meanwhile, Newton made several more trips to Toronto to meet with Gilchrist and others in the mining industry, and by the spring of 1976 they were convinced that they had come upon the existence of a world uranium cartel.

Having found the information, Kirkland & Ellis lawyers faced the problem of what to do with it. Clearly, the existence of a price-fixing cartel could form part of Westinghouse's impracticability defense in the utility cases in Richmond—although its legal impact in that proceeding wasn't so obvious. The principal legal issue in Richmond was whether Westinghouse could have foreseen the price increase and whether it had assumed the risk of a price increase—*not* explicitly whether the means used to increase the price was a legal one. After the OPEC example, shouldn't Westinghouse have anticipated the possibility of a cartel in other markets? Though undoubtedly information about the cartel would make Westinghouse's plight more sympathetic, it wasn't clear to Jentes and his partners that it would resolve the liability issue in Westinghouse's favor. What they needed was a legal mechanism to make the uranium producers directly responsible for their collusion.

To consider the problem, Jentes called Chaffetz and another litigation partner, Fred Bartlit, Jr. Though only 43 years old at the time, Bartlit was already becoming the subject of legend in the firm. A former captain in the Green Berets, Bartlit had success-fully transferred his indefatigable energy, endurance and ruthless desire for victory to the arena of corporate litigation, substituting his elegantly tailored suits for military garb. More than any other Kirkland partner, he has created the firm's present reputation for aggressive litigation, and together with Cravath's Thomas Barr, he is credited as a co-founder of the litigation-as-war school of law-yers. Bartlit's ambitions had inevitably spilled over into intrafirm politics, and after establishing himself as a loyal Chaffetz protégé and as a partner indispensable to such regular firm clients as Standard Oil and General Motors, he became one of the youngest permanent members of the firm's all-powerful fifteen-partner man-agement committee. Associates who earned his favor found their partnerships virtually guaranteed; those who failed—and Bartlit tended to make early and inalterable judgments—started looking for employment elsewhere.

For a variety of reasons, firms such as Kirkland & Ellis have always tended to defend rather than prosecute major lawsuits. The principal reason is that their clients are so large and powerful that they are understandably the target of lawsuits by smaller and less successful competitors, and they have the economic clout to re-solve their own complaints through negotiation and pressure. In the area of antitrust, their clients are the only companies large enough arguably to have monopolized an entire market. Further-more, initiating a lawsuit has never found favor in genteel society; it is contentious, it is public, and among old-line members of the blue chip bar it is avoided whenever possible. Bartlit is among a group of younger partners in major firms credited with overturning that taboo.

At the meeting of top Kirkland & Ellis partners to consider what to do about the uranium cartel, it was Bartlit who first suggested that Westinghouse sue. The only other possibility seemed to be to drag the uranium producers into the Richmond cases. But with the thirteen utility plaintiffs, that suit was already almost unmanageably complicated. Furthermore, although West-inghouse felt wronged by the uranium conspirators, it was hard to argue that the utilities should be suing the uranium suppliers rather than Westinghouse. It was, after all, a contracts case, and the contracts at issue were between Westinghouse and the utilities—not the utilities and the uranium producers. Bartlit argued persuasively that a direct price-fixing suit against the uranium producers offered the potential for treble damages—something that might more than offset any damages Westinghouse would eventually sustain in the utilities cases—as well as focus public attention on the uranium cartel rather than Westinghouse's contract default. Bartlit was also available to head up the massive worldwide litigation necessary to prosecute the case.

Galvanized by the possibility of taking the offensive, Jentes and Bartlit traveled to Pittsburgh for the first of a series of meetings with Westinghouse lawyers and eventually the chairman, Robert Kirby, and the other board members. Their proposal for a lawsuit against the members of the uranium cartel was not enthusiastically received. Westinghouse had already suffered the shock of going to court with fourteen of its most important utilities customers; it was hardly eager to alienate another major group of companies with which it did business. And the lawsuit seemed full of pitfalls. The members of the cartel all appeared to be foreign companies, some of them controlled by foreign governments. There were major questions about the extent to which United States law could even reach such defendants. And as a company that did business abroad, Westinghouse did not wish to antagonize foreign governments. Bartlit was the first to admit that within the corporate world such a lawsuit was tantamount to a declaration of war. The Westinghouse board rejected Kirkland & Ellis' recommendation and told their lawyers that the company would not sue. Besides the practical difficulties, Kirby explained that he and the board members were still not convinced that a cartel actually existed. Jentes and his colleagues were disappointed, and they were beginning to have doubts themselves.

Questions about the cartel, however, were still going to arise in the utility cases, and during the summer, investigations by Bartlit and his colleagues, document discovery and depositions continued at a rapid pace. Responsibility for gathering evidence about the cartel was given to Samuel Haubold, a junior partner who worked closely with Jentes. High on Haubold's agenda was a visit to the Atomic Industrial Forum in Washington, D.C., a trade organization of which Westinghouse was a prominent member, where the forum's mining and milling committee included representatives of most of the world's major uranium producers.

Haubold had first visited the AIF and its nuclear fuel cycle projects manager, Emanuel Gordon, in March. While Gordon was at lunch, he had let Haubold sift through his files, and Haubold had come upon a number of documents describing the participants at meetings of uranium producers, including some describing a meeting of major producers in Oak Brook, Illinois, a Chicago suburb, in 1973. Three weeks after that meeting, uranium prices had rocketed upward. Later, Haubold returned and took Gordon's deposition. That time Gordon had a lawyer present, an in-house counsel from AIF, who quickly became bored and left the deposition after ten minutes. Gordon obligingly provided all the names of representatives of the uranium companies who attended the meetings, including some from Gulf Oil. Now Haubold had a glimmer that the cartel might not be restricted to foreign producers.

Haubold's luck with the cooperative and unsuspecting Gordon, however, was not to be repeated in the other depositions Kirkland & Ellis took of uranium company executives around the country that summer. Shortly after his trip to Washington, word spread within the atomic energy field that Westinghouse lawyers were asking some pointed questions about the possible existence of a uranium cartel. The flow of information to Westinghouse abruptly stopped, and those executives being deposed were now surrounded by lawyers alert to the gist of the questions. Although uranium company executives were superficially friendly and courteous, Westinghouse discovered that its efforts to procure uranium on the world market had taken an even more menacing twist. The price had already gone above the $40 per pound level, when the producers suddenly stopped quoting any price when Westinghouse asked. Westinghouse found that it couldn't buy at any price.

Later that summer, Jentes received another call from Scannell, the lawyer inside Westinghouse, relaying some information he had received from Westinghouse local counsel in Australia, where some interesting information had turned up in a political dispute which was then raging over some uranium mining activities in Australia's barren Northern Territories. An Australian company called Mary Kathleen Mining—a wholly owned subsidiary of Rio Tinto Zinc, the vast British mining conglomerate, and one of Westinghouse's principal uranium suppliers—was strip mining uranium in an area believed sacred and worshipped by aborigines. An activist Australian ecological group called the Friends of the

Earth had taken up the aborigines' cause, and one of the group's members had infiltrated Mary Kathleen and managed to procure a sheaf of documents exposing some embarrassing political ties between the mining concern and the Australian government. This had become the center of a minor political scandal which was picked up in the Australian press.

The Australian Westinghouse lawyer had called, Scannell explained, because one of the press reports mentioned, almost inadvertently, that among the documents seized by the Friends of the Earth were some minutes of a meeting of a uranium cartel. Jentes was electrified. This could be the first hard documentary evidence of the cartel. He immediately called Haubold into his office, and told him to clear his schedule and head for Australia.

Two days later, counting one day lost crossing the international date line, Haubold arrived in Sydney, where a message was waiting for him from his partner, George Newton, Jr. Newton had already managed to get copies of the Friends of the Earth documents himself, and was sending copies to Haubold by air delivery. It turned out that soon after the Australian news report appeared, the Friends of the Earth had sent copies of their documents to a group of California ecologists organized by Ralph Nader, whom Newton knew from having worked opposite them in a suit brought against General Motors for auto emission air pollution. Though they had been adversaries, they got along well with Newton, and they agreed to send him their copies.

Once Haubold received the documents, he made appointments to see some of the Friends of the Earth representatives in Australia. But it turned out that the Friends of the Earth there were no friend of Westinghouse, a company they regarded as anathema to their own interests, and they refused to provide additional information or release any other material out of the files they had obtained from Mary Kathleen. Frustrated on that front, Haubold tried to interview some of the Mary Kathleen executives mentioned in the documents.

Haubold made something of a breakthrough with John Proud, the elderly, hard-bitten former miner who had founded Mary Kathleen. Proud was openly hostile—his stocky male secretary took down every word of the conversation—but his anger at Westinghouse seemed to make him more garrulous. Westinghouse, he insisted, was becoming too strong a purchaser of uranium, driving down prices by selling it cheaply to utilities, and "had to be taught a lesson." He ranted and raved, freely admitting that Mary Kathleen had entered a price conspiracy and a boycott against Westinghouse. Haubold recalls that "I finally knew this case was solid."

Westinghouse, however, remained unconvinced, going so far as to call a halt to Haubold's one-man investigation Down Under, a move which left Haubold frustrated. Nor were the utilities impressed or more sympathetic to Westinghouse's situation. The Nader group in California had also sent copies of the Friends of the Earth documents to Congressman John Moss, whose oversight committee made the information available to the public. The utilities, who had a long course of dealing with the uranium producers to reinforce their opinion, dismissed the allegations of a cartel as preposterous and urged that the disclosures have no impact on their own pending suit against Westinghouse.

Although Scannell and the Westinghouse executives were concerned that the Kirkland & Ellis lawyers were too caught up in what they viewed as a secondary concern, Jentes continued to look for more cartel evidence. The Friends of the Earth material gave him a solid base from which to proceed. And as he and the other lawyers began to sift through documents obtained from uranium producers in the utilities litigation, copies of some of the same documents began surfacing in the files of other companies, which gave them solid corroboration. But to convince Westinghouse to go forward with the suit, they had to find some link to the U.S. market and evidence that a U.S. company was involved.

Haubold finally stumbled upon it. In reviewing his notes from the Atomic Industrial Forum, he found the name of L. T. Gregg, a Gulf executive who was now no longer with the company. Haubold tracked him down in Atlanta, and flew there to interview him. Gregg was wary, but it was clear that he knew a great deal. Eventually, he gave Haubold the crucial information he needed: Gulf had indeed been a participant in the cartel; in fact, although none of the documents listed it as a participant, Gregg himself had represented Gulf at the formation of the cartel at a meeting in Johannesburg, South Africa, in 1972. A topic of that meeting had been the elimination of Westinghouse as a uranium middleman and competitive force in the uranium market. The Kirkland & Ellis lawyers still weren't sure of the scope of the conspiracy, but they were beginning to assemble a fairly lurid story of secret meetings around the globe, complete with bills for flowers and in one case, "two lovely ladies for the evening."

After Haubold's interview with Gregg, Jentes and Bartlit went back to Kirby and the Westinghouse executives. What seemed to make the difference this time were the continued unavailability of uranium, the evidence that Westinghouse had been singled out as a target of the conspiracy, and the tantalizing evidence that Gulf, a U.S.-based corporation, was actively involved. They may also have concluded that the situation could hardly get any worse. In late September, the Westinghouse board authorized Kirkland & Ellis to go forward with a suit against the members of the uranium cartel. On October 15, Kirkland & Ellis filed its complaint and supporting documents in Federal District Court in Chicago, charging twenty-eight uranium producers with price fixing and claiming $1 billion in damages. Fred Bartlit was designated lead counsel.

Under Jentes' leadership, the lawyers now began to use the ongoing discovery in the Richmond cases to gather evidence that might also be valuable in the Chicago case against the uranium producers. The lawyers had already discovered how difficult it was going to be to pry testimony and documents out of the foreign producers. Earlier, Kirkland & Ellis had prepared a subpoena directed to the Anglo-American Corporation, the vast South African conglomerate which controls, among other entities, De Beers Consolidated Mines. A messenger had delivered the subpoena to Johannesburg, serving it on one of the company's executives. The lawyers had never received an official reply to the demand for information, but later learned the fate of the subpoena. Haubold received a hand-addressed envelope from South Africa, and when he opened it, the tattered shreds of the subpoena fluttered out. Accompanying the remains was a handwritten note: "I found this document torn up. It looked important, so I mailed it to the address provided." Further efforts to obtain information from South Africa were abandoned. Nor was Australia much more forthcoming. Subpoenas directed to the Australian mining companies had been closely followed by a special act of the Australian parliament barring the production of any uranium documents outside the country, a blatant example of special protective legislation.

To overcome the problem of noncompliance with their discovery requests, Jentes went to Judge Merhige and asked for the issuance of letters rogatory. Letters rogatory were used in ancient Rome, but in their modern context the procedure stems from an international agreement signed at The Hague. A request for letters rogatory is made by a U.S. district court and is directed to a foreign sovereign. If the foreign sovereign issues the letters, a foreign citizen is compelled to give testimony as if he were within the jurisdiction of a U.S. federal court. Under the Hague Convention, signatory nations agree to facilitate discovery in foreign lawsuits in return for exercising the same privilege when foreign testimony is needed in suits arising in their own courts. Although the utilities opposed Jentes' request for foreign testimony, again taking the position that Westinghouse's problems with the uranium producers were irrelevant to the issues in the contract litigation, Merhige granted Jentes' request, and issued formal requests for the letters directed to Great Britain and Canada.

Though the Hague Convention supposedly makes issuance of the requested letters rogatory almost automatic, the practice is much more complicated, particularly when the defendants are foreign companies with the size and political clout of Anglo-American or Rio Tinto. In Canada, the question of whether the letters should be issued was referred to a Canadian judge who had previously been an inside lawyer for one of the Canadian uranium companies. Not surprisingly, he refused to act and Kirkland & Ellis' pleas fell on deaf ears both in his court and within the government of Pierre Trudeau, which had made American antitrust intrusion into Canada a political issue.

In Britain the Kirkland & Ellis lawyers found themselves rapidly plunged into the intricacies of the English legal system. Requests for letters rogatory are formally addressed to the Queen, who has delegated the responsibility for issuing them to a functionary called the Master of the Queen's Remembrances, who occupies a library-like chamber high in a medieval tower in the Courts of London. Master Jacob, the Queen's designee currently occupying the position, was beset by a massive protest by Rio Tinto against issuing the letters.

Kirkland & Ellis immediately sent a team of lawyers to London, including Jentes, Haubold and Goold, and they also hired Freshfields, a firm of English solicitors, and a barrister to represent Westinghouse in the English courts. In a week-long hearing, Rio Tinto raised every obstacle it could conceive to prevent issuing the letters, though they all boiled down to the mining company's complaint that the letters represented only an American attempt to harass the company with a fishing expedition launched to support a flimsy case. At the end of the week, Master Jacob ruled in favor of Westinghouse, and Rio Tinto took an immediate appeal to the Queen's Bench. There, too, after a two-week trial, the presiding justice ruled in favor of Westinghouse.

For its next appeal, to Lord Denning, Master of the Rolls, presiding over the Court of Appeals, Rio Tinto broadened its claims to embrace English public policy, which, it argued, should not enforce United States antitrust laws against a British industry that was already beleaguered by foreign competition. Lord Denning responded in kind, with a lengthy opinion drawing upon the Treaty of Rome, English common law, the developing law of the European Economic Community, and international comity. But he, too, agreed that the letters rogatory should issue. Rio Tinto then announced that it was taking the matter before the House of Lords, which acts as England's court of last resort and, much like the U.S. Supreme Court, has the final say in matters of constitutional significance, which the uranium case was now becoming. But pending that final appeal, the letters were issued.

The week following the issuance of the letters rogatory, Jentes and his colleagues began taking depositions of the Rio Tinto executives at the American Embassy in London. The first witness was the chairman of Rio Tinto, Baron Arthur Edward, Lord Schackleton. Much to Jentes' surprise, the English barrister representing Rio Tinto had been replaced by a criminal lawyer from New York named Robert Kasanof. The reason for his presence quickly became clear. When Jentes asked the first question that went beyond the witness's name and position, Lord Schackleton invoked the Fifth Amendment to the United States Constitution, the right against self-incrimination, and refused to answer. Every Rio Tinto witness subsequently called to testify adopted the same strategy.

Jentes threw up his hands. After discussions with his English lawyers and lawyers for Rio Tinto, he concluded that an American court would have to rule on Rio Tinto's Fifth Amendment claims, so Jentes called Judge Merhige, who agreed to come promptly to London to hear testimony and resolve the Fifth Amendment issue, followed closely by a flock of utilities lawyers. Becoming the first and only American judge to preside in an embassy courtroom, Merhige proceeded to hear testimony on the Fifth Amendment question, as well as a new claim interposed by Rio Tinto's solicitors—that a corporate privilege which existed in England also prevented Rio Tinto from having to answer questions about the alleged uranium cartel or produce documents. To illustrate its position, solicitors carried in a large footlocker of Rio Tinto documents each day in court which they placed symbolically in the center of the courtroom between the ranks of opposing counsel. Jentes and the Kirkland & Ellis lawyers had particular problems drawing up the briefs of the Fifth Amendment issues because of the shortage of American judicial opinions in London, but in a week the briefs were ready and oral arguments were held. Merhige became the first judge to rule against the American lawyers. In spite of the last-minute arrival of a representative of the U.S. Department of Justice carrying a grant of immunity from prosecution for the Rio Tinto executives—thereby mooting the problem of self-incrimination—Merhige upheld Rio Tinto's invocation of the English corporate privilege, saying that only a British court could order the witnesses to testify.

Several months later, the matter reached the House of Lords. The Rio Tinto appeal was argued personally by the Attorney General of Britain—a measure of the national importance that was now being attached to what had started as a request for testimony—and the argument to the Lords was attended by official representatives of France, Australia and Canada, all of whom also opposed the taking of depositions of the Rio Tinto executives. Ultimately, the House of Lords ruled that the testimony sought by Westinghouse could not be given. The company's efforts to extend the authority of a U.S. court to foreign witnesses and defendants had gotten as far as it would ever go, and it had reached a dead end.

The Kirkland & Ellis lawyers had barely returned from England when a crisis developed in the Duquesne Light case, still pending in state court in Pittsburgh. All during the summer, Duquesne's lawyer, Harold Schmidt, had insisted that he was ready to go and wanted the trial to get under way. Finally Judge Wekselman set a trial date of September 15. Given the limited progress that had been made in discovery with the uranium producers, this date was wholly unacceptable to the Westinghouse lawyers. Jentes had hired local counsel in Pittsburgh, the firm of Eckert, Seamans, Cherin & Mellott, who had gone into Wekselman's court to ask for an extension, and the judge had denied it. The Pittsburgh lawyers had appealed the order all the way to the Pennsylvania Supreme Court with no success. At last Jentes concluded that the local firm had neither the resources nor the expertise to get ready for the trial in time; and so, in spite of the press in discovery activity in the Richmond suits, Kirkland & Ellis stepped in as lead counsel in Pittsburgh. Jentes himself came to court and threw himself on Wekselman's mercy, pleading that it was "unfair and wrong" for him to force Westinghouse to trial. Wekselman didn't seem pleased, but gave Kirkland & Ellis another thirty days to get ready.

The trial began in mid-October, with three Kirkland & Ellis lawyers headed by Jentes on the scene full-time, and three others, including Haubold and Goold, shuttling from Richmond or Chicago. The first month was spent by the plaintiff establishing its uranium contract with Westinghouse, and as the time approached for Kirkland & Ellis to present its defensive case, the lawyers still didn't have the evidence they needed to establish the uranium conspiracy. Haubold was particularly frustrated. "I knew Gulf was involved in this. Here their headquarters was just two blocks down the street from the courthouse, and I kept saying to myself, 'They must have the documents just sitting in there.' "

Early in December, he decided to try serving Gulf with a trial subpoena—a discovery demand that can be issued by a judge when an issue unexpectedly becomes relevant during trial. Judge Wekselman, eager to keep the case moving, granted Haubold's request, and the surprised Gulf lawyers came hurrying into court to protest, surrounded by their outside counsel from the Washington, D.C., firm of Howrey & Simon, represented by Edward Howrey and A. Duncan Whitaker.

Howrey & Simon represents a large number of the country's most powerful companies, and its lawyers often find themselves as co-counsel in cases involving the most prestigious law firms. But it has a reputation among members of the blue chip bar that is slightly short of notorious, and the firm bears little resemblance to those firms which are the pillars of the corporate bar. Howrey & Simon has more than 125 lawyers, but they work almost exclusively on large antitrust cases. The firm prides itself on its rough "hardball" approach to litigation, an approach which frequently takes it to the very limits of ethical propriety, if not beyond. It has traditionally shunned the Ivy League as a source for new lawyers, preferring young graduates who show evidence of having weathered some hard knocks. The firm's presence in a case is, in the opinion of most other lawyers, a guarantee that the litigation will be a bitterly fought, even nasty, contest.

Edward Howrey, a former chairman of the Federal Trade Commission under Eisenhower and a founder of the firm that bears his name, has counseled Gulf Oil on various matters for more than twenty years, and Gulf has certainly had more than its share of the kind of sticky legal problems for which Howrey & Simon lawyers are known to be suited. When Gulf's inside legal staff was first presented with the legality of the company's participation in the world uranium cartel, in the spring of 1972, Gulf called Howrey to a meeting at company headquarters in Pittsburgh. Precisely what was discussed there will never be known, since no written transcripts, minutes or notes were kept, and memories of the participants are uniformly vague. But the general subject of the discussion was Gulf's participation in the cartel, and at the meeting's conclusion, Howrey delivered an oral opinion that Gulf's participation would *not* violate the U.S. antitrust laws. How seriously the Gulf lawyers took that advice is open to question. Although Gulf did go forward in the scheme, it never asked Howrey to reduce his opinion to writing, nor did it demand an official Howrey & Simon opinion. Neither did Gulf seek Justice Department clearance for its participation, which is normally done if even a question of potential antitrust violation arises. And Gulf took great pains to ensure that its participation would remain secret, an action seemingly inconsistent with Howrey's opinion that Gulf's participation was legal.

When the Howrey & Simon lawyers appeared to argue against Wekselman's trial subpoena, they had already been coordinating Gulf's document production in response to the Justice Department probe of the uranium industry, and they were confident that, as they had done from time to time in that investigation, they could simply invoke the attorney-client privilege and thus keep Kirkland & Ellis from seeing the documents. They were so confident, in fact, that they carried two suitcases of Gulf documents that they claimed were privileged into the courtroom. That maneuver proved to be a mistake. One of the idiosyncrasies of Pennsylvania law is its courts' interpretation of the attorney-client privilege, which is a narrow view that only the lawyer can invoke it to refuse testimony; it does very little to protect the client, in this case, Gulf. Wekselman demanded to look at some of the documents that Whitaker claimed were privileged, and after doing so, denied their request and turned them over to Westinghouse on the spot. He also ordered further discovery.

After the court session, Goold, the Kirkland & Ellis associate, followed the Gulf lawyers back to Gulf headquarters, where he was installed in an airless, windowless room with the radiators going full blast. But the associate quickly forgot his discomfort when he came upon a major discovery—some exact duplicates of the Friends of the Earth documents. Their presence in the Gulf U.S. files was direct evidence of the American corporation's complicity. And there was more evidence indicating that Gulf had willingly singled out Westinghouse as a victim of the cartel. There was, for instance, an internal Gulf memorandum indicating that Gulf had learned that Westinghouse, in 1973, was on the verge of cementing an agreement with an Australian uranium producer for a joint mining venture which would supply most of Westinghouse's needs for processed uranium ore. The Gulf memo concluded: "We will work with GMCL [Gulf Minerals Canada Limited] to try to put pressure on the Australians to block the proposed agreement." In June of 1973, the Westinghouse joint venture did, indeed, fall through, an event followed by another incautious Gulf memorandum which boasted that Westinghouse "was planning heavily on Australia keeping the price down—the cartel blew that."

Other documents showed Gulf quoting Westinghouse prices that were "$.20–.30/lb. higher than WMP [a reference to the cartel's World Market Price] in Japan and Europe"; furthermore, Westinghouse would be forced to take delivery of the uranium in Canada, where Gulf knew that Westinghouse would face Canadian uranium export restrictions. Another Gulf memo said that if Westinghouse didn't want delivery in Canada, "A price for U. S. delivery can be quoted which is so high that [it] will be forced to opt for Canadian delivery." Goold was ecstatic about his finds, and at the end of the day, he raced back to the hotel to call Haubold in Chicago. He recalls shouting, "We're in the money," into the telephone while dancing around the hotel room.

Goold's excitement gave way to other concerns the next day when he realized that, valuable as his previous day's discoveries had been, he was coming across evidence that a number of the documents he needed were missing from the Gulf files. Many of the documents were numbered. As he read his way through an important transaction dealing with uranium, the numbers would skip to another transaction. Angered, Goold went to the Gulf in-house lawyer in charge of the document production, and told him that, obviously, some documents were missing. The lawyer refused to comment, referring him to the lawyers at Howrey & Simon. Goold took his problem to Jentes, who raised the issue of the missing documents before Judge Wekselman the next day. Whitaker, speaking for Howrey & Simon, and appearing obviously uncomfortable at the nature of the inquiry, said that he assumed those documents were lodged in the Gulf files in Toronto, where, because of Canadian legislation that was recently, and hurriedly, enacted, Gulf was barred from producing them in a U.S. court. Immediately Wekselman wanted to know how the documents had gotten there. If they had been transported after the onset of the lawsuits or after the government's investigation began, with the deliberate purpose of concealing them, such action might be obstruction of justice. Whitaker said he didn't know how selected documents had ended up in Canada. He assumed that they had been moved in the ordinary course of Gulf's transfer of much of its Gulf Minerals work to Canada.

The mysterious and suspicious circumstances of the missing Gulf documents might have provided a fruitful line of inquiry, but the Kirkland & Ellis lawyers were never destined to pursue it. As the trial proceeded, Wekselman had begun increasingly to make pointed comments about the desirability of settling the case before he was called upon to render a verdict. One day he called Westinghouse and Duquesne executives into court, and lectured them on the importance of a satisfactory outcome of the case to Pittsburgh, and the civic danger involved in pushing Westinghouse into bankruptcy.

There were other settlement pressures. Duquesne's strategy of pushing Westinghouse into trial before Westinghouse's lawyers really had time fully to prepare their case had paid off. Jentes had to advise Westinghouse that the defensive case would not be complete, and that pushing the trial to its conclusion could lead to a finding of liability that would have a harmful impact on the much more important cases in Richmond. The last straw was Wekselman's announcement at the end of testimony that, if pushed to a verdict, he would rule *against* Westinghouse. A day later, Westinghouse's chairman announced that a settlement had been reached with Duquesne, ending the trial before verdict. A measure of Westinghouse's plight was the terms of the settlement: Westinghouse agreed to terms worth an estimated $15.3 million, or more than two-thirds of all that Duquesne had claimed. For Westinghouse the settlement approached capitulation, but it allowed its lawyers to focus all of their attention on the Richmond utilities cases and the Chicago uranium cartel case, and they avoided a formal written opinion rejecting their impracticability defense.

The Chicago uranium case had already taken some alarming twists, which gave Kirkland & Ellis its first taste of the wrath of the uranium producers it had sued.

After filing the complaint in October charging some of the world's most powerful mining conglomerates with price fixing, boycott and carving up markets, Bartlit, characteristically, had been chafing to push forward with discovery. But before he had even received a formal answer to his complaint from the defendants, he had received a threatening phone call from Thomas Johnston, a lawyer with the Chicago law firm of Chadwell, Kayser, Ruggles, McGee & Hastings, which had been retained by Kerr-McGee Corporation, the U.S. oil and mining company which was one of the defendants. Johnston mentioned that he understood Kirkland & Ellis' Washington office had represented Kerr-McGee in a congressional inquiry into the role of oil companies in the uranium market, which the lawyer considered a conflict of interest, since Kirkland & Ellis was now suing Kerr-McGee. Johnston said Kirkland & Ellis should either withdraw from its representation of Westinghouse or drop Kerr-McGee as a defendant. If not, he suggested, Kerr-McGee would have to consider a formal motion to disqualify Kirkland & Ellis for conflict of interest.

Bartlit was enraged by the threat and told Johnston tersely to go ahead and do whatever he felt like doing. He couldn't believe such a tactic would work, but he quickly called Jentes to find out what Johnston was talking about. Jentes knew only slightly more than Bartlit. He was aware that Kirkland & Ellis' Washington office sometimes did work for the American Petroleum Institute—of which Gulf, Kerr-McGee and Getty Oil, all defendants in the uranium case, were members—and he himself had sent the institute a generalized opinion on the Clayton Act in connection with some scheduled congressional hearings on the uranium industry. He recalled that the Kirkland & Ellis partner heading up the project was Frederick Rowe, the head of the firm's Washington office and a permanent member of its managing committee.

Bartlit and Jentes went to brief Chaffetz on the impending threat, and the three lawyers immediately called Rowe in Washington. Rowe's explanation only increased their concern. In late 1975, not long after Westinghouse defaulted on its uranium supply contracts, the American Petroleum Institute, one of Rowe's regular clients, had begun a lobbying campaign to defeat some legislative proposals to force oil companies to divest themselves of some of their operations in non-oil energy fields. That winter, Rowe had been retained to prepare congressional testimony and to analyze the impact of the proposed legislation with an eye to discouraging the legislation. Rowe reminded them that he had notified Chaffetz at the time. He had circulated a new matter memo to all partners in the firm, and there had been no mention of any conflict of interest.

More alarming than the assignment from the American Petroleum Institute was the scope of the work that Kirkland & Ellis lawyers had actually done on the project. They had interviewed representatives of Gulf, Getty and Kerr-McGee about their uranium activities, obtaining confidential data about market share, and had even discussed the causes of the rapid price increases in uranium. The companies had also filled out questionnaires supplied by Kirkland & Ellis, which they had submitted directly to the firm on a confidential basis. Particularly embarrassing was the fact that on October 15, 1976—the very day that Kirkland & Ellis filed its suit against the alleged members of the uranium cartel— the Kirkland & Ellis Washington office had issued a lengthy report on its findings in the uranium industry. Its conclusions: The uranium industry was highly competitive, and the presence of oil companies in the industry had enhanced competition. Rowe was not told about the suit against the uranium producers alleging exactly the opposite until after the complaint had been filed.

Bartlit was annoyed that Rowe had gone off on this comparatively insignificant research project without staying in close contact with his Chicago partners, but there was no way to correct that now. And although the situation looked bad on the surface, perhaps the threat wasn't really so serious. After all, Kirkland & Ellis hadn't been directly retained by a defendant in the uranium cases, only by their trade organization. If anything, the disarray between the two offices demonstrated that no confidential information could have moved from Rowe to Jentes and Bartlit then to be used against any of the uranium defendants. And despite the lawyers' Code of Professional Responsibility forbidding conflicts of interest, a law firm with the prestige and clout of Kirkland & Ellis had never actually been ousted from a case in these circumstances. The lawyers decided to push forward with representing Westinghouse in the uranium suit and to fight to the end any motion to disqualify the firm.

Not all the partners at Kirkland & Ellis shared Bartlit's opinion that the conflict allegations could be so easily deflected. Foremost among the dissenters was another litigation partner who, if not the firm's most powerful, was among its most visible. Don Reuben was a partner who also had other motives for fanning the flames of the conflict controversy. Reuben had been a protégé of Howard Ellis, the name partner from whom he inherited two of his major clients, the *Chicago Tribune* and the Archdiocese of Chicago. When Ellis died in the mid-1960s and those clients had turned to him, Reuben was one of the few partners with the client base to stay out of Chaffetz's rapidly growing orbit. Flamboyant and talkative, with ties to Chicago's loftiest social circles and some of its unsavory political ones, Reuben was not the kind of lawyer that other Kirkland & Ellis partners thought enhanced the firm's image; and recently, internal steps had been taken to discipline him. Reuben was forced to accept a 10 percent pay cut, from $400,000 to $360,000 a year, and he had lost his position on the firm's administrative committee. At the December meeting of the management committee, attended by Chaffetz, Jentes and Reuben, and at which the Westinghouse conflict issue arose, Reuben and Chaffetz stunned their partners by trading insults in an acrimonious screaming match.

Reuben's criticism could be shouted down inside the firm's confines, but the oil company defendants were serious about their conflict of interest threats. In mid-January, they filed formal motions to disqualify Kirkland & Ellis from the case, alleging violations of three of the canons of professional responsibility dealing with conflicts of interest. Even though they had been warned, the hard reality of the motions came as something of a shock to lawyers working on the case. Haubold, for example, attacks it as a dubious diversionary tactic, one that he himself would be very reluctant to use. Nonetheless, the defendants had embarrassed Kirkland & Ellis by finding a case where Fred Bartlit had attempted to disqualify opposing counsel for conflict of interest. They quoted him to advantage in their briefs.

It was also a motion that Judge Marshall treated seriously. He ordered affidavits from the Kirkland & Ellis lawyers to explain their conduct. Bartlit and Jentes swore that although they knew that Kirkland & Ellis' Washington office represented the American Petroleum Institute, and were aware of the identities of some of the institute's members, a "Chinese wall" had existed between the Chicago and Washington offices and no information obtained by Rowe from the oil companies had been transmitted to them. Rowe and another partner in the Washington office submitted affidavits saying that, though they knew of the utilities' cases against Westinghouse pending in Richmond, they were never told that the actions of companies engaged in uranium production might form part of the defense, nor that a separate suit might be brought against the uranium producers for allegedly price fixing.

Jentes' affidavit was the most sweeping in its denial that there had been any improper communications. "At no time prior to October 15, 1976, did I have any communications with any Kirkland, Ellis & Rowe attorneys relating to their work on horizontal divestiture legislation for API, nor have I made use of any oil or uranium company information received by Kirkland, Ellis & Rowe in the course of this case," Jentes swore under oath. He also explained why Rowe had been kept in the dark about the suit against the uranium producers: "Securities law and other related considerations dictated that every precaution be taken to guard against public disclosure of the possibility that an antitrust complaint would be filed."

Rowe explained in his affidavit that "My first information about this complaint came to me from Mr. Fred H. Bartlit, Jr., a Chicago Kirkland & Ellis partner who was visiting our Washington offices on some client matters on October 15, 1976, and stopped by to tell me in late afternoon of the filing of the Westinghouse antitrust complaint by Kirkland & Ellis in Chicago after the exchanges closed that day." But Rowe's explanation of his contacts with his Chicago partners was curiously narrow. Where Jentes had denied having "any communications" about the AIP investigation, Rowe swore only that no "company information obtained in the course of any oil company interviews in which Mr. Clark or I participated," and no "contents of any of the company survey questionnaires" had been transmitted to Chicago. His affidavit left open the possibility that there had been more general discussions of the AIP investigation between himself and someone in the Chicago office.

There was no denying that Kirkland & Ellis had taken diametrically different positions with respect to the state of competition in the uranium industry. In its reply brief to the defendants' motion, Kirkland & Ellis pinned its defense on the hardship that Westinghouse would suffer if the firm were to be disqualified in the middle of the case; the absence of a direct attorney-client relationship between the firm and any of the uranium defendants; and the existence of the "Chinese wall" between the two offices.

The importance of the matter to Westinghouse was apparent from an affidavit filed by the company's general counsel, Robert Pugliesi, who had succeeded William Letson: "Westinghouse's expenses to date for legal fees in the uranium contract cases described above . . . exceed $5,000,000, approximately 50% of which has been paid to Kirkland & Ellis," the lawyer wrote. "It is of vital importance to Westinghouse's interests that Kirkland & Ellis continue to represent Westinghouse Electric Corporation. The problems presented by a change in counsel at this point in time are almost indescribable."

Judge Marshall froze discovery in the case. He ordered Kirkland & Ellis lawyers to do nothing further until he had ruled on the disqualification motion. There the matter rested. Bartlit waited impatiently for a decision. The months passed.

The utility plaintiffs in Richmond, who had always viewed Westinghouse's flap about the uranium cartel as a wild-goose chase, continued to agitate for trial before Judge Merhige. During pretrial conferences, New York's Consolidated Edison, Kansas Power & Light and Union Gas & Electric refused to waive their rights to jury trial. Their cases were postponed until after completion of the non-jury trials. (Despite the lull, New York's Win-throp, Stimson, Putnam & Roberts, an old-line law firm which represented Consolidated Edison in the suit, managed to bill the utility more than $1 million during a year in which its case had been postponed.) The judge scheduled the start of trial for the other plaintiffs during the middle of September.

One hot, sultry afternoon during mid-August in Richmond, some of the lawyers for the utilities looked out their windows from offices they had rented across from the Ross building, and noticed several large moving vans pull up across the street. Out came some Kirkland & Ellis and McGuire, Woods lawyers from the building, who supervised a fleet of movers carrying trunk after trunk of what they assumed were documents off the trucks and into the building. Then, an hour later, they watched the process in reverse. The same cast brought all of the trunks back out of the building, loaded them onto the trucks and drove away.

Actually, what had happened was that Jentes had faced his first administrative crisis in Richmond. Once all the documents had been moved in, he had realized that the building didn't have any Xerox machines. He needed copies immediately and he had been told by Xerox representatives that they couldn't get a machine installed for several days. However, if Jentes could bring all of the documents to Xerox's huge copying facility in Alexandria, Virginia, just outside of Washington, D.C., they could be copied for him overnight. There was a bomb threat later that day at the Xerox plant in Alexandria, and Jentes spent several anxious hours afraid that the documents would be blown up. But the trucks returned early the next morning, this time with twice as many trunks to unload.

The Richmond office building served as the Kirkland & Ellis litigation facility—three paper- and file-crammed floors that Jentes wanted to look as much as possible like a military war room. Six lawyers from Kirkland & Ellis, headed by Jentes and including Haubold and Goold, began round-the-clock preparation, drafting outlines for questioning witnesses, exhibits, commuting between the litigation headquarters and their downtown hotel. As the utilities' direct cases began to near their conclusion, more and more of the lawyers' time turned to what was dubbed the "cartel show."

The Westinghouse lawyers had never made much headway in

procuring testimony from the hostile uranium producers, and since a district court can compel only the attendance of a witness located within 100 miles of the court, they simply gave up expecting any live testimony. Instead, the lawyers culled the transcripts of those depositions they had managed to take, preparing scripts of questions and answers that would be presented to the judge. It is not unusual for deposition testimony to be substituted for that of a live witness when the witness is unavailable, but it had probably never been attempted on such a scale. To keep the judge from being bored by the monotony of a single lawyer droning through the written testimony, the Kirkland & Ellis lawyers took a different approach from that adopted in the IBM case, when deposition testimony was read into the record.

Jentes "cast" the roles of the various deponents with local Virginia lawyers, including some of the best-known partners at McGuire, Woods & Battle, and then had the examining lawyer "rehearse" the lines with them so that they would sound more fresh and spontaneous while delivering the material from the witness stand. Jentes banked on his witnesses' dramatic skills, as well as his own. He himself portrayed Frank O'Hara, a lawyer inside Gulf who was involved in the suspicious document transfer, on the witness stand. In fact the judge had met some of the missing witnesses while in London during the letters rogatory proceeding, and might be able to visualize their testimony in Richmond. For some associates on the case, however, it was not what they had in mind when they thought of courtroom drama.

The non-jury trial reached its conclusion in early March 1978 after six months of constant trial—a remarkably speedy process, considering the factual complexity of the industry and the number of parties in the case, and a vivid demonstration of Merhige's administrative abilities, especially when compared to Edelstein and IBM. The Westinghouse lawyers' first indication that their efforts had not made the impression they had hoped for on the judge came when he announced after the lawyers' concluding statements that he would deliver an oral ruling very soon. Despite Merhige's reputation for decisiveness, it was hard to believe that an opinion delivered orally and quickly would rule in favor of Westinghouse. To adopt the company's theory of impracticability would have been a ground-breaking legal step, needing a carefully reasoned opinion to back it up. When Judge Merhige actually delivered his opinion their fears were confirmed. Westinghouse's defense of impracticability was unconditionally rejected. The judge ruled that valid contracts existed between Westinghouse and the utility plaintiffs and that Westinghouse was liable.

The damages to be awarded, however, were another matter. Early in the proceeding, Merhige had divided the case into two aspects: liability, to determine if Westinghouse was, indeed, excused from performance; and—only if Westinghouse was found liable in that portion of the trial—damages, to determine to what extent the utilities had been harmed by Westinghouse's default. In announcing that Westinghouse was liable, the judge indicated some "tendencies" in his feelings about the damages question. He hinted very seriously that he was not inclined to give the utilities everything they wanted. They should not let their greed run wild just because they had won on the liability issues. He also delivered his "very strong" recommendation that the utilities and Westinghouse resume their settlement negotiations. He did not believe it was really in the utilities' own interests to push Westinghouse into ruin.

Though Jentes and his colleagues could take very little comfort in the judge's ruling, they did extract some satisfaction from their dealings with the three utilities who had refused to join the other plaintiffs on the grounds that they wanted a jury trial. Not surprisingly, those utilities now came forward to say that, on further consideration, perhaps they didn't need a jury trial after all; they'd be happy to go along with the findings in the case that had just been concluded in favor of their co-plaintiffs.

This time, Jentes said that *he* wanted a jury trial, meaning that the entire case would have to be retried before a jury that might rule *against* Con Ed and the other utilities who had opted out, notwithstanding Merhige's decision. Had they allied themselves with the other utilities at the outset, they would at least have been guaranteed that their fate would be no worse than that of their co-plaintiffs. By gambling on a jury trial, those utilities now faced the expense of conducting their own full-scale trial and the risk of losing it. Jentes considers their decision one of the worst blunders of the entire proceeding. Con Ed's chairman, Charles Luce, was said to be furious with his lawyers at Winthrop, Stimson, almost as angry as he was at Jentes for now insisting on a jury trial.

The break between the liability and damages phases of the trial gave Jentes his first opportunity to return to Chicago for an extended period since the trial had begun, and he returned to discover that, in his absence, political intrigue had been brewing at Kirkland & Ellis. Judge Marshall's continued silence on the question of the conflict of interest in the uranium case was heightening the anxiety of the firm's partners, and for some, Rowe's handling of the Petroleum Institute investigation was the last straw.

Not long after the Richmond cases got under way, Chaffetz called Rowe to a meeting of top-level partners in Chicago, where Rowe's management of the Washington office came under heavy attack. Revenues there had been declining, and several promising Washington partners had left the firm, taking with them a substantial group of clients, rather than continue with Rowe. Rowe's headlong pursuit of the Petroleum Institute matter typified his failure to communicate with his partners in Chicago, many partners felt, and a conclusion had been reached that the only way to bring a halt to the disarray that seemed to be spreading through the Washington office was for Rowe to step down. If he didn't do so voluntarily, Chaffetz informed him, the partnership had the votes to force him out. He didn't need to remind the 53-year-old partner that a Kirkland & Ellis partner who withdraws or is forced from the firm loses all of his pension rights, an amount that, in Rowe's case, would have exceeded $500,000.

It was a humbling experience for Rowe, a man who had been so influential that the Washington office of the firm was called Kirkland, Ellis & Rowe. In November 1978, he announced that he was resigning his leadership of the Washington office and would be taking a six-month sabbatical away from the firm. His reward for the graceful exit: a face-saving permanent, but non-voting, seat on the firm's management committee. His name was dropped from the Washington office. Rowe departed for an extended stay in Europe, bitter that he was being made a scapegoat for the Westinghouse conflict problem.

Shortly after Jentes' return, the pace of events in the uranium case also began to pick up. In January, Westinghouse had hired another Chicago lawyer, Lee Freeman, Jr., to try to get discovery moving in that case while Kirkland & Ellis remained frozen out due to the disqualification motion. The defendants in the case had subsequently filed their answer to the complaint and a series of counterclaims, alleging that Westinghouse had been trying to hurt the producers through its own pricing practices.

Then, on April 25, the case again broke open when Judge Marshall announced his decision on the disqualification motion. He would allow Kirkland & Ellis to continue its representation of Westinghouse despite its work for the American Petroleum Institute. His opinion, however, was not a clear-cut exoneration of the firm, and the judge had obviously gone to some lengths to avoid disqualification, a step he described as a drastic remedy. He ruled that no attorney-client relationship existed between the firm and the oil companies by virtue of Kirkland & Ellis' work for the Petroleum Institute, but he found that nonetheless, the firm had violated Canon 9 of the Code of Professional Responsibility, which says that a lawyer must avoid even the appearance of impropriety. The judge wrote that he was "reluctant to exonerate Kirkland for what appears to be an error in professional judgment." Even so, he refused to disqualify the firm because of the hardship to Westinghouse, ordering the case to go forward with Kirkland & Ellis' participation while the defendants appealed his decision.

Bartlit, Jentes and the other lawyers at Kirkland & Ellis were jubilant about the decision, and felt confident that it was the kind of mid-trial order that an appeals court would be very reluctant to overturn. Bartlit plunged into assembling another Westinghouse team for the uranium suit while Jentes continued with preparation for the damages trial.

Even Rowe, now in London, was ecstatic about the decision, feeling that the decision vindicated his actions and would go a long way toward restoring his reputation within the firm. In fact, when Reuben, vacationing in Europe, took Rowe out to dinner in London shortly after Marshall's decision, Rowe wanted to talk of little else. He told Reuben then he had never understood why he was made the scapegoat of the conflict incident. He had, he said, kept Chaffetz fully informed of his activities and had even given Chaffetz a draft of his report for the Petroleum Institute before the uranium suit had been filed. Reuben was alarmed by Rowe's offhand disclosure. Did the transmittal of Rowe's report to Chaffetz mean that there had been no "Chinese wall"? Reuben later examined the Kirkland & Ellis affidavits submitted on the issue. There was no mention by Rowe that he had given a report to Chaffetz; there was no affidavit from Chaffetz at all. A stipulated premise of the litigation over the conflict issue was that no factual information had actually passed from the Washington office to Chicago. If what Rowe had told him were true, was that premise wrong, and did Reuben himself have an ethical obligation to inform the court?

Reuben's consideration of that question was very shortly to take place in a context quite different from that of a partner in the firm. When he returned from his trip to Europe, Reuben was greeted with the firm's decision to oust him from his partnership. No one at Kirkland & Ellis has commented publicly on the reasons for such a draconian measure, one which is anathema to the institutional corporate firm. Partnership is more sacred than tenure, and many a firm has long harbored partners who, for a wide range of personal problems, from drunkenness to insanity, would have been fired from most positions of responsibility. Such firms will tolerate almost anything except the kind of antagonism toward the very concept of the firm displayed periodically by Reuben, who seemed always to place his own interests before those of the firm. The very thought that a Kirkland & Ellis partner would expose details about an alleged conflict of interest like Westinghouse—in effect tattling to the court on his partners—was intolerable.

Unlike Rowe, Reuben did not go quietly. He described his outrage freely to the Chicago newspapers, denouncing his former partners to anyone who would listen, and took with him some of the firm's most prominent clients, including the *Chicago Tribune*. His departure also set off a war for personnel. Reuben took several of his allies within the partnership with him to the new firm he founded, as well as a group of associates who had worked closely with him, about twenty lawyers in all. One way that Kirkland & Ellis staved off further defections among associates was to promise them work on what was then the sexiest case in the office: the uranium suit. With the discovery program again going at full tilt, Kirkland & Ellis associates were being dispatched to Paris, to Australia and to other exotic locations. Bartlit was fond of saying that "the sun never set" on the Kirkland & Ellis litigation empire.

In retrospect, it was the high-water mark for Kirkland & Ellis' representation of Westinghouse. Bartlit and his team had collected enough information about the uranium cartel to file a 600-page answer to interrogatories filed by the defendants, one which constituted a devastating summary of practices in the uranium industry. Bartlit was beginning to press for a default judgment of millions of dollars against the foreign producers who had refused to respond to the court's subpoenas. And he had begun to feel that tactically, the uranium company lawyers were on the run.

In July, in fact, Judge Marshall had ordered a special session to hear the uranium company complaints that they were being overwhelmed by Kirkland & Ellis discovery tactics, which were pushing them at such a rate that sometimes two and three depositions were scheduled simultaneously. Marshall brushed aside their complaints and added that he would very probably enter the default judgment that Bartlit had been seeking.

The Kirkland & Ellis lawyers filed out of court that day pleased with the day's developments; then their euphoria came to an abrupt halt. Someone from the clerk's office came up waving a copy of an opinion that had just been issued by the Seventh Circuit Court of Appeals. It was a reversal of Judge Marshall's opinion on the disqualification motion. Kirkland & Ellis was disqualified and would never again be permitted to appear in court on behalf of Westinghouse in the uranium cases. Reuben now found it unnecessary to press his own evidence of the conflict.

Rarely has a major case come to such a sudden stop, and shock and dismay descended on the Kirkland & Ellis offices. Kirkland & Ellis lawyers were also barred from any contact with Freeman or any other lawyers who might be substituted in the case to avoid transmitting any taint arising out of the American Petroleum Institute contacts. Spirits in the firm were at the lowest ebb that anyone could remember. The firm had lost the utilities case in Richmond, suffered the scandal of the Reuben ouster, and now had been disqualified for violating a fundamental provision of the ethics code.

Three years later, in the spring of 1981, Kirkland & Ellis partners gathered for the gala unveiling of a new portrait to hang in the firm's marble-walled reception area: an almost photographic likeness of Hammond Chaffetz, toasted as the "master architect" of the firm during his forty years as a Kirkland & Ellis lawyer. During the festivities there was, understandably, no mention of the 1978 events which had culminated in the firm's disqualification. But it had been Chaffetz principally who had rallied his shaken partners, calmed uneasy clients, organized committees to minimize the damage to the firm and focused his partners on the future.

In 1965, Chaffetz had had his own name removed from that of the firm in order to better institutionalize its identity, and a measure of his success was the failure of the Westinghouse disqualification or even the Reuben crisis to have any long-range impact on the health of the firm. Nor did Kirkland & Ellis' disqualification have any significant impact on the course of the utilities litigation or on the uranium cartel case. Westinghouse hired Donovan Leisure Newton & Irvine to replace Kirkland & Ellis, the firm that it had already been using as local New York counsel for the Consolidated Edison and Long Island Lighting Company suits in Richmond.

The Donovan, Leisure lawyers eventually found that there wasn't as much to do as they anticipated. As Judge Merhige had urged, by 1980 all of the utilities had reached out-of-court settlements with Westinghouse which eliminated the need for the planned trial on the damages issue. Donovan, Leisure lawyers did not negotiate the settlements—they were handled internally by Westinghouse executives and the company's legal staff—and though non-monetary aspects of the agreements make them difficult to value, it is estimated that they cost Westinghouse approximately $900 million, or about half of what the utilities had claimed. If Westinghouse and the utilities had simply split their differences in 1975, before resorting to litigation, the result would have been about the same.

Nor was any significant progress made in the uranium cartel suit before it, too, came to an end in a settlement. The trial never got under way, but enough evidence emerged to raise some provocative questions about the conduct of participants in the case. For example, Donovan, Leisure lawyers sought sanctions against Gulf and some of the other defendants for refusing to produce subpoenaed documents. Among their claims were allegations that Gulf and its lawyers—including partners in Howrey & Simon— had acted in bad faith by causing documents to be shipped from the company's Pittsburgh headquarters to Canada, where they knew they would be protected by Canadian legislation forbidding disclosure. Although Howrey & Simon denied the charges, speculation about their role was further fueled by the firm's sudden withdrawal from representing Gulf in the case because lawyers at the firm were so involved in Gulf's conduct that they expected to appear as witnesses.

Those proceedings were brought to a halt in 1981, when Westinghouse's in-house lawyers negotiated a settlement with the uranium producers for a total of approximately $100 million in cash plus various options to acquire uranium ore, a settlement which most commentators considered a poor one for Westinghouse. Among those disappointed by the settlement were lawyers at Kirkland & Ellis, especially Bartlit and Haubold, who felt Westinghouse could have done better. Though no longer involved, they felt they had amassed the evidence for a devastating case, and felt frustrated that it would now never be put to use.

In any event, the cartel dissolved in the mid-1970s, and subsequent developments in the nuclear power industry have caused the price of uranium ore to plunge to historic lows. Westinghouse no longer supplies processed uranium. It has put its uranium debacle behind it, and whatever the net cost to the company, Westinghouse itself is still in business.

Nor will the full story of Kirkland & Ellis' conflict of interest emerge in court. In the wake of its disqualification, Westinghouse formed an audit committee, one of whose members was in-house counsel Ray Scannell, to assess the harm that may have been done to the company as a result of Kirkland & Ellis' conduct and to consider whether a suit should be brought against the firm. The audit committee concluded that no action should be taken. Some Westinghouse shareholders, believing the audit committee's work to be a perfunctory whitewash of the firm's conduct, filed their own derivative suit against Kirkland & Ellis. That case became dormant in 1980 when the shareholders evidently lost interest in prosecuting it.

Don Reuben has successfully gone his own way, happily pursuing the kinds of cases he likes—such as the defense of Chicago's late Cardinal Cody against embezzlement accusations—and continuing to take occasional verbal potshots at members of his old firm.

Jentes and Bartlit are unquestionably among the small group of partners who occupy the pinnacle of power today within Kirkland & Ellis. When Chaffetz retired, they were among the partners who distributed his equity shares, and their power was recently solidified further by an adjustment of equity percentages they oversaw which shifted income from some less productive senior partners to younger partners. If anything, the Westinghouse cases have ultimately enhanced the firm's national reputation and prestige. Despite the firm's losses and setbacks, it is the widespread perception among members of the corporate bar—and in the firm itself—that it was Kirkland & Ellis that saved Westinghouse.

CHAPTER FIVE

CHRYSLER
Debevoise, Plimpton,
Lyons & Gates

A haggard-looking Richard Kahn, a partner at New York's
Debevoise, Plimpton, Lyons & Gates, surveyed the crowd of lawyers packed into the Debevoise cafeteria on the 33rd floor of 299
Park Avenue. It was 7:00 P.M., June 23, 1980, the eve of the
largest corporate rescue mission ever attempted, and he mentally
checked off the presence of lawyers from Chrysler, the teetering
automaker; from the United States Treasury; from Simpson
Thacher & Bartlett, representing Manufacturers Hanover Trust
Co., the agent bank; from Shearman & Sterling, on behalf of Citibank; and some others representing pieces of the intricate financial
puzzle which, once assembled, might forestall or prevent the imminent bankruptcy of Chrysler.

Throughout the other three floors of the Debevoise offices, every
conference room was full, the conference tables weighted down
with legal and financial documents. If placed in a single stack,
they would have topped a five-story building. The documents were
so voluminous, the requirements for simultaneous signings and
ratifications so complicated, that the closing of the deal had spilled
over into neighboring law firms—to Wachtell, Lipton, Rosen &
Katz, called in by the banks as special financial counsel, whose
offices were a few floors above; to Sullivan & Cromwell, representing the European banks, whose midtown office was diagonally
across the street; to Shearman & Sterling's Citicorp offices; and to

Kelley Drye & Warren, historically Chrysler's outside counsel, now largely nudged aside by the Debevoise lawyers who had taken over as lead counsel.

Kahn had called all of them together for one last run-through of the scenario which would close the deal the next morning. As he began his instructions, a feeling of tired relief passed through him, and a sense of incredulity that this most impossible of deals had come to fruition. When he heard a voice screaming "fire" outside the cafeteria, his only thought was that it seemed an odd time for a practical joke.

Moments later a Debevoise partner appeared at the door, and announced that the fire department had ordered the lawyers to evacuate the building, although the blaze was minor and would probably be quickly contained. Expecting an interruption of only ten or fifteen minutes, the lawyers left their papers and filed out, and started walking down the thirty-three flights of stairs. As they descended, they encountered smoke, and the heat became palpable and then intense; some pulled out handkerchiefs to cover their mouths. Once outside, they crossed the street to Sullivan & Cromwell's offices, where they had agreed to wait for the signal that they could re-enter the building and continue the meeting.

But by the time they reached Sullivan & Cromwell's windows, the view had become a nightmare vision. The evacuated sky-scraper resembled a scene from *Towering Inferno*, with flames leaping from windows high above Park Avenue, casting an eerie glow on the neighboring office buildings. As the lawyers watched, horrified, firemen began breaking out windows and directing streams of water into the building. Delay would cost Chrysler $10 million per day. Even a fraction of that cost could put the ailing automaker into bankruptcy.

The prospect of bankruptcy is an even more ominous threat to a corporation than an antitrust case. The impending demise of a major corporation, such as Chrysler or Lockheed or International Harvester, is treated as a national crisis. Corporate executives will do, and pay, almost anything to stave off bankruptcy. Since that depends on arranging additional financing, either private or governmental, corporate finance lawyers are needed every step of the way. And should those efforts fail and a corporation slip into bankruptcy, the remains are guarded and parceled out by corporate bankruptcy lawyers, with their own fees exacted first from the remaining assets. The public perception that lawyers profit from others' misfortunes is particularly true in the field of bankruptcy.

Bankruptcy is a quintessential preserve of the lawyer, since it is almost entirely the product of a federal statute, the Bankruptcy Reform Act. Public policy shifted gradually from the position that debtors should languish in prison waiting for their debts somehow to be paid, to the perception that the economy and social well-being are enhanced by giving people and their businesses another chance—a rebirth unshackled by debt, another chance at productivity. Since the concept stands in blunt opposition to the common laws of contract and obligation, a federal statute was necessary to reconcile such disparate aims. To prevent conflicting and counterproductive interpretations of the statute, special bankruptcy courts were created. Once it is determined that a person or, more commonly, a business or corporation is entitled to what is euphemistically known as the "protection" of the bankruptcy courts, the chief task is to carve up the assets among the creditors. A trustee in bankruptcy, usually a lawyer, is appointed by the court to oversee the assets and to run the business while the spoils are being divided.

Where the company or the number of creditors is large, the process can take many years. All the creditors must be located and their claims established and verified. Since not all the claims can be satisfied out of the remaining assets, priorities are established to determine who is paid how much and when, all determined according to the bankruptcy laws and the laws governing loans, financial obligations and security obligations. Knowledge of this intricate process is essential in the near-bankruptcies—known to corporate lawyers as "work-outs"—as well as in actual cases of bankruptcy. When a loan is restructured, for example, a bank wants to know what chance it has of collecting its debt in the event that a bankruptcy does actually occur. A lawyer for the bank negotiating such a restructured loan will obviously try to arrange the deal so that the bank's priority in bankruptcy will be better. Lawyers for the corporation must make sure that any shift in the lender's priority doesn't impinge on any priorities that have already been entered into, say, with preferred stockholders who have their own rights in the event of bankruptcy. In a work-out situation, bankruptcy suddenly looms as the background for all negotiations. In the case of Chrysler, the background was more like a shroud.

In mid-January 1980, Debevoise's senior litigating partner, Asa Rountree, then head of the American Bar Association litigation section, received a call from J. Ronald Trost, who then headed his own specialized bankruptcy firm in Los Angeles. Trost had been working actively with Chrysler in attempts to arrange government financing to prevent bankruptcy, and Congress had indeed adopted the Chrysler Corporation Loan Guarantee Act of 1979 just before Christmas. Although Trost had also been working with lawyers at the New York firm of Kelley Drye & Warren, the law firm that had traditionally acted as outside counsel for the Chrysler Corporation, Trost said that Chrysler faced a major task in complying with the requirements of the new legislation. Frankly, he said, neither he nor Lee Iacocca and top management at Chrysler thought that Kelley, Drye was up to the assignment. Would Rountree and other Debevoise lawyers be interested in meeting with him and some Chrysler executives to discuss the possibility that Debevoise take on the role of lead counsel in rescuing Chrysler?

The question was not quite the compliment to the firm it might have seemed. Debevoise was not chosen solely because of its expertise or its reputation for quality legal work. At the time, Chrysler was in default or near default on loans and financial arrangements with nearly 400 banks, including all of the country's major lenders. Since the company was in an adversary relationship with those banks, it couldn't turn to any of the law firms which had an ongoing client relationship with the banks and might even be called upon to negotiate with Chrysler. Debevoise was virtually the only large first-rate corporate law firm that didn't act as general counsel to a major bank. Rountree agreed that a group should meet discreetly in the Debevoise offices that Sunday evening.

Rountree was not intimately familiar with Chrysler's financial plight or its efforts to arrange government support, though Chrysler news had filled the financial pages for the past several months, as had more general information about the plight of the American auto industry. Not since the Arab oil embargo of 1973–74 had the health of the carmakers appeared so precarious. The Iranian crisis had caused long lines at gas stations, and American consumers had virtually stopped buying the fuel-inefficient family-sized behemoths that were the staple of the Detroit auto producers. Chrysler especially was stuck with a huge inventory of unsold cars—the lumbering Imperials, bulging New Yorkers and Polaras and chrome-laden Cordobas—which had enabled Chrysler to keep about a 12 percent share of the U.S. auto market as the number-three American car manufacturer.

Chrysler's large unsold inventory became a growing drain on its financial resources as short-term interest rates continued creeping up to more than 13 percent. Worse, Chrysler was already behind GM and Ford in developing new models to meet federal pollution and fuel efficiency standards. It needed major outlays of capital in the fall of 1979 to convert factories for production of new models that would halt its dwindling market share in the U.S.—it fell to less than 10 percent in 1979—and meet foreign and domestic competition. Chrysler's future was pinned on its ability to manufacture newly designed and tooled "K-Cars" in time for the 1981 model season.

Chrysler's problems were painfully evident in its quarterly reports of earnings and in its sales figures. The corporation lost approximately $205 million in 1978; that figure ballooned to $1.1 billion in 1979. At the end of 1978, Chrysler had working capital of more than a billion dollars; by the end of 1979, it was $100 million in the hole and failed to meet many of its credit obligations. It had sold what assets it could to raise cash, including its European car manufacturing operation to Peugeot-Citroen, in return for Peugeot stock. By the end of the summer, Chrysler's management had exhausted its financial options and saw government assistance as the only means to prevent financial collapse. Consulting with Kelley Drye in New York, Chrysler hired a Washington, D.C., law firm to advise it with respect to obtaining federal legislation to keep the company afloat.

The Washington law firm chosen—Patton, Boggs & Blow—is a different breed altogether from the blue chip corporate firm. It is known first and foremost as a lobbying law firm, especially during Democratic congresses and administrations. One of the name partners, Thomas Hale Boggs, Jr., is the son of the late Congressman Thomas Hale Boggs and of present Congresswoman Corinne Boggs, and his political connections have stood him in good stead. Partners at Sullivan & Cromwell, at Cravath, at Davis

Polk, never lobby, though they may have personal ties and access to influential lawmakers. The reasons are partly a matter of taste and style—corporate partners are neither interested in nor fond of nor good at the kind of glad-handing conducted by lobbyists—but more importantly, the implied exchange of influence and favors could undermine their undivided loyalty to corporate clients. Lobbyists may be lawyers, their expertise valuable in drafting and examining legislation. But in the eyes of the corporate lawyers, they do not practice law.

Chrysler's lobbyists immediately encountered some stiff opposition in Congress, particularly from Senator William Proxmire, then the head of the Senate Banking Committee. Initially Chrysler sought some tax-loss carry-forwards, a tax ploy which would free immediately $1 billion in cash otherwise destined for the U.S. Treasury. The plan had been discussed with and tentatively approved by President Carter's Treasury Secretary, W. Michael Blumenthal. But when G. William Miller, the former Federal Reserve chairman and a former lawyer at Cravath, succeeded him at the end of the summer, it was clear that tax breaks smacking of special-interest legislation would never pass muster in Congress. Miller instead urged a loan guarantee program along the lines that had earlier been arranged for Lockheed. In September, Chrysler proposed a $1.2 billion loan guarantee plan, which was initially rejected by Miller. According to Carswell, the former Shearman & Sterling partner and deputy secretary, Patton, Boggs and Kelley Drye had hastily put together a proposal which was long on rhetoric and short on hard financial data that the Treasury Department could evaluate. When Carswell, Miller and their colleagues finally did receive the financial statistics and sales projections, they were so shocked by the precarious state of the company that they concluded at least $1.5 billion in loan guarantees would be needed, even more than Chrysler had asked for.

Though the Treasury came around to Chrysler's point of view about how much aid was needed, whether aid should be granted at all was far from clear. Free market proponents, who dominated the White House and executive staffs on most issues like oil price deregulation, were ideologically opposed to interfering with normal market forces to prop up Chrysler. It wasn't clear whether any economic or social policy would justify government intervention. But Chrysler was in such a rapidly deteriorating state that most of those questions could not be answered before its collapse. That time pressure, together with political pressure from some of the Midwestern industrial states and from labor, persuaded Congress to pass a Chrysler loan guarantee act by Christmas. As the Debevoise lawyers would shortly discover, passage of the act was nearly a Pyrrhic victory, in some ways more punitive than outright rejection would have been.

But as Rountree put down the phone after talking with Trost, his thoughts were on the prospect of a major new client and the headline corporate deal of the year. Trost had indicated that a significant component of complying with the conditions laid down by the government for guaranteed loans was restructuring Chrysler's existing bank agreements and privately raising massive amounts of new capital. Rountree called Michael Goff and George Adams, Jr., the Debevoise partners who headed the firm's private placement work—a form of financing that eliminated the need for compliance with the Securities Act of 1934 and which had been virtually invented by one of the firm's founders, Francis T. P. Plimpton.

They, in turn, called Cecil Wray, Jr., one of the firm's senior partners. To head the project, the partners settled on William Matteson, whose extensive work for Wheelabrator-Frye Inc. had made him among the firm's most powerful corporate partners and whose successful handling of Wheelabrator's acquisition of the Pullman company the previous year had given him experience at handling massive corporate deals. But it was also obvious that Debevoise would have to offer Chrysler some bankruptcy expertise, and that was more of a problem. Bankruptcy was actually something of a blind spot among Debevoise partners, although the firm's first major assignment was as counsel to a trustee in bankruptcy during the 1930s. The best they could come up with was Bevis Longstreth, a partner who did extensive work for the Ford Foundation and non-profit institutions, but who had some experience with a few real estate collapses during the 1973–74 recession. Longstreth was suddenly designated a bankruptcy expert.

That Friday afternoon, Matteson was skiing at Vail and had just come off the slopes when Wray called to say he wanted to broach something "which might change your life for a few months." Matteson protested that he was too busy with Wheelabrator-Frye matters, that surely there were others with more expertise. But the next morning, Matteson flew back to New York, his ski vacation at a sudden end. Sunday evening, Matteson, Longstreth, Paul Heinen, Chrysler's inside general counsel, and Trost met at the Debevoise offices. After a brief discussion, the role of lead counsel was formally offered to Debevoise and accepted. Then Trost and Heinen began outlining the company's troubles. It was obvious that the passage of the legislation was just the beginning of what would be a long and desperate ordeal.

Chrysler's decision to tap Debevoise to orchestrate the company's efforts to forestall bankruptcy hardly met with universal enthusiasm, especially within Debevoise itself. Matteson himself says the assignment was "the toughest thing I'd ever faced. I didn't panic, but I was overwhelmed." When the full partnership had its weekly luncheon meeting at the Waldorf-Astoria Hotel next door on Park Avenue the following Tuesday, Chrysler was the major topic of discussion. Matteson gave a presentation emphasizing the enormousness of the task. On the part of some of the partners, there was grave concern that, after Chrysler, the nature of the firm would be changed forever, that it would become associated with what seemed like an endless and tedious project much like Cravath had with the IBM case. After all, Debevoise had been founded as something of a reaction against the bureaucratization of the large, prestigious corporate firms that it was now beginning to resemble.

Debevoise, Plimpton is, indeed, something of an anomaly among the country's leading corporate firms. Though it is much younger than Sullivan & Cromwell or Cravath—it was founded in 1931—it has been, if anything, more old-fashioned in its style, preferring to maintain a more genteel image and approach despite the pressures that caused other leading firms to become more bureaucratic. Its original founders were Eli Whitney Debevoise and William Stevenson, both of whom were independently wealthy (Debevoise being a direct descendant of the inventor of the cotton gin) and had been associates together at Davis Polk & Wardwell. They were later joined by two Harvard Law School classmates, Francis Plimpton and Robert Page, who were associates at what is now Dewey, Ballantine, Bushby, Palmer & Wood. The founding partners all went on to illustrious careers, giving the firm early prominence and prestige. Debevoise became counsel to the High

Commissioner for Germany after World War II, John J. McCloy; Stevenson was later ambassador to the Philippines and president of Oberlin College. Plimpton served as ambassador to the United Nations in the Kennedy and Johnson administrations; and Page became president of Phelps Dodge Industries, Inc., the firm's earliest and most important industrial client.

Since its founding, the firm rapidly acquired the kind of client base to sustain a large corporate firm. Debevoise represents many large insurance companies, including Prudential, Aetna, John Hancock and Equitable; its corporate clients include American Airlines, KLM Royal Dutch Airlines, Continental Corporation, St. Joe Minerals, Tampax and Wheelabrator-Frye. The firm represents the Ford Foundation and Columbia and Princeton universities, and its non-profit work adds a luster to its regular corporate practice which has helped attract top law school graduates.

The fears that Chrysler meant an irrevocable commitment to the intense pressures and arduous working conditions of the more bureaucratic firms were soon fanned by the efforts of Chrysler partners to recruit other partners and associates to work on the deal, pulling them off of other matters entirely and leaving the non-Chrysler lawyers to cope as best they could. When Longstreth tapped associate Peter Borowitz to be his assistant, he yanked him away from seven other partners with pending matters.

The Monday after the first encounter with Chrysler, Matteson flew to Washington to meet with lawyers at Patton, Boggs and at the Treasury; on Tuesday he flew back to New York for the weekly partners' meeting; and on Wednesday he and Longstreth had an awkward meeting with Louis Warren, the partner at Kelley Drye whom they were displacing as lead counsel.

Trips to Washington and Detroit would become so frequent that Matteson maintained standing reservations for every night, including weekends, at the plush Madison Hotel in Washington, D.C., and at Detroit's Westin Hotel in Renaissance Plaza. When other lawyers from Debevoise needed the room, they simply identified themselves to desk clerks as "Bill Matteson," causing considerable confusion until the hotel staffs began to recognize the cast of characters.

After their preliminary discussions, it was clear to Matteson that the task would be enormous, requiring a division into teams, each headed by a partner, with himself as the central coordinator.

Longstreth would head the team that would interpret the Chrysler Loan Guarantee Act, act as a mediator with the Treasury and government officials, and act as a liaison between Chrysler and the government.

Corporate partner Richard Kahn was lying in bed at the Huntington Hotel in San Francisco early that Wednesday morning watching the sun rise when the phone rang. Kahn was among the group of partners most concerned about the impact of the Chrysler deal on the firm and on its work for other clients, and he wasn't happy when he heard Matteson on the other end of the line. "Chrysler needs money," Matteson told him, "and it needs you." It had been almost immediately clear that an essential component of Chrysler's rescue would be to restructure its loans from banks. Though Debevoise had no steady commercial banking client, Kahn had done sophisticated financial work for many of its insurance clients and had done some work for the First National Bank of Chicago. At first Kahn protested, then refused. But Matteson stressed both the need for Kahn's expertise, and that the firm's reputation would be publicly riding on the outcome of the deal. Though Kahn still had reservations, he had no appetite for quarreling with his partners—he had traditionally isolated himself from intrafirm politics, preferring the full-time practice of law—and he finally agreed to fly back to New York.

One measure of Debevoise's attitudes toward corporate law practice was that the firm had resisted formal departments for many years. Although gradually specialties had inevitably developed—litigation, corporate, trusts and estates, and real estate, for example—associates still are not assigned to specific departments. They may work in a variety of departments for different partners, their assignments coordinated by two administrative partners. But the partners working on the Chrysler deal, in their haste to get things under way, bypassed the usual clearance required and simply began drafting associates.

If the suddenness of the Chrysler intrusion into the firm upset some of the partners, it was even more distressing to the associates at the firm. To many of them, Matteson represented a style of practice that they had come to Debevoise to avoid. Though he had a reputation as an excellent teacher when he bestowed his undivided attention on associates, those occasions were said to be few. At other times he was abrupt and impatient, taking associates' long hours for granted and offering them little guidance. Assignments from him were viewed as strictly mixed blessings. He had the clout to make partners, but he was merciless in his disapproval of associates who didn't demonstrate his competence, stamina and dedication—and put in considerably longer hours than he himself did.

Longstreth, by comparison, represented the genteel extreme of the firm. Independently wealthy, personable and charming, he was also known as the most disorganized partner. "When you heard someone was working for Bevis," says one associate, "you'd just groan and roll your eyes." According to others, Longstreth would ask for work and then forget about it for three weeks while it sat on his desk. "Then suddenly, he'd ask, 'Where are we? Let me find this.' He'd read it for the first time, and then there'd be a crisis. He'd conclude by saying, 'I don't care if you have to stay up all night revising this.' But it was always his fault." The Matteson-Longstreth team was viewed as a marriage of extreme hard work and inaction—a deadly combination for associates.

By the time Matteson, Longstreth and their partners completed their sweep for talent, more than a quarter of the firm's associates —and many summer associates, too—would be toiling day and night on Chrysler. And though Matteson and Longstreth would rarely again have time to attend one of the partnership lunches— itself evidence of the divisive influence of such a massive under-taking—they would have witnessed the growing resentment of their partners at the disruption of their practice, resentment which would later surface within the firm.

Matteson and Longstreth's first task after organizing their man-power was to arrive at some kind of understanding of the legisla-tion passed by Congress. Such legislative interpretation is a common service rendered by law firms, especially the large cor-porate firms, since it is their large and far-flung clients who are most often affected by the economic and technical legislation that issues steadily from Congress. It is one of the few functions of the corporate lawyer that is learned in law school. Years of reading judicial cases usually teaches one, if nothing else, the deceptive simplicity of Congressional legislation and the sometimes amazing lengths to which "interpretation" can be taken by the courts. The Chrysler legislation, however, was not even simple on its face, and it had left Chrysler executives writhing in uncertainty about how to meet its terms for financial relief.

After the first week of drafting manpower for the deal, Longstreth and his chief associate, Peter Borowitz, had probably read the legislation a total of a hundred times, and still it seemed mysterious. Simply piecing it together was a major task. As they read through the 19-page bill, terms of art kept sending them back to the section of definitions, where they would often find themselves groping elsewhere. For example, the act prohibited issuing loan guarantees without some concessions by organized labor, saying, in part, that no guarantee may be issued if "collective bargaining agreements entered into by the Corporation . . . with labor organizations . . . have not been modified so that the cost to the Corporation of such wages and benefits, as determined by the Board, shall be reduced by a total amount of at least $462,500,-000." What did the act mean by "labor organizations"? Turning to the definitions, Longstreth found only that "the term 'labor organization' has the same meaning as in Section 2 of the National Labor Relations Act," which sent the lawyers to still other statutes and definitions.

But more painful than the task of figuring out what the act meant was their realization of the concessions Chrysler would have to make in return for its federal guarantees. Though all the federal government was providing was a promise to pay in the event that Chrysler itself proved unable to pay back its loans and meet its financial agreements necessary to keep it operating, no money was actually moving from the U.S. Treasury to Chrysler. Chrysler was expected virtually to sacrifice its corporate autonomy and submit to the whims of Congress. Basically, the act called for Chrysler to:

• divulge completely its corporate strategy, including detailed plans for new and improved products that would otherwise be classified as business secrets, to demonstrate that the company could survive past 1983;

• devise a new plan for improving productivity;

• negotiate wage concessions from its employees;

• submit a plan to demonstrate how Chrysler would help to implement Congressional desire to end U.S. dependence on foreign oil, a particularly galling provision, since it had so little direct bearing on Chrysler's business conduct or hopes for restoring profitability; and most importantly,

• arrange for nearly $1 billion in private financing and loan concessions from new and existing creditors.

All of these conditions, and more, had to be met before Congress would agree to implement the loan guarantee plan. And it wanted the whole package ready to go by February 15, less than a month away.

Longstreth immediately called Robert Mundheim, the former Shearman & Sterling associate who was counsel to the Treasury, and got an extension of the deadline. "The task was so enormous that it was the kind of thing that you could only grasp in an intellectual sense," Longstreth says. "The idea of a month was totally ludicrous." Mundheim was amenable. His own corporate law background had made it equally clear to him that Congress had set an impossible timetable, and he agreed to an extension. He and Longstreth were also friends. Both were lecturers at the annual Securities Institute conducted by the Practicing Law Institute, the same organization which often hosted Pillsbury, Madison's Bruce Mann, and both were fellow board members of one of Longstreth's clients.

That Friday, Longstreth and Matteson flew to Detroit for the first of what became weekly Friday meetings with Chrysler executives to discuss compliance with the act. The lawyers' first report to the Chrysler executives was not a rosy one. The thrust of their remarks was the magnitude of the task ahead—and Chrysler's rapid outflow of cash already had it chafing at the prospect of more delay. The sober truth was that Chrysler was so short of cash that it was barely meeting its day-to-day obligations, and it had exhausted its chances for obtaining more help from any of its creditor banks.

No one was more acutely aware of Chrysler's financial distress than executives at Manufacturers Hanover Corporation in New York, or Robert McKean, Jr., the bank's outside general counsel, who is a partner at Simpson Thacher & Bartlett in New York. Simpson, Thacher's relationship to Manufacturers Hanover rivals that of Shearman & Sterling to Citibank and Davis Polk to Morgan Guaranty; and McKean's office is located in the bank's midtown skyscraper. The firm also owes its presence among the country's most elite law firms to its extensive work for Lehman Brothers Kuhn Loeb and for such corporate clients as Gulf & Western Industries, Joseph Seagram and Sons, and General Motors. The firm is one of the city's oldest, founded in 1884; and among its prominent members have been former U.S. Senator Clifford Case and former Secretary of State Cyrus Vance, who is currently the firm's chairman.

Manufacturers Hanover was Chrysler's major lender, with more than $55 million in debts outstanding to the automaker, and it had been nervously calling on McKean ever since Chrysler reported its first serious loss in 1979. Unlike the case with small borrowers, the interests of a bank and a borrower which has more than $55 million of its money tend to coalesce. McKean didn't want Chrysler to go under any more than the Debevoise lawyers did. He wanted the company to pay back its debt to his bank client.

McKean had already experienced one embarrassing setback. During the summer of 1979, his principal concern had been the Chrysler Finance Company, or CFC, the Chrysler subsidiary that financed customer loans for the purchase of new cars. As he remarks, "Without financing, you don't sell cars." CFC was not itself in any financial trouble, but obviously it would be dragged down if the parent company's losses weren't stemmed. He and his partners and associates at Simpson, Thacher, especially Lillian Kraemer and Thomas Cashel, had devised a one-year revolving credit agreement that would include all 282 banks currently lending to CFC, in case the finance company needed more cash. To sell that proposal, Manufacturers Hanover executives and McKean held a midsummer meeting with representatives of twenty-six of the most important of these banks. Much to the Simpson, Thacher lawyers' dismay, the bankers listened to their proposal in stony silence. Not only did they reject the revolving credit agreement, sending the lawyers' extensive work down the drain, but they voiced a distrust of Manufacturers Hanover. They believed that the large New York bank was too tied to the interests of Chrysler to represent their interests without compromise.

Now the much larger debacle that McKean feared seemed about to happen. He had spent hours coaching Manufacturers Hanover chairman John McGillicuddy on his testimony before congressional committees in support of extending Chrysler the loan guarantees. But the banking community had been sharply divided even on that issue. Citicorp chairman Walter Wriston, for example, had opposed the guarantees in his testimony before the same committees.

Then, in early January, shortly after the act was passed and before Debevoise was hired, Chrysler came to McKean and to the lawyers for the other banks with its ideas for the banks' role in meeting the requirements of the act. Basically, Chrysler wanted the banks simply to stop trying to collect on their loans and to slash their interest rates to a nominal 1 percent for four years—a "gift" from the banks to Chrysler of about $400 million. That proposal, which had left McKean aghast, was flatly rejected even by the friendly banks. He was thus relieved when several weeks later he had a call from Richard Kahn, the Debevoise partner who was coordinating the bank work. Kahn was someone who might understand the constraints under which the banks were operating and would not make such outlandish proposals.

Kahn himself was only beginning to get a grip on the extent of Chrysler's financial plight. For two weeks, he and a team of a half dozen associates had been first locating and then analyzing the company's financial agreements to, as Kahn puts it, "get on top of Chrysler." As messengers brought pile after pile of documents from Chrysler's Highland Park, Michigan, headquarters, Debevoise's conference rooms were filled with piles of papers and associates poring over them.

What they discovered was the staggering complexity of Chrysler's financial structure. There were holders of common and preferred stock, including a substantial block owned by Mitsubishi, all of whom had various rights to Chrysler proceeds and would have to consent to various restrictions on their rights before the government would agree to any loan guarantees. There were also the holders of notes and debentures issued by Chrysler, which were also subject to representations and agreements by the company. Chrysler had different credit agreements with 482 domestic banks, from banks as large as Manufacturers Hanover and Citibank, to smaller banks like the Merchants' National Bank of Muncie, Indiana. There were financing agreements with more than a score of European and Canadian banks, as well as $100 million in loans from Peugeot. The company owned $156 million in Japanese letters of credit; and several major insurance companies—Prudential and Aetna, as well as Blue Cross/Blue Shield—held large Chrysler notes.

Every agreement would have to be renegotiated for at least one basic reason: the government, in its relief action, had insisted that it hold first priority in the repayment of any funds it extended pursuant to the loan guarantee act, thereby upsetting the whole priority system which already existed. Furthermore, the act stated flatly that no commitment would be made unless "the Corporation's existing creditors have certified to the Board that they will waive their rights to recover under any prior credit commitment which may be in default." In other words, Chrysler's creditors were expected to simply ignore default. At the same time, Chrysler was going to have to ask these same creditors for nearly $1.5 billion in additional financial assistance. Kahn found the requirements so contradictory and the likelihood of their being realized so remote that he commented that anyone who believed that Chrysler would ultimately qualify for the federal loan guarantees might as well believe in the Easter Bunny. From then on, the few optimists among the Debevoise lawyers were known as the "Easter Bunnies"; Kahn was dubbed "Cassandra" Kahn.

Talking with McKean, Kahn sorted the bank renegotiating problems into four areas: the U.S. banks, the Canadians, the European lenders and the Japanese banks and Mitsubishi. Of those, the Japanese problems were the most pressing. Chrysler had already defaulted in mid-January on note repayment obligations to the Japanese. Kahn also discovered that the Japanese had an entirely different notion of the whole problem. To them, it was a matter of national honor that Japanese banks provide for Japanese corporations that get into trouble, and they expected American banks to do the same for Chrysler. They became increasingly suspicious that the U.S. government's deal was somehow going to favor American banks at the expense of the Japanese.

But Japanese attitudes also worked to Chrysler's advantage. Because they viewed Chrysler as a trading partner, entitled to traditional Japanese respect and support, there was actually little danger that the Japanese would plunge the company into bankruptcy, as they could easily have done when Chrysler stopped its payments in mid-January. At the least, the Japanese could have wreaked havoc by stopping shipments of Dodge Colts, one of Chrysler's popular models that was actually manufactured by Mitsubishi. But the Japanese did neither. They did not want the national onus of triggering the collapse of a trading partner.

Even though the Japanese had their own ideas about national honor when bankruptcy threatened, at least they were talking to Chrysler. The European banks weren't even doing that. Though their representatives would, from time to time, agree to meet with Chrysler and the U.S. banks, they refused to take any position, apparently assuming that the U.S. government would eventually protect their interests. Not even McKean could get them to lay their negotiating positions on the table.

The Canadians posed a different kind of problem. Loans and financing agreements from Canadian banks had been made almost entirely to Chrysler's Canadian subsidiary, Chrysler Canada. Most of these loans were not unsecured, as in the case of the American banks' revolving credit agreement, for example, but secured by rights to the proceeds and assets of the Canadian subsidiary, which gave the Canadians a higher priority. The Canadians were already trying to negotiate their own restructuring with Chrysler Canada, using the superior leverage they possessed as a result of their secured loans.

Then, without advance warning, the Canadian banks froze $50 million of Chrysler deposits in Canada. When the U.S. banks found out, they were furious, since one of the premises of the loan guarantee act was a comprehensive restructuring of all the bank debt, Canadian included, and an angry McKean called Matteson demanding to know what was going on. Matteson was powerless to do anything, but he attended a meeting the next day at Manufacturers Hanover where he swore that Chrysler had had nothing to do with the freeze and would do everything it could to persuade the Canadian banks to change their approach. He had nearly to beg the U.S. banks not to abandon the recovery plan.

It was also clear to Matteson and Kahn that they had to assign the Canadian negotiations to another partner, just when the impact of the huge Chrysler operation was becoming fully felt throughout the firm. Chrysler was complaining that it was running out of money and it couldn't understand why its lawyers at Debevoise weren't making faster progress. Some other clients had been calling with requests that looked almost as if they were trying to test Debevoise—to make sure they hadn't been abandoned in favor of Chrysler. And rumblings within the partnership were steadily growing. Though Matteson hadn't attended the most recent partnership lunch, the complaints had been reported to him. Non-Chrysler partners and associates were now working almost as long and hard as those involved in Chrysler, trying to cover the needs of the firm's regular clients.

Non-Chrysler partners were also alarmed because billings to Chrysler were rising above the 15 percent of total billings which had long served as a firm limit with respect to a single client. Early in its history, the firm had decided that it never wanted to be dependent on a single client, whose displeasure and loss as a client could threaten the existence of the firm itself, and hence the exercise of its independent judgment; and it had imposed that limit. Now Chrysler was moving above it. Furthermore, the nature of the work was making it partner-intensive, which prevented the firm from capitalizing on its usual pyramid staffing structure. These concerns led one partner to propose that a cut-off be established for Chrysler work—a point at which Chrysler would be warned that the firm simply couldn't do any more. Kahn's reaction to the problem was "I told you so."

At the partnership luncheon that week, Matteson made an appearance to plead for an even greater commitment of partner time, especially for someone to take over the negotiations with the Canadian banks and government. There were no takers, but after the meeting, George Lindsay, one of the firm's senior partners and the elder brother of former New York City Mayor John Lindsay, went into Matteson's office and volunteered.

Lindsay had heard the grumbling among some of his partners, and his decision to join the Chrysler team in the firm was a quiet but effective signal that the dissension should stop and that the partners should unite behind Matteson. After Oscar Reubhausen, the firm's presiding partner, Lindsay was perhaps the most respected member of the partnership, a 25-year veteran of the firm, responsible for some of its most important clients, including American Airlines and Ogilvy & Mather, the large advertising agency. Despite his age, 61, commitments to other clients, and his need for shoulder surgery, "Lindsay went in and volunteered. That's the kind of guy he is," comments one of his partners. "And I think also there were other people who said, 'If George Lindsay can make this kind of sacrifice, then so can I.' " In any event, rash proposals such as the Chrysler cut-off point disappeared.

It would take more than Lindsay's presence, however, to handle the recurring problems with the banks. One morning Matteson scanned the New York Times and noticed an interview with Lee Iacocca. As he read the article, he groaned to himself. Iacocca was quoted as saying that Chrysler really didn't need any federally guaranteed loans and, worse, that although the banks were being extremely uncooperative, they would eventually fall into line. "I knew this would upset the banks, and as far as I knew, we desperately needed the federal money," Matteson recalls. He immediately called Iacocca, who said both that the quotes were inaccurate and that they were supposed to be only for background. In any event, Matteson had to spend a full day calling the bankers, disavowing the remarks, smoothing ruffled feathers and getting Iacocca to issue a mollifying press release.

The incident came just as slight progress was beginning to be made by the banks themselves. Meeting steadily throughout December and January, McKean had managed to impose a semblance of order on the hundreds of banks, getting them to agree that all lenders would have to share the burden of helping Chrysler survive. But the banks were almost as suspicious of one another as they were of Chrysler and the government. If even a single one of them refused to go along with the structuring, the whole effort would collapse. Even one small bank could put Chrysler over the brink into bankruptcy. Kahn's role put him in the unenviable position of having to extract as many concessions on behalf of Chrysler as possible, on the one hand, and yet not obtain any concessions from one bank so favorable to Chrysler that it caused other banks to break ranks.

"Chrysler had no bargaining power other than to threaten to commit suicide," Debevoise's Kahn points out. "It was very hard for me to say 'no' to anything they wanted. I got rid of a few of their suggestions by acting like it was an affront to my dignity, but there wasn't much I could do." Chrysler had only the threat of bankruptcy, which, unfortunately, was an even more undesirable outcome for Chrysler than for the banks. Kahn kept trying to impress the bankers with the hazards of bankruptcy, and the potential extent of their losses if that happened. But the banks had done their own studies of what would happen to them if Chrysler went under, and Kahn never knew just how bad that scenario was for them. All he could do was warn that certain provisions sought by the banks would never be approved in Washington, and hence, no federal support would be forthcoming. In short, he could threaten bankruptcy.

For example, the banks wanted the right to accelerate collection of their loans if it became obvious that Chrysler was going to fail even with its federally guaranteed loans. Under the act passed by Congress, the federal government had been given the right to accelerate—one which is usually standard in loan agreements—and the banks couldn't understand why they couldn't have the same right. The problem, from the government's and Chrysler's point of view, was that under the circumstances, the right of a bank to accelerate repayment was like giving each bank a hatchet to Chrysler's neck.

But McKean and the bank lawyers hammered away on the issue with Kahn and the Treasury lawyers, and finally the government conceded that, in the event of a true catastrophe that would imperil Chrysler—a complete shut-off of oil imports, for example—the banks could accelerate repayment. Given that toehold, the banks raced to take advantage of it. When they came back to Kahn, they had drafted a long list of covenants entitling them to acceleration. Their idea of "catastrophe" covered everything from Chrysler's failure to produce as many K-cars as it had predicted, to allowing inventory levels to rise above what the banks considered an unhealthy level.

Kahn was aghast. Though he spent Friday night from 9:00 P.M. to 4:00 A.M. trying to talk McKean and the bank lawyers out of their proposals, his only bargaining power was "This will never fly in D.C.," and he failed to get any material changes. Sunday morning he was back in the office when the phone rang. It was Roger Altman, the Deputy Treasury Secretary, asking, "Where in the hell did these acceleration clauses come from?" Altman said the provisions were unacceptable, that the government was not going to allow the banks to second-guess it about when Chrysler couldn't survive, that the whole concept of the banks' covenants flew in the face of the act. Kahn happily answered, "Yes, sir," and got on the phone to McKean. Most of the acceleration clauses quietly disappeared from the bank drafts. "I've never negotiated like this," Kahn says. "It was like after I was beaten up, I'd say, 'I'm going to tell my father.'"

While Kahn was working nights and weekends toward some long-term financial relief, Chrysler's short-term plight was becoming increasingly precarious. Originally, the company had calculated that it had until January 15 to meet its immediate cash needs, but by defaulting on its Japanese obligations and arranging an additional $100 million in trade credits it had managed to eke out the cash for another month. But now February 15 was fast approaching, the original target for federal guarantees that had been dubbed "D-Day"—Drop Dead Day—by the bankers and their lawyers. Chrysler had been busy trying to sell some of its assets, since it was plain that federal aid would never be in place by mid-February. A sale of the Chrysler Finance Company to Household Finance was in the works, but it, too, would be delayed for at least several months. Because it held a block of Peugeot stock as a result of its sale of Chrysler Europe, the company turned to its European trading partner, where it got some encouragement. Peugeot was willing to lend Chrysler another $100 million if the debt could be secured by the Peugeot stock held by Chrysler.

Longstreth cringed when he heard the proposal. The problem with the Peugeot loan proposal was that Peugeot couldn't have first priority on the Peugeot stock held by Chrysler, as it would in a secured loan, because under the loan guarantee act, the U.S. government had first priority on all of Chrysler's assets. Nor could Chrysler simply sell the stock, which, at prevailing market prices, would have resulted in a substantial loss. In early negotiations with Peugeot, the French manufacturer made clear that it would not subordinate its security interest in the stock to that of the U.S. government.

The Peugeot conundrum was typical of the many situations where Debevoise lawyers found themselves trapped between the interests of Chrysler and the government and, as a result, had to lay their own reputations on the line. Desperate for the cash, Longstreth essentially agreed to the conditions demanded by Peugeot. Then, rather than treat the transaction as a loan, he convinced the Treasury that it should properly be treated as a sale, and that the $100 million should thus count as part of the $1.43 billion in non-government financing that had to be obtained for Chrysler to qualify for the federal loan guarantees. True, the Peugeot deal looked like a loan. But because Chrysler succeeded in getting Peugeot to agree that it would have no recourse against Chrysler other than through seizure of the stock pledged as security, the loan could become a "sale" if Chrysler simply refused to pay back the Peugeot loan and Peugeot exercised its rights and took the stock. Chrysler would have its $100 million free and clear, and Peugeot would have Chrysler's Peugeot stock. But to protect Chrysler's interests vis-à-vis all of its other creditors, Longstreth had to draft one of the many "opinion letters" which would be produced before the deal was concluded.

An opinion letter is simply the representation of a law firm that a client is entitled to act on a legal conclusion provided by the firm. The law firm assumes liability for the accuracy of that conclusion, and as a result, puts its reputation on the line. A firm's opinions are only as good as its reputation, since they will be relied upon and acted upon only if clients and the public have confidence in them. In that regard, Chrysler pushed Longstreth and his partners to what Longstreth calls the "margins of confidence." "The Peugeot deal—the only cash Chrysler saw during this entire period—was really pushing as far as you can go," he says. Nonetheless, he issued a Debevoise opinion saying that the Peugeot "loan" was, for purposes of the Chrysler Loan Guarantee Act, a "sale of assets." With the $100 million from Peugeot, the February 15 D-Day was averted.

Though the $100 million was only a reprieve, it was one of the few bright spots in the course of the negotiations; and for Longstreth, at least, it suddenly made the Chrysler restructuring look possible. The following Saturday, he and associate Peter Borowitz spent the day and evening working at the Madison Hotel in Washington on information to submit to the Treasury at an informal meeting the next morning. They finished up around midnight. The long hours and his new-found optimism made Longstreth feel a bit giddy, and when he discovered that he had run out of clean T-shirts, he hit upon the idea of "fun" T-shirts that he and the Chrysler executives could wear at the next day's meetings. He and Borowitz took a cab to an all-night head shop in Georgetown, where they had Chrysler T-shirts printed with catchy phrases like "Property of the Loan Guarantee Board." The two lawyers ended up giggling in a Georgetown bar until they returned to the hotel around 3:00 A.M. It was one of Longstreth's last good laughs on the deal. By the time he dressed the next morning, wearing the T-shirt under his business shirt, the idea didn't seem quite so amusing. And at the Treasury meeting, he and Borowitz were told coldly that their latest set of proposals wouldn't pass muster. The T-shirts were not unveiled.

The atmosphere was even bleaker for the Debevoise lawyers on location in Detroit, a team of corporate lawyers headed by Paul Wilson, Jr., a bearded, relatively young partner and Matteson protégé. Wilson had volunteered for the Chrysler deal especially to prepare the prospectuses that would be necessary to support the more than $75 million which the act required be raised through the sale of notes and securities, all of which would have to be registered with the Securities and Exchange Commission in a process similar to that which Genentech had undergone.

Toward the end of January, Wilson asked senior associate Steven Gross if he wanted to "spend a little time in Detroit." That time had nearly turned into permanent residence. During the week, Wilson and Gross interrogated Chrysler executives and pored over documents, trying to compile the detailed information which would have to be included in any prospectus. During the day they interviewed company officers, accountants and outside consultants and auditors; on weekends and at night they read accounting reports and company documents.

Each Saturday afternoon, Wilson flew from Detroit to New York and ate out with his wife on Saturday evening. Sunday afternoon he took his three children to a movie, and then left for the airport. By Sunday night he was back in the Debevoise conference room in Chrysler's bleak Highland Park headquarters building. At least he saw a few movies. For the other lawyers working seven days a week, he became the Chrysler team's Pauline Kael, through whom they watched movies vicariously.

The goal of Wilson and the lawyers working with him was to come up with an accurate picture of Chrysler—its financial state and its business prospects—that was sufficiently bleak so that no one who subscribed to the contemplated offering of subordinated debentures would be misled. Chrysler executives were not eager to disclose some of the embarrassing aspects of Chrysler's plight, but the lawyers knew that the prospectuses would be closely scrutinized not only by the SEC but by skeptical members of Congress and the loan guarantee board. Wilson's target date for filing a preliminary prospectus with the SEC had been February 22, and within a few days he had finished the draft document. There was little elation, however. The night before, the U.S. hockey team defeated the Soviet Union in the 1980 Winter Olympics. Wilson had spent the night in the dank, badly lit workroom of a Detroit printer reading proofs of the debenture prospectus.

Wilson's draft prospectus contained the grim conclusion that Chrysler expected to lose as much as $500 million during 1980. At the weekly meetings in Detroit between top Chrysler executives, the Debevoise lawyers, and members of various task forces working to meet the terms of the loan guarantee act, Chrysler's chief financial officer, Jerry Greenwald, acted more and more anxious about the continuing outflow of cash. Each week he had a new timetable to give to Matteson and Longstreth, which the two partners dutifully carried with them back to New York even though they felt it set impossible targets. It put the lawyers in a bind, caught between the morale of their Debevoise colleagues, who were already overworked, and the growing impatience of their clients, who never seemed to understand what was taking them so long. Greenwald had already begun to have some doubts about the commitment of the Debevoise lawyers. Late one night, he, Lee Iacocca and some other officers had emerged from a conference room into one of the long corridors in the company's headquarters, and a rolling tennis ball had bounced off his foot. He looked down the dim corridor and perceived a group of Debevoise lawyers engaged in a makeshift game of bowling. But their antics were actually a by-product of hard work. The lawyers' average work days were stretching from 12 to 14 to 18 hours.

The strains were beginning to show up at the Debevoise offices in New York as well. Matteson, sometimes irritable in the best of circumstances, was becoming, in the opinion of some of the lawyers, positively autocratic. It annoyed them that he circulated weekly progress memos around the firm filled with terse commands to other partners and demands that they "report to" Matteson. Senior partner George Lindsay was the only exception. He was never commanded to "report to" Matteson; rather, Lindsay's entries simply mentioned that he was "working on" a particular matter.

"That was Matteson's approach," comments one Debevoise lawyer. "If you were below him on the letterhead, you worked for him. That attitude didn't sit very well." One day someone glued a *New Yorker* cartoon over the nameplate outside of Matteson's office. The cartoon depicted a king shouting, "Where are my minions?" Even Longstreth was driven into a loud argument with Matteson that spilled into the office corridors, shocking several secretaries and passing associates.

The firm seemed to be at such a crucial juncture that it scheduled, for the first time in its history, a "retreat" of all the partners to the Sterling Forest, a wooded conference center in upstate New York, for February 28, just when some of the Chrysler tensions seemed to be at their peak. "Chrysler wasn't a formal topic of discussion," Longstreth recalls, "but it was omnipresent. It was discussed as the kind of work we would be facing in the future— the notion that the large firm is going to have to handle the huge projects that require expertise from a variety of disciplines. And we talked openly about the dislocations in our lives, the resentment of our other clients." The goal of the retreat wasn't to reach any hard and fast conclusions, but to give partners a chance to talk openly with one another. In the final analysis, it may have been the Saturday evening of "light entertainment"—including a humorous song about Francis Plimpton composed by Longstreth, a series of Chrysler jokes, and a considerable amount of drinking —that did the most to boost the firm's spirits.

If Debevoise spirits were up after the meeting, those of Chrysler executives were down. Chrysler's business conditions continued to worsen during the first quarter of 1980, raising the prospect that the company's loss for the year might actually be higher than the predicted $500 million. The failure of interest rates to fall as forecast—and the government's continuing insistence on tight credit as a weapon against inflation—had depressed auto sales. Worse, the credit restrictions had caused Household Finance to scuttle its plans to buy the Chrysler Finance Company. When Longstreth went to the Treasury to report that CFC couldn't be sold—one of the conditions for guaranteed loans—he was told that CFC would also have to become a part of the Chrysler refinancing plan, with the restructuring of CFC equally subject to the approval of the loan board. It was as though the Debevoise lawyers now had to handle two Chrysler work-outs simultaneously. CFC alone had credit arrangements with 282 banks.

The bad news about CFC at least seemed to have the effect of galvanizing some of the banks, whose tough negotiating had gotten virtually no concessions out of Washington. After it became clear to Simpson, Thacher's McKean that the other banks wouldn't trust him and Manufacturers Hanover to act on behalf of all of them, a committee of the fifteen largest U.S. lenders was organized. It hired Leonard Rosen, a neutral bankruptcy specialist at New York's Wachtell, Lipton, Rosen & Katz, to act as its special counsel. The European banks had finally hired their own counsel—Sullivan & Cromwell—and the Japanese had hired Sidley & Austin, one of Chicago's leading law firms. The groups of bankers had finally begun to work out their differences together and had actually come up with a concrete plan that, although far from meeting the kind of figures called for by the loan guarantee act, looked like a starting point for real discussions. To present the plan, they arranged a meeting on April 1 with Chrysler executives and lawyers in the Pan Am building in New York.

Steve Miller, Chrysler's treasurer, opened the meeting by stating gravely that the company had given up and had, that morning, filed for bankruptcy. This attempt at humor—Miller quickly identified his remark as an April Fool's joke—drew no laughs. But coupled with the bad news about CFC, it seemed to prod the negotiators. Within a week, Matteson and his teams at Debevoise were putting the finishing touches on at least an outline of a comprehensive solution to the impasse between Chrysler and its lenders. Matteson and Longstreth took the proposal to Mundheim at Treasury, where they were reassured that if it was the best that Chrysler could do in complying with the act, the loan guarantee board was willing to be flexible about some of its requirements. The lawyers flew back to New York to begin the drafting.

On Saturday, April 12, virtually the entire team of Chrysler lawyers assembled at the Debevoise offices, along with lawyers for some of the banks. Working in offices, conference rooms and spilling over into some of the Wachtell, Lipton offices in the same building, with a full stenographic staff and Vydec typewriters working at capacity, the lawyers began drafting the agreements to restructure Chrysler's debt with its lenders. The task was enormous. As well as the restructured debt between each bank and Chrysler, which included changes in payment terms, interest rate concessions and the like, each bank had to enter into three additional agreements with Chrysler: a set-off agreement in case of bankruptcy, in which banks could immediately claim Chrysler deposits and other assets within their possession as partial satisfaction of the debts Chrysler owed them; a "stand-still" agreement in which the banks agreed that they would not sue Chrysler in the event of its default; and a "subordination" agreement, in which the banks agreed that their priority would be inferior to that of the federal government.

As a result of loan guarantee board requirements, there were also agreements defining the banks' rights to acquire preferred stock in lieu of cash repayment, and the banks had also insisted on "warrants," or rights to purchase Chrysler common stock at a set price. The theory was that if Chrysler ever recovered and its stock price rose, the banks would be able to share in the good fortune they had helped make possible by buying cheap stock. All of these documents had to be accomplished by formal written opinions from Debevoise that the transactions were legal.

For the approximately 150 lawyers from Debevoise and nine other law firms representing the various banking interests, the drafting work was intense and tedious. After initial drafts of particular sections were finished, lawyers scrutinized every line and made suggested changes. Despite Kahn's commitment to "cut out the boilerplate so dear to corporate lawyers' hearts," as he puts it, haggling among the lawyers resulted in highly technical language virtually incomprehensible to a reader untrained in law and the vocabulary of the banking industry.

For example, in the basic debt restructuring agreement, formally titled the "Amended and Restated Credit Agreement," Chrysler agreed that it would not permit its outstanding debt to rise too far above its net worth, a situation which could result in large losses for the banks in the event that Chrysler went under. In the course of the drafting and negotiating, this relatively simple concept emerged as follows:

> The Company hereby covenants that from and after the Cross-Over Date, so long as any of the Notes remain outstanding and unpaid, unless the Required Banks otherwise consent in writing:
> ... The Company will not permit the outstanding aggregate principal amount of Indebtedness for Money Borrowed at any time during the First Year and the Second Year to exceed 110% of Consolidated Net Worth, nor to exceed 100% of Consolidated Net Worth at any time after the Second Year, *provided* that for the purpose of this subsection 6.3 (including the calculations to be made pursuant to the immediately following proviso), (a) the term "indebtedness for Money Borrowed" shall include obligations of the Company and its Subsidiaries under outstanding accounts payable but only if unpaid for 105 days or more and (b) so long as the Company shall have the right to exercise the option provided in the

Preferred Stock Option Agreement, all outstanding Subject Notes (as such term is defined in the Preferred Stock Option Agreement) shall be treated as if such option had already been exercised with respect to such Subject Notes and *provided further* that, notwithstanding the foregoing, the Company shall be deemed to be in compliance with this subsection 6.3 during the First Year if Debt/Net Worth during the First year at no time exceeds 115% of Average Debt/Net Worth.

The provision cannot be understood without reference to one of sixty-one definitions contained earlier in the agreement: some of them are longer and more complicated than the provisions of the act itself. The Preferred Stock Option Agreement—an entirely separate agreement to which the reader is referred—contains twenty-one additional definitions of terms and phrases.

The creation of such an intricate jigsaw puzzle of agreements is what some corporate lawyers—those whose pleasure in the task seems directly correlated to its complexity—describe as "elegant" drafting. But for many the work can be maddening. One lawyer at the drafting session said, "This drafting was done in the course of three nearly 24-hour days. Lawyers would slump over the tables, then go out for a few hours of sleep. But what was going on was not real negotiating. The basic terms of this deal had all been already agreed upon by the banks and by Chrysler. We were just implementing them, we were technicians. We were arguing over whether a clause should be restrictive or non-restrictive, whether we should say 'any' or 'all,' whether a semicolon should replace a period. It takes a peculiar kind of mind to enjoy this sort of thing—one that likes to look for typos."

The Chrysler case required so many provisions, some of them singular, which then had to be arranged differently from anything that had ever been done before, that it was uniquely challenging. Even so, the core of the agreements was resurrected from the corporate files of Debevoise and the other law firms that were involved. Over the years, such major firms acquire an example, or a model form, of nearly every conceivable corporate transaction. Lawyers simply summon the appropriate form, usually by computer, and change a few words to adapt it to the transaction at hand, a process known as "marking up." It is by no means a mindless task, but entrenched attitudes of "What worked before will work again" have contributed to the persistent appearance of the essentially meaningless "boilerplate" that encumbers and obscures many corporate documents.

What had emerged in Chrysler's long series of meetings with the banks—their distrust of each other and of the federal government, and of course, the banks' suspicions of Chrysler—was evident in the lawyers' final product. The banks' agreements with Chrysler built in conditions that had to be met *before* the debt restructuring could go into effect. The provisions required that:

- every bank execute the restructuring agreement (the banks, especially some of the smaller ones, always remained suspicious that one or more of the banks would get a better deal by withholding its approval until the last minute);
- CFC's restructuring plan be approved by the loan guarantee board and be in effect;
- the loan guarantee board approve the Chrysler plan and guarantee the loans;
- Chrysler secure additional financing, including the successful issuance of the subordinated debentures approved by the SEC;
- legal opinions be obtained from Debevoise and from Kelley, Drye.

If even one of the conditions was not met, every bank would be released from its refinancing agreements. Now, could the Debevoise lawyers persuade Treasury that the banks had met the requirements imposed by the loan guarantee act? Had they agreed to the concessions and extensions of financial support mandated by the act? Moreover, would every bank go along with the provisions—even the recalcitrant Canadians?

George Lindsay, the senior partner who had generously volunteered for the Canadian negotiations, thinking it would be a discreet portion of the much bigger deal, had encountered a hornet's nest in Canada. He had practically moved to Toronto in order to conduct full-time negotiations with the Canadian government and the banks. Not only had the Canadian banks more secured positions than their American counterparts (which they felt entitled them to superior positions in the loan restructuring), but both the banks and the Canadian government desired redress of what they perceived to be decades of American imperialism.

Chrysler Canada sold its products in U.S. markets on 60-day

payment terms; Chrysler U.S. sold to Canada on 30-day terms. The difference in payment terms meant that Chrysler Canada financed the U.S. operation to the tune of about $100 million per year. As part of the proposed restructuring, Canada wanted the same 30-day repayment terms—something Chrysler simply could not afford under the circumstances. Such an arrangement would never satisfy the loan guarantee board, which had demanded concessions, not more favorable terms, from Chrysler's creditors.

Lindsay spent as much time negotiating with the Canadian Minister of Trade and Commerce and his top aides as with the Canadian banks. For an example, the banks decided that if they were going to extend additional credit and renegotiate the outstanding loans, they wanted the Canadian government to guarantee some of the loans as well. The Canadian government agreed that it would guarantee about $200 million of loans, but only if Chrysler could guarantee minimal levels of employment in Canada. The sensitive political nature of that issue was driven home to Lindsay one evening as he was watching television in his room at Toronto's Royal York Hotel. A few months before, the Ford Motor Company had obtained some loan assistance from the Canadian government, and had then soon closed one of its Canadian plants. As Lindsay watched the news, Robert DeCotret, the Trade, Industry and Commerce Minister with whom he had been negotiating, was pictured before the Canadian parliament as he was questioned about the Ford closing. According to Lindsay, he was "roasted" for approving the Ford loan support. Some MP's now asked him, "What are you going to do now about Chrysler?"

Lindsay realized that the Canadian government was in a political bind; it couldn't give in on the employment issue. But if Chrysler were to guarantee levels of employment in Canada it would enrage the American unions, which had been told, both by Chrysler and the loan guarantee board, that no such promise would be made. While Lindsay continued to press for Canadian concessions in negotiating sessions that often lasted until 3:00 A.M., Debevoise lawyers in New York began negotiating with Leonard Woodcock and Douglas Frazier, leaders of the United Auto Workers in the U.S. Just as those negotiations all seemed to inch forward, the Trudeau government was defeated and replaced by that of the new Prime Minister, Charles Joseph Clark. All the negotiations started over.

The Canadian loans and guarantees also had to be approved by the Ontario provincial government. While it was at first expected that this would be pro forma, Ontario officials decided to withhold approval unless Chrysler promised to build a large new research facility in the province. It seemed that everyone now had a gun at Chrysler's head, and that all Lindsay could do was try to delay their pulling the trigger. By the time the U.S. bankers and lawyers held their marathon drafting session at Debevoise on April 10 to memorialize the comprehensive agreement they had reached, Lindsay had to concede to his colleagues that the Canadian negotiations were making no progress. But he stayed at the bargaining table. In April, he postponed indefinitely surgery for the shoulder he had injured in a skiing accident the previous winter.

Despite Lindsay's problems with the Canadians, Richard Kahn pressed forward with the agreement among the U.S. and European banks. After the draft was complete, Kahn and Matteson flew to Detroit, where a meeting with representatives of Chrysler's 400 creditors was convened in Chrysler's auditorium. The terms of the amended and restated credit agreement worked out at the Debevoise offices in New York were explained to the banks' representatives, and it was emphasized that every single bank had to sign the agreement. It was left to McKean to drive home the message that the major banks, like Manufacturers Hanover, were prepared to let Chrysler go bankrupt rather than to allow even the smaller lenders to escape the provisions of the loan restructuring.

That message was impressed with force upon the twenty banks that were still holding out from the agreement. Three of them had brought lawsuits against Chrysler, forcing Debevoise to organize a litigation team to make sure that the suits didn't go forward until the restructuring negotiations had a chance to succeed. Debevoise lawyers had to worry about local counsel in Salt Lake City, Rockford, Illinois, and Fort Wayne, Indiana, where Chrysler lawyers persuaded judges not to go forward with suits against Chrysler by the First Security Bank of Utah, Peoples Trust Bank of Fort Wayne, and the American National Bank & Trust Co. of Rockford. Although those banks accounted for a relatively small amount of Chrysler's outstanding credit, any one of those suits could have destroyed the delicate overall agreement.

Though the Chrysler lawyers persuaded the judges that a successful restructuring would eliminate the need for the lawsuits—and hence, that no precipitous orders should be entered—the litigation itself had nothing to do with bringing the hold-out banks around to the agreement. Kahn, McKean, a number of other lawyers, company executives and government officials, brought every bit of old-fashioned pressure to bear that they could muster. As a spokesman for First Security later told *The American Banker*, "We did not want to be known as the bank that threw 600,000 Americans out of work." American National Bank & Trust Co. got a direct call from Treasury Secretary G. William Miller. Peoples Trust capitulated when it became convinced that the major banks would let Chrysler go bankrupt rather than excuse it from the restructuring. "I find the whole thing incredible," the bank's president insisted even in the end.

Meanwhile, delay was taking its toll on the congressional front, enabling Senator Proxmire and some of his Senate Banking Committee allies to keep up an ongoing guerrilla war against Chrysler, threatening its chances of getting the federally guaranteed loans. The urgency of the situation had been driven home late in March, when Longstreth got a call from Mundheim at Treasury asking him if he had heard about Senator Lowell Weicker's activities in the Senate that day. Longstreth hadn't and, in fact, says he was "dazzled" to learn that Weicker had introduced a Senate resolution that Debevoise's, Chrysler's and Treasury's interpretations of the loan guarantee act were "fundamentally wrong" and precluded Chrysler's getting the guarantees. The resolution was only defeated by a couple of votes. Longstreth was a little red-faced that he hadn't even known the vote was to take place and hadn't sent anyone to cover the debate.

But it made clear the fact that because Treasury or the loan board had come around on some issues didn't mean that their solutions would pass muster in Congress. For example, because of the intransigence of the banks and their insistence that all be treated equally in sharing the burden of salvaging Chrysler, the ratio of domestic to foreign bank concessions specified in the loan guarantee act had to be altered so that it was more even. The Treasury and loan board's conclusions that such an alteration was still in the "spirit" of the legislation was the kind of tampering that gave Weicker an excuse to try to derail the entire effort.

As soon as the bank agreement began to take shape in April,

Longstreth also assigned teams of Debevoise associates to draft the documents which would support Chrysler's formal application to the loan guarantee board and which would set forth Chrysler's compliance with the terms of the act. These included a number of formal legal documents, such as the "agreement to guarantee" between Chrysler and the United States, the lengthy document spelling out the details of the relationship between Chrysler and the government, replete with elaborate definitions and provisions for interpretation;* an indenture of mortgage between Chrysler and Manufacturer's National Bank of Detroit, representing a mortgage on Chrysler's real estate holdings; Chrysler directors' agreements, in which the company's directors personally warranted the validity of the factual information being put forth by the company; stock purchase warrants between Chrysler and the United States, enabling the Treasury to purchase Chrysler stock at a fixed price and thus share in Chrysler's recovery, if it ever happened; as well as factual reports prepared in conjunction with Chrysler executives and management, outside management consultants and accountants describing Chrysler's energy savings plan and its ability to continue production after receipt of the additional loans; a detailed four-year operating plan for the company; a detailed financing plan; reports on collective bargaining agreements and labor concessions; prospects for Chrysler's sale or merger; as well as other materials called for by the loan guarantee legislation. Although crucial elements of the application were still missing—notably the refinancing plan for the banks—about twenty Debevoise partners and associates spread out into various conference rooms to draw up final versions of the reports.

Late in April, the package was beginning to come together. With the bank compromise taking shape, Longstreth was again seeing a glimmer of light at the end of the tunnel. On April 18, he

---

* "This indenture shall be construed and enforced in accordance with federal law where applicable and otherwise in accordance with the internal laws of the State of Michigan except to the extent that the laws of any other jurisdiction mandatorily govern the manner or procedure for the enforcement of the lien created by this indenture on the trust estate, *provided* that any remedies herein provided which shall be valid under the laws of the jurisdiction where proceedings for the enforcement hereof shall be taken shall not be affected by any invalidity hereof under the laws of the State of Michigan.

flew to Washington for the weekly meeting of the loan guarantee board, and he was looking forward to a session where he could iron out a few remaining problems with the board and report some real progress. No sooner did he arrive at the Treasury building than he was met by an anxious and worried-looking Lee Iacocca. While flying on the Chrysler executive plane from Detroit to Washington that day, Iacocca had received a telephone call from Michigan Senator Donald W. Riegle, Jr., Chrysler's staunchest ally in the Senate. Riegle had told Iacocca that Chrysler had to take immediate action, that another congressional challenge from Proxmire and Weicker was brewing, and that it might succeed. Chrysler had to file its application for the loan guarantees that very day. Time had run out, and Iacocca had lost patience with the Debevoise lawyers. "We're not talking, we're filing," he told Longstreth. He ordered Longstreth to get the papers, telling him that he had called a press conference to announce the filing immediately after the meeting of the loan board.

Longstreth recalls, "I panicked. I thought, 'Well, okay. Let's go with it. It'll have some loose ends, but we'll just have to brush the legal niceties aside.' " Longstreth called associates Steve Gross and Peter Borowitz and told them to bring down the filing package immediately. Gross and Borowitz couldn't believe their ears. Was Longstreth kidding? They were told they had two hours to get the application done.

Gross and Borowitz galvanized every Chrysler associate they could find and sat down and started writing; besides the loose ends, there were some loose middles and beginnings. Finally, they gathered the documents together, tried to arrange them in some comprehensible order, and stuffed them into several large litigation bags. Stacked upright, the pages were more than two feet tall. Borowitz raced to the airport and arrived in Washington as Iacocca finished his press conference at which he had announced that the Chrysler application had just been filed. But when Borowitz proffered the documents themselves, he was told by Longstreth that there had been a change in strategy. He and Iacocca had decided that filing then was premature after all.

As it turned out, the associates' haste to get the package together had caused some pages to be omitted. And Iacocca's announcement, disingenuous though it may have been, succeeded in gaining the lawyers a few more days of breathing space. Ten days later, the loan guarantee application was formally filed with the Treasury Department and the loan guarantee board, even though many of its components had still not been finally worked out. Chrysler was again running out of cash, and Longstreth desperately hoped that the board would quickly approve the application.

It was Mother's Day weekend, and in Detroit the moods of Paul Wilson and his prospectus-drafting team matched the tone of the final draft of the prospectus itself—bleak. Each time Wilson would complete a version which seemed a fair statement of Chrysler's financial condition, one that would not mislead investors, it seemed that something terrible would happen. In the version he had shown the SEC in mid-February, Wilson had predicted a $500 million loss for the year. In his mid-March version the situation had worsened sufficiently so that he had to couch his $500 million loss prediction in all kinds of high-risk language. Then he started analyzing dealer sales reports that were coming in from the first quarter, and they were bad. Meanwhile, the consulting firm of Booz, Allen & Hamilton, hired by Chrysler for independent assessments of its financial prospects as required by the loan guarantee board, was making even bleaker forecasts. Beginning in early May, Wilson and his team began to revise substantially the prospectus to be filed with the SEC. The version was so pessimistic that Wilson began to wonder why anyone in his right mind would invest in a Chrysler subordinated debenture after reading it.

Wilson began by increasing the loss estimate from $500 million to $750 million. "At the beginning of 1980," he wrote, "Chrysler had a 1980 loss objective of approximately $500 million, which it has subsequently revised upward, first to approximately $650 million and then to approximately $750 million, to take into account a number of factors, including the adverse effects on the automotive industry of the recent substantial increase in interest rates and the credit restrictions imposed by the federal government during 1980 which, together with the current economic recession, have recently resulted in sharp reductions of inventories by dealers and in decreased retail sales to an extent not foreseen at the beginning of the year." But, he continued, "it is not certain that Chrysler will be able to contain its 1980 loss to approximately $750 million." If that were not discouraging enough, emblazoned on the cover of the prospectus in bold-face type was the statement that "These securities are highly speculative, involve a high degree of risk and should be purchased only by those persons who can afford a total loss of the purchase price and who are purchasing the Debentures because they have determined that it is in their interest to support the viability of Chrysler." In all, it was one of the longest and most complicated prospectuses ever filed at the SEC: 85 pages of dense text, accompanied by 43 pages of exhibits and addenda, most of it discouraging.

The strain of constant drafting in Detroit had begun to take its toll on Wilson. He had begun to do things like sneak into an isolated empty office in the Chrysler headquarters, where he would close the door, then spend a "lost" hour listening to Mozart on the radio. Saturday, May 10, had to be spent at the printer's in Detroit, proofreading copies of the final draft prospectus. But since the next day was Mother's Day, he wanted it to be a nice day for himself and the Debevoise associates who were working with him. That afternoon they took a break to cross into Canada and take a walk in what was described as a nature preserve. The weather was bad, the nature preserve looked like an ill-kept city park, and the outing was, all in all, pretty depressing.

So Wilson arranged with the printer to have steak dinners for everyone brought in to the dreary shop. When the food arrived, everyone jumped up from their proofreading, only to discover that the restaurant had failed to send any utensils. Wilson gnawed his steak using his hands; associate David Pollak used a can opener. They finished their work that morning around 4:00 A.M., and Pollak delivered the final prospectus to the SEC later that week. In a sense, however, Wilson's work on the prospectus never ended. As late as June 18 he was sending mailgrams updating the prospectus to all the debenture subscribers outlining even bleaker financial statistics, offering all the investors the opportunity to withdraw if they wished to do so.

As a selling document, the final prospectus devised by the lawyers seemed disastrously pessimistic. It was so gloomy that Chrysler chairman Lee Iacocca at first refused to sign it. It took a lecture from E. F. Hutton's lawyer to get Iacocca to sign. And Chrysler had to place all of the $500 million in debentures by the time of the deal closing with the banks in order to satisfy the loan guarantee board's conditions as well as the conditions precedent to the loan restructuring agreed to by the banks. Would anyone buy?

As it turned out, E. F. Hutton, the dealer-manager for the debenture offering, had no trouble placing all $500 million of the notes—to buyers who probably never read the prospectus or, if they did, really didn't care what it had to say. All of the notes were sold to Chrysler dealers, who, if Chrysler went under, would be out of business themselves. The prospect of a $500 million or a $750 million loss by Chrysler seemed insignificant in the face of their own loss of a business. As a result of Wilson's painstaking and time-consuming efforts, the dealers certainly knew what they were getting into when they committed themselves to Chrysler's rescue. "When people are investing their money, they have to know these things," Wilson says of his efforts. On the other hand, he concedes that his careful updating of the prospectus may have been unnecessary. "Nothing ever happened that these people hadn't been warned about, but this seemed the safest approach." The safe approach certainly consumed the time and attention of a battery of lawyers. Besides the fact gathering and drafting, formal opinions attesting to the legal validity of the debentures had to be entered by Debevoise, Plimpton; by Kelley, Drye; and by a Delaware law firm, all on behalf of Chrysler—and by Dewey, Ballantine, Bushby, Palmer & Wood, the large New York firm that was counsel for E. F. Hutton, the underwriters.

Had the securities ever been offered to the general public, the efforts of all these lawyers would surely have prevented anyone from buying them.

The Saturday before Wilson's bleak Mother's Day, Treasury Secretary Miller called a press conference to announce that the Chrysler debt restructuring agreement with the creditor banks had been resolved and that, as a result, the loan guarantee board, meeting that day, had approved the loan guarantee application submitted by Chrysler, finding that it met the requirements of the act. But the announcement was not the cause for joy among the Chrysler lawyers and executives that it might otherwise seem to be. The nearly thousand-page report was really not much more than a statement of the considerable progress Chrysler had made toward meeting the requirements of the act.

Annexed to the commitment to guarantee, were twenty-seven conditions which had to be met before any of the guaranteed loans could be drawn upon—and among them the same vexing problems remained that still plagued Chrysler's negotiations with the banks, and especially the Canadians. Condition number 3 required:

Receipt from all creditors listed on Annex A to the U.S. bank term sheet included in the Application, or their representatives, of term sheets, commitment letters or comparable assurances containing terms substantially comparable to those in the U.S. bank term sheet.

Condition number 10 required "receipt of assurances that the restructuring of the debt of Chrysler Corporation, Chrysler Canada Ltd. and Chrysler Leasing Ltd. will not preclude the dispositions of real estate." These were exactly the agreements which, so far, the Canadian banks and government had withheld.

Lindsay and the Debevoise lawyers finally threw up their hands and told Mundheim at Treasury that they were getting nowhere with the Canadians, who had steadfastly refused even to appear in the same room with the U.S. bankers. The Canadians were furious with the U.S. banks because of their insistence on identical terms with the Canadians. Finally, the Canadian bankers agreed to come to Washington for meetings with Chrysler and Treasury after some direct pleading to the Canadian government by Mundheim and Miller.

It took four days of intense negotiating as well as some intricate legal drafting for a compromise with the Canadians to be worked out. On issues of employment and maintenance of assets in Canada, a compromise was reached in which Chrysler agreed to maintain its Canadian operation as a minimum percentage of its total operations. The United States agreed to equalize Canadian and U.S. payment terms, but at a deferred rate. Construction of the Ontario research plant was made heavily contingent on Chrysler's overall recovery. In the end, the Canadian banks did get a slightly better deal than the U.S. banks, with more liberal rights to declare Chrysler in default after commencement of the guaranteed loans. Lindsay oversaw the drafting, but otherwise he sat by while Treasury and the Canadian government did the real negotiating. The final negotiations were a greater test of international politics than of legal skills.

The Canadians were the last major holdouts, though there were a few skirmishes with some of the European banks; and McKean had to make some hasty trips to Amsterdam to keep the European bankers in line. In fact, one last European crisis threatened to derail the bank agreements only days before the closing. Chrysler had sold its Brazilian subsidiary to Volkswagen, and Volkswagen had deposited the purchase price with a German bank, Deutsche Genossenschaftsbank, for transfer to Chrysler. Instead, DG had promptly seized $10 million of the proceeds to set off against money owed the bank by Chrysler. As with the Canadians, only last-minute intervention by the U.S. government persuaded the bank to return the $10 million.

By June 20—an agonizing month after Chrysler had hoped to draw down the first $500 million of its new credit—all the banks were in line; and in New York, Matteson called a meeting of the few Debevoise Chrysler lawyers actually in the office to announce resolution of the DG crisis. He seemed so tired and drawn that he showed little elation as he announced that the final parts of the package had moved into place and that the end of the ordeal actually appeared to be in sight. Borowitz began to see the possibility of a free weekend for the first time in months, and almost immediately he began to worry that it would be snatched from him at the last minute. "It's not such a disappointment when you don't even expect a break; when you do, it's terrible," he explains. Kahn, still the pessimist, wasn't convinced the deal would finally go through. The focus of his new worries was the mechanics of the actual closing.

Most closings require a few simple flourishes of pens and handshakes; but the number of parties—400 banks, Chrysler, the U.S. Treasury, and note and debenture subscribers—the number of documents, and their intricate interlocking nature, made the Chrysler closing the corporate equivalent of the signing of the Treaty of Versailles.

The federal loan guarantee was contingent on the signature of the banks to the restructuring agreement; the banks' signatures were contingent on every bank participating; the Canadian agreement was contingent on the signing of the federal loan guarantee and the participation of the U.S., European and Japanese banks; and all of these agreements were contingent on the placement of the note and debenture offerings. Technically, the closing required hundreds of papers to be signed at precisely the same moment and place—a physical impossibility. Kahn worked out an arrangement which called for preliminary closings at the four nearby law firms working on the deal. Then, at what he called the "magic moment," lawyers representing all the parties to the agreements would come to Debevoise and simultaneously exchange cross-receipts of execution—written representations that the necessary documents had all been signed in the preliminary closings. Then, Chrysler's Lee Iacocca and Treasury Secretary G. William Miller would lay their pens to the last piece of paper.

The plan was simple enough in concept, but Kahn didn't want to take any chances. He ordered everyone to be at the Debevoise cafeteria for a closing-eve dress rehearsal, planning to minimize any chance of human error. He hadn't counted on an Act of God.

Matteson felt panic creeping in on the perimeter of his thoughts as he watched the conflagration in Debevoise's skyscraper across the street from his vantage point at Sullivan & Cromwell. It was nearing midnight, and it was obvious that no closing could be held at 299 Park Avenue the next day, or probably even the next week. All he could think about was getting the documents out.

Finally Matteson crossed the street and approached one of the firemen on the scene. He told him that one of the largest corporate deals in history might have gone up in flames and that he had to get into the building to rescue the documents. The firefighter didn't seem to appreciate the significance of a Chrysler closing. To Matteson, it seemed incredible that the precarious status of Chrysler hadn't seemed to intrude into the man's consciousness at all; but the fire department officer agreed to talk to the building owner, who was on the scene. The owner seemed somewhat more responsive, if not because he recognized the importance of Chrysler then because he recognized the near hysteria of one of his important tenants. They finally agreed that Matteson could enter the building—for one trip only. Matteson seized the opening. Could he bring a few "helpers"? He raced back to Sullivan & Cromwell, and calls went out to all the other participating firms where lawyers were taking refuge. Within a half hour, Matteson reappeared at the building with more than thirty corporate lawyers, all still neatly dressed in suits and ties, ready for the ascent into a burned-out skyscraper. The firemen shook their heads.

The scene inside the Debevoise offices was chaos. Heavy black soot blanketed every surface. The stench was nauseating. But the papers were still there, dirty but intact. Commandeering the carts that the firm's messengers used for delivering mail and packages, the lawyers started wheeling all the papers into the now-functioning freight elevator.

Late-night pedestrians were greeted by a strange sight: a parade of pinstriped men, pushing supermarket carts in a parade up Park Avenue. The lawyers trailed north for five blocks, then turned east toward the Citicorp skyscraper and the offices of Shearman & Sterling. At 5:00 A.M., the documents were rearranged and in place for the closing. At 9:00 A.M. the ceremony began. Kahn, who had managed to have a shower and one hour of sleep, began to read a roll call of the participants. "Are the American banks ready? Are the Japanese? The Europeans?" he asked. All answered in affirmative, if weary, tones. Finally he came to the end of his list. "Is Chrysler ready?" There was a pause, and then Chrysler treasurer Steven Miller replied, "I guess so." The deal was over.

The day after the closing, for everyone who had participated in the deal, Iacocca threw a large cocktail party at Chrysler's offices in the Pan Am building in New York. In conjunction with the party, he held a press conference in which he went through a long list of thank-yous to those he said had made Chrysler's rescue possible: the bankers, the consultants, the accountants . . . Kahn, representing the Debevoise lawyers at the party, listened closely, but he heard no mention of "the lawyers." In his opinion, he later confided, the omission had been deliberate.

But the mutual dependence between Chrysler and Debevoise, Plimpton continued. Chrysler drew down $500 million of its guaranteed loan support shortly after the closing, but the tangle of agreements kept giving rise to new problems of interpretation and compliance. Subsequent draw-downs by Chrysler required new filings with the government and additional closings. The first major undertaking became known within the firm as "Chrysler I." Like the sequel to a popular movie, the next effort leading to the second draw-down was dubbed "Chrysler II"; and there were more on the horizon. The client/firm relationship between Chrysler and Debevoise was now stronger than ever. Paul Heinen, a former lawyer at Kelley, Drye who was Chrysler's general counsel, was encouraged to find another position after the first closing. He was replaced by Richard Goodyear, a former Debevoise, Plimpton associate recommended by Matteson.

And Chrysler lingered in the life of the firm in more indirect ways as well. Shortly after the Chrysler closing, the firm's presiding partner, Oscar Reubhausen, turned 65, the age at Debevoise when a partner must become a fixed-income "non-sharing" partner. Reubhausen had also just been named president of the Association of the Bar of the City of New York, the country's most prestigious local bar association. It was time for Debevoise to designate his successor as the firm's presiding partner.

As is the case in similar firms, the powers of the presiding partner are wholly undefined but far-reaching. At Debevoise, for example, the presiding partner makes the final determination of each partner's share of income, worked out through individual conferences with partners. He determines the agenda of the partnership's Tuesday lunches. He resolves conflicts among the partners, smooths ruffled feathers and disciplines when necessary. His selection, despite the democratic pretenses of the firm, is decidedly non-democratic. Perhaps the most telling evidence of his power is the fact that he names his successor.

There had only been two presiding partners in Debevoise's history, Eli Whitney Debevoise and Reubhausen. It was assumed by some lawyers that Matteson would be the third. He had just made more money for the firm on a single deal than anyone in its history—more than $3 million in fees by June 30—and he had worked 18-hour days, seven-day weeks to do it. Among many lawyers at the firm, it was assumed that his efforts would be appropriately rewarded. But when Reubhausen presided over his last partnership luncheon that autumn, he made some farewell remarks, then passed his mantle to his chosen successor, George Lindsay.

No one partner sabotaged Matteson's chances. In the private, lengthy discussions Reubhausen conducted with each Debevoise partner, Matteson's candidacy was discussed and sidelined in more subtle ways. The next presiding partner is actually chosen by a consensus as perceived by the present one. What was clear to Reubhausen was that Matteson had come to personify Chrysler, and that there was no consensus that Chrysler had been good for the firm.

One partner insists that he had nothing but praise for Matteson in his conversations with Reubhausen, but that Chrysler was another matter. "I think a fundamental dimension of this firm is that I find the partners here are terrific human beings. They have a breadth of interests in life, they are not just interested in practicing law, and I would say that is true across the board.

"We have an unstated policy—we don't work 15-hour days, we don't work weekends. We have the commitment, and we do what we have to do, but we don't want more than a full load. You can see what a problem Chrysler was in that regard. Everyone was working 110 percent. When that happens, you've foreclosed other things, you just don't have the time or the energy. Cravath makes no bones about this, but we're not Cravath. I know that there are partners who would like us to be, who want the associates here working round the clock. But with George Lindsay presiding, I think we're back to where we want to be."

In October 1981, Debevoise, Plimpton, Lyons & Gates celebrated its fiftieth anniversary with a new name: Debevoise & Plimpton, something shorter and more institutional. That fall, the firm opened an office outside of New York City, a branch in Washington, D.C.; it also has one in Paris. The firm now has more than 150 lawyers, and Lindsay remarks that further growth is "inevitable." For many lawyers at the firm, Debevoise may now be where it "wants to be"; it will never return to the kind of firm that existed before Chrysler. Bevis Longstreth is no longer a partner. Giving rein to a public service bent that had been overwhelmed by Chrysler, Longstreth resigned to become a Securities and Exchange commissioner in September. There seems little disagreement that when Lindsay reaches retirement age in a few years, Matteson will assume command.

In late 1981, the American auto industry entered the worst recession in its history. Despite all Chrysler's efforts, it posted third-quarter losses of $149 million. In October, it announced that it would try to draw down the last of its $1.5 billion in federally guaranteed loans, a step it had said it would never take.

There will be ample legal work for Debevoise lawyers among Chrysler's mounting calamities. But when all is said and done, what will the firm have accomplished for Chrysler? During the long, tortuous path toward the guaranteed loans, the most common feeling among the lawyers was of impotence. In the end, they never did succeed in getting Chrysler to comply with the legislation—as is evident by the Peugeot "loan," the Canadian settlement, the ratio of foreign to domestic debt—and one lawyer within the Treasury Department quit in protest over Chrysler's failure to meet the requirements of the legislation. Ultimately, it was politics, not the law, that saved Chrysler.

Nor do lawyers make or sell cars. In spite of the massive legal efforts of Debevoise & Plimpton, and the transformation the firm endured in order to achieve them, Chrysler could still fall into bankruptcy. Debevoise & Plimpton's work for Chrysler may someday come to that end.

CHAPTER SIX

KENNECOTT
Sullivan & Cromwell

Sullivan & Cromwell partner George Kern, Jr., chomped on the end of his cigar in the crowded grand ballroom of the Waldorf-Astoria hotel in New York, beads of sweat beginning to appear on his furrowed brow. He watched his client, Frank Milliken, chairman of the Kennecott Copper Corporation, the nation's largest copper producer, as he moved to a microphone on the stage to open the corporation's 1978 annual meeting of shareholders. Suddenly there was a commotion at the rear of the room, and when Kern turned and saw what was happening, he groaned and put his head in his hands. It was T. Roland Berner, the lawyer chairman of the Curtiss-Wright Corporation. Berner ran down the aisle, jumped on the stage and grabbed the microphone from a stunned Milliken. "I'm Ted Berner and I'm here!" he shouted to the murmuring crowd, waving a court order like it was a six-shooter.

It was the most dramatic moment so far in the proxy war for control of Kennecott, launched four months earlier by Berner. The pugnacious chairman had already fought his way to the top of Curtiss-Wright—the New Jersey aircraft company founded by the Wright brothers and once the world's largest manufacturer of aircraft engines—by buying up shares and ultimately persuading other shareholders to oust the company's management and replace them with him and his allies. Berner's unorthodox and brash tactics—and the legal skills he had honed while an associate at Cravath, Swaine & Moore—struck terror into the conservative blueblood management of Kennecott Copper. As soon as Berner had launched his attack several months earlier (with accusations that Kennecott's management was incompetent, which appeared prominently in the *New York Times*), Kennecott called on its outside counsel at New York's Sullivan & Cromwell.

Kern had guided Milliken and other Kennecott executives through four harrowing months of highly publicized criticism from Berner and, just the day before, had obtained a Federal District Court order barring Berner and his allies from voting their shares at the proxy meeting. But the paper Berner was waving in the air effectively undid all that. Berner had raced from the Second Circuit Court of Appeals, which that morning had heard his appeal and reversed the District Court's order. He was back in the proxy fight.

Kern signaled Milliken to delay the opening of the meeting for a few minutes and took the chairman aside. He warned him to expect a nasty and chaotic meeting, but to press forward. Despite Berner's strident campaign—and his offer to sell more than $500 million of Kennecott's assets which he promised to distribute directly to Kennecott shareholders—Kern was confident that Berner didn't have the votes to take control. He was right. Milliken and Berner traded sallies at the meeting, but when the votes were finally counted a week later, Berner fell short.

It was hard to say, however, who had won. The proxy fight was only a small battle in what looked like an ongoing war. For four months, Kennecott executives had been obsessed with virtually nothing else but the proxy fight, their attention distracted from the business of producing copper. And Kern wasn't entirely satisfied with his defensive legal efforts. He began hatching a plan which would put Kennecott on the offensive—and silence Berner as a threat forever.

If a proxy fight was anathema to the management of Kennecott Copper, it was equally so for a law firm like Sullivan & Cromwell. Considered by many lawyers to be the pre-eminent corporate law firm in the country, Sullivan & Cromwell was founded in 1897 and was one of the first firms, along with Cravath, to develop a practice that was devoted almost exclusively to the legal problems of corporations. Today the firm has one of the country's most impressive rosters of blue chip corporate clients, including Amax, General Foods, General Electric, Exxon, Phillips Petroleum and SCM. Though it is not closely tied to a major bank, it is prominently identified with various investment banking firms, including First Boston; Kidder, Peabody & Co.; Goldman, Sachs & Co.; and Lazard Freres & Co.

Sullivan & Cromwell probably comes closer to the stereotype of the Wall Street firm than does any other. Its downtown Manhattan offices on Broad Street are decorated with leather armchairs and antique prints and suggest conservative good taste and gentility. Its reception area looks much like one of the men's clubs to which many of its partners belong. The firm's lawyers, dressed almost uniformly in white shirts and gray wool suits, still bear the conservative stamp of deceased partners John Foster Dulles, Eisenhower's Secretary of State; his brother Allen Dulles, a director of the CIA; Harlan Fiske Stone, a former Chief Justice of the U.S. Supreme Court, and Arthur Dean, tapped by Eisenhower to negotiate the peace treaty which ended the Korean War. Sullivan & Cromwell lawyers think of themselves as hard-driving business lawyers, the match of any other firm, but they also think of themselves as gentlemen. And a proxy contest like the one waged by Berner is distinctly ungentlemanly.

Kern is characteristically blunt in describing his distaste for proxy fights. "They're only for the racier elements of the business and legal community," he says. "Proxies are personal, they are more like a political campaign. The fights can be dirty; the existing management almost always gets peed on. And a proxy fight is for the relatively impoverished. You can wage one for only a few million dollars." In short, proxy fights are not the province of the Wall Street lawyer. Prior to Berner's assault, Sullivan & Cromwell had only counseled one aggressive proxy battle in its history; it defends them only for its blue chip clients of long standing.

The hostile corporate takeover is another matter altogether. Once considered the proxy fight's first cousin, and relegated to the same junkyard of unseemly legal activities, the hostile takeover has been embraced by Sullivan & Cromwell and law firms like it within the past decade. Hostile takeovers are now among the firm's most lucrative and active specialties, ranking equally with friendly mergers and acquisitions as the province of the sophisticated corporate lawyer. For the company which is the target of a takeover effort, the struggle is, like antitrust cases, a life or death effort in which no expense will be spared. For the acquiring company, billion-dollar acquisitions are the fastest, surest way to conglomerate power, and even massive legal fees make up only a tiny fraction of the overall cost of the deal. It is also a field in which lawyers and the government have made themselves indispensable. In fighting off takeover bids, lawyers have erected a host of legal barricades and pitfalls. Today, even a friendly merger needs a lawyer experienced in hostile takeovers to look out for and fend off any potential raiding companies.

At Sullivan & Cromwell, that lawyer is George Kern, a living legend to younger lawyers at the firm. Kern is bigger than life, literally and figuratively. He is currently fat, although his weight fluctuates dramatically as he embraces and then abandons crash diets. During one takeover fight, he was downing two cases of Tab per day. Kern says that he has several complete wardrobes—one for each of his weight categories. He is also loud. Though his corner office is located at Sullivan & Cromwell's midtown office on Park Avenue, it is a standing joke at the firm that he doesn't need a telephone to speak with his partners several miles away at the firm's main office near Wall Street. He punctuates his stentorian delivery with highly dramatic pauses, jabbing his ever-lit cigar for effect, ashes often falling on his shirtfront. One of his partners recalls arguing with him and making the point to Kern that "saying something just doesn't make it so." Kern glared at him and rejoined, "In my case, saying something often *does* make it so." New associates are terrified of him. More experienced lawyers ascribe to him one of the softest hearts in the firm. And though he is more colorful than most of his partners, Kern has a canny business sense and is at the center of the firm's Byzantine power structure, holding a seat on its powerful nine-member management committee.

In takeover fights, Kern found a perfect match for his own volatile temperament, and he pushed and prodded Sullivan & Cromwell into following him. "I became generally aware of the [hostile takeover] phenomenon about five years ago," Kern explains. "It became clear to me that something odd was going on here. Business deals used to be put together by gentlemen, but this wasn't happening. The threat of a hostile raid was beginning to pervade the whole financial scene.

"We've always done mergers," Kern continues. "I did *Brown Shoe* myself.* When you're talking legal areas, there are really two gut areas: antitrust and securities. If Sullivan & Cromwell isn't the best at those, then we might as well just forget it. There's no reason on God's green earth why we shouldn't handle hostile tender offers."

During the years when Sullivan & Cromwell and the elite corporate firms weren't handling the hostile takeovers, other firms were. In the early 1970s, when the investment banking community began to overcome its aversion to the hostile takeovers, companies interested in acquiring unfriendly target companies and the target companies themselves began to turn to some of the firms that had not disdained proxy contests.

One New York lawyer in particular, Joseph Flom, began successfully adapting proxy fight techniques to the hostile takeover. His audacious strategies and relentless efforts met with such success that even establishment blue chip corporations began to supplement the advice they got from their regular corporate counsel by turning to Flom and his law firm, Skadden, Arps, Slate, Meagher & Flom. When Kern began observing the wave of hostile tender offers in the mid-1970s, he noticed that Flom was retained on one side or the other in almost every one of them. Though still viewed with some disdain by crustier elements of the established bar (Kern privately refers to Skadden, Arps lawyers as "Skarps"), Flom has parlayed his takeover specialty into a 230-lawyer firm that now competes directly with the established firms that once shunned him and his kind of practice.

"We live in an era where the business is going to performance," Kern acknowledges. "The institutional firms have to give more conscious attention to entrepreneurship. There's a ferment going on, and it's a different landscape on Wall Street. The business won't come to us just because it always has in the past." Kern is also aware of the risks of tender offers. "You have to assign someone to these matters who can go to the jugular and think fast. It takes a personal chemistry. There's an enormous strain on those who do this work. Basically, you know, you have a feel. If you want to do it, then you've got the chemistry." Kern says he groans

---

* A merger under the Clayton Antitrust Act which eventually was dissolved as a result of a landmark Supreme Court opinion.

when old-line firms send in one of their senior securities lawyers to discuss a takeover. "They're all wrong. Too cautious, too methodical. My God," he exclaims, "we wouldn't put me on some old lady's estate, some widow in Palm Beach!"

Kern also concedes that the reasons for launching a takeover practice are not confined to their legal mettle. The work is extremely lucrative. Sullivan & Cromwell is alone among major firms in that it never bills on the basis of an hourly rate; it claims not to even have such rates. Rather, partners charge clients what they think is fair, considering the amount of money at stake, the pressure under which the lawyers operate and the result they achieve for the client. Takeover attempts involve huge sums of money, and they are conducted under extreme pressure. And the result usually only enhances the law firm's ability to charge high fees. If the client wins, it is so grateful it will pay almost anything. If it loses, the acquiring company pays its fees—and in the magnanimous flush of victory, it is unlikely to criticize its new acquisition's legal costs. (Though they usually require fewer lawyers and are conducted under less pressure, friendly mergers and acquisitions are lucrative for much the same reason. That field has always been dominated by the established blue chip firms.)

Following Sullivan & Cromwell's lead, other blue chip corporate firms have begun efforts to develop a specialty practice in the hostile takeover. Simpson, Thacher; Dewey, Ballantine; Shearman & Sterling; and Davis Polk have been among the successful. Most others have at least a long-range commitment to this line of work. Though proximity to the financial markets and investment banking houses almost dictates that the work will remain the province of large New York firms, Kirkland & Ellis in Chicago is one of the few non–New York firms which has used its base of Midwest industrial clients to develop a takeover practice.

But in early 1977, corporate warfare had not yet received the imprimatur of the blue chip firms. Kern, Sullivan & Cromwell, and Kennecott were dragged into the fight with Berner, kicking and protesting all the way. In early 1977, the copper cycle was at one of its historic low points—copper was selling for about 60 cents a pound—and Kennecott's stock was depressed to $17 a share. Because of government antitrust problems, Kennecott had recently been forced to sell the Peabody Coal Company, which it had acquired in an attempt to diversify and make its level of earnings less dependent on fluctuations in the copper market. Peabody sold for more than $800 million, leaving Kennecott in a precarious position: it was flush with cash. So flush that the company held more liquid assets than its entire stock was worth. Anyone who bought up all of Kennecott's stock at its then prevailing market price would realize an instant profit simply by getting his hands on the Peabody proceeds.

It didn't take long for someone to figure out that Kennecott was a ripe target for acquisition. Kennecott and its lawyers couldn't tell who, but it was clear from the steady movement in sales in the stock market that someone was systematically buying small blocks of Kennecott stock. The company had to get rid of some of its cash so as to look less desirable to a purchaser, and so it fixed on an acquisition of its own: Carborundum, a manufacturer of abrasives and pollution-control devices. Sullivan & Cromwell launched that acquisition—a friendly merger—in January of 1978. It was not an action that met with the wholehearted approval of Kennecott's shareholders, some of whom couldn't understand why Kennecott wasn't relieving itself of its excess cash simply by paying it out to them in the form of dividends. On the day before Thanksgiving, one of them filed a suit for an injunction to prevent Kennecott from going forward with its acquisition of Carborundum.

That afternoon, Robert Owen, a fourth-year Sullivan & Cromwell associate, got a call from William Willis, the Sullivan & Cromwell partner in charge of making assignments. Even though it was the afternoon before Thanksgiving, Willis had an assignment that he thought Owen might like to work on—the sudden shareholder suit to stop Kennecott's acquisition of Carborundum. Even though Owen and his wife had planned to spend the long weekend with their family in Washington, D.C., Owen was eager for the assignment. One measure of an associate's progress is the importance of the clients to which he is assigned, and Kennecott was a mainstay of Sullivan & Cromwell's practice. Owen saw the Kennecott assignment as an important chance to prove himself, and he plunged into the project with first-year associate William Knull and litigation partner John Warden.

The associates worked all Thanksgiving Day analyzing the motion papers; met with Kennecott executives, investment bankers from First Boston (the Sullivan & Cromwell client acting as dealer-manager for the Carborundum acquisition) and Warden on Friday morning; and spent the rest of the weekend drafting and revising Sullivan & Cromwell's response. Owen and Knull spent Sunday night stapling and putting the final papers together, and left the office at 6:00 A.M. At 8:30 Monday, after an hour's sleep and a shower, they were back downtown in Federal District Court, ready for the argument on the motion. Warden's performance was a success. The shareholders' motion for an injunction was denied, and later that day Kennecott's acquisition went forward.

Unfortunately for Kennecott, the mysterious market purchases of Kennecott stock continued. By March of 1978, someone had acquired nearly 10 percent of Kennecott's outstanding stock, and shortly after the mystery was solved. Ted Berner, Curtiss-Wright's chairman, filed a disclosure statement with the Securities and Exchange Commission, required by law for those who intend to acquire more than 5 percent of a company whose shares are publicly traded. Kennecott's directors were distressed by the identity of the purchaser—they were well aware of his history at Curtiss-Wright—but they were positively horrified by the contents of his filing. In it, Berner mentioned the possibility of a proxy fight. He said that he would consider soliciting proxies from shareholders based on what Kennecott's directors considered to be wild and flagrant promises to the shareholders. Berner wanted to undo the Carborundum acquisition, sell off some additional assets of the company, and pay the proceeds directly to the shareholders— about $15 per share in dividends at a time when Kennecott's stock was only selling for $23. It was a proposition that was bound to be tempting to Kennecott's shareholders.

Berner's proposition caught even the lawyers at Sullivan & Cromwell by surprise. They had anticipated a hostile takeover attempt but not a proxy fight. There had hardly been a serious proxy fight for control of a large blue chip company since the 1940s. Was Berner serious? Kennecott's chairman, Frank Milliken, started immediate negotiations to find out. Berner was serious. He demanded seats on the board for himself and some of his allies, adding tauntingly that he "had great plans for Kennecott." Kennecott and its lawyers decided they had to stop Berner. Kern called Marvin Schwartz, the litigation partner who often works with him in the takeover area. Schwartz is one of the most respected litigators in the firm. He is considered especially strong in the securities area, since he and Stanley Sporkin, then the head of enforcement at the Securities and Exchange Commission, are close friends. Though anti-Semitism had never been as strong at Sullivan & Cromwell as it has been at some Wall Street firms, the fact that Schwartz, who is Jewish, was made a partner during the 1950s at a predominantly WASP firm was taken as strong evidence of his outstanding legal skills.

Schwartz bypassed the usual assignment mechanism at the firm, and called directly some associates who were familiar with the situation: Owen and Knull, also a senior associate, and Richard Urowsky, a *Yale Law Journal* editor who already had a reputation as one of the brightest associates at the firm. Kennecott also consulted lawyers at Skadden, Arps.

The Sullivan & Cromwell team plunged into round-the-clock strategy and planning meetings. Basically, they had two goals: to stop what looked like an impending proxy fight and, if possible, to get Berner out of Kennecott's hair. To achieve the first goal, the means were relatively straightforward. They could sue Berner, alleging violations of the securities disclosure laws. But even if successful, that approach would only stop the proxy fight for the time being. Berner would still have his 10 percent of the company. He would still be nagging for a seat on the board. There would be the threat of a proxy fight at every annual meeting. Legally, there was only one avenue that would actually force Berner to get rid of his Kennecott stock, and it was the same approach that had forced Kennecott to sell off its Peabody Coal acquisition: antitrust. If the lawyers could find some area of Kennecott and Curtiss-Wright business where competition would be diminished, they could add an antitrust claim to their suit and, if successful in court, force Berner to sell his holdings and eliminate the Berner threat.

Owen and Urowsky dived into analyses of the lines of business engaged in by Kennecott and Curtiss-Wright. There weren't any obvious overlaps. Kennecott was principally a copper producer, Curtiss-Wright a manufacturer of airplane components. But so tiny it was almost obscured on the Carborundum balance sheet was an operation that made something called pollution socks—cloth bags which could be installed on smokestacks and vents to diminish soot. There were only five manufacturers of pollution socks and bags in the country, even though it was a business so simple that Kern joked that the socks could be made in any home garage.

One of the five producers was Curtiss-Wright. A Kennecott–Curtiss-Wright merger would diminish competition by cutting the number of pollution bag manufacturers from five to four: a straightforward violation of the Clayton Antitrust Act. Sullivan & Cromwell had its antitrust case, even though many lawyers at the firm were skeptical. Could the fate of the nation's leading copper producer actually turn on a cottage industry like pollution bags? Around the office, Kennecott's effort to stave off Berner's proxy fight quickly became known as the "scum-bag" case.

On March 22, shortly after Berner filed his 13-D disclosure, Sullivan & Cromwell filed its own complaint, moved for a preliminary injunction, and obtained an order to show cause why Berner should not be prevented from soliciting and voting his proxies. The lawyers also filed a motion for expedited discovery. Kennecott's annual meeting was scheduled for May 2, hardly more than a month away, and the issue had to be resolved quickly. From the courthouse, Urowsky telephoned Berner's lawyers at Kaye, Scholer, Fierman, Hayes & Handler, a large New York law firm. Berner's corporate counsel was so surprised by the sudden lawsuit that he nearly dropped the phone.

While the Sullivan & Cromwell lawyers launched full-scale preparation for trial, Berner and his lawyers at Kaye, Scholer made what, in retrospect, looks like a tactical blunder. They apparently concentrated all their efforts on delay rather than on the merits of Kennecott's claims. With the annual meeting so close, the temptation for delay was undoubtedly strong. Berner reportedly played a major role in devising the strategy, and his motive was also viewed in part as harassment. In the midst of the discovery campaign, Berner and Kaye, Scholer filed a motion to disqualify Sullivan & Cromwell as Kennecott's lawyers.

The brash tactic had worked well against Kirkland & Ellis in the uranium case, but in this instance the claim seemed particularly tenuous. Berner and Curtiss-Wright had earlier tried to acquire a company called Airco, but had failed to do so. Berner had hired Skadden, Arps for that attempt—which, technically, had not yet been abandoned—and now Skadden, Arps was also supplementing Sullivan & Cromwell's advice to Kennecott. Berner argued a conflict of interest—that Sullivan & Cromwell was tainted because it was receiving advice from Skadden, Arps lawyers, who were also representing Berner in the moribund Airco matter.

Though his claim was tenuous—and Kaye, Scholer lawyers were at best unenthusiastic—Berner insisted on pressing it. It is assumed that his principal motive was to embarrass Joseph Flom, the top lawyer at Skadden, Arps, by exposing the kind of retainer agreements he had with his clients. Typically, Flom's clients paid him an enormous annual fee, upwards of $100,000. In the event they became the target of a takeover effort, Flom would represent them, even if he also maintained a retainer relationship with the company trying to make the acquisition. To alleviate what would otherwise be an obvious and unethical conflict of interest, Flom made all of his clients sign a consent agreement saying that in the event he represented another client in takeover litigation, they would not raise the issue of conflict in an effort to disqualify him. Until Berner, all of his clients had abided by that agreement, and the nature and existence of Flom's lucrative retainers were largely unknown.

Berner did succeed in airing Flom's retainers in public, though the tactic had little impact. Flom may have been embarrassed by the disclosure, but his expertise is considered so valuable that he still exacts retainer agreements from clients. And the presiding Federal District Court judge, Lloyd MacMahon, made short shrift of the attempt to derail the Kennecott proceedings, in which Skadden, Arps was not even directly involved. At the hearing on Curtiss-Wright's motion for delay and for disqualification of Sullivan & Cromwell, MacMahon looked as if he would explode with rage. He denied the motion and ordered Kaye, Scholer and Berner to trial the very next week.

Owen and Urowsky were even more delighted than the other Sullivan & Cromwell lawyers at the judge's insistence. At Wall Street firms, most litigation is conducted through discovery motions and from partners' offices. Settlements are achieved without trials, and it is rare for associates to acquire much courtroom experience. There are litigation partners who actually have never examined a witness in court. Owen was jolted one afternoon while sitting in Schwartz's office. Schwartz was on the phone discussing plans for the trial with inside counsel at Kennecott, when he mentioned the filter bag antitrust claim. Owen wasn't paying much attention until he heard Schwartz say, "Bob Owen will be trying that part of the case." It was the first Owen had heard of the plan, and he recognized it as a rare opportunity, something he had worked and waited for for six years. By the time the decision would be made about whether he would be made a partner, this might be the most important litigation responsibility he would have had.

Despite last-minute efforts by Kaye, Scholer to delay, the trial started as scheduled on April 25, and lasted four days. The night before, Kern and Schwartz agonized about going forward. Kern, in particular, was afraid that even if Kennecott won the trial, the decision might later be reversed on appeal and do more harm. Reports coming in from the investment bankers had begun to indicate that Berner didn't have enough proxy votes. If an appellate court reversal, after several months, meant that the proxy vote would have to be redone, Berner would have another chance. On the other hand, success at both the trial and appellate level on the antitrust claim offered a big prize: the elimination of Berner as a threat. The decision was to go for it.

Schwartz conducted the trial. The thrust of the Sullivan & Cromwell case was that Berner had misled the Kennecott shareholders because he had never established the feasibility of his plan to divest assets and distribute the money to the shareholders. Schwartz introduced evidence that to do so would violate loan agreements between Kennecott and its banks. As Kern put it, "Money lenders do not take kindly to assets walking out the door when a company is experiencing near-losses in earnings."

Schwartz questioned Berner when he took the stand, and Berner talked vaguely about some figuring he had done. After close questioning, and several interruptions by a skeptical Judge Mac-Mahon, Berner conceded that the only way his divestiture plan would work was if the remaining assets of the company were written up in value—a bogus accounting technique generally known as doctoring the books. According to Urowsky, when the judge caught the gist of Berner's testimony, he was so enraged that the veins in his face were visibly pulsing. Owen did get his day in court. He handled the antitrust aspect of the case, using an expert in the pollution bag field to introduce data on the number of companies in the business and their market share. His antitrust case lasted four hours.

To the Sullivan & Cromwell lawyers, Kaye, Scholer had expended most of its energies on the ill-fated disqualification motion and the efforts to delay the trial. Although Kaye, Scholer cross-examined Kennecott witnesses, in what Urowsky calls "the closest thing to total collapse by a law firm I've ever witnessed," Kaye, Scholer rested without presenting any witnesses of its own. Judge MacMahon took only a weekend to prepare his decision, and on May 1, the day before the Kennecott meeting, he found for Kennecott on all counts.

The Sullivan & Cromwell lawyers and Kennecott executives were ecstatic, especially Owen. The day of the decision he had received a handwritten note from Kern saying, "Terrific work. You have made antitrust history." At Sullivan & Cromwell, associate lawyers are kept so in the dark about the inner workings and decisions in the firm that those who attempt to glean internal secrets from external signs arc known as "Kremlinologists." That year, the Kremlinologists started saying that Owen was destined for partner.

As Kern and the other Sullivan & Cromwell lawyers learned the next day, however, their victory over Berner was to be short-lived. Immediately after MacMahon's decision, Berner had rushed to the appellate court for a stay of execution—an order which is almost routinely granted pending appeal—and had gotten it in time to come rushing in to the Kennecott annual meeting. Berner had achieved at least a semblance of the proxy fight he wanted.

More ominously for Kennecott and Sullivan & Cromwell, when the judges of the Second Circuit heard the appeal from MacMahon's decision in June, it was apparent they took a different view of the case. Judge Ellsworth Van Graafeiland, in particular, according to Urowsky, "obviously thought that an insurgent shareholder had been railroaded by a big Wall Street firm. He thought the shareholders had suffered at the hands of smart big-time lawyers. He actually shouted at Marvin Schwartz." Though the appellate judges had to grasp for the decision, given the fact that Kaye, Scholer had given them very little evidence to work with, the appellate court reversed MacMahon on every count, including Owen's antitrust claim. It was so easy to enter the pollution bag market, the court found, that it didn't matter whether there were four or five manufacturers. Kern's fears of the eve of the trial were realized. Sullivan & Cromwell's win was turned to loss. The appellate court ordered a new election. Sullivan & Cromwell started preparing a writ of certiorari to the U.S. Supreme Court, but Kern wasn't optimistic that it would be heard before another Kennecott election rolled around. It was time to try settlement.

•

Not long after the Berner proxy fight, the Kennecott board concluded that the strain of the battle with Berner was proving too much for Frank Milliken, who was 64. He was replaced as chairman by Thomas Barrow, a senior vice president and director of Exxon, another Sullivan & Cromwell client. One of Barrow's first steps was to conclude a peace treaty with Berner before the Curtiss-Wright chairman had time to mount another proxy campaign. Under the terms of the deal, Berner agreed to a three-year truce on the proxy front, promising to refrain from an attempt to wrest control of the company through a shareholder vote. In return, Barrow agreed to name Berner and three of his designates as directors on Kennecott's eighteen-member board of directors.

Kennecott flourished in the new era of peace. Per share earnings in 1979 were $3.93, up from 15 cents in 1978, the year of the proxy fight. But by late 1979, with the expiration of the truce agreement not too distant, Berner again began to rumble. This time the focus of his unhappiness was Barrow's compensation. To lure Barrow from Exxon, Kennecott had paid him more than $1 million in annual salary and bonuses, besides a lucrative pension and life insurance package. Despite the strong performance of the company under Barrow's direction, Berner began disrupting directors' meetings with complaints about Barrow's excessive salary and compensation, and tried to gather information about Barrow's performance from other Kennecott employees.

It was the last straw for Barrow, who had no intention of sitting back while another proxy fight brewed. A few months earlier, an executive in Kennecott's Carborundum subsidiary had pointed to the desirability of acquiring a Curtiss-Wright subsidiary, Dorr-Oliver, which, like Carborundum, was also engaged in manufacturing synthetic fuels. Barrow had even approached Berner about the prospect of acquiring Dorr-Oliver, but had been flatly rebuffed. Now Barrow talked to Kern, and to his investment advisers at Morgan Stanley, the New York investment banking firm. Kern suggested a bold stroke which would get Dorr-Oliver for Kennecott and eliminate Berner as a threat forever: a hostile takeover of Curtiss-Wright by Kennecott.

Kern assembled a team at Sullivan & Cromwell to consider the legal ramifications of the proposed raid, identified officially at the firm only as "Project Venetian." On the team besides Kern were

Schwartz and Neil Anderson, a corporate partner, both of whom had been working in Kern's merger and acquisition group, as well as Owen and Urowsky. Then Kern met informally with a number of the "friendly" Kennecott directors in January. But the conservative board members (nearly all were former officers of Fortune 500 companies) had a strong distaste for the prospect of a hostile takeover bid. The idea was tabled.

During September 1980, while the Kennecott directors stewed about what to do with Berner, associates at Sullivan & Cromwell had their minds on an internal issue of more immediate concern: the annual tapping of new partners which occurred each September. Those familiar with the Kennecott–Curtiss-Wright matter had considerable fuel for speculation: both Urowsky and Owen, senior associates working on the case, were apparently "up" for a partnership decision that year.

Because of Owen's handling of the Kennecott antitrust angle in the proxy case, he was deemed a leading contender. Urowsky was a bit of a dark horse. He had graduated from law school a year earlier than Owen, and technically he should have received his partnership decision the previous year. During his early years at the firm, Urowsky had amused other associates at the firm with his biting wit, often at the expense of some of the firm's senior partners. Although his comments had become more circumspect in recent years, he was still thought by many to have "attitude problems." But Urowsky had exuded none of the tell-tale signs that he had been "passed over," suggesting that he was one of a small group who had been told that another year of trial was necessary before a final decision could be made. Their principal challenger in litigation was Charles Dorkey III, an associate who had been sent to help open Sullivan & Cromwell's new Washington, D.C., office, with the senior partner who was widely perceived as his mentor, Walter Coakley.

As at Cravath, partnership decisions at Sullivan & Cromwell were once made through discussion and vote of the whole partnership, but in recent years the decision has turned on the recommendations of partners in the department where an associate has spent most of his time. In all three cases, Owen, Urowsky and Dorkey, this was litigation. Because of their work in the mergers and acquisitions group, Owen and Urowsky also had considerable contact with corporate partners. Within departments, the influence of one or more powerful partners can be the determining factor. Since later loyalties within the partnership may arise in part from gratitude for influence once wielded, partners compete with one another to bring their protégés into the partnership—to "empire build" as it is popularly called among associates at Sullivan & Cromwell. All informal polling of partners and discussions is kept secret.

That fall, the pundits at the firm were confounded. Urowsky was made a partner. Owen was told that it was "unlikely" he would be elected to the partnership, a euphemism for being passed over. Dorkey, too, was rejected, purportedly because the poor financial performance of the new Washington office had contributed to the eclipse of influence of his mentor. Owen annoyed the partners by telling his associate colleagues directly that he hadn't made partner. The partners prefer that passed over associates simply disappear into other jobs, preserving the illusion that they have decided themselves to make a change. No partner at Sullivan & Cromwell will comment, but the accepted wisdom is that Owen failed to make partner at least partly for reasons of style (he rode a motorcycle to work); for evidence of outside loyalties to family and friends that surpassed his loyalty to the firm; and for asking too many questions. After eight years at Sullivan & Cromwell, Owen would never know why.

It is assumed that it was other litigation partners, not Kern, who sabotaged Owen's partnership chances; and Kern seemed a little embarrassed when he ran into Owen subsequently. But when Kennecott started heating up again in October, Owen was dropped from the team quietly.

Since the Kennecott board had last considered the matter, Berner's behavior had become steadily more bothersome to Barrow. In March, Berner succeeded in persuading the board to appoint a special committee to investigate Barrow's compensation. Although there was no spoken criticism, Barrow had agreed to a reduction in compensation and fringe benefits. Then Berner commenced a secret investigation, probing middle management for evidence of misconduct or mismanagement by Barrow or his appointees. These distractions were the last straw for Barrow, who called Kern on Halloween to say, "Let's get serious about this." The next day, Kern and Neil Anderson met secretly with Barrow and two directors at Kennecott's headquarters in Stamford, Connecticut.

Kern and Anderson, with Schwartz on the telephone, gave Barrow a bracing idea of what he could expect during the takeover battle. "I told him he would go through hell and back," Schwartz recalls. "We candidly explained that the hostile takeover is one of the messiest and dirtiest forms of litigation. Management of the target corporation sees it as the ultimate threat to their business and professional lives. It is emotional and bitter; they act like a drowning person fighting to survive. Hysteria and fright fall like a cloud. Everything else is forgotten—the goal is to beat the takeover at all costs."

Beating the takeover usually comes down to lawyers, since the business aspect of a tender offer is relatively simple. The acquiring company simply offers to buy outstanding shares of the target company at a price which is usually considerably higher than the price that currently prevails in the market. If a shareholder wishes to sell, he simply "tenders" the shares and receives the offered price. Such transactions are usually handled by investment bankers, who acquire the offered shares on behalf of the acquiring corporation in return for a percentage of the cost of the deal. Sometimes speculators—called arbitrageurs—may buy the shares at a price higher than that offered by the acquiring company, hoping that the offerer will, in turn, purchase the shares from them at a higher price. The transaction takes place in a relatively simple marketplace of buyers and sellers.

What complicates the matter are the laws that govern tender offers, and the legal ploys that have sprung from them. Tender offers are regulated by federal statute and by the rules of the Securities and Exchange Commission. In addition to various technical requirements, they are essentially intended to help the target company shareholder make an informed decision about whether to tender shares at the offered price. Thus, the SEC requires that an offering statement—similar to the prospectuses filed by Genentech and Chrysler—be filed and approved and then made available to shareholders. The offering statement describes, in detail, the nature of the offering company, conditions of the offer, and other information that a shareholder might want to consider in reaching a decision. Failure to disclose adequately can result in the SEC's nullifying any transaction in which shares have changed hands. A common tactic of lawyers defending a target company against a hostile takeover—and one reason they become so nasty —is to force the acquiring company to disclose information so embarrassing that it either discourages shareholders from tendering or, more commonly, persuades the offeror to withdraw the offer altogether.

The other major way to stop a takeover is to invoke the antitrust laws. The Clayton Act prohibits mergers under certain conditions which might encourage monopolization; and both the Justice Department and the Federal Trade Commission can block or undo a completed merger pursuant to the Clayton Act. Target companies can invoke the threat of an antitrust action to freeze a takeover until the government antitrust regulators have had a chance to make a decision. Such a freeze often kills a takeover, even if the government never takes action. Or, delay can permit a target company to find another, friendlier, corporation to come in and make a better offer. Such a corporation is called a "White Knight."

Kern warned Barrow that there would be immediate litigation, not only in the federal courts but in any states with takeover statutes that Berner might invoke to stop the tender. Barrow's compensation and performance would be subject to hostile public questioning under oath. Claims would be made that the sole, and invalid, purpose of the tender offer was to get rid of Berner. It was important that the board members be forewarned that they could be personally dragged into the litigation. That process was made unusually difficult by the fact that Berner and several of his allies were members of the board; and it was crucial that the decision and the campaign be mounted in secrecy.

"We didn't make any final decisions in those discussions," Kern says. "There was no freight train set in motion yet. I was still wrestling in my own mind. I was haunted that the litigation process might get us enmeshed for too long a period. We were heading into the annual meeting again. I sure didn't like the prospect of a proxy fight right in the middle of a tender offer." But Kern began to gear up his team, anticipating the legal actions that might be brought by Berner and Curtiss-Wright. Eventually, Kern resolved his doubts and called Barrow. If Barrow had the stomach for a battle, "We'd pull it off." Barrow said he was ready.

During the next two weeks, Barrow met or spoke privately with fourteen friendly directors. A regular meeting of the board of directors was scheduled for November 21, and Barrow and Kern had hatched a plan for a secret meeting of the friendly directors the night before. The night of November 20, twelve of the directors met in Kennecott's suite in the Waldorf-Astoria to debate the proposed takeover raid.

For the first two and a half hours of the meeting, the directors largely ignored the Berner problem and the legal ramifications. Kern and Schwartz listened as the directors focused on the business components of the proposed transaction: how Dorr-Oliver's operations could be synchronized with its Carborundum subsidiary; the process of consolidation; the timing with respect to copper cycles; financial questions; and the availability of cash. Then they turned to Kern.

Kern delivered a speech not unlike the one he had given Barrow. The directors should be prepared to have their lives disrupted, but he saw no legal impediment to an acquisition of Curtiss-Wright. And Berner would be gone. "We all had begun to realize," Schwartz recalls, "that if Berner stayed, the company was going to be in trouble. He was determined to get control, and another proxy fight could have been disastrous." The meeting broke up around midnight, and the directors slipped out of the hotel inconspicuously. No one wanted to be sighted by Berner, who had an apartment just up the street on Park Avenue.

When the directors gathered the next morning in the General Motors building for the annual directors' meeting, there was no hint that the meeting was anything but routine. Berner and his allies seemed calm and relaxed. If they had studied the agenda carefully, they might have noticed a late addition. Buried as item number 7 was "Corporate Strategy." Kern and Schwartz were secluded in an adjoining room. In their briefcases were copies of a press release announcing the board's resolution to acquire the Curtiss-Wright Corporation. The release was timed for 11:00 A.M. —just about the time that Berner would be confronted with item 7.

After Barrow had led the directors through the first six routine items, Kern and Schwartz made an entrance and sat down at the head of the table. Berner looked startled. Their presence was unusual and signaled some major development. But otherwise he betrayed no emotion as Barrow first introduced the lawyers, then announced Kennecott's desire to acquire Curtiss-Wright. He spoke as if the chairman of the target company were not sitting in the room.

Kern watched Berner closely. How would he react? Would there be table pounding, a scene? Or more dangerously, had Berner learned of or anticipated the attempt? Were his lawyers standing on the courthouse steps waiting to file a suit to block Kennecott's efforts? It was the latter possibility that Kern feared most. If Berner were to attempt to leave the room to reach a pay telephone, Kern was prepared to use his considerable bulk to block the door.

What actually happened was the one thing that neither Kern nor Schwartz had anticipated. Berner did nothing. He sat impassively as Morgan Stanley's Robert Greenhill pursued a discussion of the business reasons for the acquisition. He made no response when Greenhill said bluntly that one of the reasons for the decision was to rid the board of Berner and his allies. Then Kern rose and gave a half-hour presentation on the legal aspects of the merger. It was similar to the speech he had made to the friendly directors the night before, though it emphasized the positive—that the acquisition wouldn't violate antitrust or securities laws—and it was edited to betray as little litigation strategy as possible. When a director asked what they could expect in terms of litigation by Curtiss-Wright, Kern demurred, saying a bit disingenuously that anything he could say would be only speculation. He looked at Berner meaningfully.

Berner seemed perplexed, looking around the room in an apparent effort to determine whether the announcement was as much a surprise to the other directors as it was to him. "In theory, Berner should have been anticipating this maneuver," Kern says. "But he must have thought it so unlikely that this conservative board would bite the bullet this way." And it was an extraordinary step for the Kennecott board, composed mostly of businessmen who had spent their lives doing business in the time-honored gentlemanly tradition of negotiation and conciliation.

Evidently still unsure that Barrow had the majority he needed, Berner called for a roll-call vote. His was the first name called. "Abstain," he said through tight lips, signaling his allies on the board. But his effort was futile. The final vote was fourteen in favor, with four abstentions by Berner and his allies. Berner realized that he had just been made the victim of a carefully orchestrated attack. As he rose to leave the meeting, he motioned to his allies and called, "Gentlemen, to the apartment." It would be remembered as his battle cry when Kern later instructed his Sullivan & Cromwell colleagues, "Knights, to your castle."

Kern was ready for war. During the past two weeks, he, Schwartz, Anderson, Urowsky, and other Sullivan & Cromwell associates had worked nearly round the clock, anticipating Curtiss-Wright's legal defenses and preparing the legal documents both to launch the takeover and to defend the expected barrage of lawsuits trying to stop it. In addition to defensive planning, the lawyers planned a three-pronged offensive assault: the filing of Kennecott's formal offering statement with the Securities and Exchange Commission, preceded by pre-emptive litigation strikes in both Delaware and New Jersey federal courts. They were designed to put Curtiss-Wright on the defensive even before its own lawsuits got off the ground.

The elaborate litigation strategy that Kern and the Sullivan & Cromwell lawyers devised was also made necessary by a new federal securities law which had gone into effect at the beginning of 1980, one which threatened to lead Kennecott into a quagmire. The Williams Act and the regulations promulgated under it by the SEC regulate tender offers and require that the offeror begin accepting tendered shares within five business days of the time it announces its tender offer. Prior to that time, the company had to have filed the necessary documents with the SEC. The purpose of the law is to permit shareholders to tender their shares promptly before speculators and arbitrageurs have distorted the market.

Unfortunately for the Sullivan & Cromwell lawyers, they had to worry not only about the federal requirements but the state laws in two states with authority to regulate the affairs of Curtiss-Wright: New Jersey, where the company had its headquarters and its principal operations; and Delaware, the state in which most American corporations are incorporated. Both states had their own interests in any attempt to get control of Curtiss-Wright. New Jersey didn't want anything to happen which might shift the corporate headquarters out of the state or that would reduce employment for New Jersey residents; Delaware didn't like corporations incorporated under its laws to be taken over by those incorporated elsewhere. Kennecott was a problem in both respects. It was incorporated in New York, with headquarters in Stamford, Connecticut.

To promote their own interests, New Jersey and Delaware had takeover laws which conflicted directly with the new regulations issued in Washington. New Jersey required that a company seeking control of a New Jersey corporation wait at least twenty days before actually beginning to purchase tendered shares. Furthermore, New Jersey's Attorney General can further delay the acquisition by ordering a hearing to determine whether the offer is "unfair or inequitable" to the target company, shareholders or employees.

Among other things, the State Attorney General can look into the financial condition of the offerer company, the competence, experience and integrity of its management, and any plans to change the management of the company it seeks to acquire. Such a hearing is a green light for the target company's lawyers to drag every skeleton out of the closet of a company like Kennecott. And because the federal law required beginning the tender offer within five days, and the New Jersey law mandated a wait of at least twenty days, there was no way Kennecott could comply with the federal requirement without violating New Jersey and Delaware law. The inconsistencies in the federal and state laws had not yet been tested in court.

To resolve that conflict—and to enable Kennecott to go forward with its acquisition—Kern seized on a litigation device called the preliminary injunction and declaratory judgment. The device is the fastest way to get action out of a court, and for that reason, it is the mainstay of takeover fights.

To handle the New Jersey aspects of the case—recognized as potentially the most serious impediment to the takeover—Kern tapped Urowsky, his new partner. Just as Owen had had his antitrust trial, Urowsky saw this assignment as a crucial proving ground. Making partner at Sullivan & Cromwell, as in other such firms, is only the beginning of a new race for power, influence, position and respect within the firm. This is certainly true at Sullivan & Cromwell, which does not pretend to a democratic partnership. It has traditionally been ruled principally by a single powerful chairman and by an oligarchical nine-member firm committee, which numbers Kern among its members. Even though he was now a partner, Urowsky's salary, for example, still depended on Kern's favor.

Urowsky got off to a shaky start. The day of the board meeting, he got caught in traffic carrying the papers to file suit in New Jersey Federal Court in Newark. It was crucial that Kennecott get into federal court before Curtiss-Wright was able to get its own case into New Jersey state courts, which were likely to be more hospitable to the New Jersey state laws, which Urowsky had to claim were in conflict with federal requirements. When Urowsky got to a conference room at Lum, Biunno & Tomkins, the Newark law firm Sullivan & Cromwell had retained to act as "local counsel," the phone was already ringing. Kennecott's announcement had gone over the wire, and Kern hadn't been able to reach Urowsky to order him forward. "George suggested—I should say he screamed at me—that it was undesirable to fall out of touch with headquarters," Urowsky recalls.

Urowsky quickly made an appointment with the clerk to see an available federal judge, and then he tried to reach Curtiss-Wright's general counsel, who wasn't available. He then called Sidney Silberman at Kaye, Scholer, who stated tersely that Kaye, Scholer wouldn't be able to get a lawyer over to Newark for the hearing. The New Jersey Attorney General's office did manage to get someone to the hearing to oppose any changes in the New Jersey statute, but the judge who was available, H. Lee Sarokin, granted the temporary restraining order barring enforcement of the New Jersey takeover statute until a fuller hearing on Sullivan & Cromwell's motion for a preliminary injunction could be held the following Monday.

While Urowsky was scurrying around in New Jersey, Berner was meeting at his Park Avenue apartment with his general counsel at Curtiss-Wright, a lawyer from Kaye, Scholer, and a newcomer, Bernard Nussbaum, a partner at New York's Wachtell, Lipton, Rosen & Katz. Skadden, Arps had pioneered the techniques of the hostile takeover, but Wachtell, Lipton was close on its heels. While firms like Sullivan & Cromwell were still disdaining takeover litigation, companies who found themselves opposite Skadden, Arps desperately needed the same kind of expertise, and Wachtell, Lipton had begun to fill the gap.

While Skadden, Arps has diversified its practice, gradually becoming more like the full-service corporate firms, Wachtell has remained a relatively small law firm, devoted almost exclusively to its original specialty. With his survival now at stake, Berner was not going to risk it on a repeat performance by the lawyers at

Kaye, Scholer. Berner's first call, after absorbing the news at the board meeting, was to Wachtell, Lipton name partner Martin Lipton, who immediately sent Nussbaum to the strategy session. Wachtell, Lipton lawyers, anxious to obtain a court injunction as soon as possible and to delay the impending takeover, began round-the-clock drafting of their own court papers for suits against Kennecott, both in the New York Federal District Court and in New Jersey state courts.

Inside Sullivan & Cromwell, the corporate team on the deal was also swinging into action. Now that the takeover had been announced publicly, the code designation "Project Venetian" could be dropped from disclosure statements that had to be filed with the Securities and Exchange Commission that were already prepared. Neil Anderson supervised the offering statement, and it was given unusual attention because of the complex motives behind Kennecott's efforts to take control of Curtiss-Wright. Anderson thought that the full history of Berner's involvement with Kennecott had to be explained in order that Kennecott's decision appear as a reasonable business judgment and that claims of shareholders being misled would be minimized. In a hostile takeover, the offering statement is always attacked by the target company as false and misleading. It has to be prepared with exceptional care in full knowledge that it will be intensely scrutinized by lawyers for the target company.

As part of his efforts to ensure full disclosure, Anderson had all of the Kennecott directors fill out a statement at the board meeting that morning disclosing any holdings of Curtiss-Wright stock, and also the dates of any transactions of Curtiss-Wright stock. The measure was a precaution. There must be no allegations of insider trading—illegally buying or selling stock, based on information not publicly available, that is likely to cause a fluctuation in the price of a stock. Clearly, any director who traded in Curtiss-Wright stock after knowing that Kennecott planned to offer a substantial premium for it would be guilty of insider trading. If nothing else, it could cause havoc by raising questions about the integrity of the Kennecott board. Anderson was relieved that there weren't any transactions which he would have to disclose or explain. Late Friday, he completed revisions and left directions to have copies of the statement ready to send to the printer on Monday.

His careful preparations were in disarray by the next morning. Anderson was home when he received a call from Barrow, who was agitated. He said he had just learned that there had been some recent transactions in Curtiss-Wright stock by members of his immediate family. Early in 1980, Barrow had borrowed $100,000 from the Texas Commerce Bank, where he is on the board of directors. He had given it to his four children to invest. Acting as a group, the four had purchased a total of 12,300 shares of Curtiss-Wright stock, 7,000 of them on November 12, just four days before Kennecott's announcement of its takeover had sent the value of Curtiss-Wright up to nearly $40 per share. Barrow claimed that his children had known nothing of Kennecott's plans, and that he had known nothing about their purchases. But the coincidence was suspicious. Anderson knew and feared that the stock purchases might be a smoking gun that could unravel the whole deal. Despite the nasty allegations that would certainly be leveled at him, Barrow said he was still determined to go forward with the takeover.

Anderson hurried into the office. He and Kern decided that full disclosure was the only way to minimize the damage from the stock transactions. All Anderson's carefully drafted disclaimers with respect to dealings in Curtiss-Wright stock had to be modified with the phrase "except as set forth above." And set forth above, a red flag for the Wachtell lawyers, was the lengthy disclosure that:

> Subsequent to its announcement on November 21, 1980, of its intention to commence the offer, Kennecott was advised that Theodore H. Barrow, Kenneth T. Barrow, Elizabeth Ann Barrow and Barbara B. McCelvey, acting as a group with each participant having a one-quarter interest and with investment discretion being vested in Theodore H. Barrow, purchased in open market transactions during the period January 25, 1980, through February 5, 1980, an aggregate of 26,800 shares. . . . The individuals included in this group are all adult children of Thomas D. Barrow, Chairman and Chief Executive Officer of Kennecott.

On Monday, however, concern over the disclosures that would have to be made in the offering statement faded quickly in the face of a sudden litigation onslaught. It is in the nature of a hostile takeover that simultaneous proceedings occur. Any one of them could derail hopelessly the efforts to acquire the stock. As a result, Kern himself rarely appeared personally in any of the proceedings. He sequestered himself in a Sullivan & Cromwell conference room, a command post he dubbed the "war room." Connected at all times by telephone, and steadily supplied with Tab and cigars, he could happily mastermind strategy on all four fronts at once.

That Monday, Wachtell launched a massive counterattack in Manhattan Federal Court. Though the attack was expected, its timing was not. Working round the clock, the Wachtell lawyers had put together a massive 50-page complaint and supporting motions and affidavits in a single weekend. Schwartz raced to the courthouse, where he argued successfully against the imposition of an immediate temporary restraining order, such as Kennecott had gotten in its New Jersey suit. He also argued for a speedy resolution of Wachtell's preliminary injunction motion.

It was already obvious that delay would be a crucial element of Curtiss-Wright's defense, as it had been during the proxy fight. But during a hostile takeover battle, delay is even more crucial, and can have an even more devastating impact. Even as much as a week's delay could enable Curtiss-Wright to find another bidder, one who would keep Berner as the company's top executive. Any longer, and the target company could sell off parts of its business, especially those that the acquiring company most wanted. It could mount an ugly and embarrassing campaign in the press, and support a barrage of lawsuits intended to harass and embarrass the acquiring company. To make the most of these possibilities, Wachtell lawyers immediately asked for more than a hundred depositions, supplemented by voluminous written interrogatories, prior to going forward with a trial on their motion for a preliminary injunction. The discovery campaign they asked for would have taken so long that probably no trial would prove necessary.

Unfortunately for Curtiss-Wright and the Wachtell lawyers, the case had been assigned to a seasoned and canny judge, Milton Pollack. He made short shrift of their discovery demands—many would be obviously irrelevant to the limited issues in the case—and granted only two of their requested depositions. The judge ordered a trial for December 23, only a month away. It was a major victory for Kennecott.

•

Meanwhile, Urowsky was facing some heavy going at his own hearing for a preliminary injunction at the Federal Court in New Jersey. Given the judge's willingness to grant the temporary restraining order over the weekend, Urowsky had anticipated a favorable result at Monday's hearing. Instead, the judge seemed to have had a change of heart, for reasons that Urowsky thought had little to do with the merits of the case. The judge seemed concerned about some arcane notions of federalism.

For most Americans, linked by interstate highways and chains of indistinguishable fast-food outlets, federalism is a dusty notion they encounter in ninth-grade civics class. For lawyers, federalism is alive and kicking in every state and federal court. And federal jurisdiction—whether or not a federal court can hear a case or is obligated to send it to a state court—is one of the first subjects one encounters in law school. The states' jealous retention of sovereignty is most strongly reflected in their systems of state courts.

Urowsky had rushed into New Jersey Federal Court with a classic clash between state and federal policy, reflected in the seemingly simple contradiction between the five-day waiting period for takeovers promulgated by the Securities and Exchange Commission and the twenty-day waiting period mandated by New Jersey law. But the problem was not just a simple one of mechanics. New Jersey didn't want its corporations taken over by outsiders unless it was satisfied that its labor force would not suffer. By and large, the federal government didn't care what happened to New Jersey workers, as long as the transaction was fair and orderly. In fact, it was actively hostile to the kind of state protectionism which conflicted with the functioning of a national economy. The SEC knew about the New Jersey twenty-day waiting period when it nonetheless insisted on a five-day waiting period in its new regulations.

Judge Sarokin was aware of that, and as a federal judge he could be expected to be sympathetic to the federal goals. But for that very reason, he was reluctant to overturn the New Jersey law if some state court might do it for him. For a federal court to declare a state law unconstitutional, or in conflict with an overriding federal law, smacks of federal imperialism. A body of court decisions dating to the states' rights era before the Civil War suggests that state courts should have the first opportunity to nullify or adapt their own laws to federal requirements.

Urowsky faced some additional hurdles because of the nature of his motion for a preliminary injunction, just as the Wachtell lawyers did in their suit for a preliminary injunction in New York Federal Court. Ordinarily, a court orders some kind of relief only after it has heard the merits of a case and has reached a decision that the plaintiff is legally entitled to some kind of relief. But a preliminary injunction is designed for plaintiffs who cannot afford to wait for a decision on the merits, for those who, by the time their case is actually tried, may have already been harmed to such an extent that no relief will ever fully compensate the damage suffered. Thus, a crucial element in getting a preliminary injunction is in demonstrating to the judge that some kind of irreparable harm is about to take place, and that it is likely that a court eventually will find that relief is required.

Judge Sarokin now told Urowsky that he wasn't convinced that Kennecott could demonstrate it was entitled to relief from the New Jersey statute until a state court had a chance to rule on its status. Nor did he see the irreparable harm, despite Urowsky's protests that by the time a state court got around to the issue, the takeover would be so delayed that, practically, it would be dead.

When Urowsky returned to the Sullivan & Cromwell offices that night, having failed to get the preliminary injunction, his excitement over Schwartz's success that morning in New York Federal Court was tempered by his own certainty that Sarokin was going to deny his motion. His expectation was borne out the next morning. If the Sullivan & Cromwell lawyers now commenced the tender offer, they would blatantly violate a New Jersey law. They could be held in contempt. They could be jailed. So could the investment bankers, a cautious breed who might now refuse to go forward with the deal. But there were still four days left of the five allotted by the SEC.

Curtiss-Wright and its lawyers at Wachtell wasted no time in taking advantage of Sarokin's order denying the preliminary injunction on Tuesday morning, and went straight to a New Jersey superior court to have a field day with the New Jersey takeover statute. At the same time, Wachtell lawyers went to the New Jersey Attorney General's office, where the state administrator had the authority to issue an administrative cease and desist order, stopping Kennecott from proceeding with the tender offer until he had the opportunity for the extensive hearings available under the New Jersey law to determine the effect of the merger on New Jersey interests. Urowsky's only hope was to beat these efforts with an immediate appeal from Judge Sarokin's order to the Third Circuit Court of Appeals, the federal appellate court which sits in Philadelphia. He spent Tuesday, Tuesday night and Wednesday working on the appellate papers, then took the Metroliner to Philadelphia. He reached the courthouse at 4:00 P.M., the day before Thanksgiving, and there was only one judge still in the building, Arlen Adams, the circuit's senior judge.

Urowsky nervously waited near the clerk's office, and just before 5:00 P.M., Adams summoned him into his chambers. The judge offered to convene an appellate panel by telephone over the weekend to hear Urowsky's arguments, but added meaningfully that it would be impossible to distribute his appellate papers to the judges, scattered for the holiday weekend. The judge had politely made his point. Faced with the prospect of pulling court of appeals judges away from their Thanksgiving dinners without benefit of briefs and papers and asking them to reverse a lower federal court judge, Urowsky conceded that the hearing could be better held the following week. That meant, of course, that the Friday deadline for filing the offering statement with the SEC would pass without a resolution of the New Jersey dilemma. Urowsky left dejected, feeling that the campaign had collapsed on his front, along with his standing in the partnership.

The Thanksgiving interruption actually helped Urowsky's cause. While Urowsky was sitting in Philadelphia, the New Jersey takeover administrator, perhaps eager to leave early that Wednesday, had hastily issued the cease and desist order sought by Curtiss-Wright and its lawyers stopping the Kennecott takeover. The timing of the order caused Kern to clap his hands in glee inside his war room. Because of his experience with a previous New Jersey takeover battle, he knew of a provision of New Jersey administrative law which provided that any such order was automatically stayed—frozen—when a notice of appeal was simply filed with the Attorney General. Kern had a junior partner rapidly prepare a notice of appeal and race to Trenton. At 4:50 P.M.—when state office workers were already beginning to filter out for the long holiday weekend—Sullivan & Cromwell filed its notice and a clerk routinely issued a stay of the cease and desist order. It was too late in the day for the state administrator to get back into a court to lift the stay. The Friday after Thanksgiving was a state holiday in New Jersey, but it wasn't for federal employees in Washington, D.C. When the Securities and Exchange Commission opened for business Friday morning, Anderson was there with the finished offering statement. Through a quirk of timing and holidays, Kennecott's tender offer started on schedule, five days after its announcement, just as provided by the federal statute, and without violating the stayed New Jersey cease and desist order.

Back in New York that weekend—no Sullivan & Cromwell lawyer had a day off for Thanksgiving—Kern and his team surveyed the situation. As Kern had anticipated, Kennecott was in the thick of a multifront war. The Delaware action was relatively quiet: Kennecott had filed in a federal court and Curtiss-Wright had filed in a Delaware state court, but both of those courts had chosen to defer to the pending actions in New Jersey before making any decisions. Urowsky was despondent about the skirmishes in New Jersey, but Kern had expected rough going there. The Curtiss-Wright counterattack in New York, too, had been expected, and was moving at a fast pace, exactly as Kern had hoped. The tender offer itself had somehow gotten off the ground. A formal opinion letter backed by the reputation and prestige of Sullivan & Cromwell that the New Jersey statute would ultimately be struck down was enough to persuade the investment bankers to go forward. The offering statement had been successfully filed in Washington, and one feared event hadn't happened.

Given the disclosures about the Barrow children in the SEC statement, Kern had expected at least an embarrassing article in the *Wall Street Journal* on the Friday after Thanksgiving, followed by a barrage of press inquiries over the weekend. But nothing had happened. The reporters seemed as lulled into inactivity by the Thanksgiving holiday as the New Jersey state office workers.

The immediate task at hand was Urowsky's appeal from Judge Sarokin's refusal to grant the preliminary injunction, which had been scheduled for argument in the Court of Appeals the next week. It would be Urowsky's first appearance at an oral argument before the Court of Appeals, and he plunged into work on the appellate briefs. Doing his research, he found that he was finding more and more cases on the issues he confronted that stemmed from litigation related to the civil rights movement. In those cases, black plaintiffs trying to secure their rights under federal law had repeatedly run into hostile southern state courts and hostile southern state laws which they had had to persuade federal courts to strike down, just as Urowsky was now trying to get a federal court to nullify the New Jersey law because it clashed with federal policy. For the first time in his career at Sullivan & Cromwell, Urowsky began to feel a little like a civil rights lawyer, and it even became a joke around the office that he was turning Kennecott into a civil rights plaintiff—a kind of litigation, lawyers at the firm hardly needed to say, that was almost never handled by Sullivan & Cromwell.

Urowsky's new strategy was actually enhanced by what continued to be a litigation debacle in New Jersey. The state administrator, furious over the stay that had been slipped in at the eleventh hour before a holiday and which had enabled Sullivan & Cromwell to commence its tender offer without violating a state cease and desist order, went straight into court Monday morning and had the stay lifted and the cease and desist order reimposed, effectively halting the tender offer. Meanwhile, he scheduled a series of hearings on the proposed acquisition which, in the hands of Wachtell lawyers skilled at delaying tactics, could cause them to drag on endlessly. The New Jersey state court judge appeared to be granting almost any request Curtiss-Wright asked for.

Unwittingly, however, Curtiss-Wright's success was playing into Sullivan & Cromwell's hands. For example, the New Jersey court forbade Kennecott from communicating in any way with Curtiss-Wright shareholders in an effort to induce them to tender their stock. Curtiss-Wright, however, remained free to barrage its shareholders with arguments for refusing the $40 Kennecott offered. Such a restriction of free speech raised an issue that is always dear to the hearts of federal courts—the First Amendment, an issue considerably more significant than federal regulation of securities offerings. As Kern remarked to Urowsky, "Sometimes you win when you lose." The more New Jersey state courts tried to clamp down on Kennecott, the more the issues did look like a civil rights case.

That was, indeed, the thrust of Urowsky's oral argument before the Court of Appeals when it convened in Philadelphia the following week. Like the District Court, the Appeals Court indicated by their questions that their chief concern was a respect for state sovereignty. There was little doubt that ultimately the New Jersey statute would have to fall, but the Appeals Court, too, preferred that it be a state court that took the step.

But by the day of Urowsky's hearing on the merits of his motion, the state courts had been given ample opportunity to do so, and had instead been enforcing the New Jersey law with what looked like a vengeance. Urowsky not only prevailed with his argument, but the court issued its order just six days later, along with a direct mandate to issue an injunction against enforcement of the New Jersey statute "forthwith." Sullivan & Cromwell received a copy of the order at 5:01 P.M. At 9:30 the next morning, the lawyers were again before Judge Sarokin, the Federal District Court judge. Acting on the Appellate Court's instruction, he enjoined the New Jersey statute. But Curtiss-Wright and Wachtell, anticipating the possibility that the Third Circuit would rule as it did, were ready with another approach. The day before, they had filed a counterclaim against Kennecott in the New Jersey proceeding, raising many of the same issues that were the basis for their suit for an injunction in New York.

That New York suit was rapidly heating up. Though the disclosure material about the Barrow children had gone unnoticed for two weeks, it had finally become an issue. On December 8, Wachtell amended its original complaint to charge Barrow and his children with insider trading, a federal offense. Noting that if the Kennecott offer were successful, the Barrow children could dispose of their recently acquired Curtiss-Wright stock at a profit of more than $140,000, Wachtell lawyers charged that:

> Mr. Barrow and the Barrow Children, by the use of means and instrumentalities of interstate commerce and of the mails, and of the facilities of a national securities exchange, have employed devices, schemes and artifices to defraud and have engaged in acts, practices and courses of business that operate and would operate as a fraud and deceit upon persons; that by virtue of the foregoing, Mr. Barrow has allegedly violated Section 10(b) of the Exchange Act and Rule 10b-5 promulgated thereunder.

Two days later, a Kennecott shareholder living in Pennsylvania who read about the insider trading allegations filed a shareholder suit to stop Kennecott from going forward, charging that the purchase of Curtiss-Wright would be a waste of the corporation's assets, "motivated by selfish motives of certain directors, including maintaining control, compensation and other perquisites of office . . . and producing a gain for Thomas D. Barrow and his children as a result of trading in shares." That suit, originally filed in a federal court in Pennsylvania, had been consolidated with the New York case, since it raised some of the same issues. If proven, those allegations could cost Barrow his reputation and his career.

When Marvin Schwartz, the partner in charge of the New York suit, learned of the Wachtell counterclaim in New Jersey, he was astounded. He looked carefully at Wachtell's 19-page affidavit, its accompanying 28-page legal memorandum, and he saw virtually the same issues that were being raised by Wachtell in the federal court in New York, and no reference to the fact that Curtiss-Wright had already sought this relief in another federal court. No federal court will hear a case that is already properly pending in another federal court, and to make sure conflicts don't occur, lawyers must swear under oath that the suit is being filed only in one place. Schwartz wondered if the Wachtell lawyers and Curtiss-Wright were so desperate that they were trying to circumvent that basic rule.

The next morning Schwartz gathered the papers, called Nussbaum at Wachtell, and asked Judge Pollack for an immediate hearing, just five days before Curtiss-Wright's motion was scheduled to be tried in the New York court.

"What's the problem?" Pollack asked when the lawyers assembled in the judge's chambers. As Schwartz briefed the judge on the counterclaim filed the day before in New Jersey, the judge became visibly upset. Referring to the sworn affidavit which accompanied the counterclaim, Schwartz said that it "contains the amazing statement—I reiterate—the amazing statement, 'No previous application has been made for the relief sought hereby to this or to any other court.'"

"Who signed that?" the judge snapped.

"A partner of Mr. Nussbaum's named Robert B. Mazur," Schwartz replied. "I don't know what else to say except to say that, at the least, I deem it outrageous that the parties should simultaneously seek injunction with respect to the same tender offer under the same sections of the statute simultaneously in two federal district courts without telling the second court that the first case is even pending."

The judge turned to Nussbaum, who argued that the issues in New Jersey were different, concluding, "I don't have a citation to demonstrate but I know the court in New Jersey has been told fully about the litigation in New York and the issues in New York have nothing to do with it, with the issues in New Jersey." But Schwartz quickly handed the judge copies of the papers filed in the New Jersey counterclaim, which made no mention of the other suit. As the judge read them, his face began to turn red, and then he turned to Nussbaum.

"I think that is an exercise in semantics," he began, referring to Nussbaum's attempt to distinguish the New Jersey proceeding from the New York case. "That doesn't sit very well with me. It indicates a form of conduct that I find difficult to associate with the high standards of your firm and the Kaye, Scholer firm.

"If indeed a member of your firm swore in an application in New Jersey that no previous application for the relief sought had been made to any other court, that was, in the circumstances, an inappropriate statement to have made and may warrant further inquiry into the professional standing at the bar of the man who made it.

"I confess that I am very seriously troubled . . . I am going to continue this matter until this afternoon to find out what voluntary response to my reaction your firm, in consideration of the interests of your clients and your firm's position, wish to do about the matter so that it can't be said that any hasty or ill-considered action is involved." That afternoon Nussbaum returned with an anxious-looking Mazur in tow and, not surprisingly, announced that he had withdrawn the counterclaim from the New Jersey proceeding. As far as Pollack was concerned, that ended the matter.

But Curtiss-Wright and Wachtell had suffered more lasting damage. The message from Sullivan & Cromwell was that it could be as tough as Wachtell. If its client was going to be publicly charged with fraud and criminal violations of the securities laws, Wachtell lawyers could be threatened with a countercharge of perjury. And what about the "professional standing" of the lawyer who made the sworn affidavit? Nussbaum brushes aside inquiries, referring to his previous explanation that Pollack had characterized as an exercise in semantics; the entire incident was to be largely forgotten within the context of the overall battle. Clearly, Wachtell had gone too far, and Sullivan & Cromwell exploited it to strategic advantage. Was perjury committed? No one really cared enough to find out.

The New York trial started on schedule December 23, the Tuesday before Christmas. Pollack's hostility toward the Wachtell lawyers quickly surfaced as he denied their requests for additional testimony from witnesses that could have delayed the case into the following week, slashing their witness list to the bare minimum. At the end of the first day, Pollack announced that he saw no reason why the proceeding couldn't be concluded by the following day, and indicated that he might have an opinion to deliver orally shortly after the end of the trial.

On Christmas Eve, Kern and Anderson waited tensely in the Sullivan & Cromwell war room for news of developments in court. Anderson was on the phone regularly with reports to the investment bankers; Kern paced in frustration at his inability to have a phone link right into the courtroom. Midway through the day, news came in from Barrow. Just before his testimony, he and Berner had been sequestered together alone in the witness room awaiting their respective appearances. Berner, Barrow reported, had seemed unusually troubled and despondent, making none of his characteristically provocative remarks.

The day wore on, and still there was no word of a decision. Around 5:00 P.M., Anderson started telephoning the clerk's office at the court. There was no answer. At 6:30, Kern gave up the vigil, assuming that Wachtell had managed to prolong the trial past the Christmas holiday. Finally, around 9:00 P.M., Anderson received a call from a *Wall Street Journal* reporter asking for comment. Anderson asked him what had happened, and learned that the trial had ended around 7:00 P.M. without a decision. Schwartz and the lawyers in court had been so exhausted that they forgot to call the command post. Anderson groaned to himself and trudged out of the deserted office.

Christmas Day offered no respite for any of the lawyers involved in the case. Judge Pollack spent the day drafting his opinion and decision. Sullivan & Cromwell expected Wachtell to try to get a stay of the Third Circuit order enjoining the New Jersey statute by going to a U.S. Supreme Court justice, so a Sullivan & Cromwell lawyer was hanging around the deserted Supreme Court building in Washington waiting to file opposing papers. No one from Wachtell appeared, so he finally left them with the policeman who sits under the stairs. At 9:00 A.M., Kern received a call from Barrow. Early Christmas morning, Barrow reported, Berner had called Kennecott's chairman and said he wanted to discuss a settlement. The Sullivan & Cromwell lawyers sensed victory.

In a sense, they got it the next day. Pollack read a lengthy longhand opinion to the lawyers gathered in court which rejected all of Wachtell and Curtiss-Wright's claims (including the insider trading allegations against Barrow and his children), leaving Kennecott free to complete its tender offer. The New Jersey threat was stayed by the Third Circuit, and it would take months for Curtiss-Wright to mount an appeal. The same day, Supreme Court Justice William Brennan, Jr., denied the last-minute attempt to overturn the Third Circuit's opinion. All systems were go—for about three hours. Berner had one last trick up his sleeve.

Immediately after Pollack's verdict, a hastily called meeting of the Curtiss-Wright board of directors convened and authorized the purchase of up to 3.1 million shares of its own stock at $46 per share, $6 per share more than Kennecott was offering in its tender offer. The announcement was coupled with an announcement that Teledyne Corporation—the western financial conglomerate controlled by the mysterious and reclusive financier Henry Singleton —would not tender the 15 percent of the Curtiss-Wright stock which it owned. The bold move by Berner could have been a disastrous one for Curtiss-Wright—where it would come up with the cash it needed to buy about half of its own stock wasn't clear—but it was tactically brilliant in blocking the Kennecott drive for control. Up until that day, Kennecott had acquired only about 25 percent of the Curtiss-Wright stock. Just when shareholders were free to tender, the market was plunged into confusion. And speculating arbitrageurs quickly drove the market price of Curtiss-Wright stock up to $41, effectively halting Kennecott's chances to get any more at $40. At midnight, Kennecott's tender offer expired.

Sullivan & Cromwell lawyers were confused themselves. As Anderson recalls, "Curtiss-Wright couldn't afford to pay $46 per share for its own stock without triggering defaults on its existing bank agreements. It wasn't rational—you don't commit corporate suicide to save your job. We've never figured it out."

But if Berner's move was just a strategic effort to follow up his settlement hints and get Kennecott and its lawyers to the bargaining table, it worked. Berner managed to ruin everyone's New Year's weekend with more round-the-clock negotiating. Meanwhile, Kennecott continued to apply pressure by acquiring additional shares of Curtiss-Wright stock in the open market, eventually getting up to about a third of the outstanding stock.

Finally a settlement was reached, and at the end of January the long battle between the two companies came to an end with something of a whimper. Kennecott did not get control of Curtiss-Wright, but it did acquire the Dorr-Oliver subsidiary and all of Berner's stock in Kennecott. In return, Berner got Kennecott's one-third interest in Curtiss-Wright stock, and the company did not default on its bank loans. Much to Kennecott's relief, Berner, deprived of his Kennecott stock, could no longer demand a seat on its board.

What had been accomplished? Kennecott spent approximately $1.5 million in legal fees to fight Curtiss-Wright to a stand-off. Reputations had been damaged. The lawyers at Sullivan & Cromwell didn't have a day off from Thanksgiving 1980 to the end of January 1981, including holidays. When Neil Anderson's wife gave birth to a baby boy on January 13, Anderson left the office for five hours. Kern gained another 60 pounds and consumed cases of Tab, his weight on another of its upswings. Although the case is in all meaningful senses finished, Urowsky continues to litigate the Kennecott case in New Jersey. Although Curtiss-Wright dropped out of the proceeding, the New Jersey Attorney General decided to fight on his own to save the New Jersey takeover statute from federal pre-emption. Owen has left Sullivan & Cromwell, but still rides his motorcycle to work—as a successful partner in his own new firm on Park Avenue.

In the end, the biggest loss in the affair was Sullivan & Cromwell's. In the spring of 1981, shortly after the truce in the Curtiss-Wright battle, Kennecott was approached by an even bigger blue chip giant: Sohio. Too exhausted from battling the Curtiss-Wright nemesis, Kennecott had no more energy for another major takeover battle. It quietly agreed to be absorbed by the oil giant, and

Sullivan & Cromwell performed all the corporate work related to the merger. It may be the last work Sullivan & Cromwell does for one of its oldest and most cherished clients. Sohio has other general counsel, Cleveland's Squire, Sanders & Dempsey. And Sullivan & Cromwell already represents one of Sohio's world rivals, British Petroleum, which will probably preclude further work for Kennecott.

It is fortunate that for Kern his satisfactions come from the thrill of the chase, the legal battle itself with its intense chesslike maneuvering. For in the end, little was accomplished. Not even the best, and most expensive, lawyers can stop the resolute flow of cash. As Kern himself concedes, they can only hope to be there when it changes hands.

CHAPTER SEVEN

ROCKEFELLER
Milbank, Tweed, Hadley & McCloy

On December 8, 1978, as former New York Governor and U.S. Vice President Nelson A. Rockefeller pondered the 64-page typed document lying on his desk in Rockefeller Center, Squire Bozorth, a 43-year-old partner at the Manhattan law firm of Milbank, Tweed, Hadley & McCloy, looked nervous. But then, Bozorth always looked nervous in the presence of one of the clients on whom his entire law practice depended, namely, one of the Rockefellers.

Now Nelson (within Milbank, members of the Rockefeller family are almost always referred to by their first names so as to avoid confusion) motioned to Bozorth. He wasn't entirely satisfied with his last will and testament as it had been drawn up. This was typical. As Milbank trusts and estates lawyers had frequently complained among themselves, Nelson was an extremely difficult client. He was, first of all, more acquisitive than any other member of the family, constantly buying up art and other tangible property, which would have to be inventoried by the lawyers and disposed of by will. Furthermore, for a former Governor and U.S. Vice President used to decision making, he was constantly changing his mind, just as he seemed to be doing again. Bozorth had drawn up this will exactly as he, Nelson and other Milbank lawyers had planned it, and would later claim that they spent more than

240 hours working on it. Nelson had already had Milbank draft twenty different wills over the years, not counting all the codicils and additions which had been attached to them from time to time; and now this one didn't seem to be satisfactory either, even though it had been completed just two days before.

As Nelson began to explain his concerns about the will, Bozorth listened closely, even though his client seemed to direct his remarks to another Milbank partner who was present, Donal O'Brien, Jr. Although Bozorth spent virtually all of his time working on trusts and estates matters for members of the Rockefeller family, he was not considered the real "Rockefeller partner" at the firm. O'Brien was. O'Brien had his own office within Room 5600 in Rockefeller Center, and rarely appeared in Milbank's downtown offices, even though he remained one of the firm's powerful partners. O'Brien seemed much more self-assured and comfortable with Nelson, and had always been the former Vice President's favorite at Milbank. Bozorth instinctively deferred to his partner's decisions.

The problem, Nelson explained to his lawyers, was his concern about a provision in which he left specific bequests of tangible property to each of his children and to his stepdaughter. One of the basic problems in Nelson's estate planning that he and the Milbank lawyers had had to confront after his second marriage to Margaretta Fitler ("Happy") and the birth of their two children, was the disparity in wealth among Nelson's children. Because the four children from his first marriage to Mary Todhunter Clark had been born while his father, John D. Rockefeller, Jr., was still alive, the older children had become the beneficiaries of a vast system of trusts that Milbank and John D., Jr., had instituted prior to the elder Rockefeller's death. The trusts, however, had made no provision for what, in the parlance of trusts and estates lawyers, are known as "afterborn" children, meaning that the young children—Nelson, Jr., and Mark—had been largely left out. In the first paragraph of his will, Nelson had asked Bozorth to explain that "a discrepancy in the economic well-being of my two youngest children and my older children still exists. It is for this reason that I make greater provision in this will for Nelson, Jr., and Mark than I do for my older children." Consistent with this approach, Nelson had had Bozorth draft a provision which left $25,000 in tangible property to each of his four living older children, and $100,000 to each of his young sons as well as to

Malinda Murphy, his wife's youngest daughter from her previous marriage, who lived with Nelson and her mother. But now he was concerned that his other children might interpret this provision as an indication of favoritism, particularly since this bequest represented gifts of personal property.

Such concern was typical of Nelson's preoccupation with the details of his will. Bozorth pointed out to Nelson that the gifts of personal property—whether valued at $25,000 or $100,000— actually were insignificant within the context of the entire estate, since $25,000 represented only .3 percent of its prospective value. But Nelson was adamant—he wanted all the bequests of tangible property to his children to be the same.

Bozorth's next problem was how to effect the change. At Milbank and at other major law firms, wills are drawn up and assembled in a fashion to deter alterations which might give rise to suspicious questions after death, especially in the case of someone as rich and prominent as Nelson Rockefeller. In an Old World fashion which seems to characterize much of the work of trusts and estates lawyers, Milbank assembles the pages of the will, ties them together with a single strip of red satin, which is then fixed with sealing wax at the time the will is signed. If Bozorth were to have the pages retyped where Nelson now wanted changes, the typeface wouldn't match those that had been prepared in Milbank's offices, which might look suspicious. So, although it looked messy and called attention to the changes, and hardly seemed the Milbank way of doing things, Bozorth—with O'Brien's approval —simply had Nelson take a pen, strike out the $100,000 bequests, write in $25,000 in their place, and initial the changes in the margin.

Then, in a ritual that traces its roots to the Middle Ages, Nelson signed the end of the document with his familiar flourish as Bozorth and two other witnesses, Edward Zimmerman and Catherine Tracy, both Rockefeller employees, watched. The three then initialed Nelson's changes and affixed their own signatures to the document, and Bozorth pressed his seal into the warm wax. Perhaps the final product was not the most elegant that Milbank had ever prepared; but given Nelson's vigorous constitution and propensity for changing his mind, Bozorth had no reason to believe that this will would be any more permanent than its predecessors.

That afternoon was the last time that Bozorth met with his

client. Less than two months later, Nelson Rockefeller was dead. Not only had he died suddenly, but in scandalous circumstances. For Bozorth, O'Brien and their colleagues in the trusts and estates department of Milbank, Nelson's awkward death would prove to be a fitting beginning for one of the most difficult, delicate and lucrative estate settlements that the firm had ever handled.

There is probably only one family in the country that could alone project its counsel into the very first rank of the country's law firms, and that family is the Rockefellers. It is not simply because the family is rich. Both the Mellon and the DuPont family fortunes have been estimated as larger than that of the Rockefellers, yet neither of those families has spawned a major law firm. It is because the Rockefeller family has kept its financial affairs so centralized and because it launched business and financial enterprises which grew into major clients in their own right. The most prominent example is the Chase Manhattan Bank, the country's third-largest, whose chairman until recently was David Rockefeller. As is the case with Shearman & Sterling and Citibank, Milbank's near total domination of the Chase bank's legal work alone would ensure it a place among the country's leading law firms.

In some ways, Milbank, Tweed, Hadley & McCloy can itself be viewed as an enterprise that was founded by the Rockefellers and that went on to have an existence at least nominally independent of the family. Although the firm now likes to trace its roots to predecessors who practiced in New York City before the Civil War, reinforcing its conservative old-line image with one of the oldest pedigrees of any firm, it began to take on its modern character when E. Parmalee Prentice moved from Chicago to New York around the turn of the century. Prentice, a moderately successful and socially well-connected lawyer, also happened to marry Alta Rockefeller, the second daughter of John D. Rockefeller, Sr., and sister of John D., Jr. Naturally, the family legal business began to flow to Prentice and his New York firm, which practiced under the name of Murray, Prentice & Howland.

It was another marriage—that of John D., Jr., to Abby Aldrich —that eventually determined the modern contours of Milbank, Tweed. After his marriage, John D., Jr., installed Winthrop Aldrich, Abby's younger brother and a Harvard law graduate, in the family law firm, where he rapidly earned his brother-in-law's respect and confidence. Although Prentice had been groomed to act as the family lawyer, he had demonstrated little interest or aptitude; in fact, he often failed to come into the office, preferring to remain at home teaching Latin to his children. Aldrich soon took Prentice's place in the mind of John D., Jr.; and his status was formally recognized when the firm changed its name to Murray, Prentice & Aldrich in 1921.

The firm's major client by 1929 was the Equitable Trust Company, the bank in which John D., Sr., had purchased a controlling interest in 1911 and which had subsequently become the country's eighth-largest bank. When its president died suddenly in 1929, John D., Jr., tapped Aldrich to be his successor; and one of the new president's first steps was to consummate a merger with the Chase National Bank, one of the country's largest and most powerful. Aldrich became the president of the new institution, which then became the world's largest bank in assets. A question which remained, however, was which law firm would act as the bank's legal counsel: Masten & Nichols, Chase's law firm, whose senior partner was Albert Milbank, or Aldrich's old firm. Merger provided the solution here as well. At the insistence of John D., Jr., and the bank, the firms merged in 1931, even though senior partners in the two firms reportedly despised one another. For a number of years after the merger, the formerly separate components of the firm continued to act almost as autonomous firms within firms. Eventually, however, Aldrich achieved dominance over the holdover personnel from the Chase bank, and so, too, did the Rockefeller lawyers in the new firm, including Harrison Tweed (the grandson of Rutherford Hayes's Secretary of State) and Morris Hadley, both of whom had been brought into the firm by Aldrich. The name of the law firm eventually became Milbank, Tweed, Hadley & McCloy.

Today Milbank's single most illustrious partner is John J. McCloy, Assistant Secretary of War during World War II, former High Commissioner of Germany after the war, and former president of the World Bank. Milbank owes the presence of McCloy, too, to the influence of a Rockefeller, in this case Nelson. McCloy had been a partner at Cravath, Swaine & Moore before accepting his wartime commission, and during the war he worked closely with Nelson, who was then heading the Office of Inter-American

Affairs. It was Nelson who helped maneuver McCloy's appointment as head of the World Bank; and when he decided he wished to return to private practice, Nelson helped him step into a partnership at Milbank. At the time, McCloy's failure to return to Cravath caused a buzz within Wall Street legal circles, and the story is still told at Cravath that McCloy was denied readmittance there because he displayed insufficient dedication to the firm during his long stints in government and public service.

Nelson's influence also asserted itself in 1972. When Nelson ended his last term as Governor of New York, Robert Douglass, a close friend, adviser and his counsel as Governor, was installed as a partner at Milbank. He has since left to become general counsel at the Chase Manhattan Bank.

The Rockefeller influence on the firm also helps explain the peculiar prominence of the trusts and estates department within Milbank. Although all the blue chip law firms maintain a trusts and estates practice, the department is usually regarded as the poor stepchild of the corporate and litigation departments, maintained principally to provide secondary services for the firms' more important corporate clients and their executives. To rise above the mundane practice of will drafting and estate administration, it is necessary to have a major bank client with a large trust department or some very wealthy individual clients. Most of the elite firms meet this requirement. Shearman & Sterling and Debevoise & Plimpton have Citibank trust business; Cravath has IBM's Watsons; Davis Polk has the J. P. Morgan heirs and Morgan Guaranty Trust; Sullivan & Cromwell has the Mellons and the Mellon Foundation. Even so, the departments are small compared to others in the firms. Cravath has only eleven trusts and estates lawyers; Sullivan & Cromwell has only twelve; Davis Polk, eleven; Kirkland & Ellis, ten; Pillsbury, Madison, only eight.

Milbank, on the other hand, has both a major family *and* a major bank in the Rockefellers and Chase. Its eighteen trusts and estates lawyers, including eleven partners, compose the largest such department of any firm in the country. And if a principal function of the trusts and estates department is to keep major clients of other departments happy, then keeping the Rockefellers contented is one of the most important tasks at Milbank.

This is not to suggest that the Rockefellers and their far-flung interests take up *all* the attention of lawyers at Milbank. The firm acts as general corporate counsel to some major corporations, such as Alcan Aluminum, Amerada Hess Oil, Cummins Engine Co., General Tire and Rubber Co.; it has the requisite brokerage house, Blyth Eastman Paine Webber; and it represents the New York Stock Exchange. The firm's litigation practice has been led by William Jackson, son of the former U.S. Supreme Court justice. But there is no other major firm which would undergo a precipitous decline in the event that it incurred the wrath of, say, David or Laurance Rockefeller. Much of the credit for the fact that such a calamity has never happened—that, indeed, the firm's hold on the Rockefellers has strengthened over the years—must be bestowed upon the firm's trusts and estates partners.

There is also no question that the trusts and estates partners at Milbank pay their share of the rent and contribute to the firm's profits. Like the other aspects of legal practice which characterize the practice of the elite corporate firms, the trusts and estates practice involves large sums of money which change hands under circumstances which do not limit the firms to an hourly rate. The economics of the practice, however, are probably as curious as any aspect of major firm practice, obscured by centuries of tradition, by a genteel aversion to the discussion of fees, particularly in connection with death, and by the secrecy which shrouds the practice of trusts and estates to a greater extent than any other department in what are already secretive institutions.

Traditionally, the preparation of a will and estate planning are viewed as "loss leader" work. Though a will may take hours of preparation in anything but a routine estate, and may be billed by a major firm such as Milbank for as little as a $100 flat fee, the payoff comes when the client dies and the firm acts as counsel to the decedent's estate. The executor of an estate (who may or may not also be the lawyer for the estate) receives a percentage of the total estate which is fixed by statute at a rate ranging from 2 to 5 percent, depending on the size of the total estate. The executor is responsible for reviewing the legal bills from counsel to the estate and approving them, but in practice the legal fee is almost always the same as the executor's commission, based on the same percentages, dating from the days when bar associations published fixed fee schedules for trusts and estates work which were identical to executors' commissions. The whole process is made more palatable for clients by the fact that both executors' commissions and the legal fees are paid out of the decedent's estate, so that, in a sense, no money has to leave anyone's pocket —anyone who is alive, that is.

The system almost invites abuse—and no one, no theorist, is able to articulate a good reason for charging estates on a percentage rather than hourly basis. One practitioner offered the rationale that "hourly rates invite slow work," a defective argument in any competitive business, and one that would undermine billing systems in most professions and, indeed, in most of the legal profession. The system has been so often abused—usually by small practitioners who latch onto an estate and bleed it for the last penny—that judges are giving the question of fees increasing scrutiny, especially in the case of large estates. In an estate of $1 billion, a 2 percent legal fee comes to $20 million, far more than almost any amount of estate planning or will drafting could possibly justify.

The result for firms like Milbank, with wealthy and sophisticated clients (as a rule of thumb, Milbank will not act as counsel to an estate of less than $1 million), is that provisions are written into the will which limit the size of the executors' commissions and, by extension, the size of counsel fees. Every current Rockefeller will requires the executors to waive their rights to statutory executors' commissions. Furthermore, when the administration of an estate is concluded, an accounting is prepared and submitted to the court for review. If legal fees appear excessive, a judge can refuse to discharge the executors from liability until questions about the fees are resolved. That same procedure also subjects counsel fees to public scrutiny, since probate files are available to the public, and embarrassingly high figures (if examined, which they tend not to be) could lead to calls for reform.

Milbank received legal fees of $900,000 for its legal services to the estate of John D. Rockefeller, Jr., who died in 1960 with a gross estate valued at $160,598,584. While nearly $1 million in 1960 was a considerable sum of money, it represented only .6 percent of John D., Jr.'s gross estate, far less than the percentage allotted the executors by statute. (A Milbank partner also acted as an executor in John D., Jr.'s estate, and executor commissions amounted to another $800,000.)

From the perspective of law firm economics, there are problems with the trusts and estates department. At Milbank, there are eleven partners and only seven associates—a partner/associate ratio that is higher than one-to-one in a firm where the overall partner/associate ratio is less than one-to-two. The pyramid partner/associate structure which is so important in generating firm profits is inverted in trusts and estates, and the nature of the work makes it unlikely that the situation can be corrected. Trusts and estates work is much more personal, and clients tend to rely more closely on a particular lawyer. It is not easy to delegate portions of the work to associates, and some of the Milbank partners have found that it takes less time to do almost all of the work themselves than it does to explain a problem to an associate and involve him or her in a project.

There is also the problem that trusts and estates partners tend toward a genteel aversion to mundane concerns such as billing and firm finances. Despite the patently exploitative system for billing, there is not even a hint of greed from the trusts and estates partners at Milbank. In a recent financial study of the firm done by an outside business consultant, the trusts and estates partners were shown to be among the least businesslike lawyers in the firm. They "wrote off" time charges (failed to bill clients) more often than the lawyers in any other department. They were notorious in not submitting bills on time. Their percentage contributions to firm profits were lower than the litigation, banking and corporate departments at the firm. Sometimes they were simply careless. When Edward Little, the former president of Colgate-Palmolive, died recently, it turned out that Milbank's counsel fees had been fixed in the will, which had been drafted more than twenty years before and were grossly below current billing rates.

It also seemed that trusts and estates partners were too public-spirited for the firm's financial good; they spent extensive time on *pro bono* charitable and non-profit activities, although they argue that in their field such activities are important in generating wealthy clients. And finally, the trusts and estates lawyers did not put in as many hours of work as did their counterparts in other departments.

In this sense, trusts and estates lawyers seem to come closer to representing the self-image that many corporate lawyers like to have of themselves: urbane, refined, too concerned with lofty concepts of the law to worry much about bills or profit or hours worked. And no one better personifies this image at Milbank, at least on the surface, than the chairman of its trusts and estates department, Alexander Forger. It is hard to imagine anyone who could better comfort bereaved widows and children than Forger. He is tall, and still strikingly handsome at 58 years. His voice is clear, confident, instantly reassuring and sympathetic. It is obvious that he cares deeply about his practice, and about the law itself. In 1977, when he was named president of the Legal Aid Society of New York—one of many civic and professional organizations to which he has dedicated himself throughout his career—he told an interviewer from the *New York Law Journal* that his only hobby was law.

Forger is an articulate spokesman for the trusts and estates practice, a role he refined as chairman of the trusts and estates section of the New York State Bar Association and, more recently, as president of that organization. Nevertheless, he is perceived as an anomaly within the trusts and estates department at Milbank. He is, for example, a liberal Democrat. He was chairman of the McGovern presidential campaign in New York State; he himself ran unsuccessfully for a State Senate seat as a Democrat in a suburban upstate district which is 3-to-1 Republican. Even more significantly, in a department where one of Forger's predecessors used to keep a copy of the Social Register on his desk and remark that he had no need for a telephone book, Forger was, for many years, the only Milbank trusts and estates partner who was not included in the Social Register.

What is perhaps most striking about Forger's career within the trusts and estates department is that his success has come, for the most part, independently of the Rockefellers. Although he did extensive work for the trust department of the Chase Manhattan Bank, he never developed a close personal relationship with any member of the Rockefeller family, nor did he devote himself to any of their individual estates. It is rumored that Forger's partnership was preordained by entirely different circumstances. During World War II, he saved the life of the son of one of the firm's senior partners, who in turn arranged for Forger to begin practice at Milbank and who shepherded his interests thereafter. Forger corrects the rumor, however. It was the life of a client's son he saved, and he claims his heroism had no impact on his career. In any event, no one disputes that Forger deserved his trusts and estates partnership on the basis of merit, even though merit has never been an exclusive basis for promotion to a Milbank partnership.

Since becoming a trusts and estates partner at Milbank, Forger has also made a splash that at times has seemed to generate resentment among other members of the department. Despite his middle-class origins, he is the chief source of new clients for the department. It was to Forger that Jacqueline Kennedy Onassis turned after the death of Aristotle Onassis in 1975. She had reportedly been recommended to Forger by Mrs. Paul Mellon, another of Forger's wealthy clients. Forger negotiated Mrs. Onassis' comparatively small $250,000 bequest under Onassis' will into a $20 million settlement.

Since then, he has handled an expanding number of personal problems for members of the Kennedy family, including the arrest of one of Robert Kennedy's sons on drug charges, Mrs. Onassis' property disputes on Martha's Vineyard, Caroline's lawsuit against an annoying photographer and, most recently, Joan Kennedy's divorce from Senator Edward M. Kennedy. Despite the secrecy which has surrounded all of this activity—even the identity of Mrs. Onassis as a client of the firm was felt to be so sensitive that she was identified only as "special 1" on client matters and billing statements—some partners have worried that celebrity clients are bringing Forger, and by extension Milbank, dangerously close to publicity and exposure to the media.

No one at Milbank is more apprehensive about this prospect than Squire Bozorth, the partner who acts as principal counsel at the firm's offices at 1 Chase Manhattan Plaza to members of the Rockefeller family. Most members of the Rockefeller family abhor publicity—at the least the kind of publicity over which they have no control—and Bozorth mirrors their attitudes. Bozorth is the opposite of Forger in almost every significant respect. He is the least popular partner in the department among the trusts and estates associates. While Forger rarely brings associates into his work, Bozorth relies on them heavily—in some cases, the associates say, to mask his deficiencies. They also say Bozorth is disorganized, particularly for someone in a field which requires an unusually meticulous attention to detail. "Squire was impossible to work with, at least for me," one former associate reports. "He was always asking for something to be done 'immediately.' You would get it to him the next day, and then hear nothing about it for two weeks, when he would get around to asking about it. Or even more frequently, he would just let something go until the last minute, then suddenly remember he needed it done. This often happened on Friday night."

While Forger disdains artificial social distinctions, associates say that Bozorth seems to revel in them. He is listed in the Social Register, but only by virtue of marriage. His own origins were modest. He was born in Oregon and educated at the University of Oregon and New York University. For many years, however, John Lockwood, a senior partner in the trusts and estates department, who acted as the Rockefeller family counselor and had an office in Room 5600, took it upon himself to have parties at which eligible young lawyers at Milbank were introduced to the "right" kind of young women.

"Lockwood took a deeply personal interest in these affairs," one Milbank lawyer recalls. "He never had any children himself, and he took an active interest in the lives and careers of the children of his friends, almost as though they were his own children." Bozorth met his wife at one of Lockwood's house parties. After the marriage, "It was almost as though he had become Lockwood's son," a colleague recalls. When Lockwood retired as chief counsel to the Rockefeller family—Room 5600 has a policy of mandatory retirement at age 65—and returned to his office at Milbank, however, he did not install Bozorth in his old position. At the insistence of Rockefeller family members, particularly Nelson, that position went to a contemporary of Bozorth's among the trusts and estates partners, Donal O'Brien. But Bozorth received a consolation prize; he became the liaison partner between Room 5600 and O'Brien and the rest of the firm.

It is a position for which Bozorth proved to be well suited. Whatever his legal skills or intellectual abilities may be, he has demonstrated that he has a crucial ability to get along well with the diverse members of the Rockefeller family. "For many years," a former Milbank lawyer says, "I wondered how on earth the partnership tolerated Squire. As far as I could tell, the bulk of his work was performed either by O'Brien and the lawyers at Room 5600, or the senior associates at 1 Chase. Bozorth was not even particularly efficient at coordinating their work. He was, for example, always late getting out his bills. But gradually I realized that Bozorth was the one partner there who could, or would, tolerate anything these clients did. Not only tolerate, he genuinely seemed to revere them. When Happy was having her drinking problems, Squire could still talk to her. The Simpson daughters—many of us referred to them as the 'bitches'—somehow Squire was able to deal with them. In this sense, he was very valuable to the partnership."

In the eyes of some of the other Milbank lawyers, Bozorth's own modest origins have bred an awe of great wealth and a close personal identification with the Rockefeller family and their interests and attitudes.

Some of the other trusts and estates partners at Milbank certainly would feel no such awe for their clients, having, as they do, pedigrees which are even more aristocratic than most of the firm's wealthy clients. Carroll Wainwright, Jr., is a descendant of nineteenth-century financier Jay Gould and former New York Governor DeWitt Clinton; he is a fixture in New York society and served as president of Easthampton's exclusive Maidstone Club for a number of years. Wainwright acted as counsel to Nelson Rockefeller while he was Governor; he is a trustee of the National Trust for Historic Preservation and Cooper Union, both Rockefeller philanthropies. Wainwright handles much of the trusts and estates department's work for non-profit institutions, most of which are also Rockefeller interests: Lincoln Center, Rockefeller University, the American Museum of Natural History, for example.

Another partner, Samuel Polk, is a descendant of U.S. President James K. Polk; he is part of the same family that contributed the Polk name to Davis Polk & Wardwell. Polk oversees most of the work for the Chase Manhattan Bank's trust department. Both he and Wainwright exhibit the charm and sophistication often associated with the well-born. However, while Wainwright is considered haughty and distant—he was notorious for short hours and long weekends—Polk is popular among associates for his civility and consideration. Polk has even shown some democratic leanings within the highly stratified firm. After being made a partner, he continued to use the associates' washroom until his behavior was evidently corrected by more senior partners.

It is still the perception within Milbank that to become a trusts and estates partner, social connections are essential, the most dramatic example being the case of Thomas McGrath. McGrath spent more than ten years as an associate in Milbank's trusts and estates department, from 1957 to 1969, after working at the firm in the managing clerk's office while attending law school at night. He was viewed by his colleagues as a superb lawyer, but when it came time for the partnership decision, his self-made credentials did not stand him in good stead. He was not made a partner, reportedly blackballed for lacking the right social and educational credentials. He subsequently left Milbank, moved to Simpson, Thacher, divorced his wife and married a wealthy film starlet. He is now a partner at Simpson, Thacher.

It is thought by some that the youngest partners in the department, Carolyn Clark and Jeffrey Brinck—neither of whom is listed in the Social Register—represent a democratic departure from tradition. Others are not so sure. Clark was the firm's first— and until very recently, only—woman partner, and in the eyes of one colleague, "She was simply in the right place at the right time." In the early 1970s, Milbank had been sued, along with a number of other large New York firms—including Sullivan & Cromwell and Davis Polk—for sex discrimination; and according to this lawyer, the firm "was desperate for a woman partner." Clark was in the suitable field for women of trusts and estates. She had ingratiated herself with Bozorth, and her partnership decision also happened to coincide with the death of Winthrop Rockefeller, Nelson's younger brother, in 1973, a time when there were especially heavy demands on the trusts and estates department.

After Bozorth, with whom she continues to work closely on Rockefeller family matters, Clark is the least popular of the trusts and estates partners. "While she was an associate, she was known as Goody-two-shoes because of the way she ingratiated herself to Squire," one colleague recalls. "Now she's known as Jaws." That she is a highly competent and effective attorney is not questioned. However, the peculiar confluence of circumstances that contributed to her being made a partner seems so unique that no trend is detected by others at the firm.

Jeffrey Brinck, the youngest of the trusts and estates partners, is an enigma even to some of the other members of his department. That he would not make a point of any social connections underscores his close relationship with Forger. Brinck is a Forger protégé, and works almost exclusively with the department chairman and his clients. It is also said that his intellectual reputation within the firm was such that Forger was told by other partners in the firm that if Brinck could not be made a trusts and estates partner in the firm, he would be made one in another department. In any event, Brinck's circumstances are also considered too unique to generalize from.

According to Samuel Polk, social connections "should not be discounted" but "are not as significant a factor as they once were. Rich people want the person known for his expertise. Performance is the key. Social connections may establish a contact, but once the client is in the door, they don't matter." Whatever their individual differences, the strongest factor that binds the Milbank trusts and estates partners together is the Rockefeller family. Even as the family itself has grown more numerous, diverse and far-flung, the role and influence of Milbank has become entrenched.

The Rockefeller attitude that has given rise to this state of affairs is perhaps best expressed in the statement of purpose to the Rockefeller Brothers Fund, drafted by Milbank lawyers in 1940. In it, the sons of John D., Jr.—John D. III, Laurance, Nelson, Winthrop and David—expressed the goals of the non-profit private foundation they were about to endow:

> We the undersigned, being brothers and having interests and objectives in common, have joined together in our desire to continue the tradition of public service and fearless leadership established by our grandfather and carried forward and extended by our parents. In uniting our efforts and coordinating our activities, we hope to be more effective in aiding in the preservation and development of the republic form of government. . . . In line with those convictions, we are prepared to subordinate personal or individual interests as and when necessary for the sake of accomplishing our broader objectives. We propose to use our individual abilities and those material resources which are at our disposal to further these objectives. By acting together with a common purpose, we will be in a stronger position not only to promote our common interests, but also to foster and effectuate our individual interests.

The most concrete evidence of this intention to "subordinate personal or individual interests" was the family office, which, due to its location in Rockefeller Center's RCA Building, became known as Room 5600, even though it occupies several entire floors. Its personnel, in turn, became so intertwined with the lawyers at Milbank that at times the institutions seemed functionally indistinguishable.

The key to this amalgam of Rockefeller interests was Nelson's installment of Milbank partner John Lockwood as the family's chief counsel in 1947, which came at a crucial juncture in the development of the family and its enterprises. That year, Thomas Debevoise, who had acted for many years as chief personal counsel to John D., Jr., as the family office's resident legal expert, was easing out of his dominant position in the family organization. Debevoise wanted to name Vanderbilt Webb, a lawyer from another Manhattan firm, as his successor; Nelson advocated Lockwood, knowing, as Peter Collier and David Horowitz wrote in *The Rockefellers,* that "by controlling the allegiance of the family *consiglieri,* he would control the family."

John D., Jr., ultimately deferred to Nelson and the new generation he represented, allowing Lockwood to be named as the new family counselor. Webb and his law firm, today known as Patterson, Belknap, Webb & Tyler, were consoled by being named counsel to the Rockefeller Foundation—one of the few Rockefeller institutions which has slipped out of Milbank's grasp. When Nelson himself abdicated his position within the family office by pursuing public office, the advisers he had named, among them Lockwood, assumed even more power. Lockwood, unlike his predecessor Debevoise, was in a position to name his own successor when he retired in 1969, and he made sure it was another partner from Milbank.

Since then, Milbank and Room 5600 have exercised immense control over the financial affairs of the various family members. As Collier and Horowitz wrote, the family office functioned "in loco parentis, a bureaucratic guardian of elaborately complex proportions handling everything legal and financial for its wards, from the doling out of their income to preparing their tax returns, and even to relatively simple tasks like the purchase of automobiles and house insurance. . . . By insulating the cousins [the brothers' children] from the facts and processes of their wealth, it made them dependent to an extraordinary degree, adding a sense of helplessness to the sense of guilt they already felt as recipients of the awesome legacy." Harvard professor Walter Kaiser, when he divorced Neva Rockefeller in 1981, revealed that he had been made to pay his modest $39,000 annual salary from Harvard over to Room 5600 and accept an allowance in return.

It is only within such a context that Milbank's dominance of the family's legal work can be understood. The firm has drafted nearly every will in this far-flung and numerous family, and their collected provisions reveal an intricate master plan of trust pour-overs and bequests to the Rockefeller philanthropies which have maximized the family's economic power as a whole and minimized estate taxes. There have been only a few defectors from this scheme, and ironically, they have tended to secure Milbank's monopoly. In 1961, Nelson's son Michael died while conducting an anthropological expedition to New Guinea. He died without a will, a condition known as dying intestate, and one which was embarrassing to the lawyers at Milbank, all of whose clients are supposed to be the beneficiaries of elaborate estate planning.

Michael was only 23 at the time he died, but his special guardian appointed by the probate court which investigated his death was at some pains to explain why he had died without a will. The guardian testified that Lockwood "had endeavored on several occasions to have my ward execute a will, but that my ward was always too busy to do so. Mr. Lockwood testified that on March 16, 1961, before my ward started on his final trip to Dutch New Guinea, he had lunched with him and had once again reiterated to him the need for a will, without result. On being questioned on whether he thought my ward might have employed other counsel who might have prepared a will, Mr. Lockwood replied that he did not think it at all likely." It was, in fact, almost unthinkable, since Lockwood routinely had prepared all the family wills when members of the family reached 21.

The only real exception to this hegemony was Nelson's brother Winthrop, who broke completely with Room 5600 for a time and actually had a new will prepared by counsel in Arkansas, where he moved in 1953. Winthrop had always been the rebellious brother, the one least comfortable with the family legacy and the fraternal competition with Nelson. But in 1972, when he visited Sloan-Kettering in New York for surgery and chemotherapy to halt the spread of cancer, the prospect of death reconciled him to Room 5600 and his old financial advisers. Milbank lawyers quickly drew up another will, naming O'Brien as one of the executors.

And the lawyers were almost gleeful at the discovery that Winthrop's unsophisticated Arkansas lawyers had seemingly committed a major error in will drafting. The Arkansas will contained a provision which provided that estate and income taxes be paid out of the residue of the estate, a common provision in ordinary wills. But no Rockefeller estate is an ordinary estate. Winthrop's residue went principally to charity, which meant that it was not subject to estate tax. But to the extent that estate taxes had to be paid out of funds that would otherwise have gone to charity, the amount of the charitable deduction is reduced, since money in an estate which goes to taxes *is* itself taxable. In turn, additional money must be taken out for the incremental tax, and the charitable residue is again reduced, in a circular process that can end up costing an estate the size of Winthrop's enormous amounts in additional tax. In Bozorth's view, the error was an object lesson in what happened when a Rockefeller strayed from the Milbank fold.

Members of the Rockefeller family themselves seem uncomfortable with the public perceptions that they are eternal adolescents dependent on Room 5600 and Milbank for their allowances and financial planning; yet such is their concern about Milbank's reaction that if any have strayed to other lawyers they are not admitting it publicly. Former press secretary to New York Mayor John Lindsay, Thomas Morgan, who is now married to Mary Rockefeller, one of Nelson's daughters, says, "The impression that the Rockefellers are some unified force is erroneous. It's absurd. These people are very individual and distinct. I know that they [Milbank] are not doing it all." However, he can't—or won't— name any member of the family not using Milbank. "I just don't know. Who does and who doesn't use them would be very private. I don't know who would know." And, in fact, Milbank drafted Morgan's own will.

The Milbank lawyers themselves do not like to call attention to the extent of their work that is performed for the Rockefellers or their interests. But with the exception of Forger, who has developed an independent practice, the vast majority perform Rockefeller work, directly or indirectly. At the core are the family members and the private foundations: the Rockefeller Brothers Fund, largely endowed by the four brothers, sons of John D., Jr., and the Rockefeller Family Fund, established to pursue the philanthropic interests of their offspring, commonly known as the "cousins." Then there are the principal Rockefeller institutions: Rockefeller

University, Lincoln Center, Rockefeller Center, the American Museum of Natural History, the National Trust for Historic Preservation. And then there are the more indirect Rockefeller interests, like the Urban League. Even Milbank's other prominent family client—the McCormicks—is tied to the Rockefellers through marriage.

While many of the firm's clients have ties to the Rockefellers, the kinds of problems which end up in the trusts and estates department are not so easily categorized. As other departments in the large corporate firm have become increasingly specialized, the trusts and estates department has become, if anything, less so. Its function has become so broad at a firm like Sullivan & Cromwell, for example, that the department name has been changed to "individual clients," meaning that any legal problem relating to a single person or family ends up there.

Much of the work remains estate planning, will drafting and the planning and drafting of trust agreements. The probate estates and trusts, either created during a client's lifetime or at death, remain the principal legal structures through which wealth is passed from one generation to another, and both are governed by legal concepts which date from feudal England. The most fundamental of these is the legal notion of the fiduciary, which requires that the lawyer administering an estate or acting as trustee act in all respects in the best interests of the client, even though the client may be dead.

Estates and trusts, however, is also a field which has been heavily overlaid by legislation, particularly tax statutes, and much of a trusts and estates lawyer's work today is actually tax work, much of it based on the elaborate provisions of the Internal Revenue Code dealing with estate tax and the income tax on earnings of an estate. At Milbank, for example, one of the tax partners spends almost full time working with trusts and estates partners on trust and estate tax matters. Non-profit organizations, too, are subject to specialized tax regulations, and their problems can span the full range of legal problems which arise in business: employee relations problems, contract disputes, labor problems, pension funds, copyright problems and the like. And individuals typically view their estate planning counsel as the family lawyer, turning to him for nearly every problem which can arise, from real estate and small business problems to brushes with the police.

Forger resents the image that has grown up around trusts and estates departments at major firms. "The financial practice is viewed as the mainstream of these firms," he says, "and trusts and estates is seen as a fringe department that is safe for women lawyers—where they will deal with corpses instead of corporations. Or as a place where, through our shrewd maneuvering, the rich get away without paying taxes." On the contrary, Forger perceives trusts and estates as "one of the most personally rewarding areas of practice. You get to a more basic kind of relationship with the client—you deal with the real person. You must like people. There is no substitute for that. You're a counselor and adviser and an advocate from time to time. There is no problem that you don't get into. You want to serve the family's needs. This work goes way beyond drafting a will or a trust agreement."

Jayne Kurzman, a 31-year-old senior associate in Milbank's trusts and estates department, waited patiently by the Xerox machine for copies of Nelson's latest 64-page will. It was not customary for Milbank associates to do their own Xeroxing, but Bozorth was so anxious about leaks that he insisted that a Milbank associate personally supervise the copying of all Rockefeller documents, particularly when there were financial schedules involved, rather than allow a secretary or paralegal to see the papers. There had been a major explosion recently when Bozorth, while prowling around the copiers, had found the original of a final page of a Rockefeller financial schedule inadvertently left in the machine.

Kurzman had never aroused Bozorth's wrath, even though she had worked closely with him for years. She was clearly perceived as the "Rockefeller associate," a position which traditionally meant that she had bright prospects, either as a partner in the firm or as a lawyer within the family office at Room 5600. She did not come from a socially prominent background, but in other respects she seemed perfectly suited for Milbank and the upper reaches of trusts and estates practice. She is attractive but professional, with a demeanor that is both businesslike and soothing. She is a trustee of Vassar—a visible symbol of competence and public-spiritedness viewed favorably within Milbank, which also acts as counsel to her alma mater. Most importantly, she has an amazing grasp of the intricacies of estates practice, at least in the eyes of other associates who worked with her. It was obvious, for example, that she was indispensable to Bozorth.

Much of the draft of Nelson's will coming off the copier was actually her work, and it had been an unusually difficult task. Nelson was a demanding member of a family whose affairs were unusually complicated. She couldn't imagine, for example, a problem in will drafting that would be much more complicated than Nelson's disposal of his property interests in the family's estate at Pocantico Hills.

What to do with the family's 3,600-acre estate north of New York City had been the subject of discussions within the Rockefeller family and with the lawyers at Milbank for many years. The property had been sold to a corporation closely held by the four brothers before John D., Jr.'s death. During the late 1960s, Nelson and Laurance were contemplating the development of the area around a central park area into towns with housing and commercial and recreational sites. John D. III and a number of the Rockefeller cousins opposed the plan, preferring that the estate be maintained intact and donated for public use as a park and historic site. By the time Milbank prepared John D. III's will in 1979, the family's plan for Pocantico was expressed as follows within the text of that will:

> My brothers, Nelson, Laurance and David, and I own considerable real property located in the area known as "Pocantico Hills" in Westchester County, New York. Our collective holdings form a unique body of undeveloped real estate in close proximity to New York City and its increasingly urban environs. We have given full and careful consideration to the disposition of this property and it is our decision that substantially all of it should be preserved for park purposes benefitting the general public. Accordingly, I ask my executors to work with my brothers in evolving a suitable park plan, or if such a plan is already being implemented at the time of my death, in bringing the plan to fruition.

John D. III, however, didn't actually live at Pocantico, and held only a 7.25 percent interest in the shares of the holding corporation which was the nominal owner of the property. Nelson, on the other hand, maintained two residences there, the "Japanese House" and the "Hawes House"; he owned 30 percent of the corporation's shares; and his wife and two young sons lived there. Although he had agreed with his brothers to carry out a plan for turning Pocantico Hills into a public park, he told Bozorth and O'Brien that he wanted his wife and children to be able to remain in their home if he predeceased them.

It fell largely to Kurzman, working closely with another associate, Robert Sheehan (widely perceived as next in line as the "Rockefeller associate"), to implement what were Nelson's somewhat conflicting wishes. After long discussions with each other and with Bozorth, who then consulted with O'Brien and Room 5600, the lawyers drafted three separate articles of the will to dispose of Nelson's Pocantico Hills property interests.

Article I read:

> I give, devise and bequeath to my wife, Margaretta Fitler Rockefeller [referred to as "Happy" by the Milbank lawyers], if she survives me, the house designed by Junzo Yoshimura and all of my interest in the house known as the "Hawes" house, both of which are located within the area known as the "Park" . . . together with all of my interest in all other structures on and all interests owned by me at the time of my death in the following described real property and any other real property which I may own individually at the time of my death located in the Park.

Following was a lengthy and detailed geographic description of the specific land and property located in the park which was bequeathed to Happy. Article II provided for all the property owned jointly by Nelson and his brothers, whether or not in the formal boundaries of the proposed park.

> I give and devise to my wife, Margaretta Fitler Rockefeller, if she survives me, all interests in real property (excluding, however, for purposes of this subdivision C, such real property as shall be effectively devised pursuant to subdivision A of Article Third hereof) owned by me jointly with one or more of my brothers, Laurance and David, and the Estate of my late brother John, or any legatee under my brother John's will, at the time of my death and located in Westchester County, New York.

Finally, subdivision A of Article III provided for the contemplated public park. However, since John D. III's death in 1978 the brothers' thinking, especially Nelson's, had taken on a somewhat more grandiose cast. Nelson now wanted the estate to become a national park. Thus, the provision in Nelson's will specified:

I give and devise the following described property to the United States of America, for inclusion in the National Park System, but only if the United States has enacted enabling legislation authorizing the establishment of a national park in the Pocantico Hills area prior to my death.

In the event that the United States did not enact such legislation, the property was to go to the National Trust for Historic Preservation, and if it declined the bequest, to "one or more of any State or other political subdivisions of the United States of America, in all cases for exclusively public purposes."

Nelson wanted more control even after his death over the family assets than had his brother John. He insisted that his wishes be spelled out in greater detail for the disposal of the park area and his father's house, Kykuit; and Article III concluded with the language "It is, however, my hope that they will be interpreted as a structure and area reflecting the lives of three generations of the Rockefeller Family and their interests."

Despite whatever agreements might have existed among the brothers prior to the death of John D. III, Nelson had already managed to segregate a substantial amount of property from the park area and bestow it upon his wife and children. This did not mean, however, that the comprehensive park plan was lost. The will also contained the provision "It is my hope that the Japanese House and Hawes House properties will ultimately go to a charitable entity. . . . To assist the entity, if any, ultimately receiving the Japanese House and Hawes House tangibles, I have had photographs prepared of the Japanese House and Hawes House properties which may be used as guides in restoring these properties to their present state."

Once it was bequeathed to his wife, Nelson could not actually dictate the property's subsequent disposal by her. However, he could rest assured that her will would be prepared by Milbank, the same lawyers who had prepared his own, and the language of his "suggestions" indicates that he had every confidence that those wishes would be observed by his wife in her own estate planning. Indeed, when his father, John D., Jr., had died, approximately one-half of his gross estate went to his second wife, Martha Baird Rockefeller, whom he had married late in life and who had given birth to no Rockefeller children. Upon her death, however, she obligingly bequeathed almost everything she had inherited back into Rockefeller philanthropies—pursuant to a will drafted by Milbank.

The Milbank associates in their drafting, however, couldn't assume that Nelson's wife would survive him, and in the event that she didn't, they provided elaborate alternative bequests, principally to his two young sons or, if they had not reached the age of 21 at the time of his death, in trust to them. Such contingency planning is customary in any will, but was largely precautionary for members of the Rockefeller family, since whenever there was a death in the family, all the wills were reviewed and redrafted if necessary. Such contingency planning, however, covered the possibility of both Nelson and his wife dying simultaneously, or within a very short period of each other.

The real estate intended for a national park was only one of a large number of specific bequests that Nelson intended for charitable purposes, and much of his vast art collection was designated for museums. His collection of primitive art, for example, much of it collected by his son Michael in New Guinea, he gave to the Metropolitan Museum of Art, where it is housed in a specially designated Michael Rockefeller wing; much of his contemporary art was to go to the Museum of Modern Art. (His large collection of American art, however, he bequeathed to his wife.)

The bulk of the rest of his estate was disposed of in only two articles: a bequest of one-half of the total estate to his wife, and the creation of a testimonial trust for everything left over, known as the "residue."

Nelson's bequest to his wife, known among the trusts and estates lawyers as the "marital bequest," is a standard provision in every Rockefeller will where there may be a surviving spouse, and it is a cornerstone in estate planning to minimize tax. Until the most recent tax law change, an estate tax deduction, commonly known as the "marital deduction," was allowed for a bequest to a surviving spouse for an amount up to one-half the gross value of the estate. (Under the current law, the deduction has been expanded to cover the full value of the estate.) The deduction was conceived in an era when most men predeceased wives with no independent means of support who needed the bequest to survive. Tax was, in effect, deferred until the last surviving spouse died. In estates the size of the Rockefellers', such a deferral results in enormous tax savings. When John D., Jr., died, nearly $60 million passed to Martha Baird Rockefeller tax-free.

Thus, Nelson's will provided:

> If my wife, Margaretta Fitler Rockefeller, survives me, or if she dies simultaneously with me or in such circumstances as to render it impossible to determine who predeceased the other, I give her an amount equal to a) one-half the value, as finally determined for federal estate tax purposes, of my adjusted gross estate, less b) the value, as finally determined for federal estate tax purposes, of all interests in property which pass or have passed to my wife under other provisions of this will.

The lawyers had to insert the subtraction to prevent the amount going directly to Happy from exceeding the half of the gross estate which qualifies for the marital deduction.

The remainder of the estate fell into what is usually called the "residuary clause"—everything which is not otherwise specifically disposed of in the will. In most of the Rockefeller wills drafted by Milbank, the residuary estate, usually taking up most of the one-half of the gross estate not covered by the marital bequest, was assigned to charity. Since a bequest to charity also qualifies for an estate tax deduction, the use of both a marital bequest and a charitable residue can almost eliminate the payment of estate tax, entirely lawfully, no matter how large the estate. In John D., Jr.'s estate of more than $160 million, more than $75 million went to charities, most of them Rockefeller-controlled. His taxable estate amounted to only $17,790,450.78; his estate taxes, at the then-prevailing rate, were only $3,071,394.66—less than 2 percent of his gross estate. John D. III, in a similar fashion, had bequeathed half his gross estate to his wife, Blanchette, and the residue to charity.

This option, so useful from the tax perspective, was one that

Nelson did not feel was available to him. As the Milbank lawyers often point out to their clients, avoiding taxes isn't everything. There may be more important family needs to consider. In Nelson's case, these needs were to provide for the two young sons from his marriage to Happy. All of John D. III's children and Nelson's from his prior marriage, for example, were, as Nelson indicated in the first paragraph of his will, "amply provided" for by John D., Jr. The cousins were the beneficiaries of the huge trusts set up during John D., Jr.'s lifetime to reduce the amount of his own estate which would be subject to tax, especially what were known as the "1934 Trusts."

Those trusts, endowed by John D., Jr., with roughly $50 million each, were established to benefit each of his five children and their descendants. These trusts were of the common "income to my children for life, principal to their descendants in equal shares" type, often known as "generation-skipping" trusts, so called because there was no tax to the children on the principal which produced the income during their lifetimes. The creation of any trust must satisfy one of the best-known relics of Old English law: the rule against perpetuities.

The rule has bedeviled law students for generations, but, simply put, it forbids keeping property in trust forever. The principal must devolve, free and clear, on someone within "lives-in-being and 21 years," that is, the remainder of the lifetime of any of the trust beneficiaries plus an additional 21 years. In practice, the New York version of this rule prevented Nelson's young children from becoming beneficiaries. They were not "lives in being" by the time John D., Jr., died in 1960. Nor were they beneficiaries of the 1950 Standard Oil trusts he set up for all of his then-living grandchildren, each of which was valued at more than $5 million.

As a result, Nelson, O'Brien and Bozorth worked out a trust arrangement for the residuary which would help redress this imbalance. At the same time, it helped cement the Milbank hold over its beneficiaries: O'Brien was made a trustee. As drafted by Kurzman, the residual clause read:

I give, devise and bequeath all of the rest, residue and remainder of my property and estate, both real and personal, of whatsoever kind and wheresoever situated of which I shall die seized or possessed or of which I shall be entitled to dispose at the time of my death (my "residuary estate"), to the Trustees hereinafter named, IN TRUST, NEVERTHE-LESS, to hold, manage, invest and reinvest the same, to collect the income thereof, and to pay over to or apply for the benefit of my wife, Margaretta Fitler Rockefeller, during her life so much or all of the net income and principal thereof as the Trustees, in their sole and absolute discretion, shall deem advisable. . . . Upon the death of my wife, . . . the principal of the trust, or my residuary estate, as the case may be, shall be transferred, conveyed and paid over, and I give, devise and bequeath the same, to my then living descendants born of my marriage to Margaretta Fitler Rockefeller, in equal shares *per stirpes*.

The trust clause further provided that if his sons were not yet 40, the principal would continue to be held in trust for their benefit until the youngest turns 40, and if neither son lives until age 40, that the principal should go to the Rockefeller Brothers Fund. Nelson was not exactly precipitous about bestowing his estate on his children, but his residual estate would eventually help compensate for their late birth.

Those provisions took care of almost all of the estate's assets, but there were still some loose ends that the lawyers had to tie up. One problem in particular that had worried Bozorth was Nelson's habit of bestowing "loans" on his friends, colleagues, allies and servants. After Nelson's death, it would be the obligation of his estate's executors to seek repayment of those loans, and if Nelson actually wanted the loans treated as gifts, he had to do something about them in his will. And that meant that once the will was filed with the Surrogate's Court, the existence and identity of the loan recipients would be made public.

This had been a particular problem some years back, when Bozorth had taken pains to have Nelson delete someone from the clause in his will which forgave existing debts. One of the recipients of Nelson's lending largesse—the sum of $100,000—had been L. Judson Morhouse, a former chairman of the New York State Republican Committee who had played an instrumental role in Nelson's 1958 gubernatorial nomination and later was close to Nelson as an Albany lobbyist. His was one of the loans that Nelson did not want repaid, and his name appeared in the clause of his will discharging some of the loan recipients from any obligation to repay his estate.

In 1966, however, Morhouse was convicted of bribery in connection with a scandal in the New York State Liquor Authority. Whatever the actual nature of the relationship between Nelson and Morhouse, Bozorth recognized that the presence of Morhouse's name in Nelson's will might give rise to some awkward questions and, at the least, would taint Nelson's memory by calling attention to an unsavory association. In 1973, Nelson was persuaded to simply forgive Morhouse his loan outright, and Bozorth wrote Morhouse out of the will. (The Morhouse connection, nevertheless, did become a target of scrutiny in Nelson's vice presidential confirmation hearings—which seemed to confirm Bozorth's concern about the presence of Morhouse in the will.)

In the current draft of Nelson's will, the number of loan recipients mentioned had been trimmed to three: "I release and discharge each of Susan Cable Herter, Megan R. Marshack and Hugh Morrow from any indebtedness, including interest thereon, which he or she may owe to me at the time of my death, and I direct my Executors to cancel any promissory notes or any other evidence of his or her indebtedness to me." Bozorth had no reason to believe that any of those names would cause trouble: Susan Herter was the daughter-in-law of former Secretary of State Christian Herter, a close friend of Nelson's father and a long-standing family friend; Megan Marshack was working closely with Nelson as the coordinator of a series of books on his art collection; Hugh Morrow had long acted as Nelson's and the family's chief press aide.

Almost all of the remaining twenty pages of the will related to executors and trustees and their respective powers to oversee and administer the estate. Although these provisions would not, at first glance, seem to have much substantive bearing on the disposition of the estate, in the case of someone whose financial affairs are as complicated as Nelson's and for whom the process of estate administration can be expected to last for many years, even decades, they are extremely important, bestowing most of the power that Nelson would have had himself. They are particularly important for the lawyers at Milbank, since O'Brien is one of three executors named. The provisions cover the amount of executors' commissions and, by extension, the legal fees for counsel to the estate, as well as all the powers that the executors can exercise.

Lawyers at Milbank make a point of the fact that they discourage their clients from naming the same lawyer or law firm that drafts the will as an executor; and within the upper reaches of the trusts and estates practice, to act as both counsel to an estate and as executor is considered highly questionable, if not outright unethical. According to Richard Covey, a partner at the New York firm of Carter, Ledyard & Milburn, a comparatively small firm which has a prominent old-line trusts and estates practice, "There is great potential for abuse when the lawyer for the estate acts as executor. First of all, the lawyer/executor is entitled to two fees. He may be paid twice for what is essentially the same work. But more significantly, it is the executor who hires the counsel for the estate. He is supposed to scrutinize their work and exercise independent judgment. Although it is customary for the executor to hire as counsel the lawyer who drafted the will, that too should be an independent decision reached by the executor." Despite Milbank's official endorsement of Covey's position, a Milbank partner is *always* named as executor in a Rockefeller will; and, not surprisingly, Milbank is always hired as counsel to the estate. Ultimately, a Milbank partner approves the fees paid by the estate to his partners.

The Rockefellers, of course, are presumably not the kind of unsophisticated clients who could be bilked by blatant and exploitative collusion between executors and counsel to the estate, and O'Brien is not the sole executor of Nelson's estate. Laurance and J. Richardson Dilworth, until recently the head of the family office, are also named as executors, and presumably act as a check on Milbank's activities.

Some of the members of the family have, in fact, been almost stingy about executors' commissions and legal fees, which led to some revisions of those provisions in Nelson's will. When Abby Mauzé, Nelson's sister, died in 1976, her will limited executors' commissions to $150,000 each, paid in five annual installments of $30,000. Martha Baird Rockefeller, John D., Jr.'s wife, who died in 1971, was only slightly more generous, limiting executors' commissions to $175,000. More common were the provisions in Winthrop's and John D. III's wills, which set executors' commissions using a percentage of the estate's assets and income to the estate (for example, one-half of 1 percent of the principal in John

D. III's estate). Even so, the administration of Winthrop's estate was so complicated and time-consuming that Milbank lawyers had to go back to the family office and renegotiate their fee upwards.

Nelson was persuaded to abandon these limitations. With respect to his brother Laurance, he simply eliminated executors' commissions altogether, assuming that Laurance didn't need the money and would be happy to act as an executor anyway. For O'Brien and Dilworth, he provided "such commissions and/or other compensation as may be agreed upon between him and my brother Laurance S. Rockefeller." And in the event that Laurance died or was otherwise unavailable, Nelson simply let the executors set their own fee: "If my said brother is unable to act, my Executors and the Trustees hereinabove named shall receive as compensation for their services such commissions and/or other compensation as they may agree to among themselves."

This unusual indication of trust in the discretion and restraint of his executors was also indicated in the long and comprehensive list of their powers which filled the remaining pages in the will. As one lawyer at Milbank explained the detailed provisions, "We wrote in everything but the kitchen sink. We wanted to give the executors as much authority as we could." In case anything had been overlooked, the provisions in Nelson's will concluded with the statement:

> [It is] my intention that my Executors, with respect to my general estate, and the Trustees of each trust estate, with respect to such trust estate, shall have all of the general powers of Executors or Trustees, as the case may be, appropriate to the particular circumstances, all of the special powers herein expressly granted, and all powers necessary or incidental to or reasonably to be implied from, the proper exercise of the special powers herein enumerated.

Jayne Kurzman pulled the final page of the will draft from the copying machine—making sure that she hadn't inadvertently left any papers lying around—and reviewed the final version with Sheehan. They agreed that all the document needed was Nelson's signature, an event which was scheduled to take place two days later at Nelson's office in Rockefeller Center. Neither of the two associates had been invited to attend the will signing, however. In fact, it was extremely rare for even senior trusts and estates associates to meet members of the Rockefeller family or even O'Brien, for that matter. They almost never came to the firm's 1 Chase office. A measure of this firm/client relationship was that the trusts and estates partners almost always traveled to the Rockefellers, even if it meant a time-consuming drive up into Westchester County.

Several years before, Milbank trusts and estates associates had banded together and formally requested what they called more "pre-mortem" client contact. The partners had ignored the request and offered no explanation for their continuing refusal to allow associates much contact with the firm's clients, especially the important ones. "Our assumption," one of those dissident associates recalls, "was that they were afraid that the clients would develop an attachment to some of the associates who did most of their work. Then, if the associate didn't make partner at Milbank and left to go elsewhere, the client might leave too."

Even though Kurzman and Sheehan weren't attending Nelson's will signing, they knew the procedure by heart: Nelson would state that the document was his last will and testament and sign it in the presence of three witnesses, one of whom would undoubtedly be Bozorth, who would then sign their own names.

Two days later, Nelson's signed and altered will was back at Milbank. It was placed in the firm's will vault in the Chase Manhattan Bank, to repose with the hundreds of other Milbank wills, ready for use in the event of death. Bozorth, Kurzman, Sheehan and the Milbank trusts and estates department would again be poring over Nelson's will much sooner than they expected.

Less than two months later, on January 27, 1979, Nelson ate dinner with his wife and sons at their Fifth Avenue Manhattan duplex cooperative, then left around 9:00 P.M., explaining that he needed to do additional work at his midtown office. At 12:00 A.M. the next day, Nelson was pronounced dead at Lenox Hill Hospital, the victim of a heart attack.

Any sudden death comes as a shock, even to such seasoned veterans of the event as the Milbank trusts and estates lawyers. But what associates at the firm perceived as the anguish being suffered by Bozorth in the following days was not Nelson's sudden death alone but the circumstances in which his death had occurred. It was Bozorth's idealization of and identification with this client, they felt, that made those circumstances so hard for him to bear, so vulnerable to the fact that even a Rockefeller was, in the end, merely human.

It is unlikely that Bozorth, O'Brien, Forger or any of the Milbank partners know precisely what happened during Nelson's final hours. The one person who certainly does, however, was a name with which they were quite familiar: Megan Marshack, Nelson's aide who had just been made a beneficiary in his will. Marshack was the only person with Nelson when police officers arrived at a town house on West 54th Street and found no signs of breathing, pulse or heartbeat in his body. Marshack lived next door in a cooperative apartment which had been purchased for her by Nelson and which was, in fact, the subject of the debt from which she was discharged in his will. It had apparently been she who called the 911 emergency number at approximately 11:15 that night.

Even as tributes poured in from around the world and dignitaries and family members gathered for the funeral, at which Milbank partners O'Brien and Lockwood served as ushers, daily news disclosures about the circumstances of Nelson's death kept public attention focused on his private life. It turned out that Nelson had not been stricken shortly before Marshack placed her emergency call, but a full hour earlier. A friend of Marshack's, a local television personality named Ponchitta Pierce, had actually placed the 911 call after being called by Marshack. Family spokesman Hugh Morrow was caught in a web of inconsistent pronouncements. Marshack disappeared into seclusion. And everywhere, including the 1 Chase offices of Milbank, the conclusion was reached that Nelson had died in the presence of yet another mistress.

Not that that conclusion was discussed in anything above a hushed tone within the firm, and outwardly there was no acknowledgment by Bozorth or the other partners that Nelson's death had been anything but an unavoidable tragedy—not even any expected denunciations by Bozorth of the sordid press coverage. One associate in the trusts and estates department at the time recalls, "It was almost perverse that there was *no* mention of the circumstances of Nelson's death. I mean, there were legal questions involved: Might his life have been saved, and if so, had Marshack acted negligently? Might she be liable? But in the Milbank trusts and estates department, there was to be no talk about the personal affairs of clients. No one ever talked about that sort of thing. You were only supposed to talk about law. At the department lunch after Nelson's death, it was like nothing had happened. An associate gave a report on the planned topic, which was probably something like 'Recent Developments in Generation-Skipping Tax Transfers.' " Another associate recalls that "There was definitely gossip, some of it, I might add, pretty lurid. But people were very cautious. They'd look around in the cafeteria to see who was there before saying anything."

Nelson's death also triggered so much work for the Milbank lawyers that there wasn't much time to speculate extensively about the circumstances. One of the first steps was to file a copy of Nelson's will with the Surrogate's Court in Westchester County, the location of Nelson's official residence. Ordinarily, the task of transporting the will to the courthouse and handing it to the clerk who makes sure that it conforms to the standard requirements is so simple that someone in Milbank's managing clerk's office does it. This time, Bozorth himself decided to take the will up to White Plains. The previous summer, after John D. III had been killed in an auto crash near the Pocantico Hills estate, he had sent Jayne Kurzman up with a copy of his will. But someone within the Surrogate Court clerk's office must have tipped off the press that the will was being filed, because Kurzman ran into a horde of reporters and had to slip out a rear entrance to avoid them. In Nelson's case, the situation was bound to be even worse, especially with the mention of Megan Marshack in the will. Bozorth managed to submit the will without making any comment to reporters, but they were lurking in the courthouse. Much to his annoyance, the New York Times carried a short item the next day that Nelson's will had been filed, and it mentioned Bozorth's name.

Filing the will itself begins the formal process by which a will is "admitted to probate," that is, formally designated as the deceased's last will and testament which will control disposal of the estate. Once a will is admitted to probate, the surrogate issues the official "letters testamentary" to the executors, which formally authorize them to act on behalf of the decedent with respect to the estate. It is the process of admitting a will to probate which traditionally gives rise to the kind of conflict so often and richly chronicled in literature: the will contest.

Except for the occasional sensational examples like billionaire

Howard Hughes, who apparently died intestate but for whom scores of conflicting wills materialized, wills are generally not contested. To discourage heirs from doing so, Milbank lawyers sometimes wrote clauses into wills which provided that if any of the beneficiaries challenged the admission of the will to probate, they would lose their bequests. In Nelson's case, however, they had inserted a clause which provided that:

> Should any person . . . successfully contest to any extent the testamentary dispositions made herein for benevolent, charitable, educational, literary, scientific, religious or missionary purposes, I give, devise and bequeath the interests which are the subject of such testamentary dispositions, to the extent successfully contested, to the descendants surviving of my father, John D. Rockefeller, Jr., other than my own descendants, in equal shares *per stirpes*.

This clause was inserted by the Milbank lawyers for a somewhat different reason, however, and is an example of what Bozorth called "writing around the law." Under a New York State statute applicable at the time Nelson's will was drafted, any beneficiary whose interest under the will would *increase* if charitable bequests in excess of one-half the gross estate were shifted to the residuary had the right to sue to overturn that portion of the charitable bequests.

It wasn't clear that Nelson's charitable bequests would exceed half the value of the gross estate, because that depended on the value of his art collection and other tangible property at the time of his death. But in case they did, this provision in his will eliminated the possibility that anyone would challenge them, despite the statute. The only people who could challenge the excess charitable bequests were the residuary beneficiaries: Happy and the two boys. But their interest would not increase in the event they challenged the charitable bequests, since the will provided that the descendants of John D., Jr., *other than* Nelson's own descendants would get it. Hence, under the statute, no one had the right to challenge the charitable bequests. The New York State legislature has since changed the language of the statute to try to prevent such clever Catch-22-like circumvention.

Practically speaking, however, Nelson didn't have much to

worry about. The admission of a Rockefeller will to probate has *never* been challenged, probably because all the family members have been so well provided for that such a challenge would only be motivated by unmitigated greed or malice. And even if someone wanted to make the challenge, who would they have to turn to to carry it out? Milbank.

Will contests are also rare because the grounds on which a will can be denied admission to probate are so narrow. The only permissible grounds for contesting a will are whether the decedent had the capacity to make the will—whether he possessed the mental state to knowingly dispose of his property—and whether the formalities of a valid will were observed: that the signature be that of the decedent and that there be three attesting witnesses. Furthermore, the New York trusts and estates law sharply limits the number of people who have the right to contest a will's admission to probate to those who would inherit if the decedent had died intestate, and spells out in considerable detail how assets are divided in the event someone dies without a will. In Nelson's case, his wife would have received a third, and the remaining two-thirds would have been divided equally among his four surviving children from his first marriage and the two children from his second. Thus, they were the only people who *could* contest the admission of his will, even if the proper formalities had not been observed.

Nelson's wife, Happy, was also further eliminated as a threat by the size of her marital bequest. Under the law in New York and in most states, a surviving spouse has a right to what is known as the "elective share," whether or not he or she is a beneficiary under the will. The elective share is one-third the gross estate. Thus, Nelson's bequest to Happy was not necessarily an act purely of devotion, nor was it merely a tax dodge. When the Milbank lawyers had prepared the will for the $60 million estate of Josephine McIntosh, a cousin of Huntington Hartford, it bequeathed one-third of the estate to her husband, even though the couple disliked one another and had been separated for years. Had the will failed to do this, the husband could simply have appeared in Surrogate's Court and demanded a statutory one-third, and thereby upset the rest of the planned distributions.

Under New York law, when Nelson Rockefeller died, his two children from his second marriage were "infants" under 16 years old. The Surrogate's Court was required to appoint an independent lawyer, someone *not* associated with Milbank, to act as a "guardian *ad litem*" for Nelson, Jr., and Mark, and to decide whether it was possible, or in their best interest, to mount any challenge to the will.

The Westchester surrogate, Evans Brewster, appointed a well-known White Plains trusts and estates lawyer, Henry Smith, to examine the position of the two minor children under the will, and Smith prepared a detailed report for the court. His conclusions indicated that the children had not fared nearly so well as their bequest of the residual estate, in trust, might at first have indicated, and indeed would probably receive less than they would have had their father died intestate.

Based on his conversations with O'Brien and Bozorth, Smith estimated the value of Nelson's probate estate at approximately $68 million. (Comparing this figure to the $200 million of Nelson's net worth at the time of his vice presidential confirmation hearings indicates the extent to which his assets had devolved through trusts that were not part of his probate estate.) Nelson, Jr.'s and Mark's share of that amount, had Nelson died intestate, would have been one-sixth of the non-marital half, or $5 million, although that figure does not account for potential changes in estate taxes owed had Nelson died intestate.

In analyzing the children's share under the will, Smith reported that:

> The concept remain[s] clear enough that the residue will be what remains of the non-marital half after paying out a $500,000 bequest to an existing trust; the $175,000 in value of personal property to six children and the stepdaughter described above; presumably minor gifts of debt forgiveness and completion of pledges; the huge, absolute, charitable gifts of real property and personalty; and estate or similar taxes of the Federal government and at least three states. The best current estimate of the value of such deductible gifts of the New York property alone, i.e., realty and personalty at Pocantico Hills and the two gifts to the New York City museums, is about $26,000,000.

As a result, he concluded that the value of the residue was only about a million dollars, and, "considering the preresiduary gifts of $25,000 in tangible personal property to each of my wards, I therefore estimate the value of their absolute interests under the will in a total of $1,050,000, or $525,000 each."

Such a conclusion—that a bequest falls more than $4 million short of the beneficiary's intestate share—would be cause for alarm for the lawyers who planned the estate in more ordinary estates. But in Nelson's case, the Milbank lawyers had made sure that even if it were in the children's interests to contest the will, the chance that they would succeed was almost nonexistent. There was no evidence that Nelson's final will was defective. The great care he showed in poring over it and even changing aspects of it the afternoon he signed it indicated his presence of mind; and the witnesses, O'Brien and two of Nelson's employees, were bound to be loyal witnesses to the validity of the will. But Nelson had had so many wills over the years that to challenge the latest one would be to embark on a virtually unending task. For, in the event that an existing will is successfully challenged and denied admission to probate, the court turns to any prior will. In Nelson's case, that meant his children would have to successively dispose of at least twenty wills that the Milbank lawyers had prepared for Nelson during the preceding years.

But the most significant factor in Smith's final recommendation —that Nelson's will be admitted to probate—was probably the unfaltering Rockefeller tradition of keeping the money in the family. Smith concluded that "the most valuable and significant boon lies in the absolute gift to their mother, of whose bounty they are the natural objects or are among the natural objects with her four other children, consisting of the huge marital half of the estate." And Smith could rest assured that O'Brien, Bozorth and their Milbank colleagues were drafting Happy's will with those "natural objects" in mind. Without further incident or question, Nelson's will was admitted to probate on March 14, 1979. Letters testamentary were issued to O'Brien, Dilworth and Laurance, and the real work of administering Nelson's massive estate began.

There was another loose end for the Milbank lawyers to tie up with the Westchester surrogate. Bozorth had not gotten out the bill for the recent work by the firm on Nelson's estate, which meant that he had to seek the court's approval for the estate to pay the amount of legal fees outstanding. Such a request would probably be routinely granted, but it was, nonetheless, rather embarrassing for Bozorth to have a copy of Milbank's bill placed in a public probate file. In it, Nelson was charged $23,500 for "preparation of will executed on December 6, 1978, including review of assets and pledges, preparation of estate planning schedules and tax computations and extensive revisions thereof to reflect requested changes and alternatives; review of gifts to descendants; conferences and telephone conferences therewith."

In typical Milbank fashion, the bill contained no further specific information, such as how many hours that work might have taken or who performed it—partners, associates, paralegals, accountants or secretaries—but then, Milbank was accustomed to have its bills paid without question.

In an affidavit he submitted with the bill, however, Bozorth indicated that the will preparation had taken more than 240 hours. Accepting that claim at face value (it would seem unusually high for updating an ongoing estate plan, but given Nelson's attitude about changing his will it would not be implausible), Milbank's fees average out to slightly less than $100 per hour. Such a rate is not quite "loss leader" work, but it is probably significantly less than the average hourly rate generated elsewhere in the firm.

The bill also provides a glimpse of some of the work provided by trusts and estates lawyers at Milbank that is not strictly will or trust planning. Included were charges of $2,375 for "counsel and advice with respect to appearances in or defenses against actions arising out of the Attica Prison riot, including review of testimony; extensive conferences and telephone conferences in connection therewith" (both O'Brien and Bozorth had also been on hand for Nelson's vice presidential confirmation hearings), and a $300 charge for "review of agreement with Harrah's concerning a Rolls Royce automobile" and "counsel and advice with respect to various personal matters."

The "estate planning schedules and tax computations" referred to in the bill formed a large part of the work at Milbank both before and after Nelson's death. Milbank maintains a staff of what are known as "fiduciary accountants" to work exclusively with the trusts and estates lawyers to estimate and calculate the tax implications of various versions of an estate plan. Before Nelson's death, various "mixes" of bequests were run through computers to determine the tax consequences; the final plan chosen was one which maximized the tax savings within the overall contours of Nelson's wishes for the disposal of his assets.

The use of such calculations and computer runs became even more intense after Nelson's death, although the emphasis was no longer on the mix of bequests, since that was obviously now fixed by the will, but on tampering with valuations of the tangible property bequeathed. Changing the valuations can have an enormous impact not only on the amount of taxes eventually owed but on the real extent of the bequests themselves—the size of the residual estate, for example, or the amount of liquid assets in Happy's marital bequest. Valuing Nelson's property caused enormous problems for the lawyers at Milbank in dealing with his estate. It also raised the most serious ethical questions about the propriety of the firm's exclusive representation of all members of the Rockefeller family and of the overlap within the firm between O'Brien as an executor and his partners who acted as counsel to the estate.

The tax implications of differing valuations are relatively straightforward. Nelson's estate could be divided by the lawyers into three broad components: the marital bequest to Happy of half the gross estate, which was not taxable; the gifts to charity, which were not taxable; and the residue in trust for Happy, the principal to devolve upon the children, which *was* taxable. All of the real estate and tangible property, such as the artwork, which composed a large part of Nelson's assets, would have to be valued for purposes of computing the tax. Assume, hypothetically, that the "real" value of Nelson's estate were as follows: property and tangibles bequeathed to Happy, $50 million; tangibles bequeathed to charity, $50 million; property and tangibles falling into the residue, $50 million; liquid assets, $75 million. In that hypothetical situation, Happy would get a total of $100 million, half the gross estate, made up of $50 million in property and tangibles and $50 million in liquid assets. Charity would receive $50 million, and the residue would get its $50 million in tangibles and no liquid assets. Tax would be paid on the $50 million residue.

Now, change the valuations. Assume an appraiser can be found to overvalue Happy's property and tangibles at $75 million and, similarly, to overvalue the charitable tangibles at $75 million. However, he *undervalues* the residual property and tangibles at $10 million. Again, there is $50 million in liquid assets. In this case, Happy's share of the gross estate comes to $105 million, divided between $75 million in property and tangibles and $30 million in liquid assets. Charity gets $75 million. And this time the residue gets the same property and tangibles, valued now at $10 million, *plus* the remaining $20 million in liquid assets. And the tax paid by the estate would only be on the $30 million in the residue. Note too that, based on the real values, Happy's $105 million interest would actually be worth only $80 million; and the residue going to the sons, though valued and taxed at $30 million, would actually be worth $70 million. By disguising a transfer of wealth from Happy to the children, through valuation, the lawyers for the estate can save tax on $20 million.

These manipulations, of course, are entirely hypothetical. But the fact is, the Milbank lawyers routinely ran various valuation permutations through the computers while administering estates for members of the Rockefeller family, at the same time they acted as counsel to the estate and represented the various beneficiaries, whose interests, as the example vividly demonstrates, may be adversely affected. In short, the situation gave rise to a classic conflict of interest.

"There is no question in my mind that Happy should have had her own counsel, separate from Milbank, at this stage in Nelson's estate," one source at Milbank acknowledges. Bozorth was representing both Happy and the estate and, for example, was intimately involved in the final decision about the valuation of the American art she was bequeathed. Within limits, the ultimate appraisal would invariably conform to the numbers most likely to achieve the lawyers' estate tax objectives. "Who's to know what these things are really worth," the Milbank source continues. "I can tell you that some of the decisions were adverse to Happy."

The artwork in Nelson's estate, by its very nature, was particularly subject to widely fluctuating potential valuations. For example, when Michael died intestate in New Guinea, Milbank grossly undervalued the primitive art he had collected there. This valuation was subsequently challenged by New York State tax authorities, and Milbank eventually agreed to a sizeable increase. Obviously there was a tax incentive to undervalue those artworks. Some lawyers within the department were so concerned about the situation that they raised the issue with Bozorth. They were brushed aside with the claim that "it's nothing."

The existence of a conflict of interest, while it can often be embarrassing, is not automatically a violation of the Code of Professional Responsibility, if both parties to the conflict knowingly waive objections to it. It is possible, though unlikely, that O'Brien or Bozorth explained the situation to Happy and the children and obtained their consent to represent everyone's interest in this and every other Rockefeller estate. There is no evidence, however, that such consent was ever obtained. One source at the firm reports that Happy actually complained that Nelson's estate has left her burdened with tangible property and real estate that has left her relatively "cash poor," since it accounts for most of her half of the gross estate, and it is certainly the case that Nelson's estate carried with it an extraordinary amount of tangible property.

Did or does Happy understand that she can disclaim bequests of tangible property, which would increase the liquid portion of her marital bequest? Have the Milbank lawyers explained these options to her and their other clients and the implications of such disclaimers? (So far, Happy has disclaimed only a single jet aircraft, in papers drawn up for her by Milbank.) These are the kinds of questions which presumably would not even have to be asked if Happy had her own counsel, questions that Milbank partners will not answer.

At least one of the firm's clients has been alert to this kind of problem. The estranged husband of Josephine McIntosh, mentioned earlier in connection with the elective share, retained Sullivan & Cromwell to represent his interests in his wife's estate. His valuation problems were of a somewhat more drastic sort, however. The bulk of his wife's $60 million estate consisted of A&P stock, which during the period of the estate's administration fell from roughly $40 per share to $7 per share, dragging the estate value down to about $4 million. (Fortunately for Milbank, the executors' commissions and counsel fees were calculated as of the time of death.)

Meanwhile, as valuations, tax computations and accountants' schedules continued to pour forth in Nelson's estate, the process of cataloguing and inventorying Nelson's vast possessions continued at a breakneck pace. The federal estate tax filing must be made within nine months of the date of death, and although extensions can be granted in exceptional circumstances, Milbank takes pride in meeting the deadline, even for Rockefeller deaths. "Nelson's estate was incredibly difficult," one of the Milbank lawyers recalls. "We had to poke into warehouses, crates, boxes. People had to travel to Texas, where he ran a wild game preserve, to South America, where he had the Venezuelan property. It seemed unending." But the Milbank lawyers made it on time. Exactly nine months after Nelson's death, they filed with the Internal Revenue Service the Form 706 estate tax return along with 34 volumes of exhibits, each three to four inches thick, cataloguing his property and possessions—the most voluminous filing the firm had ever made.

Filing the return, of course, did not mark the end of Nelson's estate for the Milbank lawyers. All the routine aspects of estate administration continued—tending to sales of the Rockefeller art reproductions at the Manhattan retail outlet, for example, or making sure the wild animals at the game preserve were properly cared for. Winthrop's estate—which for a time had Milbank lawyers who couldn't tell a sow from a boar flying to Arkansas to run Winrock Farm—is still open, as is John D. III's. The Internal Revenue Service is auditing the returns on both of those estates, which requires constant work by the lawyers; and it is expected that it will do so for Nelson's.

The carefully laid plans for the national park at Pocantico Hills have made no progress. The National Park Service was not interested; the National Trust for Historic Preservation didn't want it without a bequest of an endowment with which to maintain the property and transferred its interest to Sleepy Hollow Restorations —a Rockefeller philanthropy. Somehow, Nelson doesn't seem to have had quite the stature to be memorialized as a national hero —and there is nothing the Milbank lawyers can do about that.

It is customary at the conclusion of an estate administration for the executors to file what is called an accounting, which includes a statement of executors' and counsel fees. Based on that submission, the surrogate formally relieves the executors of their fiduciary responsibilities and of any potential liability for their handling of the estate. In the most recent Rockefeller estates to be concluded, however, those of Abby Mauzé—the brothers' sister—and Martha Baird Rockefeller—their father's second wife—no such accounting has been submitted. The same effect can be achieved by a process known as "receipt and waiver," in which all the beneficiaries waive any claims against the executors. That process avoids judicial and public scrutiny, which is evidently the route now preferred by the publicity-shy Rockefellers and their lawyers.

Nelson was the third of John D., Jr.'s children to die within ten years. During the same period, his widow, Martha Baird Rockefeller, also died. With estimated legal fees to Milbank ranging from $150,000 to $1 million (the latter for Nelson's estate and for his trusts) per death, the passing of a generation of Rockefellers is the most lucrative event the Milbank trusts and estates partners will experience. At the same time, it seems almost as much an end of an era within Milbank as within the Rockefeller family itself.

After Nelson's death, and despite her extensive and important work on the estate, senior associate Jayne Kurzman was not made a partner for reasons, associates there report, that had nothing to do with her competence and ability. Given the pessimistic conclusions of the outside financial consultant, there was simply no more room within Milbank for additional partners in the trusts and estates department. And, citing to her colleagues the Byzantine family politics that have always dominated the internal life of Room 5600, Kurzman did not follow in the footsteps of some former "Rockefeller associates" and vanish into the family office in Rockefeller Center. The circumstances of her departure contributed to associate Robert Sheehan's decision to leave the firm shortly after. Both are now in private practice at other smaller but distinguished New York firms. Neither has been replaced within Milbank. Today there really is no "Rockefeller associate," and the total number of associates has been allowed to shrink. Those that remain report an uncharacteristic, and ungentlemanly, emphasis on the production of billable hours.

With so many of the older generation of Rockefellers dead, the trusts and estates department's prospects are simply not as bright as they once were. Discussions among the partners have focused on the fact that the number of Rockefeller offspring is proliferating, and eventually some are bound to break away from Room 5600 and Milbank, and the fact that the members of the youngest generation, individually, aren't all that rich.

As Covey, the Carter, Ledyard partner puts it, "Rockefellers, Mellons, DuPonts—these are the household names of the past. I want the new money. I want the guy who has made it. These are not the household names." Milbank's partners are putting more emphasis on attracting new business, and there is even a "new business" committee within the department. Milbank is actively pursuing the once taboo matrimonial and divorce work, a move which was supported even by the cautious Bozorth. It is an acknowledgment that the nature of trusts and estates work is changing. The most recent tax law changes have drastically simplified estate planning for 99 percent of the population, since they eliminated estate tax on estates smaller than $600,000, and doubled the size of the marital deduction to the full value of the gross estate.

These trends indicate that even at Milbank there may be an awareness that the firm's trusts and estates department is too dependent on a single family. As long as individual Rockefellers remain wards of the family office, their lawyers will be able to exercise considerable power and influence over their decisions. But in the end, it is Milbank that is much more dependent on them than vice versa. The lawyers who surround someone as strong-minded as John D., Jr., or even as independent and vigorous as Nelson, were really only there to do their bidding. As Thomas McGrath, the Simpson, Thacher trusts and estates partner who was once a Milbank associate concedes, "The Milbank trusts and estates partners deal with great wealth. That's true. But no trusts and estates department is that powerful. Compared to the power of the Rockefellers themselves, the power of the law firm is almost insignificant."

The trusts and estates lawyer still comes closest to the traditional image of the upper crust lawyer: dignified, urbane, reassuring, genteel—someone for whom money and conflicts of interest are not polite topics of conversation, someone who mixes with the well-to-do and acts as their personal counselor and confidant. Theirs is not the world of cutthroat finance or hard-fought litigation, and they have resisted the personal sacrifices long since made by their colleagues in other departments of the firm. Unfortunately for many of them, theirs may no longer be the world of the elite corporate law firm at all. At such blue chip corporate firms, trusts and estates lawyers are in danger of becoming an anachronism.

CHAPTER EIGHT

KODAK

Donovan Leisure Newton & Irvine

Samuel Murphy, Jr., the star litigating partner at Donovan Leisure Newton & Irvine, was grim as he welcomed five of his partners, all members of the firm's executive committee, to his large corner office in Rockefeller Center early Tuesday morning, January 9, 1978. Murphy had interrupted a business trip to Atlanta and flown back to New York the night before, and the importance of the occasion was underlined by the presence of both George Leisure, Jr., and Ralstone Irvine, two of the firm's most senior partners. "I know you are finding this hard to believe," Murphy told the worried group, and proceeded to unfold a tale of scandal and intrigue which, unknown to the committee members, had been brewing within the firm for months. As he continued, "a state of shock began to take hold," Murphy recalls.

Conspicuously absent from the high-level secret meeting was John Doar, probably the firm's best-known partner as a result of his national prominence as counsel to the Senate Judiciary Committee throughout the Watergate crisis. That morning, Doar was sequestered in a Donovan, Leisure litigation office in lower Manhattan working on the closing statement to the jury in *Berkey* v. *Kodak*, an antitrust case he had just tried for one of Donovan, Leisure's most important corporate clients, Eastman Kodak. The closing argument, Doar realized, might be his last chance to salvage what was rapidly turning into a disaster of nightmare proportions.

That disaster had already struck was manifestly clear to the stunned executive committee members gathered in Murphy's office. And as the details of what was happening sank in, their concern quickly expanded beyond worry about losing the Kodak case. They had to face the fact that the Kodak debacle now threatened the continued existence of Donovan, Leisure itself.

A private antitrust case like the one filed by Berkey Photo against Eastman Kodak is usually quite different from a government antitrust suit, such as that brought by the Justice Department against IBM, although both kinds of cases stem from the Sherman Antitrust Act. Typically, the plaintiff does not put such an emphasis on economic planning, is less concerned about divestiture, and is more interested in the prospect of money damages—especially since the damages in antitrust cases are trebled automatically.

The private antitrust case is, nevertheless, equally the preserve of the elite corporate firm. Generally, the clients of these firms are defendants in such cases—so successful and wealthy that inevitably less fortunate competitors raise claims of unfair competition and attempts to monopolize. As IBM discovered in the Telex case, the amount of damages in such cases—even before they are trebled—can be huge. Berkey eventually claimed that it had been damaged by Kodak to the tune of more than $300 million, trebled to almost $1 billion. In dollar terms, private antitrust cases are often the highest-stakes litigation of all, and even massive legal fees remain a small percentage of the overall potential for loss.

Donovan, Leisure had advised Kodak on antitrust matters ever since the Depression. Donovan, Leisure, like Debevoise & Plimpton, is a relative newcomer to the ranks of the country's most elite firms, and it arrived there by a somewhat different route. More than any of the other firms, it owes its presence there to its antitrust work for major corporate clients, which in many cases has evolved into broader representation as well. Its major client today is Mobil Corporation, but it has a long list of other corporate clients, including American Cyanamid, Ford Motor Company, Walt Disney Productions (for which it maintains a Los Angeles office) and Westinghouse.

Donovan, Leisure was founded in 1929 by General William Donovan, who was to become known as "Wild Bill" during his days as head of the Office of Strategic Services during World War II. Donovan had headed the antitrust division of the Justice Department during the 1920s, and was well known to Kodak executives in Rochester, New York, Donovan's home town. He and Thomas Hargreaves, Kodak's chairman, were close friends. Another early partner was J. Edward Lumbard, Jr., who later became the chief judge of the Second Circuit Court of Appeals in New York. Among their landmark cases was the defense of the Socony-Vacuum Oil Company in the Madison Oil case in 1940, which led to the firm's ongoing representation of Socony-Vacuum, later renamed Mobil. Donovan, Leisure was one of the first firms to develop the litigation capacity to handle massive industry-wide cases, which helped compensate for a lack of strong ties to a major bank.

One of the firm's perceived strengths was its ability to settle such cases, which were invariably complicated and expensive. Typical was Donovan, Leisure's work for Kodak in 1953 and 1954, when the Justice Department began an investigation of Kodak's refusal to sell film without a commitment to use Kodak film processing. (This is known as a "tying" arrangement—the link of one product or service to another to restrict competition.) In that case, Donovan, Leisure partners James Withrow, Jr., Ralstone Irvine and Vernon Carnahan worked out a settlement which headed off a lawsuit. Kodak agreed to share its photo-finishing processes with competitors in the photo-finishing market, and not to require use of Kodak developers. As a result of the settlement, color photo-finishing companies sprang up all over the country, and one of the most successful was a New York company called Berkey Photo, Inc.

In 1972, Kodak introduced its 110-Series Instamatic camera. Launched with an intensive advertising campaign, its small size and easy-loading features quickly captured a significant percentage of market sales—and rendered Berkey Photo's own recent technological developments largely obsolete. By late 1972, executives at Berkey had become nearly obsessed with the notion that Kodak's dominance of the photography market kept Berkey perpetually at the mercy of Kodak's latest innovation, a situation which threatened Berkey's continued existence. Such frustration leads inevitably to thoughts of antitrust suits, and the Berkey executives called in their outside counsel at Parker Chapin Flattau & Klimpl.

Commensurate with Berkey's own limited status in the photography industry (1976 annual sales were $56 million, compared to Kodak's more than $5 billion), Parker, Chapin is not a firm on the lines of Donovan, Leisure; Shearman & Sterling; or Cravath, Swaine & Moore. Berkey is not the kind of company that can afford to ignore the cost of legal counsel, no matter what the stakes in a particular case; and Parker, Chapin is a smaller, more cost-conscious firm. Berkey's inquiry was referred immediately to Alvin Stein, who heads Parker, Chapin's twenty-five-lawyer litigation department. Stein conferred with the Berkey executives; he made a few overtures, which were rebuffed, to Kodak to express Berkey's concerns; and he began to put together some theories for an antitrust case against Kodak.

Stein and Berkey were not alone in their thoughts of an antitrust suit against the photography giant. Earlier in 1972, Bell & Howell, then active in the home movie camera industry, had actually filed charges of monopolization against Kodak. As they had done in the past, Withrow and Carnahan stepped in and negotiated a settlement. Stein also spoke to lawyers at one of Kodak's much larger and more powerful competitors, GAF Corporation, which was represented by a firm that was in the same league as Donovan, Leisure: Simpson Thacher & Bartlett in New York, which represented Manufacturers Hanover in the Chrysler deal, and whose senior partner for GAF litigation was Cyrus Vance, who would later become Secretary of State. GAF announced that it, too, was contemplating an antitrust suit against Kodak, suggesting that Berkey would not be alone in its efforts. Though he and his firm had never tried an extended antitrust case, Stein believed that settlement would closely follow the filing of a complaint. On January 29, 1973, Berkey formally charged Kodak with monopolization.

Unknown to Stein, there had been some changes at Kodak since the Bell & Howell settlement, changes which would have a direct effect on the progress of his case. Kodak's general counsel, the lawyer inside the company who had overseen all its legal affairs, including the work of its outside counsel in various law firms, had been Homer Brereton. Brereton's presence ensured that a steady stream of outside legal work continued to flow in Donovan, Leisure's direction. But in 1972 he retired. He was succeeded by Kendall Cole, an associate not at Donovan, Leisure but at one of

Donovan, Leisure's archrivals, New York's Sullivan & Cromwell, the firm which had traditionally handled much of Kodak's outside corporate work.

Like the Bell & Howell matter, the Berkey complaint was routinely referred to Donovan, Leisure, where it was in turn handed over to Withrow and Carnahan. But Cole wasn't happy with their assignment. Withrow was already in his sixties, probably too old to try a case, and both he and Carnahan were counseling settlement. Cole disagreed. He was part of a new generation of corporate counsel who were fed up with what they believed to be blackmail by faltering competitors armed only with hollow antitrust complaints. Give in to Berkey, he reasoned, and there would be an avalanche of frivolous lawsuits hoping for settlement. Cole took the unprecedented step of scheduling a meeting between Walter Fallon, Kodak's present chairman, and Samuel Murphy, Jr., the head of Donovan, Leisure's litigation department.

Murphy does not bear a formal designation as the firm's top litigator, and until recently he didn't sit on the firm's executive committee. He is, nonetheless, the most powerful lawyer in the firm, the man who has attracted or held many of the firm's major clients. Associates fear and admire him. "If John Wayne had been a lawyer, he'd have been Sam Murphy," notes one. Though he is far from the most senior partner at the firm, Murphy became the protégé of Irvine, who informally anointed him his successor. Murphy is assertive, handsome, brilliant—the kind of lawyer who instantly inspires confidence in clients.

Murphy flew to Rochester in early 1973. At the meeting, Fallon announced that Kodak had concluded it was time to draw the line. The company wanted to fight the Berkey charges—and the GAF charges which had followed them by a few weeks—with all of its resources. And it wanted Murphy to handle the litigation—not Withrow, Carnahan, or any of Donovan, Leisure's aging senior partners. In fact, Fallon was armed with a typed list of Donovan, Leisure partners that Kodak would be willing to have head its litigation, and the list wasn't very long. Fallon made clear that, while Kodak had enjoyed a very long and satisfactory relationship with the Donovan, Leisure firm, it could not take Kodak's outside legal work for granted. Several other firms were also being considered for the antitrust cases, among them, Sullivan & Cromwell.

Murphy accepted the assignment—to preserve his firm's relationship with one of its oldest and most valuable clients he had little choice—and the terms of his acceptance remain a matter of some dispute. Murphy was then trying what were known as the "tetracycline cases"—an avalanche of litigation which resulted from defective births due to use of the drug by pregnant woman— on behalf of another of Donovan, Leisure's important clients, American Cyanamid. He expected those cases—which had already been dragging on for fourteen years—to be finished in a few months, freeing him for the Kodak matter. Murphy says that he told Fallon that either he would personally try the cases or find an outstanding trial lawyer to take his place. Cole later claimed that Murphy's promise was unconditional.

Murphy returned to New York and immediately set about assembling a team of lawyers to handle the suits against Kodak. Carnahan and Withrow continued to work on the case, and three other partners were added: James Magee, Mahlon Perkins, Jr., and Helmut Furth. George Leisure, Jr., son of one of the firm's name partners, oversaw their work when Murphy was tied up with the tetracycline litigation. It was a blue ribbon team, obviously designed to impress Kodak. Perkins, in particular, added luster to the group. A quiet, dignified, scholarly man, he had been an Oxford scholar, president of the World Federalist Organization, and was known as the firm's best brief writer. He was not, however, the kind of lawyer that Donovan, Leisure would assign to the front lines in a hotly contested litigation. As Murphy puts it, "Perkins was not a real courtroom lawyer. There are all kinds, you know, and he is a very bright man. But he doesn't get up on his feet." Thus, though Perkins was nine years senior to Murphy, he plainly labored in Murphy's shadow. He attracted few clients on his own, spent most of his time working behind the scenes, and was ultimately dependent on the business-getting abilities of lawyers like Murphy for his own livelihood. For many lawyers like Perkins—and his counterparts are found in every major firm—the large corporate law firm provides a haven from the competitive pressures of the world of business and affairs, much like medieval monasteries. "I always thought Perkins was happy with his niche," Murphy says.

Thus, when Murphy promised that either he or a first-rate trial lawyer would try the Kodak case, Perkins was not the man he had in mind. Nor were Withrow and Carnahan, already rejected by

Kodak; nor was Furth, whom he thought too young and eccentric. By mid-1975, discovery in the Kodak cases was ready to go forward, and it was apparent that the tetracycline cases could not be finished anytime soon. Murphy couldn't try the Kodak cases, and he didn't know whom to offer Kodak in his place. Donovan, Leisure's two leading litigators who had been groomed to take over the mantle left by Leisure and Irvine had been lost to the firm. Roy MacDonald had died suddenly; Walter Mansfield had left the firm to become a federal district court judge in Manhattan. Murphy discussed the situation with members of the firm's executive committee, and the conclusion was reached that the firm would take an unprecedented step. It would look outside the firm for a litigating attorney of the first rank, and offer him a partnership in the firm as well as leadership of the Kodak case.

It was a step that Donovan, Leisure had never taken in the past, and it breaks one of the rules of the corporate law firm: never admit an outsider into the partnership. Despite their reservations, however, the Donovan, Leisure partners felt they had no choice. Murphy first approached a federal court judge: Harold Tyler, Jr., who was known to be interested in returning to private practice (he eventually did join the New York firm now called Patterson, Belknap, Webb & Tyler). Tyler wasn't interested, but he had another suggestion: John Doar, who would shortly become nationally known as counsel to the Senate Judiciary Committee during the Watergate crisis, and who had worked for Tyler in the Justice Department during the Eisenhower administration.

Murphy had several meetings with Doar, who was then president of the New York City Board of Education and had been counsel to the Bedford Stuyvesant urban renewal project, one of whose board members, Rawleigh Warner, Jr., was chairman of Mobil, one of Donovan, Leisure's major clients. Doar did not have the background of most partners in major corporate law firms. He had grown up in Wisconsin and, after graduating from the University of California Law School at Berkeley in 1949, had returned to private practice in Madison. Later he joined the civil rights division of the Justice Department and came to the attention of then Attorney General Robert Kennedy.

Murphy recalls that at their meetings Doar appeared interested in joining Donovan, Leisure, but the firm itself ultimately decided against him, principally because other members of the executive committee felt that he hadn't had enough experience managing the kind of complex cases he would encounter at Donovan, Leisure. But then Doar was tapped for the Watergate investigation, and he became nationally prominent just at the time Kodak was insisting that Donovan, Leisure assign a nationally known trial lawyer to its antitrust cases. Doar was suddenly exactly what Murphy and Donovan, Leisure wanted. The firm's earlier reservations were forgotten in the afterglow of Watergate celebrity.

In January of 1975, Murphy, George Leisure, Jr., and John Tobin, a corporate partner and member of the executive committee, met with Doar over dinner at the Gloucester House, a seafood restaurant in midtown Manhattan. After final financial details were worked out—Doar was told he could expect a minimum six-figure salary—Leisure formally extended the offer of partnership, and Doar accepted. Murphy reminded Doar that the firm had the Kodak litigation in mind for him, though his assignment to that case would be contingent on Kodak's approval. Doar pointed out that he hadn't had any real antitrust experience, but that the cases sounded challenging, and he liked challenges. Neither Doar nor any of the Donovan, Leisure partners that night had any idea of how overwhelming that challenge would prove to be.

As soon as Doar arrived at the firm in February, Murphy scheduled a meeting in Rochester with what Kodak called its management task force, consisting of Walter Fallon, the chairman; Kendall Cole, its chief inside counsel; David Wier, another inside lawyer who was an alumnus of Donovan, Leisure; and several of Kodak's financial officers. Murphy had prepared a little speech with which to "sell" Doar, but it turned out he didn't have to use it. Fallon was delighted with the choice of Doar, and plunged immediately into the details of conducting the litigation. Kodak wanted the best and most thorough representation it could get, and he insisted that the Donovan, Leisure lawyers and Doar begin by immersing themselves totally in Kodak and its business. Within a week, Doar had practically moved to Rochester, absorbing everything he could about the photographic equipment industry. But the assignment left Doar little time to get to know his new partners at Donovan, Leisure.

Staffing of the case at Donovan, Leisure was also restructured. During the time when Murphy had been nominally in charge of the case, he had delegated much of his authority. Carnahan was in charge of the motion practice, Perkins headed up the economic theories of the case, and Furth was in charge of developing the legal theories. When Doar arrived, that delegation largely ended. He assumed principal responsibility for all those areas, and the three partners were delegated to less significant roles. Furth was assigned to manage discovery in the GAF suit; Perkins was assigned to document production and analysis in the Berkey case. Their new assignments were regarded as demotions in favor of a newcomer.

During 1975, the Kodak cases settled into a routine characteristic of any litigation of such a large size and scope. Stein had made several discovery motions before Judge Marvin Frankel, the federal district judge to whom both the Berkey and GAF cases had been assigned; and the judge had been relatively generous in granting them. As a result, Donovan, Leisure associates began to comb through the files at Kodak, making copies of the hundreds of thousands of documents requested by the plaintiffs' lawyers. To coordinate the production of documents, the Donovan, Leisure team was assigned space in offices maintained by Kodak in New York City at 77 Broadway, known as the Wanamaker building. There, lawyers and paralegals scrutinized the documents, coded them, entered them into an elaborate computer system installed for the litigation, and then gave copies to lawyers for GAF and Berkey.

As Cravath's had been in the IBM case, the strategy was to drown the opposition in documents, most of which were harmless or irrelevant, hoping that they would lack either the manpower or the willpower to pore through each and every one of them. Similarly, litigants schedule depositions—pretrial question-and-answer sessions—with as many of the opposing party's executives as possible, as much to harass as to gain information that may later be used as evidence at trial. All such "discovery" activities are designed to minimize surprises at the trial itself.

By the end of 1975, the Donovan, Leisure lawyers under Doar's direction had produced more than 500,000 documents from Kodak's internal files. Their opponents at Parker, Chapin and at Simpson, Thacher had not moved nearly as quickly. They had not computerized their operation—Stein's firm couldn't afford the system—and had produced only about 100,000 documents.

Furth, in particular, sensed that Donovan's heavy document production had stunned the opposition, and he moved quickly to exploit what he perceived as an advantage. He made a motion to Judge Frankel for immediate commencement of depositions of all of GAF's top executives, which Frankel—a judge who was known for his efforts to speed up lengthy litigation—granted. Simpson, Thacher's Vance tried to stop the program from going forward (he, like Murphy, was preoccupied with other cases), but when he failed, he assigned defense of the depositions to a highly regarded partner, John Guzzetta, and an associate, Eric Vitalliano.

Furth's strategy was first to depose Jesse Werner, the chairman of GAF, and James Sherwin, the executive vice president, to, as he puts it, "draw first blood." That deposition began in Kodak's office space in the Wanamaker building shortly after Frankel's order. Such procedures usually take a few days, at most a week. Werner's deposition took a solid month, and as the days wore on, Werner's temper became shorter.

To Furth's surprise, he didn't think the lawyers from Simpson, Thacher took the depositions very seriously. To the untrained eye, the lawyer who represents the person being questioned at a deposition doesn't have much to do. Occasionally, the lawyer may instruct the witness not to answer a question, but such an instruction can be appealed to the judge or a magistrate and is not often given. Ordinary courtroom objections have no effect. In many depositions, the defense counsel seems to do little more than listen, and for these reasons, corporate law firms often send their less experienced litigation associates to cover them. In Simpson, Thacher's case, the firm rotated lawyers at Werner's and Sherwin's depositions, beginning with Guzzetta, who then occasionally assigned others to take his place.

One deposition objection frequently made is that a question has already been asked and answered, but it requires a defense counsel familiar with what has already happened at the deposition. According to Furth, when he saw Simpson, Thacher sending in new lawyers, he deliberately began to ask the same questions over, prolonging the deposition and rattling Werner and Sherwin. While the witnesses became increasingly agitated, the Simpson, Thacher lawyers listened to the repetitive questions for the first time, not noticing Furth's ploy.

Guzzetta adds that Furth did not restrict his repetitive questioning to days when substitute Simpson, Thacher lawyers were present. "I did attend all of Werner's deposition," Guzzetta insists, "and it was rattling, all right. Furth asked the same questions not just twice, but sometimes three, four or more times. I filed a complaint with the judge."

One area of questioning during Werner's deposition was GAF's profitability, since GAF alleged in its suits that unfair competition from Kodak had held down its profits. Such an allegation is routine in any private antitrust case, and becomes an important part of determining damages if a plaintiff wins.

During World War II, GAF had been taken over and run by the government under the Trading with the Enemy Act (GAF was then a subsidiary of the German manufacturer I. G. Farben), and a point that Furth planned to make at trial was that GAF's profitability had been hurt not by Kodak but by inept administration during the 23-year period after the war when it was run by the U.S. government. Furth had also noticed that during the early 1970s GAF had been granted an exemption from wage and price controls. Why? Might GAF itself have argued that government control had so harmed its business that application of wage and price controls would be unfair? Furth wondered.

The next day, Furth asked Werner about the effect of government administration during and after World War II, and the chairman emphatically denied that it had had any effect on GAF's profits. But Furth was still suspicious. He later asked Guzzetta for any letter Werner had written to the wage and price council requesting an exemption. Guzzetta answered that if such a letter hadn't already been produced, it had been lost or destroyed. The next day, Furth called Vitalliano at Simpson, Thacher. Feigning innocence, he indicated that the price control issue was coming up in his questioning and said, "We're ready for that letter Werner wrote to the wage and price council." Vitalliano took the bait. Werner had indeed written such a letter, and Vitalliano answered that he'd have to review the document, but otherwise he'd be happy to send it. By Monday, Furth had a document in his hands that he hadn't even been sure existed.

As soon as he had the letter, Furth made the unsuspecting Werner repeat his sworn testimony that government administration had had no effect on GAF's profitability. Then he pulled out a copy of the document in which Werner had argued the opposite position to the wage and price council. Werner was surprised and embarrassed. Whatever he might have planned to say at trial on the subject would now be undermined. When Vance later left the firm to become Secretary of State, GAF dropped Simpson, Thacher from the case.

Furth considered his deposition campaign in GAF to be a litigation coup, but it was not so regarded by his new superior at Donovan, Leisure, John Doar. Doar confided to one associate that Furth's technique had amounted to little more than a cheap trick, one unbecoming to the profession. Doar told Guzzetta that he was having "problems" with Furth. When Furth later offered his opinion that the Kodak cases should be tried before a judge and not a jury, his advice was disregarded. And when GAF successfully obtained an indefinite postponement of its case in order to change counsel (GAF first asked Stein to handle its case as well as Berkey's; when he declined, it turned to Skadden, Arps, Slate, Meagher & Flom in New York), Furth was left in charge of GAF. His legal staff dwindled to two associates, and he was in the law firm's equivalent of exile.

Helmut Furth was not the only partner at Donovan, Leisure who became disenchanted with Doar; and several went to Murphy to complain. Besides Furth, Mahlon Perkins and James Magee told Murphy that they had reservations about Doar's ability to handle a complicated case. His major problem, they agreed, was an inability to delegate authority and to trust the results of his partners. They felt his problem was exacerbated because it was coupled with what they perceived as a kind of self-righteous arrogance, an excessive concern with personal rectitude. An associate who worked closely with Doar during this period describes him as "a very good lawyer who could do the work of three. But give him thirty lawyers—and still he only produces the work of three. He didn't trust, didn't rely on us. It made me furious." But Murphy disregarded these complaints, ascribing them to personality differences and the natural pique of those who resented Doar's being placed above them in the partnership order. But Murphy himself didn't feel comfortable with Doar, and he never relayed his partners' complaints to him.

While Donovan, Leisure lawyers were busy scheduling and conducting depositions of Berkey and GAF executives, Stein was finally getting his own discovery program under way on behalf of Berkey. After conducting depositions of Fallon and most of Kodak's top executives during the course of 1976, Stein scheduled the deposition of Yale economist Merton J. Peck, whom Donovan, Leisure lawyers had chosen to be Kodak's principal economic expert witness in the case.

It is hard to overestimate the importance of an economic expert witness in an antitrust case, especially one being tried before a jury. After the basic facts have been introduced, the economist enters and attempts to explain what all the seemingly disconnected bits of information mean in terms of economic theory. In the end, the expert's testimony purports to resolve the inherent contradiction in antitrust law: Do all of these facts paint a picture of healthy competition? Or are they a portrait of an anticompetitive monopolist?

The care and feeding of an expert witness by lawyers takes time and money. The experts must review all of the facts in the case, thousands of documents, and must develop an economic theory which coincides with the legal theory being presented by the lawyers. For their efforts, such economic experts command fees of up to $4,000 a day; Peck received more than $100,000 for his work with Donovan, Leisure. In theory, the testimony of such an expert is supposed to represent the independent judgment of the expert, untainted by any favoritism toward either party. In practice, the economists, who otherwise subsist on academic salaries, know to whom they owe their six-figure yearly incomes. Highly respected experts have been known to ask lawyers, "Tell me what I'm supposed to say."

Early in the Kodak case, Perkins had been given the assignment of selecting and preparing Kodak's expert witnesses. It was an assignment that appealed to the scholarly side of Perkins' nature, and to assist him, he asked that associate Joseph Fortenberry be assigned to work with him. Fortenberry, too, had a professorial air, though at times it bordered on that of a mad professor. Other associates and partners at the firm describe him uniformly as an odd-ball, a loner who most enjoyed library research assignments, whose oddities concealed a shy and sensitive nature. After Perkins had selected Peck and Morris Adelman from the Massachusetts Institute of Technology as Kodak's economic experts, he and Fortenberry set about developing the economic theories, submitting various reports and analyses to the experts for their review, and developing positions through exchanges of memoranda.

On March 29, 1977, Stein finally scheduled his deposition with Peck, and Doar assigned Perkins and Fortenberry to the task of defending his deposition. While it was a logical extension of his work in developing Peck's testimony, Perkins was not looking forward to the deposition. As hard as he had tried, Perkins had never delighted in the kind of tough litigating tactics that had characterized Furth's work, for example, and that might be called for in the deposition by the opponents' lead counsel of Kodak's single most important witness. But the need to prove himself was weighing heavily on Perkins since Doar's arrival, and he went into the deposition determined to take a hard line.

Peck's deposition began on April 20 in a conference room at Donovan, Leisure's Rockefeller Center offices. Peck was nervous; Stein recalls that it was quickly apparent to him that "Peck wasn't strong in the personal sense; he seemed vulnerable, very suggestible." Stein began, however, by focusing his questions at Perkins. At the time he scheduled Peck's deposition, Stein had also made a request for all the documents that Peck had received and everything he had written about the Kodak litigation.

While the request was a broad one, it wasn't unreasonable. Over the years, courts have ruled that almost anything that a lawyer shows an economic expert witness must be disclosed to opposing counsel, the theory being that everything a witness sees relating to the case becomes a part of his thinking and should be subject to cross-examination at trial. An expert's opinion, the theory goes, is only as good as the information on which it is based. The lawyers at Donovan, Leisure had already taken a hard line about producing some of the documents that Stein had demanded, to the point that an exasperated Stein called for a special hearing before the magistrate to determine what Donovan, Leisure had to produce. Doar attended the hearing—not Perkins—and the magistrate ruled that even "interim" reports had to be produced if they had been discussed by the expert with counsel. Doar had argued that only "final" reports had to be turned over, but Doar sent a memo summarizing the ruling to Perkins in anticipation of his deposition with Peck.

When Stein began his questioning of Peck, the lawyer naturally focused on the existence and whereabouts of such documents that

Donovan, Leisure might have failed to turn over to him; and in the course of his questioning, Peck told him that he had returned all of his written material, including his handwritten notes, to the lawyers at Donovan, Leisure. Stein hadn't gotten any handwritten notes. The lawyer stopped his questioning to demand that those papers be produced, and almost casually Perkins replied that the material "had not been retained."

Peck then babbled on about what had happened: "The practice I followed when I accumulated a substantial bulk of material is to send it by REA Express to Donovan, Leisure, because a lot of the material was covered by a confidentiality order, and I had no storage facilities as well as I had no room. . . . I just kept it in a cardboard box and when the box filled up I sent it off. I told them I didn't want it anymore and I had no further use for them." Stein's suspicions were aroused. Was Peck being defensive, a little too effusive in his explanation? Again Stein turned to Perkins: "I ask that I be provided with the dates when materials prepared by this witness and returned to Donovan, Leisure was [sic] destroyed by Donovan, Leisure, and I ask that there be identified to me the persons who participated in that destruction."

"I have no way of knowing," Perkins answered irritably. "All I can state is that no materials were destroyed subsequent to the receipt of your notice of production." Fortenberry, Perkins' associate who was sitting beside him, interrupted to whisper in Perkins' ear, but Perkins brushed him aside as Stein asked again who at Donovan, Leisure had destroyed the Peck documents. "Well, I am the person responsible for destroying or seeing that they were destroyed," Perkins finally admitted.

Stein moved on to another area of questioning, but he had on the record what he wanted for the time being: three admissions from Perkins that a substantial number of potentially important documents had been destroyed, and an admission that Perkins himself had destroyed them. Stein thought that the situation smelled suspicious. There is nothing wrong with destroying documents in the ordinary course of business—such behavior is routine at many corporations as a result of cases like Kodak—but if they were destroyed *after* they are subpoenaed it is a crime: destruction of evidence. Even if not subject to a particular subpoena, destruction of documents related to an ongoing case by counsel seemed extraordinary. "My feeling was that all along what they'd done was so contrary to reasonable practice—this was a perfect example which would reflect seriously on the credibility of Peck's testimony," Stein recalls. He made a note to himself to again explore the subject of the missing documents at trial, before the judge and the jury.

It had been a bad day for Perkins, whose fears about the ugliness of litigation had been confirmed. When he returned to the Wanamaker building, Perkins asked to talk with Doar, and Fortenberry began examining documents for the next day's examination. Perkins told Doar what had happened at the deposition, mentioning that he told Stein that he had disposed of documents that had been returned to him by Peck. Just as Stein had been suspicious, Doar was troubled by the explanation. In a case involving hundreds of thousands of documents that had been successfully computerized and accounted for, it was inherently odd that three entire briefcases of documents had disappeared, apparently destroyed by one of the top partners in the case. Why? What could account for such extraordinary behavior?

It was a critical juncture in the case and one where Doar, with some vigorous questioning of Perkins, might have prevented all that was to happen. But inexplicably, Doar simply accepted Perkins' explanation. He didn't ask him any questions. He didn't call in Fortenberry to find out if he knew anything about the matter. He told Perkins only that he was "troubled" by the destruction of the documents, that it suggested that there was something untrustworthy about Donovan, Leisure, and by implication, Doar himself. His chief concern seemed to be his own reputation, not Perkins' shaky explanation; and he told Perkins to find other copies of the documents in question and produce them to Stein.

Doar may have been preoccupied by the fact that he had already made a more significant blunder with respect to materials relied upon by Peck. About a month earlier, Doar had prepared some looseleaf notebooks which contained all the information he would need to conduct his examination of Peck at trial, including a draft of the actual questions that he intended to ask and the answers he expected to receive from Peck—a virtual script for Peck's testimony at trial. Though trial testimony is always intended to sound spontaneous, such script preparation is common. Showing it to the witness is not. Because of strict discovery requirements, it must never be shown to an expert witness economist, from whom it could actually fall into the hands of opposing counsel. Doar had given his notebooks to Peck to read, but he had not turned them over to Stein pursuant to his discovery request. The next day, Doar planned to attend Peck's deposition and admit to Stein that he had shown the books to Peck while arguing that they were protected by a lawyer's work product privilege and didn't have to be produced. At the same time, Doar wanted Perkins to produce copies of all the documents that he could recall had been destroyed. Perhaps such a display of candor and cooperativeness would restore some of Doar's reputation for trustworthiness.

Doar made his appearance, but his explanations did not satisfy Stein, and in fact only heightened his suspicions. He took the matter to the magistrate in the case, who ordered Doar to produce the four notebooks he had shown Peck. Doar was desperately afraid of turning over those materials, and had in turn to appeal the magistrate's order to Judge Frankel, bringing the whole unpleasant business to the attention of the judge. The hearing on that appeal was set for May 5. Knowing that the issue of the destroyed documents was also likely to come up then, Doar brought Perkins along to the hearing.

The subject arose almost immediately, and Perkins delivered the explanation he had worked out with Doar. Yes, Perkins told the judge, the documents had been destroyed, but he had searched through his files and come up with duplicates; those had been turned over to Stein. The story seemed a bit implausible to Frankel. "And you are able to know just what it was that was destroyed, is that what you are saying?" the judge asked skeptically. Perkins didn't answer, and Frankel ordered Perkins to produce an affidavit, sworn under oath, explaining what had happened to the documents and how they had been reproduced. Then Stein tried to exploit what he saw as a crucial weakness in Perkins' explanation:

"The witness has testified, Peck, that over the period of years he received a whole host of documents from a whole host of sources. He has made notes and memoranda of what he saw over the years," Stein pointed out.

"He then testifies that all of this material, every shred of it, was returned to Kodak's counsel. And Kodak's counsel now says that every bit of that, or virtually all of it, was destroyed." Stein had managed to make the story sound even more implausible.

"Including memos that the expert made?" the judge asked.

"Including *handwritten* memos and drafts of what he prepared, yes," Stein emphasized. How could a handwritten memo be reproduced from Kodak's files?

"Is that right, Mr. Perkins?" the judge asked incredulously.

Perkins evaded the question, answering, "Your Honor, I haven't reviewed all of the record."

The judge, noting the still unanswered questions, ordered Perkins to have his explanatory affidavit in court by the following Monday morning.

After the court hearing, Perkins returned to his office in Rockefeller Center and began drafting his affidavit. Doar went back to the litigation headquarters in the Wanamaker building. The next day, Doar received a call from another partner working with Perkins on the case, James Magee, who said that he was concerned that Perkins' affidavit wasn't responding sufficiently to the questions that had been posed in court, but was simply making the same recitation that the documents had been destroyed and that duplicates had been produced. Incredibly, Doar didn't call Perkins directly to discuss the affidavit or to query him further about the events in question. (How, for example, had the documents been destroyed?) Rather, Doar drafted an elaborate memo setting forth the questions which he felt should be answered and how, and he called Magee to arrange a meeting for the next day.

Sunday afternoon, Doar, Perkins and Magee met in Perkins' office. But nothing further was said about Perkins' statement in court, nor were any questions asked about the document destruction. The affidavit was discussed briefly, and Doar gave Perkins a copy of the memo he had prepared, telling Perkins to make sure that his affidavit conformed to it. Then Doar changed the subject to other aspects of the case. "It never occurred to me that Mr. Perkins had in fact not destroyed the documents which he said he had destroyed," Doar later said. Nor did he realize that the documents, now stored in a large suitcase, were at that moment hidden in a closet in Perkins' office, inches from where Doar sat.

By the summer of 1977, the discovery phase of the trial was over. Despite all of its resistance, Donovan, Leisure eventually turned over nearly all the documents it had with respect to Peck, though the judge spared Doar from having to produce his note-

books. The trial began on July 18 in Federal District Court in
downtown Manhattan. Stein did all of the questioning in presenting Berkey's case, which—keeping the presence of the jury always
in mind—was short and to the point. Doar began his direct questioning immediately after. He did virtually all of the examination
of Kodak's witnesses. Neither Perkins nor Furth was ever seen in
the courtroom, though Doar was always accompanied by several
associates.

Given his "niche" within the firm, Mahlon Perkins would not
have taken a visible part at trial in any event. But by the time
Doar began introducing Kodak's case, Perkins' activities on the
Kodak matter had further dwindled. Some time after submitting
the affidavit about destroying the documents, Perkins went to
Doar and asked him to relieve him of responsibilities related to
the expert witnesses. Whether he felt his reputation as an effective
lawyer had been so damaged within the firm, or whether he was
simply fed up with everything related to Peck is unclear; but Doar
granted his request and assigned him to the preparation of legal
memoranda which might be submitted during the trial—an assignment befitting a first-year associate out of law school. Two associates—Fortenberry and Phyllis MacSheain—took over Perkins' remaining work with Peck.

Peck himself was scheduled to provide the trial's finale as
Kodak's last witness. One day before Christmas, as the day Peck
would take the witness stand approached, Furth—still banished to
the long-dormant GAF case—bumped into Peck in the Wanamaker offices. Peck was petulant, complaining that he had nothing
to do, that "I'm here to prepare for my testimony but no one
seems to have time for me."

Furth saw an opportunity, since he didn't have anything to do
either. Furth also had some experience with Peck, since the two
had worked together early in the proceedings. Peck had written a
letter to Furth in which he explained an old 1915 antitrust consent
decree in which Kodak had admitted attempts to monopolize.
Furth hurried in to Doar, who was preoccupied with the ongoing
trial and agreed that Furth could help prepare Peck for his testimony. Furth promptly began drafting some questions for Doar to
use with Peck at trial, including one which posed to Peck the
source of Kodak's monopoly power. The question was a crucial
one, and it was intended to provide a summary of Kodak's basic

position. The answer Peck was supposed to give was that Kodak, to the extent it had monopoly power, had earned it through product innovation and service to the consumer. If the jury believed it, that explanation would virtually assure a finding that Kodak was innocent.

Peck took the witness stand on January 5, 1978. One topic which was excluded from his examination was the 1915 case he had discussed with Furth, since the Donovan, Leisure lawyers had argued that the old ruling against Kodak might prejudice the jury if they knew about it. Then Doar, on the very first day of Peck's examination, asked him the broad question that Furth had drafted, and Stein immediately objected. If Peck was going to discuss the source of Kodak's monopoly power, he argued, he should be permitted to question him about the 1915 consent decree, which Berkey contended had contributed to Kodak's dominant position in the market. The judge let Doar proceed with his questioning, but indicated that he would rule on Stein's request to ask about the 1915 case the following day.

When Peck and the lawyers got back to the Wanamaker building, Peck went over to the drinking fountain and started talking with Furth, with whom he seemed to have established a rapport, and who had not been in court. As soon as Peck mentioned the dispute over the subject of the 1915 case, Furth's eyes lit up. Furth has an amazing memory for detail—Donovan, Leisure lawyers conceded that no one rivals Furth's command of the Kodak facts—and he immediately recalled a letter he had received from Peck that discussed the 1915 decree. "That's no problem," Furth told Peck, and proceeded to refresh the economist's memory of the now four-year-old letter.

But Peck was troubled. Already anxious that the lawyers hadn't given him enough attention during his preparation for trial, he went to MacShein and asked why he hadn't been shown the letter he had written to Furth in 1974, and asked if he could see it now. This was the first that MacShein had heard about a 1974 letter, and she went to Doar to ask him about it. "Peck shouldn't worry about it," Doar told her. "Tell him if Stein asks him about it to identify it," Doar said, even though he had never seen the document himself.

Later that evening, around 9:00 P.M., Doar, MacShein, Fortenberry, a lawyer from Kodak and Peck met in Doar's office to review for the next day's examination. Furth was excluded, as usual, even though he was the only one who actually recalled the substance of the 1915 memo. When the subject of the 1915 case came up, Doar finally asked to see a copy of the letter. He looked at it briefly and said that if Frankel ruled the next day that the 1915 case was relevant, he would have to give copies of the document to the judge and to Stein. Peck was upset, saying that he didn't want to be asked questions about a document he hadn't seen in more than three years, so Doar gave him a copy to review. No one bothered to ask why a copy of the document hadn't been provided Stein before during all the discovery. According to Doar, he was preoccupied with proposed instructions to the jury that would follow Peck's testimony and was busy making sure that all the documents had been properly admitted into evidence.

The next morning, Frankel began the court session with a ruling that information about the 1915 case appeared to be more prejudicial than relevant, and hence questions about the 1915 case would be barred. A sigh of relief went through the Donovan, Leisure ranks, for now it would not be necessary to unveil Peck's letter. But Stein was still suspicious that Peck had produced some work that had not been turned over to him during discovery, so he again asked the economist if he had produced any such memoranda. With the 1915 letter now fresh in his mind, Peck said, "Yes, there are." With that, Doar was forced to hand out the copies of Peck's memo on the 1915 antitrust case.

Stein's retaliation was quick and harsh: "A vital, relevant document has been deliberately withheld, and in this case I am compelled to say by counsel as well as the witness . . . it is particularly shocking since it relates directly to the matters we have been wrestling with these past few days trying to find out whether there is a reason . . . for bringing in the 1915 decree," Stein exclaimed. The document itself was innocuous enough, as Furth had earlier noted, but in the present context it was a disaster. Since its whole premise was whether the 1915 case had contributed to continued unlawful dominance of the market by Kodak, it indicated that the Donovan, Leisure lawyers thought that was a relevant question in the case—precisely opposite to the position they had been arguing to Judge Frankel, who had ruled in their favor that morning. The judge immediately asked why the memo hadn't been produced, and Doar—evidently facing that question for the first time—volunteered that a magistrate's ruling had exempted it from production. Incredibly, Doar couldn't remember which ruling, remembering vaguely only that one had been made. Doar was speculating desperately, for there had been no such ruling. Judge Frankel, skeptical, noted that the case was becoming "explosive" and ordered Doar to produce an affidavit explaining why the memo had not been produced before.

The day had been a humiliating nightmare for Doar. When the glum litigation team returned to the Wanamaker building, Doar shut himself in his office and refused to see his colleagues.

The next two days in court were spent discussing the proposed jury instructions, but the incident over the 1915 memo had put all of Stein's complaints about Donovan, Leisure's discovery tactics in a new, harsh light. The destroyed documents had continued to nag at Frankel, and at the close of the day on January 8, he ordered Doar to include with his affidavit about the 1915 letter yet another affidavit explaining how and why the Peck documents had been sent to Donovan, Leisure and destroyed. Doar assigned responsibility for the preparation of the affidavits to Magee, who went to the Rockefeller Center offices to tell Perkins that he had to provide a fuller explanation.

At the Wanamaker litigation center, further concern about Perkins and his missing documents, if any, was lost in the gloom over the Peck debacle. As Furth recalls it, "There was no question that Peck had been lost at this point. He was completely at sea. He looked like a fool, he sounded terrible, he wasn't answering properly, he wasn't making any sense." A more secure witness might have staved off disaster. After all, nothing of any great substantive importance had been uncovered. But Peck lacked the strength of character to fight back from the accusations of lying and hiding evidence, and Doar offered no support. Peck crumbled before the jury's eyes, looking less and less believable as his testimony neared its agonizing conclusion.

But the worst revelation occurred outside the courtroom. Late on January 8, Perkins arrived at Doar's office in the Wanamaker building visibly upset. Magee had been to see him about another affidavit, he explained to Doar, and then his speech faltered. Looking tired, haggard, and with tears in his eyes, Perkins finally confessed to Doar: No documents had ever been destroyed. With his earlier affidavit, Perkins had committed perjury. He couldn't do it again.

•

As the case continued to collapse around him, Doar remained coldly professional. He immediately called John Tobin, the corporate partner who headed the firm's executive committee, at Tobin's home in Westchester, and broke the news. He told Tobin that he and Perkins were leaving then for the Rockefeller Center offices, where the documents were stored, and advised Tobin that he planned to take the entire matter before the court once he had had a chance to look at the documents. Tobin was astounded and confused—the facts were hard for him to grasp—he couldn't believe that "Perk," his friend, colleague and former classmate at Harvard Law School, was involved.

Tobin called George Leisure, Jr., the son of the firm's patriarch, who was also a litigator and was more familiar with the Kodak case. Leisure left immediately for the Wanamaker building to intercept Doar and Perkins. But by the time he had arrived, Doar's mind was already made up about the course that had to be taken. He was taking Perkins to his office to review the documents, and as soon as he had determined what had been withheld, he intended to notify the judge and opposing counsel. Doar was unwilling to wait for the advice of Donovan, Leisure's executive committee, and at about 10:00 P.M. Doar and Perkins left for the Rockefeller Center offices, where they spent the remainder of the night poring over the documents in the suitcase, trying to identify which had been produced, and numbering and indexing those which had not.

Stein was asleep in his home on Long Island at about 6:00 A.M. the next day when he was awakened by a phone call from Doar. Doar "was obviously very distressed," Stein recalls. "He told me that he'd discovered that these documents we'd been told had been destroyed were in the possession of Donovan, Leisure lawyers all along, and that he'd have them in court that morning." Stein told Doar only that he'd be interested in seeing them, concealing his surprise. "I realized instantly that it meant that obviously false affidavits had been filed. There is a limit—I mean, even with their already questionable ethics in this case, I never believed they would go that far."

The new disclosure was ammunition that Stein was prepared to use that very day in court—the last sorry day of the beleaguered Peck's testimony. Peck had spent the previous evening at the Wanamaker building getting ready for his last day, oblivious to the Perkins disclosure taking place only a few doors away from where Fortenberry and MacSheain were rehearsing him for his final questions. Nor did the Donovan, Leisure associates and most other partners know what had happened the night before, or why Doar was looking quite so haggard and worn. Only Magee had joined Leisure, Doar and Perkins the previous night, and all agreed to keep the matter a secret until it was formally disclosed to the court. Only in the limousine heading to the courtroom in downtown Manhattan did Doar explain to Peck that yet another miserable day lay ahead, and that the fact that Perkins had not destroyed the documents would be revealed.

The day proved to be all that Peck and Doar feared. Doar began his presentation by stating on the record that certain documents previously described as having been destroyed were actually intact, and he produced them for Stein. Frankel was expecting the admission—Doar's phone call had gotten him out of the shower that morning—but not Doar's attempt to minimize the impact of the disclosure by asking that the document destruction issue not be brought to the attention of the jury. "All the documents that I know of have been produced to Mr. Stein for his cross-examination with respect to Dr. Peck's opinion," Doar argued. "The matter of the destruction of the documents seems to me to be so prejudicial to Kodak . . . that the prejudice would outweigh any issue of credibility."

But the judge's patience with respect to Donovan, Leisure's disclosure of evidence had reached its limit, especially since Stein, after looking at the documents Doar produced, noticed from their dates that some of them had been found in Peck's files *after* the time Peck testified he had sent them all back to Donovan, Leisure. Frankel snapped at Doar, "I don't understand how you can say that when a few minutes ago Mr. Stein told me that at your instance Peck looked in his files over the weekend and found some that were not sent back and not destroyed . . . and if that doesn't go to his credibility, I don't know what does. For his [Peck's] $60,000 or $70,000 he ought to look in his files."

Frankel then allowed Stein, in front of the jury, to question Peck at length about the supposedly destroyed documents and Perkins' false statements under oath; and it gave Stein the material he wanted for a blistering final characterization of Peck and his testimony: "That sordid spectacle of dissembling, evasiveness, deception and concealment disgraces the dignity of this court, this proceeding, and you jurors. . . . And there is no doubt, I believe, based upon the evidence presented to you, and the conclusions to be drawn from that evidence, that the witness deliberately and purposefully concealed material evidence, and—I think it has got to be said—lied to you under oath. Not once, repeatedly." Stein finally concluded that Peck "has proven himself utterly unworthy of belief."

Back at the Wanamaker building, the Donovan, Leisure litigation team continued its work drafting proposed instructions to the jury. None of them yet knew of Perkins' disclosures, Peck's humiliation or the debacle in the courtroom—facts that now made most of their work irrelevant.

The secrecy which still shrouded what was rapidly becoming known as the "Perkins affair" was a conscious policy of Donovan Leisure's executive committee, which had rapidly perceived the explosive potential of the incident, not only for the Kodak case itself but for the future of the firm. It was just after Tobin had spoken to Leisure on Sunday night that he had called Murphy at a hotel in Atlanta where he was waiting for an appearance in Federal Court the next day. As soon as that hearing was over, Murphy flew back to New York and convened the meeting of the executive committee in his office on Tuesday morning.

Attending the meeting besides Murphy were Tobin, Withrow, David Teitelbaum, a corporate partner, and the firm's two active senior partners, Irvine and Leisure. Doar was not invited, and at any rate was busy preparing his closing statement for the trial. Most of them had been called by Tobin on Sunday evening, and Murphy outlined the situation as he perceived it. "Hearing the story out loud did not make it any easier to believe," Murphy recalls.

As the partners sorted out the facts, one option was clearly unavailable. Even if it had been possible legally and ethically, Perkins' false affidavit could not be concealed. Doar had already made a full disclosure to the court and to opposing counsel. As one lawyer close to the case recalls, "There was hardly universal admiration for Doar's unilateral action. It had been hasty, seemingly without much thought for the consequences or how they might be alleviated. Was it possible, for example, to delay raising this matter until the case had already been submitted to the jury?

Perhaps not, but Doar didn't even give his partners the chance to raise the question. He seemed more concerned about establishing his own innocence than about the welfare of the client, or of the firm."

The next pressing problem was how to explain the situation to Kodak, and how to minimize the damage to one of the firm's oldest and most important clients. There, too, the firm's options had been limited. Doar had also called Kendall Cole on Sunday evening, and Cole had been in court the next day to savor the full, devastating impact of the disclosure. "We didn't know where we stood with Kodak," Tobin recalls, "but a partner had done something that seemed injurious to their interests. They needed advice divorced from the situation of the trial." The partners reluctantly concluded that Kodak needed to be advised by counsel from outside Donovan, Leisure, since the firm faced a potential conflict of interest. Its desire to protect Perkins might obscure its obligations to Kodak.

Kodak, of course, was not the only client that worried the members of the executive committee. Though so far the incident had been kept under wraps, it was only a matter of time before details emerged in public; and the lawyers concluded that it might be devastating for other clients to learn of the matter from news accounts. Together they drew up a list of about twenty of the firm's most important clients, including Mobil and Disney, and began the painful task of telephoning individually the various general counsel and chief executive officers to describe what had happened. The partners also decided that the firm itself had to be notified as well. For the first time in memory, a meeting of the entire firm was convened—all partners, associates, paralegals, secretaries and other personnel crowded into one of the firm's midtown conference rooms. Murphy outlined what had happened. In the shocked silence that followed, John Tobin pledged that the firm would carry on, that it would weather the crisis, and that no one's job would be jeopardized. "Let's don't point fingers," Tobin urged, emphasizing that the firm's energies would be devoted to putting the crisis behind it.

In the opinion of most of the lawyers who attended the all-firm meeting, Tobin's plea was intended not so much to exculpate Perkins as to deflect criticism of Doar. Word of the problems with Doar's management of the case and style had reached many of the firm's associates who were not working directly on Kodak, corroborated by some of their own experiences in dealing with him. "Cold," "distant," "morally arrogant," are the phrases which most quickly come to the minds of these associates in describing Doar, while Perkins is still praised in almost extravagant terms. "He was one of the kindest, gentlest, most thoughtful men I've ever known," says one associate—who also worked directly with Doar —of Perkins. "My first thought when I heard about this incredible incident was that Perkins could not have done something like that." Tobin agrees, though he said nothing at the time. "Perkins was sixty years old, with forty years of professional experience. It was utterly uncharacteristic. He didn't know Doar well, and I'm sure that contributed," Tobin now says.

Whatever their private thoughts, Donovan, Leisure's executive committee concluded in what seemed like an unending stream of conferences that Doar had to be protected from the scandal. After all, the trial was proceeding. Doar concluded his summation to the jury on January 11, but preparation for possible appeals and a separate trial on the extent of damages should Kodak be found guilty lay ahead. The only way to salvage the firm's relationship with Kodak, the partners concluded, was to stand behind Doar. If possible, they also wanted to stand behind Perkins. He stayed away from the all-firm meeting, though he was in his office, and afterward Murphy went in to talk privately with him. Murphy recalls that Perkins seemed dazed, remote, and offered no explanation of what had happened. Murphy tried to reassure him, saying he "hoped it would all turn out all right," that the firm's partners "wanted him to stay," and that they "wouldn't throw him out of the firm."

Unknown to Murphy and his partners, the chance to save either Perkins or Kodak had already been lost.

The day after the first executive committee meeting in Sam Murphy's office, Kodak general counsel Kendall Cole flew to New York to attend the remaining sessions of trial and to hear Doar's summation to the jury. At lunch, he met with Tobin and Murphy. Again at dinner, the three sat down to discuss the future of the case and of Kodak's relationship to Donovan, Leisure. Cole seemed sympathetic, concerned about who would replace Perkins on the case. He was in "complete agreement," Tobin recalls, that the firm had taken the proper steps and that the defense of the case should proceed with Donovan, Leisure at the helm.

Cole also agreed that Kodak needed independent advice with respect to the Perkins incident itself, and indicated that Simon Rifkind, a former judge and partner in the prestigious New York firm of Paul, Weiss, Rifkind, Wharton & Garrison, had been retained for that purpose. Two days later, after the jury retired to deliberate, Tobin and Murphy flew up to Rochester with Cole and met with Walter Fallon, Kodak's chairman. Fallon, too, reassured the Donovan, Leisure partners that they had Kodak's full confidence. Murphy asked point-blank if there was any unhappiness with the conduct of the trial, and Fallon said, "Everything is okay."

But it wasn't. After Cole learned on Sunday night about Perkins' disclosure about the documents, he secretly boarded one of Kodak's private planes and flew to New York. On Monday morning, he was at the downtown Manhattan offices of his former law firm, Sullivan & Cromwell, where he met with litigating partners John Warden and Robert MacCrate, who had been Cole's college roommate at Dartmouth, and Sullivan & Cromwell's litigation patriarch, William Piel, Jr. The Sullivan & Cromwell lawyers agreed to begin immediate full-scale preparations to take over the case from Donovan, Leisure and agreed that their work had to be kept secret until the right moment came for them to step in. By the next day, Sullivan & Cromwell had assembled a litigation team of three partners and four associates, with Warden assuming the lead role. On January 11, the day that Cole reassured the Donovan, Leisure partners at lunch that they would continue at the helm of the case, there was a strange face among the spectators in the courtroom—a Sullivan & Cromwell associate. From then until the end of the trial, Sullivan & Cromwell associates—but never partners, out of fear that they might be recognized—rotated into the courtroom. Each Friday, the Sullivan & Cromwell associates assembled inside the firm's offices and delivered oral accounts of their observations at trial. No new-client memo was circulated at the firm, and nothing was put in writing.

Meanwhile, within Donovan, Leisure, debate continued about how to handle the Perkins matter. As previously expressed by Murphy, the sentiment of the executive committee was still to do what it could to protect Perkins' status as a partner in the firm and as a member of the bar. But Doar soon removed that option, as he had done earlier by bringing the matter to the attention of the court and to opposing counsel. As soon as Doar finished his closing argument and the jury retired on January 13, he determined unilaterally "to make a more complete report to the Court as to what Mr. Perkins had said to me Sunday night."

Perkins, on the advice of Murphy and Tobin, had retained his own counsel, Harold Tyler, the former federal judge who had been approached to join Donovan, Leisure at the time Doar was hired. Perkins had since refused to talk to Doar about what had happened, so Doar called Perkins' lawyers and advised them that he intended to go into court the next morning and tell the judge everything Perkins had told him during their Sunday meeting. Since Perkins' earlier statement to Doar admitted that he knew he was lying when he prepared the affidavit about the destroyed documents, Doar's account was likely to result in a perjury indictment. Faced with that threat, Perkins called Tobin and said he would be willing to discuss the incident with a member of the firm and with Doar before Doar went into court the next day. That Friday night, Perkins came into the Rockefeller Center offices and met with Doar for about three hours. By the time they emerged, Perkins agreed that he would personally appear in court the next morning and make his own statement before the judge.

The next afternoon, a Saturday, Perkins, his lawyer Tyler, Doar and Stein met in private session in Judge Frankel's chambers. No one from Kodak was present, nor were other Donovan, Leisure partners. Though a transcript of the proceedings was made, it was promptly placed under seal, and Frankel stressed the need for secrecy, warning that he had already refused to take calls from several reporters. Then Perkins began his account:

"I think I should probably start by saying that the things or most of the things I am going to tell you, I haven't told anybody before now except to my lawyers," he began in a quiet, halting voice. After referring to his work with Peck and the shipment of documents, he turned to the Peck deposition. "Mr. Stein was asking Professor Peck about documents that he said he had sent to Donovan, Leisure. He asked me where the documents were and I said they had been discarded. He asked me who destroyed them, and I said, 'I did.' That was not the truth, Your Honor. As I recall it now, that answer came into my head for some reason at the deposition. I had not planned to make that answer. I don't believe that I had really considered it." Perkins explained that the evening after the deposition, his associate Fortenberry, acting on his own, had taken the briefcases containing the documents Perkins testified had been destroyed up to the Rockefeller Center offices, where the documents were stored in a locked closet. Perkins said he never looked at the documents until the night he opened the suitcase with Doar. Rather, "I know this is difficult to explain," Perkins said, "but I simply treated those documents as if they had in fact been destroyed. I did not discuss them with Mr. Fortenberry."

Perkins seemed at particular pains to explain exactly Fortenberry's involvement in the matter. After discussing his conversation with Doar about the affidavit he prepared, and the redraft he did with the help of Magee, he added, "It's my best recollection that Mr. Fortenberry had no knowledge at the time of the contents of that affidavit. Following this whole episode, I just didn't discuss the matter with Mr. Fortenberry. He didn't bring it up with me. I knew that he was aware of it, because he brought the suitcase up." And then Perkins remembered that Fortenberry had interrupted him during the Peck deposition: "During the morning of the second day of the deposition [when Stein was pursuing the matter of the destroyed documents] . . . Mr. Fortenberry . . . whispered in my ear, something to the effect . . . 'You have forgotten about the suitcase.'"

Perkins also made clear, perhaps inadvertently, that the destruction of the documents had only brought to the surface what seemed to be a pervasive sense of despair about his career and about his stature in the firm. "This whole thing had become something that I kind of wanted to forget about, and hoped it would go away, and put out of my life." He added that "I felt that John Doar could not be happy at all . . . I had a conversation with him, I think in my office, at one point which I suggested to him, or I don't know exactly how to put it, that perhaps he wouldn't want me any longer on this case, or could I be useful and how."

It was at that point that Doar had assigned Perkins to work on a motion for a directed verdict and relieved him of responsibility for the economic witnesses. Perkins said he realized that the motion for a directed verdict "would be kind of a futile thing to do," that there were "more important things for us to be doing," and that he had been virtually exiled within the firm. "My role in that case after that point changed completely."

Not long after that discussion with Doar, Perkins recalled that the judge had ordered him to draft yet another affidavit explaining the destroyed documents. "I started to revise it," Perkins recalled, referring to his affidavit, "and then it began to grow on me that I shouldn't be handing in any more affidavits to Your Honor." It had been that evening that Perkins had gone to Doar and confessed. Only when Perkins opened the suitcase with Doar that night did he learn that virtually all the documents it contained had already been produced to Stein. The few papers that hadn't been produced proved to be entirely inconsequential, and were never submitted as evidence by Berkey. The attempt to conceal them, in the end, did nothing to benefit Kodak.

"I am not going to go into my feelings on the subject of the documents which were not destroyed in the suitcase and my affidavit to you, but I understand absolutely that what I did was wrong," Perkins sadly concluded. "I injured many people as a consequence."

The following Monday, Perkins came into his office as usual, where he found a note asking him to speak with Tobin. The previous day, the Donovan, Leisure executive committee had again met to consider Perkins' status. After reading a copy of the sealed transcript of Perkins' statement to the court—and the judge's assertion that at some future point all the information would be turned over to the U.S. Attorney for possible prosecution—the committee members painfully concluded that Perkins could no longer maintain a practice within the firm. Tobin, Perkins' closest friend on the committee, was delegated to convey the decision.

Even now, Tobin finds it difficult to talk of his meeting with Perkins. "It was a very difficult thing for me to do, but I personally relieved him of all assignments within the firm. I spoke to him, I just told him that we had to . . . It was painful, but he understood and agreed. We talked about replacements for his other clients (principally the Advertising Association of America). He tried to talk about what had happened, but he couldn't explain it. He was in shock." Though Perkins stopped coming into the office, he remained a partner in the firm pending a further investigation of the incident.

•

Attention was shortly diverted from the plight of Perkins by yet more bad news for Donovan, Leisure. After nine days of deliberations, the jury returned to the courtroom on January 22 and announced its verdict. It found Kodak guilty of monopolization. Judge Frankel ordered commencement of a separate trial for damages—Berkey claimed damages of approximately $300 million, which, when trebled, would result in an award of nearly $1 billion—and Walter Fallon, Kodak's chairman, quickly issued a press release denouncing the verdict and pledging an immediate appeal. Decisions about how to handle the damages trial and the appeal of the verdict had to be made quickly, so Tobin and Murphy flew to Rochester to meet with the senior Kodak executives.

It was at this meeting, the day after the verdict, that the Donovan, Leisure partners were first made aware of Kodak's displeasure with the conduct of the trial. It had nothing to do with the Perkins matter, the Kodak executives claimed; but according to Cole, sentiment had been growing for some time within Kodak that Doar was not handling the case properly. Would Donovan, Leisure consider replacing Doar as lead counsel for the damages trial? Murphy asked for some time to consider the decision, but his instinct was that Doar should not be replaced. "It didn't make any sense," he says. "The trial was in its last stages. Doar had put together the defense; no one was in a better position to go forward with it. It really was in no one's interest to replace him, and it would have been a devastating blow for Doar."

Murphy and Tobin returned to New York, where they met with members of the executive committee. After considerable discussion, they reached the decision that Doar would not be replaced unless Kodak left the firm no alternative. To do so would have implied an admission of fault on Doar's part, a total lack of support by his partners, and, by implication, an admission of wrongdoing on the part of the firm. That was not the official position that had been worked out, a position that looked beyond the Kodak case to the impact on present and future clients. An internal investigation conducted by a senior associate not involved in the case, John Gordan, concluded that the Perkins misconduct was an isolated incident, and that no one was responsible or could have prevented it but Perkins himself. Perkins had betrayed the trust of his partners; he now had to be excised to save the institution.

The position the firm adopted and tried to convey to Kodak was not enhanced by the reaction of Judge Frankel, who, after further reflection, made the following statement after the jury rendered its verdict: "I listened sadly and sympathetically as Mr. Perkins went out of his way to take all the blame to himself and to absolve substantially everyone else, except possibly an associate. But I was left with a nagging sense of uneasiness about that—a feeling that didn't diminish as other circumstances developed and came into focus."

Frankel proceeded to cast aspersions on the conduct of the other lawyers at Donovan, Leisure: "The strange and suspicious story of destroyed documents obviously called for inquiry. The upshot is that this matter, without questioning anybody's honesty, seems to have been characterized in its handling by defense counsel by . . . a course of self-help, mistake, and/or extreme carelessness. All of this," the judge continued, "reflects a kind of single-minded interest in winning, winning, winning, without the limited qualification of that attitude that the court, I think, is entitled to expect and which I feel must have infected Perkins." The judge's suggestions that the improper attitudes of top partners on the case—Doar obviously included—had "infected" Perkins provided ammunition for the growing group within Kodak that wanted Doar off the case. Shortly after the judge's remarks, Cole called Murphy to tell him that Kodak not only wanted Doar off the damages case, they wanted him off all Kodak matters.

It was becoming apparent to Murphy that a showdown with Kodak was approaching, despite his efforts to dramatize the firm's continued commitment to its client and to the case. Shortly after the earlier meeting, Murphy assigned to Kodak the partner he describes as his "right-hand man," Kenneth Hart—a fiercely hardworking litigator who once posed for Marine Corps recruitment posters—and also several new associates to work on the damages case. He personally visited the exhausted litigation lawyers at the Wanamaker building in an attempt to boost morale.

In a last attempt to soothe Kodak, Murphy and Tobin chartered a private jet on Friday, March 10—the only time either had ever done so—to meet with Kodak executives in Rochester and to explain the firm's decision that it would not replace Doar. But in his heart, Murphy says he already knew that "Kodak was lost." Tobin, too, now says, "I went up to get fired. That wasn't my purpose. But we had reached the point where we had to know if, in light of our refusal to replace Doar, we were going to be replaced and if so, how it would be handled." The same Kodak executives who attended the earlier meeting assembled. When Tobin delivered the firm's final position—that it would stand behind Doar—Fallon revealed for the first time that Kodak had been consulting with lawyers at Sullivan & Cromwell, and had determined to change counsel.

"Everyone there was upset," Tobin recalls. "No one wanted this to happen, and the decision was delivered as nicely as possible."

But Murphy was stung. "It wasn't so much that they were going to change counsel. It was that they had already made the decision without telling us. That hurt," he says. Fallon agreed that he personally would fly to New York the next day to convey the decision to Doar.

As soon as they returned to New York, Tobin and Murphy notified the other members of the executive committee of Kodak's decision. They agreed that it was unnecessary to notify major clients again, all of whom had indicated their continuing support at the time of the Perkins incident; but the occasion did call for another all-firm meeting on the following Monday. Associates were assured that their jobs were secure and that the firm would have no difficulty assigning Kodak lawyers to other cases and clients. Privately, however, the executive committee members were worried. With a total of thirty lawyers working full-time on Kodak matters, the sudden loss posed a serious problem of transition and loss of income.

Not until March 28, two weeks later, did Kodak issue a terse statement announcing that Donovan, Leisure was being replaced as counsel by Sullivan & Cromwell. Cole justified the decision with a statement to the press saying that "an unfortunate incident" (the Perkins matter) had given rise to a potential conflict of interest with Donovan, Leisure, making necessary the change of counsel. But both Cole and the lawyers at Donovan, Leisure knew that the potential conflict had had nothing to do with the decision to drop the firm altogether. A lawyer at Sullivan & Cromwell recalls that the pretext of the conflict of interest was nothing but a face-saving fib, and that at the time Sullivan & Cromwell was assigned the case Kodak said nothing about any concern over a conflict.

Most lawyers at Donovan, Leisure were not surprised by Kodak's decision, rare as such action is in the world of major law firms and their clients. After the seemingly endless bad news, to most it seemed an inevitable culmination. Not so to Helmut Furth, the partner who was still toiling away on his preparation for the long-dormant GAF case.

Furth had been on the sidelines of Kodak matters for some time, and was kept even further away after the incident over the letter about the 1915 antitrust consent decree, which he had brought to the attention of Peck and which, however inadvertently, had triggered the whole Perkins disclosure. But Furth himself knew nothing of the Perkins matter at the time it happened; he remained oblivious to all the executive committee meetings, to the closed-door conferences taking place steps from his own office. He learned about Perkins' false affidavit only when it was announced at the all-firm meeting. Similarly, he knew nothing about Kodak's decision, or about Donovan, Leisure's decision to stand behind Doar, until that, too, was told to the entire firm. But what shocked him most was that Kodak was not only sending the Berkey case to Sullivan & Cromwell—it was sending them all the pending cases, including GAF, his own pet project.

Furth hurried to his office after the meeting, closed the door, and phoned Cole at Kodak. "I didn't know why they wanted new lawyers on GAF," Furth says. "I thought things were going fine; we really had them [GAF] on the run after they changed counsel." Cole explained to Furth that the Perkins matter played only a small role in Kodak's decision, and that the company's real concern was Doar's overall direction of the case. Then Cole dropped a bombshell that drove Furth into a rage. After the loss of the liability case, Kodak had asked that Furth—and not Doar—be assigned the principal role in the damages trial which was to follow. Murphy had refused to grant the request.

Furth charged into Murphy's office demanding an explanation and threatening to quit the firm. "He was furious, very angry, especially at me," Murphy says. "He felt that Donovan, Leisure had wrongly and unfairly prevented him from being able to take the spotlight." Murphy tried to explain the firm's decision, saying that it didn't reflect personally on Furth, and that he should talk to

Irvine before he did anything rash. Furth wasn't assuaged. A week later, he called Kodak again. He said he would rather resign from Donovan, Leisure than stop working on the case. "Everything I had been working on was about to go down the drain," Furth recalls, his face reddening in anger when he thinks about it. "I knew it would be risky to devote myself like this to a single case. But I thought Kodak would need me in the transition." Kodak agreed, and said it would be happy for Furth to continue to work if an acceptable arrangement could be worked out with Sullivan & Cromwell. Early that summer, Furth negotiated an "of counsel" relationship with Sullivan & Cromwell and angrily withdrew from partnership in his old firm.

The Sullivan & Cromwell litigation team had gone into high gear as soon as the announcement was made that it was taking over the case. Less than a month later, the firm managed to put together a lengthy motion for a judgment notwithstanding the verdict, which was denied. During the spring, Donovan, Leisure lawyers gradually cleared out of the Wanamaker building, and to ease the pain of the transition, only one Sullivan & Cromwell partner oversaw the transition at the building itself. One afternoon that spring, however, a Sullivan & Cromwell associate recalls being given a tour of the litigation center by a Kodak executive. "It was terribly uncomfortable," the associate recalls. "There were still a few Donovan, Leisure associates around, and they were virtually ignored. We were being hailed as the lawyers who could save Kodak; they were described contemptuously as the lawyers who had nearly destroyed it."

Following the transition period during the spring, most of the Donovan, Leisure lawyers on the case were sent on vacation—the firm had nothing else for them to do. Doar himself went on a six-week trip to Ireland with his wife, and when he returned he submitted his resignation to the firm.

Doar was never told that Kodak had demanded that he be replaced, nor did the firm ever seek his resignation. But he realized that his position in the firm had become untenable. "It was entirely his own decision to leave," Murphy says, "and I tried to talk him out of it. I think he was held responsible by my partners for things that really weren't his fault, and because of the case, he really didn't know any of them besides me and Tobin. He undoubtedly felt pressure."

Furth is more blunt in his characterization of Doar's position within the firm: "It was intolerable. Kodak was Doar's loss, his responsibility. There wasn't another partner in the firm that would ever let him handle another major case. He had no big clients of his own. [Doar's only other matter had been a small case for the International Ladies Garment Workers.] I wasn't surprised when he left, and I don't think anyone else was either. He had little choice."

At the time he left, Doar told his partners that he missed the small practice he had had as a lawyer in Wisconsin, and had reluctantly concluded that a large firm wasn't the setting for him. Today he maintains a solitary practice in a small office in midtown Manhattan, still handling occasional matters for the Ladies Garment Workers and waiting for litigation referrals. Divorced by his wife, he is described by one lawyer who has dealt with him recently as "hiding what seems to be bitterness behind a cold and taciturn facade." Still revered by much of the public for his Watergate role, his legal career is viewed by many other lawyers as in shambles.

Furth became "of counsel" to Sullivan & Cromwell but is an outcast in his new firm. Sullivan & Cromwell partners have banished him to his office in the Wanamaker building, where he pores over files and presides over a suite of now largely deserted offices. He has no illusions about his future with Sullivan & Cromwell, and hopes that when the case is over, Kodak will reward his loyalty with a position on its in-house staff in Rochester.

Joseph Fortenberry, too, is no longer at Donovan, Leisure. Though all other senior associates who toiled on the Berkey case have been rewarded with partnerships—a visible symbol of the firm's promise that no one's future at Donovan, Leisure would be handicapped by the Perkins affair or the loss of Kodak— Fortenberry was passed over and is now a lawyer with the Justice Department in Washington. It is doubtful that, despite being implicated by Perkins, Fortenberry really knew the true story about the destroyed documents. (If he did, he would have been obligated to reveal Perkins' misconduct to the bar association, or at least to senior members of the firm.) Fortenberry claims that a paralegal, not he, carried the suitcase of documents from the Wanamaker building to Rockefeller Center, and says he "does not recall" whispering anything about the suitcase to Perkins at the deposition.

At any rate, Fortenberry's role in the scandal had nothing to do with his failure to be made a partner. The firm had actually passed him over two months before the Perkins matter ever came to light. It later lied about its decision so as to enhance Fortenberry's chances of getting another job, keeping him working so that prospective employers would not see his immediate dismissal from the firm and conclude that Fortenberry was indeed implicated in Perkins' wrongdoing. Even so, Fortenberry was not hired by every private law firm at which he applied for a job.

Ironically, Perkins may have emerged relatively well. In the fall of 1978, he appeared in Federal District Court and pled guilty to a reduced misdemeanor charge of contempt of court. His lawyer, Harold Tyler, commented that "there, possibly but for the grace of God, go I, because of the pressures which come upon men and women who practice law in big cases." Though Perkins spent 30 days in jail for the offense, he retains his firm pension and has never been disbarred. Since his release, Perkins has traveled extensively in the Far East, where he taught English to Japanese students for some time, and is now devoting himself to his duties as president of the Greenwich, Connecticut, Philharmonic Society. He has little contact with his former partners at Donovan, Leisure; but one lawyer who spoke with him recently describes him as "happier, I believe, than he had been as a practicing lawyer."

By the end of the summer of 1978, anyone at Donovan, Leisure responsible, or perceived to be implicated, in the scandal, was gone or on the way out. A malignant tumor had been excised, and Donovan, Leisure, as a firm, very shortly regained its health. When Westinghouse needed a massive litigation staff to handle its uranium litigation after Chicago's Kirkland & Ellis was disqualified, it was satisfied that the Kodak debacle would not be repeated. Though Donovan, Leisure was not its first choice to take over the job (both Cravath, Swaine & Moore and Jones, Day, Reavis & Pogue had to turn down the assignment because of conflicts with other clients), it got the assignment. This time Murphy and Leisure themselves supervised the work, and by early in the fall, the entire Kodak litigation staff that had been idled was shifted to the Westinghouse cases. Later, the firm was swamped with work related to Mobil's efforts to take over first Conoco and then Marathon Oil.

Kodak, too, has emerged unscathed. On June 25, 1979, based

on the briefs submitted by Sullivan & Cromwell, the Court of Appeals for the Second Circuit, in a precedent-setting opinion that was later cited by IBM, reversed the jury's verdict for Berkey. The reversal was, in practical terms, an unqualified victory for Kodak. It eventually settled the case with Berkey for a comparatively paltry $4.75 million in cash and $2 million of credit.

Thus did the Kodak case come to an end. As in the IBM case, it is hard to say what impact the lawyers actually had on the ultimate result. The Donovan, Leisure lawyers themselves maintain that the Court of Appeals reversal of the jury verdict vindicates their own efforts at trial. In any event, the law firm of Donovan, Leisure, as an institution, has emerged relatively unscathed.

The same cannot be said for Doar, Perkins, Fortenberry and Furth. The intense pressures which exist for partners in all of the elite corporate firms forced them outside the self-contained world of Donovan, Leisure, and into the arena of public scrutiny and prosecution. At all such firms, institutional self-preservation comes first. For the lawyers within them, the resulting personal sacrifices can be great indeed.

Appendix 1

THE ELITE CORPORATE LAW FIRMS

NAME	LOCATION	SIZE	DATE FOUNDED	KEY CLIENTS	NOTES
Cravath, Swaine & Moore	New York	213	1819	IBM, CBS, Chemical Bank	The archetype of elite corporate firms
Davis Polk & Wardwell	New York	230	1849	ITT, LTV, Morgan Guaranty	Long known as the top "white shoe" firm
Debevoise & Plimpton	New York	154	1931	Chrysler, Prudential	A relative newcomer; strong in corporate
Donovan Leisure Newton & Irvine	New York	185	1929	Mobil, Westinghouse	Litigation strength, firm's standing threatened by Kodak
Kirkland & Ellis	Chicago	290	1908	Standard Oil (Indiana)	Awesome reputation in litigation
Milbank, Tweed, Hadley & McCloy	New York	211	1860	Chase Manhattan, the Rockefellers	Pre-eminent in trusts and estates
Pillsbury, Madison & Sutro	San Francisco	245	1865	Standard Oil (California)	The established West Coast firm
Shearman & Sterling	New York	341	1860	Citibank, United Technologies	The ultimate banking firm
Simpson Thacher & Bartlett	New York	211	1884	Manufacturers Hanover, Gulf & Western	On the rise; strong banking and corporate
Sullivan & Cromwell	New York	215	1897	Exxon, General Foods, GE	The quintessential business practice

Appendix 2

The following excerpt, though published in 1948, is the best articulation of the principles which underlie today's elite corporate law firms. The preceding chapters demonstrate the extent to which these principles still hold sway, as well as ways in which the firms have failed to live up to these standards.

THE CRAVATH FIRM*

Since 1906

The dominant personality of this volume is Paul D. Cravath. He was the authoritative head of the firm until his death in 1940, and his conceptions of the management of a law office still control its operations. Henderson and de Gersdorff in corporate work, and Wood in litigation, were long active with him in developing the "Cravath system" and the Cravath tradition; they have now passed on, leaving the firm to new generations of partners.

The firm's practice, even in litigation, has dealt primarily with corporate and financial problems, and the character of the work from year to year has been increasingly determined by national economic conditions. Cycles of security issues in boom times have been followed by cycles of receiverships and reorganizations in times of depression, while, without letup, problems arising from the constantly heavier impact on business of Federal taxation and regulation have pre-empted more and more of the time of partners and staff.

THE CRAVATH SYSTEM.

Cravath had a definite philosophy about the organization of his law firm, its partners, its practice and its relation to its associates.

* This is Chapter VII of *The Cravath Firm and Its Predecessors, 1819–1948,* by Robert T. Swaine. Privately printed, New York, 1948, Ad Press Ltd. Most footnotes have been deleted.

As to recruiting the legal staff:

Cravath believed that a staff trained within the office would be better adapted to its methods of work than a staff recruited from older men who, in practice elsewhere, might have acquired habits inconsistent with Cravath methods, and hence he insisted that the staff should be recruited, so far as possible, from men just out of the law schools.

He believed that these men should have had a thorough preliminary education in the arts as well as in the theory of the law. Cravath believed that disciplined minds are more likely to be found among college graduates than among men lacking in formal education; that mastery of the fundamental theories of the common law is a *sine qua non* of legal competence; and that such mastery can better be taught in the law schools than by practitioners in a busy office. The best men, too, are most likely to be found in the law schools which have established reputations by reason of their distinguished faculties and rigorous curricula, and which, by that very fact, attract the more scholarly college graduates.

Cravath believed in seriousness of purpose—a man with a competent mind, adaptable to practicing law according to Cravath standards, should have made a good scholastic record at college. But he recognized, without full approval, the tradition of the early decades of this century—that "gentlemen" went to college primarily to have a good time and make friends. Hence, while a good college record was always a factor in favor of an applicant, lack of such a record was not necessarily an excluding factor. Cravath himself had not made an unusually distinguished college record. As the playboy traditions of college life became obsolete in the stern realities of the depression of the '30s, however, college records of applicants came to have added importance. For a poor law school record Cravath never had tolerance. He believed that a man who had not attained at least the equivalent of a Harvard Law School "B" either had a mind not adapted to the law or lacked purpose and ambition; in either case, the man was not for the Cravath office.

The scholastic standards of the "Cravath system" thus made a Phi Beta Kappa man from a good college who had become a law review editor at Harvard, Columbia or Yale the first choice. Such standards are commonplace today among New York offices; when Cravath came to the Seward firm in 1899 they were regarded as somewhat eccentric—not to say stuffy. As other offices have adopted the same standards, the supply of the theoretically first-choice men has not equaled the demand, and from time to time quite a number of B-men, and occasionally C-men, have been employed. Experience has proved the reliability, for the purposes of the Cravath office, of the scholastic standards to which it endeavors to adhere. Few of the B-men and none of the C-men have been able, within the office, to equal the accomplishments of their contemporaries of higher scholastic achievement. Of the 23 partners on May 31, 1948, 15 are Phi Beta Kappa and 15 were law review editors.

Cravath did not, however, want colorless, narrow-minded book-worms. From applicants who met his standards of scholarship, he wanted those who also had warmth and force of personality and physical stamina adequate to the pressure to which they would often be subject because of the rugged character of the work. It is, of course, difficult to judge these qualities in the brief interviews which the partners are able to have with most of the many applicants. This was especially true during the conventional "rushing season" of December which prevailed prior to World War II, when applicants came to the office in scores in a concentrated period of a few weeks. Despite the care taken in interviewing and checking the men finally chosen, misjudgments have sometimes been made in taking men not adapted in their personal qualities to the Cravath practice; probably many more mistakes have been made in adversely judging men on inadequate contact.

There were two exceptions to Cravath's general standards during his active leadership. Because he found that most of the more brilliant young men strongly preferred handling concrete matters to library research, he thought the office should always have at least one associate of mature experience with capacity and preference for legal research. He also believed that for real-estate work and litigation it was well to have a few men who had been trained in other organizations where there was more of such work than in his own office. There was some reason for such exceptions in the first decades of the Cravath firm, when its legal personnel numbered less than forty. But as the organization has grown to more than a hundred lawyers and the fields of its practice and its own expertness have become more comprehensive, Cravath's early exceptions have tended to disappear, and the same standards are applied to all the men in the office, whatever their work.

As to training associates:

Cravath preferred that men should not specialize in such branches of the law as real estate or administration of estates or, later, taxation, until they had attained a general experience over several years. The objective required that a man should not be confined to the work of one client or even be assigned to one partner for any undue length of time.

At the outset of their practice Cravath men are not thrown into deep water and told to swim; rather, they are taken into shallow water and carefully taught strokes. The Cravath office does not follow the practice of many other offices of leaving small routine matters entirely to young men fresh from law school without much supervision, on the theory that a man best learns how to handle cases by actually handling them. Under the "Cravath system" a young man watches his senior break a large problem down into its component parts, is given one of the small parts and does thoroughly and exhaustively the part assigned to him—a process impracticable in the handling of small routine matters. Cravath believed that the man who learns to analyze the component parts of a large problem involving complicated facts, and to do each detailed part well, becomes a better lawyer faster than the man who is not taught in such detail. Matters involving small amounts often involve difficult, complicated law problems, and a man may be misled, perhaps made careless, by being allowed to handle such a matter without adequate analysis and supervision.

Cravath's insistence that the legal staff be recruited from men just graduating from the law schools, rather than from older, experienced lawyers, was based not only upon his desire for a Cravath-trained staff but also upon his belief that the office and its clients would get the best service from men confident of unimpeded opportunity for advancement. When a former associate asked, in 1916, whether there might be an opportunity for him to return to the office and make it his career, Cravath referred to the "office policy of filling advanced positions from the ranks of the young men who enter the office as beginners," and added: "I feel that if our office has been successful it is very largely because of our adherence to this plan, which has enabled young men to feel that if they remain with us during the years of preparation they will have the first chance when opportunities for responsible positions from time to time develop."

It is a fundamental part of the Cravath training that a man's responsibility shall be increased as his growing competency permits. There are partners in the firm today who, after only two years in the office, handled effectively as associates, with little supervision from partners, matters involving millions of dollars. On the other hand, there have been men of the finest scholastic records and personalities who could not acquire capacity for independent responsibility.

As the men grow in professional stature, those who evidence capacity for delegation are given opportunity to expand their own activities by the use of younger assistants to whom they can in turn give the same kind of training they have enjoyed. The art of delegation in the practice of the law is difficult, requiring nicety of balance which many men with fine minds and excellent judgment are unable to attain. There have been many cases—some even among the partners—of inability to find the happy medium between doing all of a job personally and turning it over completely to an assistant. The more nearly he attains the right compromise between these two extremes, the greater the amount of effective work a man can turn out, and hence the greater his value to the firm.

As to compensation:

Before Cravath came to the firm, law students in the office and several of the admitted associates received no compensation. Those associates made their living by doing what business they could develop for themselves and paid for desk room by assisting in office business. Cravath could not tolerate the inefficiency and divided loyalty implicit in such an arrangement. He abolished the study of law within the office, and every associate, including the man fresh from law school, was put on a salary.[1] Because its demands in time, energy and competence are heavy, the Cravath office tries to keep annual advancements and ultimate compensation at least as high as those of any other office in the City.[2]

Adoption by other City offices of many of the same principles on which the "Cravath system" is based led, about 1910, to competitive bidding for the highest-ranking men of the leading law schools. This gave a few men inordinately high beginning salaries, sometimes double those of the generally applicable scale. The discrimination among the men just coming out of law school became unfair and made the initial salary offered too important a criterion in the choice of offices. Within a few years the evils of the practice were admitted by the offices and strongly objected to by the faculties of the law schools; on their suggestion it was abandoned after World War I, following a conference among the managing partners of the larger offices. Beginning salaries thereafter tended to become uniform, and at increasing rates, until the disruption of education during World War II and elimination of the regular annual crop of law school graduates made it impossible to apply uniform standards to men of widely varying ages who had spent years in Government service.

As to tenure:

Every lawyer who enters the Cravath office has a right to aspire to find his life career there—but only by attaining partnership.

Men who are willing to stay only a year or two are not desired, for the "Cravath system" cannot train a man in that short time. They are expected to remain as long, but only as long, as they are growing in responsibility. Cravath used to say that, except for a few research scholars and specialists, no one should be permitted to stay in the office more than six years unless the partners had determined to admit him into the partnership. Most of the partners admitted up to 1926 had been in the office for five or six years. As the work of the office, the complexity of the problems, the number of partners and the size of the staff increased rapidly during the '30s, the period of apprenticeship for the partners admitted in 1940 lengthened to about eight years. The dislocations due to World War II further lengthened the period; the partners admitted in 1946 all graduated from law school before 1936.

Ten years is too long for a man to remain a Cravath associate under normal conditions unless he has been told that the chances of his

---

[1] That element of the "Cravath system" was put into effect when Cravath became a member of the Seward firm in 1899. The beginning salary then established was $30 a month; by 1901 it became $40, and by 1908, $50, increasing $5 bimonthly during the first two years; thereafter the top annual increases were about $500.
[2] Just before World War II the beginning salary was $2400 and top annual increases had reached $1500.

being made a partner are still good. A man who is not growing professionally creates a barrier to the progress of the younger men within the organization and, himself, tends to sink into a mental rut—to lose ambition; and loss of ambition induces carelessness. It is much better for the man, for the office and for the clients that he leave while he still has self-confidence and determination to advance. The frustrated man will not be happy, and the unhappy man will not do a good job.

Under the "Cravath system" of taking a substantial number of men annually and keeping a current constantly moving up in the office, and its philosophy of tenure, men are constantly leaving. Where do they go? Associates with good records have no difficulty in finding promising and profitable opportunities if they do not stay too long, causing potential connections to question their success and hesitate to gamble on advanced age or salary levels. The firm constantly has requests from clients and other leading industrial and financial organizations to supply men for legal and executive positions. Other high-ranking law firms of the City and elsewhere have taken Cravath men as partners; many Cravath men have formed successful law firms of their own; and quite a number have become members of law school faculties. It is often difficult to keep the best men long enough to determine whether they shall be made partners, for Cravath-trained men are always in demand, usually at premium salaries. Because among the many called to the staff only a few can be chosen as partners, even good men are likely to feel that the odds against them are so great that they should accept flattering offers from others.

Almost without exception, the relations between the Cravath partners and the men who have left the office to compete professionally have remained friendly, and often intimate. Cravath partners take great pride in the success of the alumni. Business which such men have been doing while with the firm has frequently been encouraged to continue with them; new business is often referred to former associates.

As to choosing partners:

The "Cravath system" has given the firm a multiplicity of talent from which to choose its partners. While recognizing the risks of too much inbreeding, Cravath insisted that new partners should be chosen from within the office, unless special requirements otherwise compelled. Young partners and young associates are seldom subjected to the discouragement of seeing someone come in over them from the outside. During the four decades of the Cravath firm there have been but three exceptions: the two advocates, Walker D. Hines and Frederick H. Wood, and the present senior tax partner, Roswell Magill.

Obviously not all the men competent to be partners can be taken into the firm—for that would make the firm unwieldy. The choice is difficult; factors which control ultimate decisions are intangible;

admittedly they are affected by the idiosyncrasies of the existing partners. Mental ability there must be, but in addition, personality, judgment, character. No pretense is made that the ultimate decisions are infallible. Only infrequently have mistakes been made in taking men into the firm; more often, mistakes not so easily remedied have been made in not admitting others.

As to interests outside the firm:
Probably the most rigid feature of the "Cravath system" has been insistence that for every man in the office, from the senior partner to the neophyte law clerk, the practice of law must be the primary interest and that that practice shall be solely as a member of the Cravath team.

This is not to say that the great advantages of interests outside the law are not recognized. On the contrary, Cravath himself gave much time to charitable, educational and artistic activities. He wanted his partners and associates to have such interests, and believed that the few who allowed office work to pre-empt all their energies were harming themselves and the firm. Neither partners nor associates, however, are encouraged to have outside business interests, and they may not have any such interest which would impair their work at the office. There are no half-time partners or associates. Nor is there any such thing as the business of individual partners or associates: all the business in the office must be firm business. This means that there is no division of fees between the firm and its associates, as there is in many other offices. The problem of the firm is to do effectively the business which comes to it; by so doing that business, more comes in. Hence, business-getting ability is not a factor in the advancement of a man within the office at any level, except in so far as that ability arises out of competence in doing law work, as contrasted with family or social connections.

Cravath early came to believe that in most cases the client is best advised by a lawyer who maintains an objective point of view and that such objectivity may be impeded by any financial interest in the client's business or any participation in its management. Accordingly, he made it the policy of the firm that neither its partners nor its associates should hold equity securities of any client, or serve as a director of a corporate client, or have a financial interest, direct or indirect, in any transaction in which the firm was acting as counsel. Occasionally, more frequently in recent years, clients have insisted upon exceptions permitting partners to occupy directorships and own qualifying equity securities, but the exceptions have been few.

As to the relations of the partners inter se:
Every partner is expected to cooperate with every other in the firm's business, through whichever partner originating, and to contribute to all the work of the firm to the maximum of his ability. The formation among the partners of cliques practicing independently of

each other, which developed under Guthrie, would not be allowed today.

Attainment of partnership does not mark either the limit of potential growth or accession to any automatic hierarchy. The younger partner who evidences capacity to win the confidence of clients with whom he works so that they continue with the firm, who impresses others who come into contact with his work so that other business comes to the firm through him, and who takes responsibility for a number of varied matters, at the same time supervising the work of members of the staff and sometimes of other partners, may well rise, and indeed often has risen, within the firm more rapidly than some of his seniors. The partners are judged *inter se* just as are the associates, and adjustments are made to reflect the evaluation of the younger partners by their seniors.[1] Complete objectivity in such appraisals is not easy, for the most companionable man is not always the best, or the most effective, lawyer.

As to the scope of the practice:

The practice of the office is essentially a civil business practice. Cravath desired a staff equipped to serve corporate and banking clients in any of their legal problems.

After the withdrawal of Guthrie, the office work in litigation did not attain standards fully acceptable to Cravath until Wood joined the firm in 1924. With the assistance, first, of Bruce Bromley and later, also, of William D. Whitney, Alfred McCormack and Albert R. Connelly, Wood was able to build that practice up to the standards of the rest of the office and the traditions of Blatchford, Seward and Guthrie.

As the importance of tax questions increased, a partner was delegated to become an expert in taxation. First it was Hoyt A. Moore, then Hugh Satterlee, then Charles A. Roberts, then Maurice T. Moore; and in 1943 Roswell Magill was brought into the firm.

Anomalously, only in the fields of patents and admiralty, in which the firm was once premier, has it failed to provide expert service within its own staff. As early as the Seward era the specialized patent practice was almost wholly superseded by the nearly equally specialized corporate practice, and patent law specialists have been brought in as co-counsel in most of the patent work developed by the office. The partners have, however, handled patent-licensing problems, as well as those involving the impact of the antitrust laws upon patent licenses. In recent years this work has greatly increased, and currently several cases primarily involving patent law problems are being handled by the litigating staff.

The firm has a substantial practice in the administration of estates and personal trusts; but domestic relations cases are not encouraged.

---

[1] Cravath partners are true partners, not salaried associates given the nominal title of partner.

As to "influence":

Not since the retirement from practice of Richard Blatchford has the firm trafficked in political influence. While Cravath recognized that acquaintance of the partners with judges and administrative officials, commanding their confidence, was an asset to the firm, he followed the tradition of Clarence Seward in never purporting to have special influence with a judge or governmental officer, or ability to produce a magic result, which could not be exerted or produced by anyone else of equal legal ability and diligence. It was Cravath's philosophy that the politically "right people" are transitory, hence that political influence is evanescent, and that a practice based or dependent upon such an approach to legal problems is unlikely to have permanence. He also believed that those (of whom there have been so many in recent years) who purport to have special connections enabling them to accomplish results not capable of being accomplished by any other skillful lawyer usually oversell their wares; that most courts and administrative bodies decide cases on the merits rather than by favor; and that, notwithstanding the frequent gullibility of clients, skill and diligence in developing the law and the facts are much more important than "influence." That is still the firm's policy.

As to the firm's management:

Cravath believed that a law firm, like any other successful organization, must have strong executive direction, and until the mid-1930s his firm was under a dictatorship in his person.[1] Details of office management were, of course, left to the conventional managing clerk, and there has always been a managing partner, chosen from the younger partners, charged with supervision of managerial detail and, in effect, the liaison between the senior partner and the staff.

Cravath never completely delegated to anyone ultimate determination of office policy or evaluation of associates and partners. However, as the legal and clerical staffs began to increase rapidly after World War I, he relied more on the judgments of his partners. Weekly firm meetings started about 1923, where matters of general policy and of management, as well as current law problems, are discussed. Today every partner has a voice in the decision of every important question, as well as the benefit of the views of all his partners.

[1] It has never had a written partnership agreement.

Appendix 3

LAW FIRM ECONOMICS

The large corporate law firms are also businesses, evidenced by the imposition of more formalized management and cost-control systems in the firms, the hiring of professional administrators, usually with MBA degrees, and a growing preoccupation by partners with the bottom line. The key to profitability in such firms is the partner/associate ratio and "pyramid" staffing of client matters. There must be more associates than partners—the bigger the disparity the better—since the firms make money from associates by billing their clients for their work at rates which more than compensate for associate salaries and overhead.

To determine billing rates, the top firms generally use a formula; they double associates' salaries and divide by 1,000. Thus, a new associate who is paid $43,500 per year would be billed to the client at a rate of $87 per hour. If that associate bills 2,500 hours in a year (a large but fairly typical figure), he will generate $217,500 in revenue for the firm. Generously assuming that overhead per associate (rent, secretarial, etc.) is about the same as the associate's salary of $43,500, the firm is left with $130,500 in profit per new associate.

Assume a corporate law firm with 150 associates and 50 partners. Associates earn an average annual salary of $50,000. The associates alone generate $37,500,000 in annual revenue, which amounts to $500,000 per partner. The fifty partners, themselves billing an average 2,500 hours apiece at an average hourly rate of $200, generate another $25,000,000. That's total gross revenue of $62,500,000. Figuring overhead at $50,000 per lawyer, and after subtracting associate salaries, the firm generates profit of $45,000,000. That amounts to almost $1,000,000 per partner, on the average. These figures are rough estimates, but they indicate the exponential impact of the associate staffing pyramid on firm profits. The numbers are correspondingly lower for the firms where the associate to partner ratio is not as high as 3 to 1.

Calculating price by simply doubling costs and passing them on to clients is not the way that prices or fees for services are set in competitive markets. But the elite corporate law firms make little pretense that they behave in an economically competitive fashion, though partners may occasionally complain that associate salaries are getting too high. Rather, they see themselves as exercising a natural monopoly over the upper reaches of the profession, brought about, in their own antitrust terms, by "skill, foresight and industry." The monopoly is one, nonetheless, that their secrecy—especially about fees and costs—their policies, and their images have served to maintain.

Index

About the Author

James B. Stewart writes regularly about the legal profession and is executive editor of *The American Lawyer* magazine. Born in 1951 in Quincy, Illinois, he is a graduate of DePauw University and Harvard Law School. Before embarking on a writing career, he practiced law with the New York City law firm of Cravath, Swaine & Moore. He is a member of the New York bar and the Association of the Bar of the City of New York, and lives in New York City.